Creating Ourselves

CREATING OURSELVES

AFRICAN AMERICANS

AND HISPANIC AMERICANS

ON POPULAR CULTURE

AND

RELIGIOUS EXPRESSION

Anthony B. Pinn and

Benjamín Valentín,

editors

DUKE UNIVERSITY PRESS

Durham and London

2009

© 2009 Duke University Press

All rights reserved

Printed in the United States of America

on acid-free paper ∞

Designed by Amy Ruth Buchanan

Typeset in Scala by Achorn International

Library of Congress Cataloging-in-

Publication data appear on the last printed

pages of this book.

Contents

Acknowledgments

This project developed over the course of a good number of years. We first discussed it in late 2000 as we read through the proof pages for *The Ties that Bind*. Many people encouraged and helped us maintain focus on this book, and we would like to take this opportunity to thank them. Miriam Angress, our editor at Duke University Press, worked hard to bring this volume to its readers. We are grateful for her patience, hard work, and good cheer. We would also like to express our gratitude to the anonymous readers for Duke University Press whose comments and questions helped us improve the project.

From Anthony Pinn: I would like to thank Caroline Levander, Ramon Rentas, Eli Valentín, Alexander Byrd, Michael Emerson, and Edward Cox for their kind words, encouragement, and friendship. Finally, I thank my graduate student Torin Alexander who worked to ensure that the manuscript met Duke's formatting requirements. And to my family, thanks as always!

From Benjamín Valentín: I would like to thank my beloved wife, Karina, for her unfailing love and support. Also, I am grateful for the unconditional love and care of my family—Angel, Santa, Betsy, and Elieser Valentín. I offer thanks to my colleagues at Andover Newton Theological School for their support through the years.

Introduction

Rarely have African American and Latino/a theologians and religious scholars inquired into the possibility and even necessity of cross-cultural communication with respect to the two communities and their scholarly traditions in theology and in religious studies.[1] This is the case despite the unique web of historical and cultural relations that links African Americans and Latinos/as; despite the parallel history of struggle against multiple forms of jeopardy that have variously threatened their well-being; despite the fact that they share a comparable history of both subversive activity and the preservation and celebration of life; despite the current growth in tensions developing between these groups and the consequent need for more communication and collaboration between them; and despite the many interesting and potentially advantageous themes and issues that can be comparatively and jointly explored by them. It is indeed surprising that African American and Latino/a intellectuals in general and theologians and religious scholars in particular have not made more of an effort to explore both the possibility and desirability of communicative exchange, comparative analysis, and collaboration. But while this lack is surprising, it is nevertheless an unfortunate fact that little substantive interaction has taken place.

The reality is that the academic exploration of African American and Latino/a religious expression has been carried out with little substantive cross-dialogue between the two groups. That is, although black and Latino/a scholars have worked under the assumption that theology and religious studies are best understood as a dialogical practice and best carried out *en conjunto*, the analysis of theologies and religious expression coming from these two communities has occurred independently of each other. Furthermore, even a brief perusal of the bibliographies and indexes of books and articles written within either one of these discursive traditions reveals a lack of attention to academic resources from the other tradition.

Given this regretful state of affairs and our sense of the advantages of further dialogue between the scholars of these two ethnic communities, we have in various instances sought to bring together African American and Latino/a theologians and religious scholars for the purpose of comparative dialogue. In *The Ties That Bind,* for instance, we sought to bring together for the first time the rich, complex, and mature theological discourses of these two groups. That project provided a view of the development of these two theological systems, and it compared and contrasted key issues and elements relevant to both forms of theological reflection. It also touched on the important theological and ethical messages that these two traditions offer not only to the African American and Latino/a communities but also to the larger community of the United States. But in addition to that work we have also made an effort to bring together scholars from these two communities to engage in broad and collaborative conversation by way of academic forums and symposiums, and as such we can say that this book represents another attempt along these lines.

We must admit that our involvement in this effort at cross-cultural or cross-group exchange is motivated by an impulse that is at once political and intellectual. Politically speaking, this effort is to a good extent fueled by our unwillingness to relinquish the utopian dream of broader-based public connection, collaboration, and coalition. We are of a mind that it is important that progressive intellectuals and scholars, who aspire to ameliorative and transformative social relevance in their work, seek to revitalize coalitional energies wherever and whenever possible. It seems to us that the need for connection, alliance, and coalition across racial, gender, class, and religious lines is especially pressing today as a result of the increase of social antagonism, the fracturing of social movements and progressive energies, the deterioration of a spirit of solidarity, the growth in economic insecurity, the waning of broad public sympathy for minority persons who have suffered the most from racial, cultural, and economic exclusion, and the surge in racial antagonisms and xenophobic reactions experienced in our era. In times such as these, coalition building is extremely important. It is perhaps especially so for those historically subordinated and disadvantaged persons and groups that may lack the power to single-handedly transform present institutional structures. And to be sure, it is not solely the members of racialized minorities and disadvantaged ethnic or cultural groups in society who stand to gain from the political empowerment that coalitions can engender; indeed, the inequities, antagonisms, insecurities, and pathological consequences that result from inequality and injustice eventually affect us all in one way or another. Therefore, all who are concerned with the existence and effects of cultural and social inequality in our nation; all who are concerned with the fracturing of utopian energies in our time; all who are concerned with the deterioration of a spirit of solidarity; and all who remain committed to the ideals of equality, the common good, justice, and substantive democracy should be supportive of efforts at coalition building.

Still, although there is a definite need for coalitions today the truth is that we lack the holistic and integrative processes that can abet progressive connection and collaboration across lines of difference. And in the absence of these arrangements, the desire for transformative connection and coalition will remain at the level of wishful thinking. So before we can dream of collaboration and coalition building across lines of difference, we must first desire and foster cross-cultural and cross-group communication or dialogical exchange. We need, in other words, to get into the habit of engaging the "other" in substantive conversation. To put it boldly and simply, it would be premature to assume a collaborative or coalitional posture in the absence of the kinds of dialogical exchanges that can help us to know each other at least a little bit better. In a word, dialogue is essential. But the sort of cross-cultural dialogue we are talking about here is still a rarity in our time. This must change if we are to work toward mutually enhancing alliances.

For sure, occasional cases of meaningful communication and interaction can occur between members of these two cultural groups. But sustained dialogue is still not the norm between these two communities, even though they represent the two largest so-called minority groups in the United States and even in spite of many good (if not pressing) reasons for conversation. Dialogue has certainly not been standard among black and Latino/a theologians and religious scholars. And this communicative disconnect prevents us from more potentially fruitful cooperative interaction in our institutional efforts. How can we cooperate or collaborate with each other when we hardly know each other? We, if honest, know very little about each other, and we surrender against our better judgment to assessments based on stereotyping. This lack of awareness needs to be overcome if we are to collaborate with each other in our yearning for institutional change, and this rise above ignorance can only come through dialogue. Is dialogue "enough"? No it is not! But it is a vital starting point—one that allows us to compare experiences, exchange perspectives and opinions, and deliberate over our shared problems, aspirations, and hopes.[2]

For all that, it is important to mention that our involvement in this effort or experiment in cross-cultural or cross-group exchange is motivated not only by a political desire but also by an intellectual stimulus. It is our belief that there are many themes that scholarly members of these two communities can explore together. The fact is that the history and identity of African Americans and Latinos/as is inexorably linked. And so the material, symbolic, decorative, and expressive cultures of these two groups show similarities that can be analyzed. At the same time, a glance at the theological and religious scholarship produced by these two communities in recent times reveals comparability in the ways that these two discursive traditions have emerged and evolved both methodologically and thematically. Yet the differences or dissimilarities between these groups can also be explored. And it is our belief that both of these theological and religious studies traditions, though still relatively young, are developed enough to allow for fruitful and rigorous exploration. Black theology, for instance, has been in existence as an academic discipline since 1968 and can be said to be in its third wave of expression, while Latino/a academic theology has been around since 1975 and also reveals a kind of third unfolding.[3] The broader explorations of religious studies coming from these two communities also would seem to roughly correspond in regard to historical development. Thus at this point in their respective histories it would be interesting to compare and contrast the scholarly production of African American and Latino/a theologians and religious scholars. Such an intellectual curiosity can only serve to expand the thematic and methodological considerations being explored by these two scholarly communities.

The discussion generated by our first edited volume *The Ties That Bind* (2000) has been highly beneficial. That book directly led to various moments of interchange between black and Latino/a theologians and religious scholars, including two dialogical sessions sponsored by the Association of Theological Schools in 2002 and 2006; an American Academy of Religion session in 2003; and a consultation sponsored by the Fund for Theological Education and the Hispanic Theological Initiative that in 2005 brought together African American and Latino/a Ph.D. students in theology and religious studies to engage in each other's work. Still, we believe that this dialogical exchange can go further. And so in this volume we have brought together a group of scholars to explore the religious and theological significance of cultural production, or what we can call "popular culture." The reason why we selected this particular theme for our comparative and collaborative analysis is simple: cultural production has historically been of great importance to the theological and religious scholars in both communities. African American and Latino/a theologians and religious scholars have both in parallel ways converged on modalities of popular cultural expression coming from these two communities, and they have done so in an attempt to build theology and religious scholarship from the "stuff of life" that is to be distinctively found within black and Latino/a peoples. Hence, we perceive that the rubric of "the popular," or the realm of popular culture in other words, can offer a good intellectual framework from which to engage each other in comparative and critical conversation.

Much attention has been given to the fundamental nature and meaning of "the popular" within African American and Latino/a theology and religious scholarship. However, it is our view that much more work is possible and indeed necessary regarding the analysis of cultural production as popular expression within both of these communities. When African American and Hispanic and Latino/a scholars in theology and religious studies have dealt with the religious dimensions of cultural production their efforts have tended to be limited to music and to "popular religion." Examples include Michael Eric Dyson's *Holler If You Hear Me: In Search of Tupac Shakur* (2001); Anthony B. Pinn's edited collection *Noise and Spirit: The Religious and Spiritual Sensibilities of Rap Music* (2004); and Jon Michael Spencer's *Blues and Evil* (1993) and *Self-Made and Blues Rich* (1997). In terms of "popular religious practices" we might think in terms of the recent volumes on African-derived practices or Dwight Hopkins's work on popular practice in African American religious history—for example, in his *Down, Up, and Over: Slave Religion and Black Theology* (2000). On the other side, Latino/a theologians and scholars of religion have mostly focused on the study of religious expressions that may be characterized as "popular," such as Guadalupana devotion, patron saint devotion, and Afro-Caribbean religion. This focus is visible in texts such as Anthony Stevens-Arroyo and Ana Maria Diaz-Stevens's edited volume *An Enduring Flame: Studies on Latino Popular Religiosity* (1994); Jeannette Rodriguez's *Our Lady of Guadalupe: Faith and Empowerment among Mexican-American Women* (1994); Alex Garcia-Rivera's *St. Martin de Porres: The Little Stories and the Semiotics of Culture* (1995); Virgilio Elizondo's *Guadalupe: Mother of the New Creation* (1997); and Orlando Espin's *The Faith of the People: Theological Reflections on Popular Catholicism* (1997), among others. Much work thus has been done in both communities to explore the possible religious meanings of music and some forms of popular religious practices. Still, many other examples of popular culture have remained underexplored.

What about literature, the visual arts, movie and television production, food, the body as a cultural signifier, and other such examples of the popular? Unfortunately, these areas have not received the attention they deserve as expressions of black and Latino/a popular culture and agency and as cultural signifiers with great religious and theological meaning.

In this book we are fundamentally concerned with unpacking, in a comparative manner, the religious and theological significance of diverse expressions of African American and Latino/a cultural production— expressions that often as a whole are referred to as "popular culture." For the purposes of this project, popular culture is defined as the signs, symbols, aesthetics, behaviors, practices, and assumptions that disclose and explain the life and agency of a given community. The sections of this volume correspond to particular (and an admittedly limited number of) dimensions of cultural production as popular process, including body construction, Hollywood production, music, literature, visual arts, and the art of food. Other dimensions and modalities of "popular culture" can and should be explored. Here, however, we start with a fuller exploration of "the popular" found within these two communities by looking into these particular examples of popular culture, and we delve specifically into some of these because they have thus far been overlooked·and underexplored within black and Latino/a theological and religious study.

More broadly, however, we undertake the exploration of these examples of popular culture with two guiding aims: first, we seek to better utilize popular cultural production and agency as a theoretical, methodological, and descriptive source in theology and religious studies; second, we aim to more appropriately undertake comparative analysis that cuts across communities of concern. Underlying the analysis of popular cultural production found in this text is a certain intuition: basically, we are of the mind that popular cultural production entails a useful way of framing and forging dialogue beyond wrestling for sociopolitical crumbs premised on a warped sense of entitlement vis-à-vis the size and depth of "battle scars" and markings of struggle. Such thinking is too often premised on at least a soft embrace of assumed ontological arrangements of race and ethnicity or of a rigidly construed politics of identity (e.g., "ontological blackness and brownness" and the type of essentialism, exceptionalism, and localism often entailed by these). We believe that the terrain of popular cultural production can offer us a more useful conceptual framework in which to house this proposed dialogue, given the fluidity of being it suggests in various forms. As we see it, engagement with popular culture can serve to flood the frameworks of our often reified models of being and belonging—what it means to be "black" and "brown." This is so because when we analyze black and Latino/a forms of popular culture we hit upon the fact that African American and Latino/a life and agency represent a messy blend of identity factors that cannot so easily be construed, circumscribed, and detangled. Thus the study of African American and Latino/a popular culture requires at least a subtle challenge to fixed boundaries to expose their porous and somewhat illusionary nature. Popular culture, then, puts us in touch not only with the stuff of African American and Latino/a life but also with the messy nature of life for African Americans and Latinos/as in the United States. And in this way it can serve to undermine the logic of limited identity politics and even notions of membership in the United States.

This last point brings up one other possibility that comes from engaged scrutiny of the contours and possible meanings of popular culture: the study of popular culture can point us in the direction of a more hemispheric orientation. This is so because popular cultural production, particularly as it is found to be created and expressed within these two communities, represents a modality of meaning making that is not restricted to the mechanism of race and nation in a strict sense. And this is quite understandable when it comes to African American and Latino/a cultural agency. For both of these groups life involves, after all, holding together distinct cultural worlds taking root not only in the American hemisphere—North, South, and points in between—but beyond it as well. So the very nature of African American and Latino/a popular culture requires confrontation with the messy exchange of ideas, languages, images, aesthetics, patterns, customs, identities, and so on. In exploring popular culture we confront each other, but we do so in the fuller sense of our hybridity.

In uplifting the category of culture and popular culture we do not mean to suggest that race and ethnicity do not matter. Rather, our effort aims to argue for an understanding of race and ethnicity as an unstable and "constructed" marker, one that is shot through with an assortment of messy arrangements and relationships. Hence, race and ethnicity are not to be excluded; to do so is to dismiss the manner in which the discussion of, for example, Puerto Rico in the early twentieth century played off notions of race at work within the United States. And issues of immigration and the like are often viewed and analyzed through a hermeneutic of race. So rather than exclude the category of race, we recognize the manner in which race and ethnicity is infused in thought and action in ways that reinforce notions of belonging and meaning. The fact is that race and ethnicity shape and arrange the body (as both biochemical reality and symbol of sociopolitical arrangements) in ways that fix it as valuable or unimportant, as a source of normality or dis-ease. African Americans and Latinos/as to some degree have at points in history been viewed as "foreign" elements in the nation-state—that is, as persons whose presence and practices have been deemed to be a threat to national meaning. These ways of thinking still pop up from time to time today, and they must be counted against and resisted. And thus the category of race and ethnicity is still important as a critical construct. Yet we must admit that at times it can prove to be limited and more of a hindrance than a help in certain kinds of discussions, particularly when these are construed in ontological and narrow ways. And so, from time to time, it is good that we ask whether or not dialogue between these two particular social groups should either explicitly or implicitly maintain such narrow categorical arrangements. This is all to say that at least occasionally such categories or arrangements need to be troubled, and that more fluid ways of thinking about identity and meaning are necessary.

On some level the pieces in this volume suggest motion or movement, the fluidity of identity and meaning, as the guidepost for dialogical exchange. Each in their own way points toward the potential viewing and use of popular culture as a dialogical mechanism that synchronously serves to note and trouble the construction of individual and collective identity, thereby allowing for visibility of like and dissimilar bodies without necessarily doing damage to them in the way that reified arrangements might. Popular cultural production is deeply entrenched in the "stuff" of life arrangements found in these two communities and in the American hemisphere, but it also serves in important ways to undermine the logic of limited identity politics and notions of membership in the United States. In this way, popular cultural production suggests the messy nature of life for African Americans and Latinos/as in and between our shared geography of the United States (and beyond).

Admittedly, we hint at something that is not developed adequately in this text: the ways that cultural production is or can be used to trouble assumed frameworks of nation-state and rigid or closed forms of group identity politics by maintaining a porous and more hemispheric orientation. In borrowing from Paul Gilroy we might talk in terms of the Religio-Atlantic as the conceptual framework and geography for a new study of religion in this hemisphere, with a theological underpinning that cuts in numerous directions drawing from the Europe of Martin Luther to the language of balance in traditional African religion to the liberationist grammar of the Americas.[4] Such a move has already taken place in other fields such as history and literature. This volume entails merely a nod in the direction of such a project, an invitation to converse in ways that we hope will force the next step by begging us to enquire whether our existing frameworks and assumptions in the study of religion do us a service or a disservice as we attempt to come to grips with the overall cultural agency and religiosity of peoples within the Americas.

Notes

1 Throughout this introduction we use concurrently the terms theology and religious studies (and theologians and religious scholars) because they are sometimes differentiated and because this volume includes articles written by individuals who identify with one or the other in terms of their approach to the study of religion—that is, the study of the perennial human effort to make sense of life and the world through observable patterns of ritual, stories, beliefs, and cultural expressions. As this definition indicates, we take the term religion to stand for a wide network of human doings or actions. Theology and religious study, however, are reflective practices that involve the description, comparison, interpretation, and critical analysis of these actions. This implies a distinction between religion and theology or religious study on the one hand, and a connecting line between theology and religious studies on the other. However, at times the enterprises of theology and religious studies may be otherwise differentiated. This issue of differentiation is deeply complex and unsettled, and we cannot here sort through all of the different attempts at its settlement. However, we will note that one approach suggests that theology deals with one particular religious tradition, while religious studies reckons with the phenomenon of religion more generally. Another pathway to the distinction suggests that theology contributes to the interpretation, evaluation, and extension of a religious tradition or the practice of religion, while religious study contributes to the description, comparison, and critical analysis of religion. This assumes that theologians are interpreters of religion or have an interest in the maintenance, nurture, and endurance of religion, while the religious scholar does not.

2 Michelle Gonzalez's *Afro-Cuban Theology: Religion, Race, Culture, and Identity*, published in 2007, pushes for a move beyond dialogue to collaboration. We too hope for meaningful collaboration between blacks and Latinos/as in every level of the academy and society in general. However, we believe that collaboration and coalition building require some degree of forethought and intention that is not possible without dialogical exchange between members of these two groups. In effect, collaboration and alliance presupposes dialogue,

and so before we can collaborate with each other we must first talk with each other.

3 For a helpful overview of the historical emergence and unfolding of black and Latino/a theology, see Anthony Pinn's "Black Theology in Historical Perspective: Articulating the Quest for Subjectivity" and Benjamín Valentín's "Strangers No More: An Introduction to, and an Interpretation of, U.S. Hispanic/Latino(a) Theology," in *The Ties That Bind.*

4 Gilroy, *The Black Atlantic,* chapter 1.

PART ONE  THINKING ABOUT RELIGION AND CULTURE

Anthony B. Pinn

回

CULTURAL PRODUCTION AND NEW TERRAIN:

THEOLOGY, POPULAR CULTURE,

AND THE CARTOGRAPHY OF RELIGION

This essay, drawing from and building on earlier work, involves an effort to correct what I consider the troubled relationship to popular culture (i.e., signs, symbols, behaviors, postures, and frameworks recognized by and used to express meaning and place) that shapes black religious studies in general and theological discourse in particular. The corrective I propose involves a change in the conceptual posture revolving around the significance of religious "cartography" as a plausible theoretical framing of the study of black religion. In addition, I will also give some attention to thinking through this proposed reframing in light of the purposes of this book—namely, the dialogical possibilities between African American and Latino/a scholars of religion. As a context for this constructive work, I begin with a few descriptive thoughts on the purposes of African American cultural production.

The Changing Purpose of Popular Culture

Classic works by African Americans during the early formation of the United States are marked by an effort to address existential and ontological discomfort through apologetics in the form of expressive culture. One might explain in this manner the eighteenth-century sermonic-like prose of Jupiter Hammon, an early literary figure who sought to understand the presence of Africans in North America but did so in ways that did little damage to the religio-political and white supremacist paradigm used to structure the new nation.[1] Cultural production in this case sought to make sense of a rather absurd situation through the tools available. This eighteenth-century literary apologetic, a verbal alchemy, usually discounted (or at the very least did not adequately recognize) the significance of black bodies and the rights of those bodies to occupy with comfort and freedom this space called the United States. Poetry and prose framed a process of alchemy to transform into a meaningful existence by creative manipulation the terror and dread that marked the realities of the death and rebirth of life as chattel. African Americans made use of their historical memory and the culturally derived materials available in order to do this work. An apologetic, yet one more self-assured and assertive, is present also in the nineteenth-century autobiographical writings of Frederick Douglass. Such is also the case with the visual arts during the late nineteenth century as provided by artists such as Henry O. Tanner, whose *Banjo Lesson* (1893), for instance, portrays the humanity of African Americans to an American audience that held such a possibility suspect.

Following the tracks of the Great Migration and other historic developments after the socioeconomic and political reckoning called the Civil War and Reconstruction, the psychosocial posture of African Americans changed radically, particularly after the first decade or so of the twentieth century. That is, the emergence of the twentieth century is marked by a change in perspective—a movement of both bodies and ideas—expressed in significant ways through the increasingly unapologetic language of cultural production.

While the expression of cultural sensibilities has always served as an outlet for African American reflection on pressing existential questions and dilemmas, the twentieth century involved a shift in this work based on a new ontology—what Alain Locke noted as the emergence of the "New Negro." Locke traced the rise of this new consciousness, this new personhood, via the cultural self-expression dotting the landscape of African American communities. This "New Negro," representing more than simply a cosmetic makeover, marked a changed relationship between African Americans and themselves, and African Americans and the larger population of the United States. "The migrant masses, shifting from countryside to city, hurdle several generations of experience at a leap," wrote Alain Locke in *The New Negro*, "but more important, the same thing happens spiritually in the life-attitudes and self-expression of the Young Negro, in his poetry, his art."[2] There is something to be said for the paradigm shift noted with such brilliance by Locke: it represented a new cultural period and, like a category five hurricane, it cut an impressive if not systematic path through the landscape, forever changing what could and would grow on the exposed cultural soil.

Locke's Renaissance: The Texture of Cultural Epistemology

What Locke speaks to is a change in the nature of cultural production within African American communities—change that is marked in substantial ways by a move from apologetics, say in literature, to realism, to an appeal to the full range of emotions, thoughts, and activities framing African American life. For the purpose of this essay, of paramount concern is the manner in which this cultural creativity informed and was informed by the religious sensibilities and the religiosity of African Americans. Locke gave attention to the manner in which African American cultural production spoke to an alternate, defiant, and proud shaping of the geography of American life in spiritual terms. That is, "gradually too," according to Locke, "under some spiritualizing reaction, the brands and wounds of social persecution are becoming the proud stigmata of spiritual immunity and moral victory." As of the early twentieth century African Americans are, Locke continues, "at last spiritually free, and offer through art an emancipating vision to America."[3]

Harlem, for Locke, was during the early twentieth century a "prophetic" place—a special geography marking cultural energy and creativity from the African diaspora. It is in New York, Locke reflects, that African Americans built "fuller, truer self-expression" beyond the confines of the racial status quo. Yet, this has not simply involved the reconstituting of individual self-recognition and understanding on the part of African Americans *for* African Americans. Rather, this renaissance—the period of this profound artistic growth—marking the intellectual terrain of African American communities involved the "enrichment of American art and letters and . . . the clarifying of our common vision of the social tasks ahead."[4] It called forth a reenvisioning of American life, one that recognized without flinching and as a matter of psycho-cultural realism the full range of life activities and of group promise and foibles.

There developed during the early twentieth century an alternate aesthetic by which African Americans understood the maturation of their sociopolitical, economic, and cultural selves as a project of "wholeness" and beauty. It exposes beauty embedded in "raw" life episodes rehearsed, celebrated, and at times lamented. And the dimensions of this aesthetic were presented in the various layers and levels of African American cultural production. Thereby African Americans began a transformation with deep ontological and existential consequences—a transformation that marked a revised sense of self, and of self in relationship to community and world.

No wonder Locke comments near the end of his foreword to *The New Negro* that "negro life is not only establishing new contacts and founding new centers, it is finding a new soul. There is a fresh spiritual and cultural focusing. We have, as the heralding sign, an unusual outburst of creative expression." And those coming of age during the period of which Locke speaks are credited with ushering in a new ontology and a radicalized re-working of existential themes and categories filled "with arresting visions and vibrant prophecies; forecasting in the mirror of art what we must see and recognize in the streets of reality tomorrow, foretelling in new notes and accents the maturing speech of full racial utterance."[5] The shattering of old notions of African American life undertaken through these cultural developments spoke in graphic terms to the depth of the yearnings within African Americans for a fuller sense of meaning and "space." And this shattering and reconstitution of life is based on a deep feeling for and expression of the world as encountered by African Americans *and* as recounted for the benefit of African Americans.

Theological Imagination and Popular Culture

Scholars of African American literature and history, for instance, have mined African American cultural production, particularly the developments stemming from the two waves of the "Harlem" renaissance and the cultural geography of New York City. However, the significance of cultural production for an understanding of the religious yearnings and experiences of African Americans has not been lost on theologians and other scholars of African American religion.

One finds particularly intriguing examples of this recognition beginning in the late 1960s within the theological discourse known as black theology of liberation. In fact, this modality of theological discourse lists as a primary resource for the doing of theology the culture and cultural production of African Americans. In an effort to move beyond European theological models as well as to deconstruct American theology's relationship to the status quo, African Americans began to assert theological independence and to seek alternate modes of construction. Such a move involved a process of introspection—a searching through the "stuff" of African American life.[6]

James Cone penned *The Spirituals and the Blues* after joining the faculty of the Union Theological Seminary in New York during the early 1970s. Within this text, his third major publication, Cone responded to the critics who argued that his first two books failed to specify a theological framework that was deeply connected to and grown out of the intimate details of the African American experience. That is, the critics lamented the lack in those books of a deeply recognized "blackness"—cultural and otherwise—as the organizing principle of theological discourse. According to his brother, Cecil Cone, James Cone's theological formulations were much more indebted to the neo-orthodoxy of Karl Barth than to the theological formulations found implicitly and explicitly in African American religious culture. Further, Cecil Cone notes, black theology during its early phase carried the imprint of European cultural and religio-theological sensibilities deep in its organizational matrix, in its "soul." Hence the question arises: What is "black" in and about black theology?

The apparent theoretical and methodological genealogy of black theology, the critique goes, made the religious sensibilities and outlook of white Westerners the lens by which the world was viewed. Consequently, white supremacy in the realm of religious reflection was reinforced. This move, from the perspective of the critiques, was odd considering James Cone's broad appeal to African American culture as a major source for the doing of black theology. For Cone black culture is "the creative forms of expression as one reflects on history, endures pain, and experiences joy. It is the black community expressing itself in music, poetry, prose, and other art forms." And, he continues, in order to be organic to the black community, black theology had to take seriously black cultural production because "black culture . . . is God's way of acting in America, God's participation in black liberation."[7]

With the critique made and its legitimacy recognized, Cone attempted to reverse this theological trend by turning attention to musical production—namely, spirituals and the blues. In doing so he sought to mine from these forms the theological insights and liberation agenda of the African American community prior to the development of formal modalities of theological inquiry (e.g., churches). According to Cone it was through these musical forms that African Americans expressed their theological and religious sensibilities and presented an alternate ontology and epistemology. While Cone gave little attention to the visual arts for their theological insights, music and literature of various kinds served to enliven his presentation of a black theological epistemology. In moving from the spirituals and the blues as modalities of theological discourse, Cone gives attention to literary genres such as the slave narratives, autobiographies, folk wisdom, and other "texts" outlining the relationship of African Americans to the world and the divine.

James Cone's students have continued this tradition of exploring various types of popular culture, particularly music and literature, for their theological wealth. James Evans, for instance, has given considerable attention to the theo-religious qualities and pronouncements of African American literature.[8] More recently, Evans's work has branched out to include issues of the theoretical framework and methodological sensibilities informing black theology. Furthermore, Cone's student Dwight Hopkins has given consistent attention to an explication of the cultural sources (e.g., slave narratives) for black theology, at times to the exclusion of other vibrant source materials.[9] Like Cone, Hopkins argues that the basic dimensions and characteristics of black theology as a formal enterprise are found in the nascent theological discourse of African Americans housed in their popular expressions and modalities of engagement. Hence, according to Hopkins, contemporary black theology in part must concern itself with mining early sources and thereby building a theological discourse that mirrors and is consistent with the development of the African American community. In this way Hopkins seeks to promote the doing of theology as a reflexive enterprise that is community committed and community responsive.

At times Hopkins's work implies a connection between African American cultural production and theological discourse so intimate and strong that no real distinction need be made—that is, cultural production *is* theological discourse. Literature and other forms of the arts thus become simple carries of a particular cosmic message. I believe this link is made, for example, because of the slippage between popular culture and popular religion found in some of his work. That is one way to interpret the following statement by Hopkins: "If religion suggests a sacred, comprehensive, and integrated style of being for all reality[,] and culture suggests the site of popular religious dimensions of black experiences, then black theology claims its God-talk and God-walk from the popular religion of the folk's total way of life."[10]

On one level the approach outlined above runs the risk of doing precisely what Cone warns against: an equating of human words and wants with divine will or, in the language of Karl Barth, a neglecting of the infinite and qualitative distinction between God and humans.[11] On another level it seeks to limit to one dimension (i.e., the institutionally and doctrinally recognizable as "religious") of the range of African American creative responses to existential conditions and metaphysical questions. Based on certain religious assumptions held by black theologians of liberation, this is most commonly articulated in terms of the Christian religiosity celebrated in popular culture. At the very least it is a (mono)theistic reading that privileges notions of a loving and liberative divinity. This issue is depicted in Riggins Earl's reading of folk wisdom accounts of Brer Rabbit in which he sees nascent forms of contemporary liberation paradigms. Regarding "Brer Rabbit's Hankering for a Long Tail," for instance, Earl interprets the story as possessing a clear moral: "God in the primal act of Creation had given the oppressed the necessary intelligence for its own preservation."[12] However, lines such as the following might suggest an alternate reading, one that is more concerned with a type of religious naturalism than with traditional notions of a transcendent divinity. In what follows, Brer Rabbit has completed all the tasks required by God in order to secure the long tail he desires. But rather than an exercise of divine power resulting in the growth of the desired appendage, he is first ignored by God. Then, after nearly being struck by lightning, finally he receives this word: "You are so smart get your own long tail."[13] The actual story, as summarized here, suggests other alternative readings—ones that do not privilege a positive take on theism. While Earl paints this as a story of the resources for survival that God provides, as well as God's great wisdom in denying certain forms of assistance in order to foster human growth, the story also allows for religious naturalism as the proper reading. Attention to this story is not meant as an apology for a particular reading of Brer Rabbit as religious devotion. Rather it is meant to point to the potential of multireadings of popular culture and to the fact that black theological discourse tends toward a rather myopic approach to the religious meanings of cultural production.

Studying popular culture as a theological exercise can become a way of simply establishing signposts for certain understandings of the encounter between human and divine. The study of popular culture is appreciated, in such instances, to the extent it serves traditional theological reflection and religious sensibilities. This effort, however, can easily result in a distortion of popular culture's depth and competing robust intentions and meanings. Often when this type of reading cannot be easily accomplished, popular culture is relegated to the background of theological discourse. This, for instance, accounts for the general disregard for rap music by most scholars within black religious studies. It can be difficult to wrap the conservative religious mind (e.g., those thinking about religion in strict institutional terms) around the bald and raw depictions of life found in the music and lyrics of figures such as The Game. In such instances when the rapper asks an epistemologically driven question put simply as "Ya heard?" the black scholar of religion might respond, "No, thank God!" This is problematic in that the scholar believes herself or himself to have opened academic exploration to the realities of popular culture, but this is done without allowing popular culture to actually penetrate and inform the academic's work.

Black male theologians are not the only scholars to engage popular culture in various ways with varying degrees of success. Unlike black (male) theology, womanist theology is premised on a direct appeal to popular culture for its theoretical and methodological foundation. In fact, womanist scholarship argues that black women have been excluded from the more traditional modes of power, and that they have voiced their theo-religious sensibilities through creative outlets. Cultural production for womanists, as their name would suggest, draws its epistemological sensibilities and posture from the popular writings of Alice Walker, particularly *In Search of Our Mothers' Gardens*, where she defines and applies the term *womanist* as a style of life and as a hermeneutical device for dissecting the experiences of black women in the United States:

> 1. From *womanish* (opp. of "girlish," i.e., frivolous, irresponsible, not serious). A black feminist of color. From the black folk expression of mother to female children, "you acting womanish," i.e., like a woman. Usually referring to outrageous, audacious, courageous or *willful* behavior. Wanting to know more and in greater depth than is considered "good" for one. Interested in grown-up doings. Acting grown up. Being grown up. Interchangeable with another black folk expression: You trying to be grown: Responsible. In charge. *Serious*.
>
> 2. Also: A woman who loves other women, sexually and/or nonsexually. Appreciates and prefers women's culture, women's emotional flexibility (values tears as natural counterbalance of laughter), and women's strength. Sometimes loves individual men, sexually and/or nonsexually. Committed to revival and wholeness of entire people, male and female. Not a separatist, except periodically, for health. Traditionally universalist, as in "Mama, why are we brown, pink, and yellow, and our cousins are white, beige, and black?" ans.: "Well, you know the colored

race is just like a flower garden, with every color flower represented."
Traditionally capable, as in "Mama, I'm walking to Canada and I'm taking you and a bunch of other slaves with me." Reply: "It wouldn't be the first time."[14]

Based on this early association of womanist scholars in religious studies to African American literature, it was a natural move to highlight for investigation the fiction (and to a lesser extent the nonfiction) writings of black women as a way of framing theological studies. Using these materials has been important from their perspective because such texts house the voices of black women, indicating "the operations of the ordinary theologies of black women's daily lives as rich sources for theological constructions, emphasizing the importance of spiritual and communal life."[15] One sees this, for example, in the early work of the pioneering figure Katie Cannon, who maps out a womanist approach to ethics using the writings of Zora Neale Hurston. Hurston's writings, according to Cannon, exposed the "elaborate façade of myths, traditions, and rituals erected to couch systems of injustice in America." And, while so doing, she celebrated the creative ethical and audacious ways in which African Americans express "understanding and manifestations of courageous living."[16] For Cannon, close attention to the voices of black women expressed in short stories, etc., can foster the formation of religious studies as an intellectual practice that is community responsive and liberating.

For Delores Williams, more so than for some other womanists, this work does not distinguish particular cultural sources as much as make available a proper hermeneutic for the exploration of all source material: "Where would I be in order to construct Christian theology (or god-talk) from the point of view of African American women?" In responding to this question, Williams recounts the following exchange: "I pondered this question for over a year. Then one day my professor responded to my complaint about the absence of black women's experiences from *all* Christian theology (black liberation and feminist theologies included). He suggested that my anxiety might lessen if my exploration of African-American cultural sources was consciously informed by the statement 'I am a black WOMAN.' He was right. I had not realized before that I read African-American sources from a black male perspective. I assumed black women were included."[17] Mindful of this need for a mode of interpretation in favor of black women, Williams explores the unexceptional stories of black women, such as the biblical figure Hagar, for the exceptional qualities of creativity, ingenuity, and perseverance they present to the careful reader. In this way Williams undertakes the development of a theological discourse that is healthy for the African American community because it takes seriously the voices of those most often forgotten.

A Cartography of the Religious through the Popular:
An Alternate Conceptual Posture

While womanist scholarship is creative and insightful, much of it is insular and tends to shape popular culture to fit the religio-theological sensibilities of the scholar as opposed to allowing cultural production, or popular culture, to influence in a deep sense the work of the scholar of black religion. Furthermore, it seems that many womanist scholars make use of a hermeneutic of familiarity when drawing on popular culture to inform their understanding of the history, experiences, thoughts, and voices of black women. By this I mean that many womanists siphon into comfortable existential containers the "raw" material of life presented in literature, music, and so on regardless of "fit." Hence, for example, the character Celie from *The Color Purple* can provide a strong critique of the traditional Christian doctrine of God and theological anthropology without it having any visible impact on the manner in which womanist scholarship by and large understands the nature and meaning of religious experience.[18]

Furthermore, Alice Walker's panentheism is noted, at times, without challenging the existing narrow theories of religion and religious experience popular with womanist scholars, although Walker's thought frames womanist methodology and theory.[19] To put it bluntly, the typical theories of religion within womanist scholarship remain deeply (and often narrowly) Christian in spite of Walker's openness (in fiction and nonfiction) to a more naturalistic conception of divinity and religion.[20] Walker and her characters such as Celie recognize the plurality of ways in which the significance of the universe is expressed, but many of her interpretations do not.

The vague shape of this dilemma is present, it seems to me, in the work titled "Roundtable Discussion: Christian Ethics and Theology in Womanist Perspectives," which was published in the *Journal of Feminist Studies in Religion* in fall 1989. In this publication, Cheryl Sanders raised questions concerning the appropriation of Walker's womanist concept in light of its departure from traditional (read narrow) Christian theological sensibilities. This critique represented a minority opinion to be sure, but we still await the formation of a response to Sanders that offers a deeply conceptual pluralistic sense of religious experience and a comparative theologi-cal framework. While the cultural production that black women offer to the world is diverse and at times contradictory, the interpretation of this material by womanist scholars of religion is often singular in focus and teleological in perspective.[21]

Both womanist scholarship and black male scholarship within the arena of theology in particular and religious studies in general harbor a similar problem—namely, a notable discomfort with popular culture. Cul-tural production is touted as a means by which to explore and unpack the depth and texture of African American religious thought and experience. However, it often is handled poorly in both theological camps in that the deep richness and variance it represents is not fully depicted. This being the case, popular culture as a theological tool for black male theologians and womanist scholars does not inform in a significant way epistemology of African American theological life. It strikes me that theological work has involved in large part an attempt to explain away the messy nature of existence, to make sense of complexity and paradox. It often understands history as being teleological in nature and provides a rather "flat" depiction of the African American religious landscape.

Popular Culture

Popular culture studied within the context of black religious studies can provide thick and textured examples of the ways in which humans make meaning. In this regard, popular culture might offer an open and public discourse on the large questions of life, even when these questions are cov-ered in such nonspectacular ways as a Jerry Springer wrestling match, a *Fear Factor* meal of something decayed, or the vexing refrain of a disco-era hit. The point is not acceptance of particular approaches to questions fram-ing life and relationship but rather the various and messy ways in which people seek to uncover who, what, when, and why they are invaluable to the scholar concerned with issues of ultimate concern and orientation. Popular culture is a public and rich terrain, it is a space where so many find themselves, and it is a varied and complex development. Paul Gilroy is correct in his view that cultural production connects social groups and communities in a web of mutuality and ontological and existential concern that merits attention.[22]

The geography of human creativity and angst takes on a different look when popular culture is given serious attention. And some of what this geography entails via popular culture is deeply religious and is the proper business of those whose professional lives are committed to better understanding religion and religious experience. In light of these views, questions naturally come to mind: What are the key issues and questions one should address in the study of religion and popular culture? What methodological issues need to be clarified and addressed to enable increasing sophistication in advanced research in this field? I would like to combine these questions by asking: What are some key theoretical and methodological considerations needing attention as we push forward the study of religion and popular culture? With respect to this question, I would like to offer a particular way of framing black theological studies of popular culture by way of a metaphor. I do so because I believe that a significant hindrance to such work involves the problematic nature of our theological vocabulary and grammar.

Popular culture is messy, contradictory, confusing, and complex. And so traditional elements of black and womanist theological vocabularies do not adequately, or even necessarily, address this messiness without doing damage to it. This is certainly the case with discussions of theodicy. Furthermore, does soteriology really capture what 50 Cent might mean by "Get rich or die trying"? No, it does not. Or does theological anthropology as often formulated adequately address the nature of self and self-consciousness sloppily noted in shows like *The Bernie Mac Show*, or *Run's House*? I doubt it. Furthermore, does our theological discourse that privileges the written word have the flexibility and creativity necessary to properly handle nonwritten texts?

Popular culture—say, in the form of visual arts—holds in tension material existence and nonmaterial impulses, and it brings to the mind of the viewer the presence of this nonmaterial impulse in ways that influence relationships with historical realities and materials. Like the paintings of Jean-Michel Basquiat, it has the ability to affect us by drawing into the open concealed realities, possibilities, and meanings, and thereby teach us about the connections between historical developments and inner urges. In the area of theological and religious studies what is perhaps necessary is a rethinking of our grammar and vocabulary in ways that allow our work to be deeply influenced by the public sensibilities of popular culture. Mindful of this challenge I favor a mutlidisciplinary approach whereby the various layers, textures, and tones of popular culture are unpacked.

I suggest an alternate posture concerning this enterprise—one that involves viewing this work as a type of religious cartography. There has been spotty use of this term in some black and womanist theologies, yet it is typically meant to resemble a teleological depiction of black life—a charting of God's cropping up in human affairs.[23] By way of a working definition, however, I mean by cartography a less Christian-specific presentation of material—an arranging and fixing in time and space of the contours and routes of meaning making. The term connotes by way of relationships between various elements the parameters and shape of reality. By so doing cartography frames our sense of ontology as well as our awareness of and response to existential situations. This metaphor of cartography might also suggest a mode of analysis, one that is comfortable with the tensions, paradoxes, inconsistencies, and often nonwritten nature of popular culture in that it allows for a visual description of the religiously centered concerns, questions, and so on that mark popular culture.

The novelist Peter Turchi is correct when he notes that there are ways in which the writer can be understood as a cartographer. For the writer involved in religious studies, this might involve using signs and symbols along with words and rituals as a means to express by charting the nature and meaning of the religious sensibilities and activities of various communities. This is a rather loose use of terminology—one that involves some linguistic slippage that professionals in cartography might find troubling—but I think it is a potentially important application for those of us in theological and religious studies.

Religious and theological studies as cartography (combined with what I noted a few years ago concerning theology as archaeology)[24] is a vital shift in symbolism and metaphor in that the process of mapping is sensitive to the more straightforward dimensions of religious experience (such as location of rituals and doctrine). Furthermore, it hints at a corrective for the inadequacies of our language for capturing what I have described as the significance of religion in a more general quest for complex subjectivity—the elemental nature of religion not completely known through physical structures, rituals, doctrine. In this sense religious studies as cartography both marks the known and is sensitive to what is beyond our ability to fully comprehend.

Plotting Out the Religious and the Popular

On our metaphorical map there are blank spots that play a role in pointing out patterns of life and the arrangement of relationships. These spots correspond to the activities for transformation operating outside the status quo and outside the normative structures of society, and these developments are precisely those with which liberationists are concerned. Expressing this concern as a liberation theologian involves mapping the efforts on the part of the oppressed that resonate with what Rolland Paulston notes as a turn in his own work as a cartographer to a focus on "current efforts by individuals and cultural groups seeking to be more self-defining in their sociospatial relations and how they are represented."[25] Such a mapping, I believe, allows for a vital tension and an important two-way focus on both the center and periphery of meaning-making efforts, and as such recognizes the situational nature of religious developments manifest in this case through popular culture.[26] Yet, mapping does this in a way that sees the significance of both the content and form of this meaning making without trying to flatten out, for the sake of consistency and uniformity, the rough terrain that is religiosity in popular culture. In this case, popular culture serves as the material for this new mapping, this detailed cartography of religion and religious life.

Signs and symbols, words and rituals, are used to chart the nature and meaning of the religious sensibilities and activities of various communities. For the scholar concerned with issues of transformation or liberation, for one with a sense of the historical development of terror, this might involve mapping the tone and texture of meaning making or sketching the geography of what Charles Long labels the crawl back through history toward the first creation of the self.[27] Such a thick analysis allows for perspective and for a framing of life in the context of our portion of the world that notes the pleasures and tensions premised on the logic of construction resulting in what we know and feel as "black" and "brown" bodies. Yet, it does so in a way that sees the significance of both the content and form of this meaning making. It involves a thick, complex, and dialogical process of recognition.

What is more, for the religious scholars mapping the religious landscape or world of particular communities, this cartography is shaped or influenced in some ways by forces that transcend the individual. Even for the ethical humanist, such a mapping even when premised on the rightness of naturalistic sensibilities is informed by the push and pull of the unseen and the transcendent, but in this case such a reality is framed by the large sense of community of which the individual is a part but whose logic supersedes his or her own reasoning. Whereas the theist might note the need for faith as the proper posture toward this grand otherness, the humanist or religious naturalist might push for imagination or, more important, a sense of fantasy as providing needed flexibility when approaching the contours of our strange world. I find Turchi's words to be a suitable framing of this process for the cartographer of religion when dealing with the religious landscape of any community. "It seems," he writes, "that no matter how many discoveries we make, we tell ourselves we've reached the end of the knowable world. Maybe some of us are always inclined to claim we've done all we can do, while others of us refuse to rest; or maybe it's that one day we're defiant, the next we're humbled, awed by the scope of the mysteries around us."[28]

What is of fundamental significance is the manner by which exposing or rendering radically visible social boundaries through mapping allows for a questioning of their necessity and their permanence. Boundaries are chosen. What we have is recognition of the various fields of power as well as their logic. Such cartography of the religious is best, I believe, when it puts in relief a cross-section of communities involved in this enterprise. By its representation of sameness and difference, the cartography metaphor may in fact provide deep value in the ability to present comparative and complex arrangements of "realities," contested sites of knowledge and meaning, as well as competing conceptions of socioeconomic want and need.[29]

The Challenge of Mapping Twos

In a somewhat horrifying way, mapping with respect to the Americas is stamped on the bodies of African Americans and Latinos/as, thereby providing the manner in which these bodies are read and regarded. Such a plotting provides an alternate, nonspoken vocabulary and grammar for the articulation of certain formations of the real, the visible, and by extension the invisible. Yet there is a tension in that these bodies have never been content with the traditional mapping—the mapping of conquest through the logic of (re)construction. Rather, by their very existence they propose other mappings, at times in conflicting formulations, and other possible directions and routes for meaning making. That is, the presence of African Americans and Latinos and Latinas serves as an example of the truth of any mapping—there are alternate possibilities and the authority of one over others is contested and must be fought for continuously.

Mindful of the above, the essays in *The Ties That Bind* as well as in this volume are for me first an exercise in negative cartography—that is, the recognition of the limits or "lies," to borrow from Mark Monmonier, that shape the process of re-presenting reality. Or in more explicit terms, "a good map," writes Monmonier, "tells a multitude of white lies; it suppresses truth to help the user see what needs to be seen. Reality is three-dimensional, rich in detail, and far too factual to allow a complete yet uncluttered two-dimensional graphic scale model. Indeed, a map that did not generalize would be useless. But the value of a map depends on how well its generalized geometry and generalized content reflect a chosen aspect of reality."[30] In applying cartography as metaphor, Turchi makes a similar remark when he states, "How we see depends, in part, on what we want to see . . . Every map intends not simply to serve us but to influence us."[31] While Monmonier and Turchi note the presence of "deliberate falsification or subtle propaganda in map making," I want to highlight and problematize the presence of these distortions. In short I value a heightened skepticism concerning map making. Based in part on my appreciation for Paul Gilroy's reframing of modernity through the black Atlantic as heuristic device, I want to hold in tension, to see as the source of the problem, Monmonier's understanding of certain lies as required and his rendering of value based on how well the "lie" addresses a "chosen aspect of reality." Further, I want to think this through in terms of the realities and theological mission of African Americans and Latinos and Latinas.

Perhaps some shortcomings in mapping are unavoidable in order to adjust for scale, loss of dimension, etc., but the general idea of deception is given weight and a charge by sociopolitical connotations and a historical context (Why are certain dimensions of reality distorted; and what guides this process?). This process of distortion, in other words, buttresses certain sociopolitical arrangements and sensibilities. Should a member of a community that is in part shaped through such a lie written across a certain arrangement of sociopolitical, economic, and cultural frameworks see the ability to render visible and invisible, to enlarge or shrink, elements of reality any other way?

Religion in the Americas, in this case the portion called the United States, involves certain "lies." This involves a mapping of reality that gives central importance to the "city on a hill" ideology that guided many early colonists—one that allowed for the use of slave labor and the destruction of indigenous populations. In short, a religious mapping of the Americas gives some shape to the realities of Latinos/as and African Americans. Even more recent mappings of life in the United States—ones that seek to be multicultural in orientation are often drawn from older mappings—are never completely free from the flaws that marked earlier interpretations of life and reality in the United States. Yet this status quo mode of mapping is not the only possibility. It is not the only way to articulate and arrange the meanings of existence.

Mapping Twos and Studying Religion

It became clear to me, and remains so, that there are shared existential and epistemological realities that the "children" of the New World such as African Americans and Latinos/as might discuss and utilize in theologically productive ways in order to begin a process of undertaking a more positive cartography of the religious landscape of the United States. However, such mapping, if it is to have felt meaning, must involve more than narrowly contextual materials and insular conversations. We must face and address the silences that punctuate our collective reality, and maneuver through the uncomfortable, and at times awkward, gaps in our mutual knowledge that represent another dimension of what it has meant to be "othered." Mindful of this need, as well as of an already shared theological language and grammar, the next effort should be a reimagining of the religious landscape of the United States in part through the often overlapping movements of the popular cultural production of both groups.

There is little doubt that within the United States Latinos/as and African Americans share a similar socioeconomic and political position—that is, related existential and ontological "spaces" and a certain mapping of reality. To borrow from Charles Long, both communities have undergone a certain type of "creation"—a second creation—by which the contact and conquest that marked the formation of the New World overdetermined and fixed their identity.[32] In simple terms, both communities bear in their flesh even today, perhaps to differing degrees, the consequences of the travel across the Atlantic. Both wrestle against the terror and dread associated with the warping of self-consciousness, of one's sense of being, that stem from being rendered the "other." Both face destruction of their physical bodies stemming from an unequal distribution of economic resources, while both are plied with the rhetoric of politicians who recognize the significance of these voting blocs but who offer little in the way of renewed and vibrant life options. Both groups have responded creatively to ontological and socioeconomic trauma through the praxis of liberation theology shaped in part through attention to cultural production.

Within this theological work of liberation there is a concern with sustained reflection on the proactive dimensions of humanity and well-being captured in both communities' religious life. In this way, theological studies at their best within both communities have highlighted the manner in which African American and Latino/a religious experience and identity entails a creative tension between reaction and creativity (or initiative) within a troubled historical moment. In fact, a comparison of the theological books and articles by thinkers within these two communities reveal substantial similarities in their theoretical framework and approach. But a shared sense of what it means to do theology, how one does theology and for whom theology is done, has seldom resulted in theologians initiating and sustaining deep or "thick" exchange.

Some might speak of this disconnect as the result of differing cultural sensibilities that promote, if not necessitate, insular conversations and encourage the maintenance of an insider-outsider paradigm for discourse. Yet even if one recognizes cultural distinctions this should not point to an inability to converse but rather to rich differences that might play a role in healthy and complex theological exchange. Furthermore, theologians from both communities operate from a position of stability and intellectual "legitimacy" that makes dialogue possible. That is, the theological work of both communities is recognized in the academy—with the presence of groups devoted to both within the American Academy of Religion serving as only one example—and this provides a space in which to wrestle with theological issues of mutual concern. At its best the exchange generated by these and other questions has involved a genuine, "gloves-off" approach to exchange—the sharing of theological agreement and disagreement—with the intention of increased understanding and greater cooperation.

I would like to begin this process with some attention to the religious terrain marking this dialogue. Christianity dominates the religious terrain of both groups, but there are other traditions that are supple, vibrant, and very much alive. And the boundaries between these various traditions are soft, thereby allowing for some ritual, theological, and doctrinal exchange between them. That is, the process of making meaning, of developing a fuller sense of humanity, that marks all of these traditions allows for overlapping intent that on some level makes some of the "soft" elements of these various traditions translatable and transferable. For example, physical bodies have merit and theological weight. Yet the sense of embodiment articulated in connection to liberation theology is highly spiritualized and discussed in terms of the historical (i.e., sociopolitical and economic) placement of these bodies. I suggest that theologians from both communities have fallen short through their inability to articulate theologically the value of these bodies as both sources of pleasure (including the relationship with the "divine") and as pleasured, within the context of the erotic, in the sense put forth by Paul Tillich.

Furthermore, the kind of dialogue we undertake ought to be sensitive to and comfortable with paradox and difference—the complex nature of relationship. Hence we must recognize the theological weight and epistemological centrality of competing claims if theological education is to progress in ways beneficial to the dialogue recently started by Latino/a and African American theologians. In other words, this dialogue must grow to encompass a comparative component—one that recognizes the diversity of religious experiences. I have made this argument before and I restate it here.

I am pushing for a mode of discourse framed by a post-apologetic modality of inquiry that entails a method of exploration that can respond to our religiously complex and shifting terrain. This is not to suggest the complete removal of liberation theologies, for instance, as a method of exploration. Rather, I am calling for the "death" of a certain illusion regarding theology's work, and a deconstruction of a myopic, religiously chauvinistic, and provincial understanding of theological discourse. This entails a movement beyond theologies as a general (and religiously biased) theory of religious experience, along with the recognition that Christian liberation theology speaks to and about only one dimension of what it means to be and to be religious.

It strikes me that theological dialogue sensitive to competing religious claims can only develop through a willingness to creatively adjust both theological language and grammar. A case in point is that the transformation as expressed in liberation theologies done by these communities—even in its limited articulation as two-dimensional—is housed in flesh. That is, these two modalities of liberation theology are in fact theologies of embodiment. There is an explicit and profound appreciation for the physical form, for black and brown bodies. By body I mean both the physical form (flesh) and the megasymbol connoting all things foreign and dangerous in the popular imagination of modern (white) America. In this sense the body rendered visible through a certain history of race and ethnicity represents the physical world of work and pleasure, and it also serves as a prime symbol of chaos. In either case, in physical terms or as symbolic representation African Americans and Latinos/as connote something both appealing and repulsive within the historical development of North America, and serve as "things" to be controlled vis-à-vis their

categorization as inferior. Hence, the language used to discuss the placement of bodies serves to reinforce social sensibilities and structures. As
David Davis reminds us, language has often been religious and theological, and the implications of this practice should be a part of the ongoing
dialogue between these two communities.[33] It is in response to the terror
and dread of this predicament that we react in our religions and find representation in our popular culture, and it is these various responses that we
should appreciate and map in our theological and religious studies.

Finally, liberationist scholarship as done in both communities has involved, to some extent, an expansion of the language of theology to include
culturally informed nuances of and alterations to categories of meaning
and perception. Yet, we have maintained the same theological grammar,
with the same rules of usage for mapping out patterns of meaning. This
can change, and popular culture may provide both the content and form
of this linguistic transformation. This is because complex cartographies
of religiosity using the resources of popular culture promise thickness of
discourse as well as a deeper appreciation for the varied and fluid nature of
the boundaries between the ways in which we express our lives.

Notes

This essay, particularly the last section, is drawn from Anthony B. Pinn, "Facing
Competing Claims," *Theological Education* 38, no. 2(2002): 87–95.

1 See Jupiter Hammon, *America's First Negro Poet: The Complete Works of Jupiter
Hammon of Long Island.*
2 Locke, *The New Negro*, 4–5.
3 Ibid., 53.
4 Ibid., 10.
5 Ibid., xvii, 47.
6 The genealogy of black theology has been examined in various publications.
See, for example, Pinn, "Black Theology in Historical Perspective," 23–35;
Cone and Wilmore, *Black Theology*; and Hopkins, *Introducing Black Theology
of Liberation.*
7 Cone, *A Black Theology of Liberation*, 27–28.
8 See, for example, Evans, *Spiritual Empowerment in African American Literature.*
9 See Evans, *We Have Been Believers*; Hopkins and Cummings, *Cut Loose Your
Stammering Tongue*; and Hopkins, *Shoes That Fit Our Feet, Down, Up, and
Over,* and *Being Human.*
10 Hopkins, "Black Theology on God," 99.
11 Cone, *A Black Theology of Liberation*, 27–28.

12 Earl, *Dark Symbols, Obscure Signs*, 154.

13 Abraham D. Rogers, *African Folktales*, cited in Earl, *Dark Symbols, Obscure Signs*, 55.

14 Walker, *In Search of Our Mothers' Gardens*, xi.

15 Mitchem, *Introducing Womanist Theology*, 72.

16 See Cannon, "Resources for a Constructive Ethic," in *Katie's Canon*, 89.

17 Williams, *Sisters in the Wilderness*, 1.

18 See, for example, Walker, *The Color Purple*, 175–79.

19 See, for example, Walker, "The Only Reason You Want to Go to Heaven Is That You Have Been Driven Out of Your Mind," in *Anything We Love Can Be Saved*.

20 More recent womanist voices, such as that of Melanie Harris (who teaches at Texas Christian University), have raised questions concerning the nature of womanist appropriations of Alice Walker. However, as opposed to the conservative and narrow Christological critique offered by Cheryl Sanders in the 1980s (see the discussion below), Harris's critique is meant to enlarge the use of Walker and the religious meaning of this appropriation. See Melanie Harris, *Uncovering Womanism*.

21 An exception to this posture is presented in Stewart, *Three Eyes for the Journey*.

22 See Gilroy, *Black Atlantic*.

23 See, for instance, Dwight Hopkins's passing reference to cartography in "Black Theology on God," 109, 110.

24 Pinn, *Varieties of African American Religious Experience*, chapter five.

25 Paulston, *Social Cartography*, xviii.

26 Smith, *Map Is Not Territory*, 101.

27 See Long, *Significations*.

28 Turchi, *Maps of the Imagination*, 225.

29 See Paulston, "Preface: Four Principles for a Non-Innocent Social Cartography," in *Social Cartography*.

30 Monmonier, *How to Lie with Maps*, 25.

31 Turchi, *Maps of the Imagination*, 78, 88.

32 Long, *Significations*; see the chapter titled "The Oppressive Elements in Religion and the Religions of the Oppressed."

33 See David Davis, *Inhuman Bondage*; *The Problem of Slavery in Western Culture*; and *In the Image of God: Religion, Moral Values, and Our Heritage of Slavery* (New Haven: Yale University Press, 2001).

Benjamín Valentín

◨

RESPONSE TO THE ESSAY BY ANTHONY B. PINN

Anthony Pinn's essay emboldens my belief that there is much that relates black theology and Latino/a theology in the United States, and it strengthens my hope for further comparative and collaborative work between representatives of these two theological communities. The reason for my views is that the essay makes it clear that these two discursive traditions not only share similar and estimable developmental trajectories, methodologies, and aspirations but also similar limitations and inadvertencies. Clearly, black theologians and Latino/a theologians in the United States have analogously granted the realm of culture great importance in their theological undertakings. It seems clear too that this convergence on culture is equally motivated by a shared concern and aspiration—namely, the felt need to counter an unjust cultural-valuational structure in an attempt to remedy gender, sexual, and racial-ethnic injustice, and the desire to allow for the assertion and vindication of group identity. In this sense representatives of these two intellectual communities correspondingly view the realm of culture as neither an optional extra nor an idealist distraction for their "liberationist-inspired" theological enterprise but rather as a terrain for both political struggle and communal empowerment. And so both of these theological traditions in the United States share not only a methodological turning to the realm of culture from very early on in their developmental stages but also similar reasons for doing so.

According to Pinn's essay as well as my essay in this volume it would seem that both of these theological communities unfortunately share a similar problem in regard to their treatment of popular culture and culture more generally. In Pinn's essay he laments a problem that he sees in both womanist and black male theological scholarship—that is, a poor handling of the deep richness and variance of black popular culture. Ironically, he suggests that although the black cultural production of black men and women is touted in black theology in the United States as a means by which to explore and unpack the depth and texture of African American religious thought and experience, black theologians seem to display a discomfort with the variety, messiness, paradoxes, and complexity of black popular culture. As he explains it, sometimes this discomfort reveals itself in an attempt to "Christianize" black cultural agency and creativity, while at other times it is displayed either in an unwillingness to deal with certain expressions or modalities of popular culture or in the attempt to "explain away" the messy nature of cultural agency. I would note that this critique is not very different from the one I vocalized in my own essay on Latino/a theology. There I called for a greater level of immersion in Latino/a popular culture, and a better recognition and acceptance of the disparateness, changeableness, and contradiction of Latino/a culture and of all human cultures generally. And so it would seem that Pinn and I are making similar calls to our respective discursive communities.

In his essay Pinn proposes a method of "religious cartography" to correct the tendency to "flatten" the multiformity and depths of black cultural agency in African American theologies. In my essay, I simply propose a different way of conceptualizing "culture." Rather than seeing culture as a bounded or fixed set of beliefs, conventions, practices, and characteristics assumed to "belong" to a social group, I have proposed that it be conceptualized as a sphere of signification and practice shot through with at times willful and at other times indeliberate action, power relations, struggle, contradiction, transverseness, and change. Thus although we go about it differently Pinn and I are both calling for and proposing correctives that may be conducive toward a fuller and higher-grade portraiture of the variety and complexity of African American and Latino/a agency. Indeed, it is my hope that not only Pinn and I but also our two theological communities can address this call together.

I do wonder, however, whether foundationally there might be some differences at the level of what "culture" actually means that may need to be examined in our future collaborations. I think it might be a good thing if we took some time in the future to explore more deeply the ways in which we may be defining terms such as "culture" and "popular culture" and what this might mean intellectually or conceptually as well as socially and corporeally. To take it a step back, I think it would be fruitful to explore what we mean by the term "culture" to begin with, and whether or not there might actually be different definitions of this word or concept within our works.

Clearly, the term "culture" is a most complex word. As Raymond Williams reminded us in *Keywords* (1976), there are actually few more problematic words than "culture." The complexity of the term and the idea of culture is traceable to its elasticity in meaning. In popular usage the meaning of the term oscillates between a habit of mind, the arts, a general summary of the conventions, practices, and assumptions of an ethnic or social group, a signifying system, or a whole way of life and, therefore, everything from economic production and the family to political institutions. In short, the term stands for many things. At times, therefore, although the terms "culture" and "popular culture" are being used repeatedly, it is difficult to know how we are actually employing the term or what we mean by it. More to the point, I think sometimes we use the word "culture" in different senses. I note, for instance, that at least in the way that Pinn interprets things black theologians in the United States have tended to use the term "culture" to point to those practices, behaviors, postures, and creative or artistic works that express meaning in black communities. Culture here means an activity. Although this sense of culture as "creative agency" is certainly found in Latino/a theology, I submit that Latino/a theologians have thus far tended to use culture more in the sense of identity. Culture in this sense denotes an entity. Although these two senses of the word need not be deemed incommensurate, they are in fact different. How are these different? Does it matter at all that inclinations toward different senses or meanings of the term "culture" might be evident in our works? Does this hinder the purposes of joint and comparative work together? Or, on the contrary, is it not only to be expected but actually welcomed that different conceptions, definitions, and uses of culture are revealed in the annals of these two theological communities? Why is it that these two intellectual communities have gravitated toward these different senses of the word "culture"? Might this say something about their perceived struggles and locations within the broader social realm? In the case of Latinos/as, for example, could it be that the gravitation in their intellectual work toward a use of culture in the sense of identity is reflective of a struggle against nonrecognition (being rendered invisible by means of representational, communicative, and interpretive practices in our social order that often constrain perceptions of race, class, and cultural identity to a black or white structure) and against disrespect (being routinely disparaged as inadequate people, as people who do not belong, as a problem people, and as people who need to be assimilated; and being viewed as "perpetual aliens" in the nation, regardless of citizenship status and years of residence)? These kinds of questions are worthy of some consideration as our two communities continue to explore the possibilities of working together on a theology of culture and holistic liberation.

Benjamín Valentín

▣

TRACINGS: SKETCHING THE CULTURAL

GEOGRAPHIES OF LATINO/A THEOLOGY

In the last few decades a radical change has come about in the theoretical foundations of the humanistic disciplines. Since the early 1980s the intellectual basis for the study of the humanities has been steadily transformed by the importance given to the idea of culture, by the refashioning of "culture" as an analytical category, and by the increase in works on culture. Intellectuals frustrated by some of the limits of a generalist approach to the study of history and society, and by some of the constraints of a solely materialist analysis of the social, have increasingly turned toward an analysis of culture to elucidate the cultural contexts in which individuals and groups act. More and more they have focused on the ways in which humans construct the character of their individual and collective lives through group living. By directing their thinking to the analysis of symbols, rituals, discourse, and cultural practices, intellectuals have opened the doors to a deeper understanding of and appreciation for the particular histories, contexts, experiences, and identities of peoples and social groups.

This more recent interest in the concept and theorization of culture has swept over a wide range of academic disciplines, including the field of theological study. Latino/a theologians in particular have been for quite some time turning to an emphasis on culture in their theologies. From its beginning, Latino/a theology in the United States has placed emphasis on the idea and realm of culture. In fact, the very first text written from a fully intentional and uniquely Latino/a theological perspective, published by

Virgilio Elizondo in 1975, was appropriately titled *Christianity and Culture*. This book not only offered a full-length theological study and expression of the consciousness that emanates from the culture and popular religion of the Mexican American people, but also called attention to the possibility and desirability of a theological interpretation that emanates from the space of the self and of identity. In doing so it began with a contextualized cultural reading of the Hispanic and Latino/a experience. This stress on the idea and realm of culture was to receive continued expression in the subsequent work of Elizondo as well as that of other Latino/a theologians. Indeed, much of the uniqueness of Latino/a theology in the United States derives from the centrality that it has given to matters of culture and from the creativity with which it has treated and employed the category of culture.

The theme of culture has informed much of Latino/a theology in the United States and thus has influenced both its theological and political imagination. Theologically, for instance, it is perceptible in the recurring use of and significance attributed to the concept of *mestizaje* (i.e., cultural hybridity) in the consideration given to the surreptitious activity and potentiality embedded within forms of Latino/a popular religious expression and in the ongoing attempts to theologize Latino/a agency. Politically, the importance of culture is usually expressed through a discourse that seeks to defend and advance Latino/a identities, end cultural domination, and win recognition for Latinos and Latinas. In these ways and others Latino/a theology demonstrates a commitment to the realm of and theorization of culture.[1]

In this essay I want to bring to the surface some of the reasons why Latino/a theologians have generally turned to the realm of culture. In addition, I want to illustrate some of the ways in which Latino/a theologians have employed the idea of culture, and I wish to suggest some ways in which Latino/a theology's turn to culture can be furthered or enhanced.

Why All the Fuss about Culture?

The reasoning behind the emphasis on the realm of culture in Latino/a theology is easily grasped, I believe, when we examine the general history of Latino/as in the United States. To put it simply, from the very beginning we Latino/as have always had to struggle zealously to keep alive our distinctive historical and cultural heritages while also claiming our rightful place as legitimate citizens and active agents in this nation. In light of the cultural devaluation, negative stereotypes, ethnic prejudice, and social marginalization with which Latino/as have often had to contend, Latino/a theologians in the United States have come to the conclusion that there may be sources of oppression other than economic—cultural imperialism, assimilatory pressures, racism, and sexism, among others—affecting the lives of Latino/as in our society. Appropriately, these theologians have turned to the realm of culture in order to unearth, define, and validate a certain set of beliefs and practices connected to Latino/a peoples in the United States in both the past and the present, to promote cultural affirmation among Latinos and Latinas, and to find within that realm a potential space and medium for subversive consciousness that both offers a creative defense of Latino/a cultures and a basis from which to foster positive self and group identity.

As this last commentary should already make clear, the interest of Latino/a theologians in culture is fueled to a good extent by a political concern. Surely other concerns and interests motivate this turn to culture, such as an interest in history and in the aesthetic dimension of Latino/a life past and present. But alongside these other interests there exists an implicit if not explicit political motivation fortifying the interest of Latino/a theologians in culture. In their view and in their theological enterprise culture is neither an optional extra nor an idealist distraction but rather a terrain for and even the very grammar of political struggle. Simply put, Hispanic and Latino/a theologians have devoted a great part of their reflective energies to questions of culture not only in the interest of finding there an inbred source for theological reflection but also in the hopes of resisting unjust social patterns experienced by many Latinos and Latinas, such as cultural domination, assimilatory pressures, nonrecognition, and disrespect. In Latino/a theology, therefore, "culture" is defined in political rather than merely aesthetic terms in the sense that it is understood as the texts, symbols, signs, values, meanings, and practices of everyday life and also as a terrain of conflict and contestation.

This political disposition has in turn laid the foundation for two distinct yet interrelated uses of culture within Latino/a theologies: namely, culture has been employed by these in the sense of identity and in the sense of creative agency. In the first instance the idea of culture is used to refer to the particular historical, experiential, and identity-determining configurations that seem to constitute Latino/a life. In the second case culture is used to refer to the space in which and the process by which meaning is produced, contended for, and continually renegotiated.

To explore these uses of the idea of culture as well as their political undertones within Latino/a theology I turn to the work of two Latino theologians: Virgilio Elizondo and Orlando Espín. Elizondo is perhaps best known for his theological interpretation of hybridity, or more specifically Mexican American mestizaje hybridity. Espín has come to be noted for his exceptional work in the interpretation of Latino/a popular religion. I suggest that the work of these two theologians serves at once to make manifest the emphasis on culture, the political understanding of culture, and the two uses of culture that I see as prominent within Latino/a theology.

Theologizing Mestizaje: Virgilio Elizondo's The Future Is Mestizo *and* Galilean Journey

As the feminist cultural critic Susan Friedman puts it, the discussion of hybridity has "emerged explosively in the late-twentieth century as both rallying cry for anti-purist ways of thinking about 'race' and as a widely used term in postcolonial studies, anthropology, and cultural studies to suggest different forms of cultural mixing and interactive exchange."[2] The term most commonly used within Latino/a literature to speak about these different forms of biological and cultural mixing, as they are found among Latino/a peoples, is mestizaje. This term principally refers to "the process of biological and cultural mixing that occurs after the violent and unequal encounter between cultures."[3] The term, however, is more generally used within Latino/a literature to deal with the multilayered hybridity that lies at the heart of Latino/a cultural history and identity. Latino/a cultures and identities are, after all, the result of a syncretic, eccentric, and disjointed fusion of Iberian, Amerindian, African, and Euro-American influences or cultures.

The particulars of the multidimensional biological and cultural fusion—the mestizaje—that marks Latino/a history began to emerge in the sixteenth century with the arrival in the Americas of the Spanish conquistadores and are related to the rather rapid Spanish conquest and colonization of most of Central and South America, Mexico, large segments of the Caribbean, and much of what is now the southern and western United States. Historians of the Spanish colonial period have established that much of the early Spanish interest in these territories centered on mining.[4] The development of these mines, however, required a larger supply of labor than the Spanish colonizers were willing or able to provide on their own. The result was that the conquered indigenous populations were soon forced into mining labor. But the oppressive labor conditions, scant nourishment, broken family life, and disease that were part of this harsh life of indenture under Spanish rule combined to bring about a swift and dramatic decline in the native populations. This mass extermination affected not only the native Amerindian population but also had tragic consequences for the people of Africa because in order to augment a rapidly declining indigenous labor force the Spaniards took to introducing large numbers of African slaves from the western coast of Africa to the Americas.[5] The proximity of these three groups of people in the Americas occasioned the emergence of a new biological and cultural context as the Spanish and Portuguese, Native American, and African populations increasingly intermingled, thereby creating large populations of mestizo and mestiza and mulatto peoples (i.e., peoples of mixed ancestry). In turn, the mixing between these hybrid, bicultural populations and other peoples commonly took place so that almost innumerable racial, ethnic, and cultural mixtures came into being in the Americas. Present-day Latin American and United States Latino populations have been especially marked by this history and are in some way the biological and cultural result of the tempestuous and startling encounter of these cultures during the Spanish colonial period.

But in the case of Latinos and Latinas in the United States the term mestizaje takes on an added element, for in this instance we also need to take into account the influence of cultural traditions and life experiences in this country. Latino/a identity and culture are the result of a confluence of contexts and cultural heritages that at the very least includes Iberian, Native American, African, and Euro-Anglo influences. Hence, the search for and reconstruction of a denied positive cultural identity must eventually come to terms with the hybrid experiences that shape so much of Latino/a life. This search must also negotiate the ambivalences and transgressive possibilities that mark Hispanic mestizo and mestiza consciousness, one that always emerges from "the dynamics of moving between worlds, and feeling at home and not at home in more than one."[6]

The process of translating lived mestizaje into written discourse can be traced back to the writings of the Latin American intellectual José Vasconcelos in the late nineteenth century and the early twentieth century.[7] In more recent years, however, this process has crossed the U.S. border and found a home in the writings of Latino/a scholars and activists such as Daniel Cooper Alarcón, Guillermo Gomez-Peña, Cherríe Moraga, and especially Gloria Anzaldúa—writers who have given mestizo and mestiza discourse newfound recognition. Even before discussion of hybridity and mestizaje became popular in cultural scholarship in the United States during the late 1980s, however, a Mexican American theologian by the name of Virgilio Elizondo had been working on the interpretation of Latino/a mestizaje. Already in the early 1980s he was employing the concept of mestizaje as a theological starting point from which to interpret the historical experience of Latino/as in the United States. Following his influential lead, most Latino/a theologians have come to see mestizaje, and the matter of cultural identity as a whole, as an important and fertile locus for theological reflection.

In the introduction to *The Future Is Mestizo*, a theological autobiography of sorts that takes the form of a quest narrative, Elizondo discloses that the turn to mestizaje specifically and to culture and matters of identity more generally in his theology finds its beginnings in a personal identity crisis that he had felt since early in his life. "All my life," Elizondo recalls, "I had been pulled in two opposing directions—the U.S. way of life and the Mexican way of life. Sometimes I felt the pull would be so great that it would rip me apart."[8] He elucidates the roots and contours of his Mexican American identity as follows: "I lived on the border between two nationalities. I was an inside-outsider to both. I was 'Mexican' in the United States and *gringo/pocho* in Mexico. . . . I gradually became more and more aware of the many things I was not: I was not and would never be, even if I wanted to, a regular U.S.–American. Yet neither would I be a *puro Mexicano*. There were identities that I knew that I was and was not at the same time: U.S.–American, Mexican, Spanish, Indian. Yet I was!"[9] These declarations are immensely helpful for understanding Elizondo's work because they reveal, among other things, that his theology emanates from the space of identity—both self and collective identity. Particularly, they disclose that the starting point of Elizondo's theology is a preoccupation with the Mexican American's struggle for positive self and communal identity amid the contradictions that abound in the physical, emotional, and spiritual borderlands of the southwestern United States.

The struggle against cultural oppression and identity suppression has had a long legacy in Mexican American history, and it is no wonder that Mexican Americans have had to grapple long and hard with such matters. After all, the foundational narrative of "Mexicanness" intrinsically involves a dual story of conquest, colonization, and miscegenation. The first conquest involved the Spanish subjugation of the indigenous peoples of what is now Mexico and the southwestern United States during the sixteenth century, and it included the imposition not only of Spanish rule but also of Spanish culture. The second conquest consisted of the U.S. invasion and subsequent colonization of the great northern regions of Mexico, from California to Texas. The aftereffects of these conquests continue to reverberate within the Mexican American psyche. Mexican American culture and consciousness continue to rest firmly upon dynamics that unfolded during these two conquests. And what unfolds from this history of conquest is in every sense an ambiguity, for it at once grants the resources for the creation of a new being, a new race or mestizo/a people, and also "a site for wounding, a space for the exercise of power over others."[10] Indeed, to this very day Mexican Americans continue to grapple with this site for wounding at the United States borderlands. As Gloria Anzaldúa puts it, in many respects this site continues to be a *"herida abierta* [open wound] where the third world grates against the first and bleeds."[11]

Quite possibly, Elizondo reflects, this wound has most afflicted Mexican Americans at the inner level of the self, and in the realm of signification, of symbolic culture. Manifesting his strong focus on the realm of symbolic culture and identity, Elizondo suggests that the most poisonous aspect of these conquests lay in the attempt to destroy the worldview, rituals, symbols, and the very means by which the conquered peoples sustained meaning in their existence: "Beneath the violence of physical conquest," he states, "there is the deeper violence of the disruption that destroys the conquereds' worldview, which gave cohesion and meaning to their existence."[12] And surely wherever there occurs a disruption in the realm of culture, in the region of symbolic action, one will also necessarily witness obstruction and perplexity in the province of existential identity.

Complicating matters further, Mexican Americans have also long confronted the hurtful biases that often accompany a mixed race and culturally hybrid identity, and these are prejudices that have not yet completely disappeared. In light of the widespread influence of Western racialism, and the hold that purist ways of thinking about race have had in the Western world, the tendency in our societies has been to speak of interracial and intercultural mixing mostly in derogatory terms. Human biological and cultural hybridity has varyingly been denigrated as the mongrelization of humanity, as the degeneration of pure race or pure culture, and as a source of inferior beings and ghettoized cultures. To be sure, although there has been some change in both the law and culture of our nation, the concept of a multifaceted identity is still not easily accepted in the dominant discourse of the United States. To claim and affirm an identity marked by hybridity, therefore, one must still go against the grain.

In view of all of these pressures, Elizondo opts to place his attention firmly on the critical area of culture and self-definition. Moreover, in the process of his own inner quest and struggle he comes to the conclusion that the achievement of both an adequate resistance against cultural oppression and an affirming self-identity inheres in the ability of the Mexican American and Latino/a to reclaim and live out the radical potential that exists in a mestizo/a existence. Additionally, by affirming their hybrid identities, Elizondo suggests, Mexican Americans may actually usher in new life not only for themselves but also for the betterment of everyone. Briefly put, Elizondo's answer to the cultural hybridity of his own Mexican American identity, and the physical, sociopolitical, and psychic pressures that come with it, is a full embrace of the vulnerable yet transcendent and utopic "in-betweenness" that a mestizo/a existence offers. Accordingly, he fully undertakes in his theology a revaluing of mestizaje and an elucidation of the power embedded within it. Mestizo and mestiza identity, as Elizondo conceives it, admits for much more than pain and dislocation; it is also a liminal space filled with potentiality, and it is a prospective site of grace.

In his yearning to uncover the potential that exists in the "third space" created by a mestizo and mestiza existence—the positive synergy that lies waiting to be discovered within the dual or multiple identity of culturally hybrid individuals—Elizondo draws an interesting analogy between the mestizaje of Mexican Americans and that of the historical Jesus. The basic intention of his analogy is to elucidate both the abstruse evocations of rejection, pain, and spiritual searching that mestizaje evokes in a racially stratified social context, as well as the healing, indeed redemptive, transcendence that it holds for self and society. To build such an analogy, Elizondo turns his attention to the earthly identity of Jesus—that is, to Jesus's sociocultural identity.[13]

So who was this Jesus? And what was his earthly sociocultural identity? Elizondo points out that he was a Galilean Jew—a native of the town of Nazareth in the region known as Galilee. According to Elizondo, what is noteworthy about the Galilee of Jesus's time is that it was a great border region between the Greeks and the Jews of Judea that also served as a natural crossing place for travel routes. "It was," therefore, "a land of great mixture and of an ongoing mestizaje" where different cultures were continuously clashing, interweaving, and fusing to create new syncretic or hybrid cultural traditions.[14] Elizondo points out that whereas subsequent generations of Christians have glossed over Jesus's earthly identity, the early Christian communities highlighted his Galilean origin and gave it special significance, as evidenced by the fact that "it is mentioned sixty-one times in the New Testament."[15]

Elizondo asserts, however, that this mestizaje was not regarded favorably by the dominant social, cultural, and religious hierarchies of Jesus's time. Galilean Jews were often doubly rejected as hybrid and as border persons. They were on the one hand scorned by those Gentiles who despised Jews, and on the other hand were regarded with patronizing contempt by the pure-minded Jews of Jerusalem: "The natural *mestizaje* of Galilee was a sign of impurity and a cause for rejection. The Pharisees looked down upon 'the people of the land' because they were ignorant of the law. The Sadducees looked down upon them because they were somewhat lax in matters of religious attendance and familiarity with the rules of temple worship."[16] Moreover, says Elizondo, "The Galilean Jews spoke with a very marked accent and most likely mixed their language quite readily with the Greek of the dominant culture and the Latin of the Roman Empire. Peter could deny Jesus, but there was no way he could deny he was a Galilean. The moment he opened his mouth he revealed his Galilean identity."[17]

The point of Elizondo's excursion into the particulars of the historical Jesus is to describe the kind of racial and cultural hybridity that characterized Jesus's sociocultural identity and the pathologies of oppression that it faced. A biological and cultural mestizo identity was a source of ridicule and rejection in Jesus's time, just as it often is today. As a cultural mestizo who was born in Galilee, Jesus likely was culturally vilified as a deviant. It was no wonder, then, that the pure-minded Jews despised him and became indignant when Pilate proclaimed him king of the Jews: "A scandal to all the pious and the pure of society. How could such a one be their savior and king."[18] Yet as a Galilean Jew he also was marginalized from the Roman political establishment and was considered an outsider within the dominant "Gentile" cultural and intellectual mainstreams of his time. In short, as a mestizo Jesus experienced firsthand the vulnerability that comes with a borderlands existence—the uneasy feeling of never being quite at home in any of the dominant cultural geographies of his time and, perhaps, on occasion not even in his own body. Elizondo puts it this way: "When the Epistle to the Philippians says that Jesus became nothing, it is no mere figure of speech. In a very existential way, he became the nothing of all human groups—the *mestizo* whose existence is the nonexistence of permanent exclusion. No matter where you go or where you are, you are never fully accepted because you are the other."[19]

Although Jesus's mestizo identity undoubtedly was regarded with disfavor by most people during his time, Elizondo emphasizes that it nevertheless was also a source of healing, indeed redemptive, transcendence. Jesus's beginnings in the highly mixed environment of Galilee, Elizondo suggests, allowed him the opportunity to learn not just from his Jewish faith but also from the many other traditions that enriched his home territory. This provided fertile ground for the cultivation of an inner capacity in Jesus to move beyond the social and cultural borders of his time and to break the barriers of separation that these borders engendered. Being at once an inside-outsider and an outside-insider to the cultural geographies of his time, Jesus inhabited an "in-between" space that uniquely privileged him to see and appreciate the best and worst of the cultures that prevailed in ancient Judea. It was in Galilee, Elizondo intimates, that Jesus first learned to juggle cultures and to develop a plural personality in order to survive sanely; and it was through the process of this learning that he came to offer something new to his world: a mode of being that demonstrated a tolerance for contradictions and challenged the fixity of the delimiting human borders and categories of his time.

Moreover, Elizondo intimates that Jesus's identification with the most rejected of society and the affinity that he demonstrated toward these people during his ministry were at least in part the result of his mestizo origins and his own experience of rejection as a borderlands dweller. Having learned of the virulent side of society's absolutes through his own marginalization and suffering as a mestizo, Jesus, Elizondo suggests, was better able to understand the virtue and necessity of an inclusive sensibility and ministry. In encapsulating his intimations on Jesus's mestizo identity in the language of a traditional soteriology, Elizondo surmises that "the apparent nonimportance and rejection of Galilee are the very bases for its all-important role in the historic eruption of God's saving plan for humanity. The human scandal of God's way does not begin with the cross, but with the historico-cultural incarnation of his own Son in Galilee. . . . What the world rejects, God chooses as his very own."[20] For Elizondo's purposes, then, it is of great consequence that in the biblical narrative of Jesus's life ultimate redemption is shown to spring forth from the margins and, more precisely, from the interstitial site that a mestizo and mestiza experience generates. The core of the Christian Gospel, as Elizondo sees it, announces that "one of the marginated ones became the source of solidarity and messianic hope among the masses of hopeless people."[21]

The ultimate intention of Elizondo's tracing of Jesus's sociocultural identity is to draw an analogy between it and the Mexican American mestizo/a experience. Accordingly, therefore, his reflections in *Galilean Journey* and *The Future Is Mestizo* end with a comparison of Jesus's mestizo identity and the condition of Mexican American cultural identity today. "Being a Jew in Galilee," Elizondo writes, "was very much like being a Mexican-American in Texas." Just as the Jews of Galilee were "considered too Jewish to be accepted by the gentile population" and yet "too contaminated with pagan ways to be accepted by the pure-minded Jews of Jerusalem, so have the Mexican-Americans been rejected by two groups": namely, the Anglos in the United States and the Mexicans in Mexico.[22] Yet just as Jesus was able to generate new life from the margins, and just as he was able to come to terms with his status as an inside-outsider, Elizondo believes that Mexican Americans too find themselves in a unique position to advance a liberating mission not only for their own well-being but also for that of others. In reflecting on Mexican American mestizaje as a force for social good, Elizondo points out the following:

> In the light of the Judeo-Christian tradition, the Mexican-American experience of rejection and margination is converted from human curse to the very sign of divine predilection. . . . It is in their margination from the centers of the various establishments that Mexican-Americans live the Galilean identity today. Because they are inside-outsiders, they appreciate more clearly the best of the traditions of both groups, while also appreciating the worst of the situation of both. It is precisely in this double identity that they have something of unique value to offer both . . . As *mestizos* of the borderland between Anglo America and Latin America, the Mexican-American stands in the midst of both worlds and what in effect appears an unfinished identity can be the basis for personal understanding and appreciation of two identities.[23]

As it regards our tracing of Latino/a theology's turn to culture and its employment of culture in the sense of identity, I want here to highlight that the issue taken up by Elizondo is the struggle for positive identity among Mexican Americans and Latino/as and the creative defense of their cultures. The goal is fully to help Mexican Americans, and Latino/as as a whole, to come to terms with the racial, cultural, and religious hybridity that marks their identities; to enable them to maintain their marginalized cultural traditions in the United States; and to elucidate the uniqueness of that culture and identity.[24] Hence, while Elizondo cursorily deals with issues related to geopolitics, race, national identity, and social analysis in his theological writings, he is chiefly concerned with the realm of self-identity and local culture, and particularly with the preservation of a salutary cultural identity among Mexican American and Latino/a communities. Toward this end he theorizes and employs the notion of mestizaje as a construct that synchronously allows for the accentuation of Mexican American and Latino/a cultural indistinction and syncretism, the celebration of the racial and cultural hybridity found within Mexican American and Latino/a identities, and the promotion of resistance against conceptions of self and culture that prejudicially privilege the colonizing West and "white" Anglo-Saxonism.[25] In sum, Elizondo's theological affinity to the concept of mestizaje demonstrates a turn to the realm of culture and a concern with culture in the sense of—or in the interest of—identity.

Interpreting "The Faith of the People":
Orlando Espín and the Study of Popular Religion

The turn to cultural analysis in Latino/a theology is revealed not only in the special role granted to the theorization of mestizaje in the writings of most Latino/a theologians but also in the prominent status accorded by them to the study of Hispanic popular religion in the United States.[26] This theological fascination with popular religion proceeds, I believe, from the perception that it gives witness to a site of ongoing, albeit covert, form of Latino/a self-definition and communal resistance against assimilatory pressures in the United States. To put it plainly, Latino/a theologians perceive that the study of Hispanic popular religious expression may provide a window onto one of the central ways that Latino/as in the United States have attempted to maintain their marginalized cultural traditions and thus regain their identity. In the bounds of this study of popular religion by Latino/a theologians, culture (and religion as a central component of culture) is shown to be defined or utilized in the sense of creative agency—that is, as the space in which and the process by which meaning and identity is produced, contended for, and continually renegotiated. The work of Orlando Espín offers, I believe, a propitious example of the way in which the study of popular religion within Latino/a theology in the United States manifests a turn to culture in the interest of Hispanic identity and cultural affirmation.

Espín's interpretations of popular religion are fundamentally grounded in one orienting conviction. According to Espín, regardless of their cultural differences, one common experience binds all Latinos and Latinas: they are all here, Espín maintains, "as the result of vanquishment." As he explains:

Some Latino groups are the result of the rape of their ancestors by the conquering Spaniards, while others are the outcome of willing *mestizaje*. There are communities that trace their roots back to the violence of the *encomienda* and others to the violence of the African slave trade. Many were here when the United States militarily conquered and illegally expropriated their land in the nineteenth century. Still others came because they had become the losing victims of political and economic struggles in other lands. But in *all* cases, the Latino cultural communities are here as the result of vanquishment, of having become the losing victims of someone else's victory. All of the communities, (Mexican-American, Puerto Rican, Cuban-American, etc.) are distinct, with their own histories and cultures, as well as with the shared elements of language, religious symbols, and worldview. Yet, behind all the distinctions, and even divisions, there lies this common experience of vanquishment that—however they might explain it—does bind them together. . . . Latinos are in the United States as the vanquished. And the dominant Euro-American culture treats them as such.[27]

It is from this vantage point that Espín claims popular religion as a means for opposition to cultural oppression and as a device for the establishment of positive self-identity and social identity among Latinos. "Popular religion," Espín submits, "allows its practictioners to discover power there where hegemonic ideology had veiled the possibilities for self-determination. Instead of utter powerlessness, through popular religion's symbols, the people can define themselves as empowered" (128). Popular religion, Espín argues, provides oppressed Latino/as a clandestine yet subversive vehicle by which they can attain meaning and hope.

Undergirding Espín's thought is the sense that in an oppressive context rarely will the resistance of a disenfranchised people take on direct or overt forms. Rather, oppressed peoples have often taken to the domain of symbolic activity to oppose marginalization and to defend their dignity. Whether through the use of semantic reversals, the fusion of different forms of belief and practices, or the preservation of autochthonous icons and symbols, disempowered groups have frequently turned to culture and religion as an insidious conveyor of counteraction and communal self-expression. Espín has creatively integrated this insight into his reading of Latino/a popular Catholicism by viewing it as a prominent, though covert, site both of cultural resistance and self-affirmation for Latino/as in the United States. Espín writes:

> Popular Catholicism is the "shape" that Latino Christianity, doubly vanquished in history, found most meaningful for the affirmation and survival of its cultural identity and of its faith heritage and life . . . Latino popular Catholicism can be characterized as an effort by the subaltern to explain, justify, and somehow control a social reality that appears too dangerous to confront in terms and through means other than the mainly symbolic. However, this popular religion is founded on the claim that the divine (identified by the people as the Christian divine) has been and is encountered by them in and through the symbols (ritual, ethical, and doctrinal) of popular Catholicism. (58, 92)

Two interconnected goals lie at the heart of Espín's work on popular religion. On the one hand as a theologian he endeavors to defend popular religious expression, in particular Latino/a popular Catholicism, as a legitimate site of faith and an authentic religious form that mediates the triune Christian God and can, therefore, be deemed a principal resource for Christian theology. On the other hand his desire is to demonstrate how Latino/a popular Catholicism operates as a province for the protection and affirmation of culture and identity. In regard to the first of these symbiotic yet distinct aims, Espín comments that popular religion has too frequently been considered as a blemish on or source of shame to Catholicism. "It has," Espín remarks, "been derided as the superstitious result of religious ignorance, a product of syncretism, a vestige of the rural past, and an ideologically manipulated tool in the hands of those who would abuse simple folk" (63). While he does not dismiss the fact that some of these charges do provide reason for concern in certain situations, Espín contends that there is much more to popular religion than what these simplistic dismissals convey.

Popular Catholicism, Espín argues, can actually be theologically understood as "a cultural expression of the *sensus fidelium*" (64). Here, Espín's reference is to a rather underexplored and undisclosed tradition within Catholicism that places attention on the living witness and faith of the Christian people; his basic intention in excavating and assigning great consequence to this tradition is to infuse the "faith-full" intuition of the common Christian practitioner with as much credibility as the written texts of institutional Catholicism. He puts it this way: "The whole Church has received the revelation of God and accepted it in faith. And, as a consequence, the whole Church is charged with proclaiming, living, and transmitting the fullness of revelation. Therefore, the necessary task of expressing the contents of scripture and Tradition are not and cannot be limited to the ordained ministers of the Church. The whole Church has this mission, and the Spirit was promised to the whole Church for this task. Members of the Christian laity, consequently, are indispensable witnesses and bearers of the gospel—as indispensable as the magisterium of the Church" (66). In short, according to Espín, the living intuition, witness, and faith of the people, in this case mediated through their culturally infused popular religious expressions, are as inspired and valid as are the written documents and texts of the church's magisterium. And in view of this premise Espín proposes that Latino/a popular Catholicism may be regarded as "the culturally possible expression of some fundamental intuitions of the Christian faith" (68).

This theorem brings us to the second of Espín's goals: his attempt to interpret popular Catholicism as a site of cultural resistance and identity affirmation. Here again Espín's theorizations are sufficiently nuanced to incorporate some of the possible oppositions or skepticisms toward popular religion. He acknowledges, for instance, that popular religion has frequently appeared to function as a compassionate sedative to injustice among oppressed peoples. He also points out, however, that for Latinos and Latinas, as for other subordinated groups, it has acted as an important preserver of dignity, positive identity, and hope. With respect to this conviction, Espín writes:

> Today's Latino popular Catholicism still bears the marks of its history, of its Iberian roots, and of the traumatic conquest of Amerindians and African slaves by Christians. It still displays, often through powerful symbols, the expressions of the despair of the vanquished and of their hope for justice. . . . Religious in expression, content, and experience, this language has long been the code through which hope and courage have been shared and maintained as plausible by generations of Latinos. Fundamental cultural values have found their place in and their medium of dissemination through popular religion. Lastly, and perhaps ultimately more importantly, popular Catholicism embodies a rebellious hope by its very existence as religion. If . . . religion is the

socialization of the experience of the divine, and if in Latino Catholicism the divine is identified with the Christian divine, then this religion of the subaltern claims that the *Christian* God is to be found in and through the culture and experiences of those considered insignificant by American society and Church. (103)

Espín fleshes out and substantiates his claim for the role of Latino/a popular Catholicism in preserving culture and identity by pointing to various historical examples. He contends that during the independence movements in the Spanish colonial period it was the popular version of Catholicism that served as the religion of the Hispanic proponents of independence. "It became commonplace," Espín writes, "to find the symbols of popular Catholicism used as gathering banners for the people against Spain" (134). He also correctly points out that the symbols of popular Catholicism have prominently appeared and been associated with some of the most recent and important social and political movements among Hispanics in the United States. "The *Virgenes* of Hispanic popular Catholicism," Espín reminds us, "have appeared prominently in gatherings, publications, and even on neighborhood walls where cultural identity and pride are consciously emphasized." Furthermore, "the United Farm Workers have proudly and frequently displayed images of the Virgin of Guadalupe and of the Virgin of San Juan de los Lagos," and Cuban Americans "have been emphasizing the Virgin of Charity as a unifying cultural (and political) symbol since the 1960s" (155). These "Virgin" symbols, along with the plethora of Santos and other popular religious practices and devotions that are so much a part of Latino/a life seemingly point to the importance of popular Catholicism and other forms of autochthonous spiritualities as a means to safeguard and affirm the distinctiveness of Latino/a cultures and identities in the United States.

All of these religiously imbued forms of communal cultural expressions have continued to live among the different Latino/a communities in the United States in spite of their ancient heritages and despite the availability both of many other "official" or "mainstream" religious persuasions and of many efforts to suppress these expressions. Espín posits that one of the reasons for their longevity and continued relevance can be found in their functioning as a form of "epistemology of suffering." That is, Espín believes that popular Catholicism is one of the most fundamental ways through which Latino/as have attempted to understand, deal with, and make sense of their sufferings, particularly those that stem from human moral evil. To support this position, Espín draws attention to the ubiquity of the "suffering Jesus" portraits among Latino communities, and he suggests that for Latinos this portraiture conveys the idea that "just as Jesus endured victimization but not been ultimately conquered, so will their suffering not lead them to be *only* victims at the end." Espín also points out that the symbols of popular Catholicism mostly tend to portray God as provident not in a conquering way but rather in a radically caring one. "The God sensed through these symbols," he offers, "is not the powerful, conquering divinity of the victorious and successful, but a parental (maternal!), familial, communal God whose providence is encouragement and support, shared suffering and quiet determination, and final justice-building." Espín reads Latino/a popular Catholicism, as a whole, as "an active creation of symbols and means to foster hope, to sustain communal solidarity, and to prepare for the alternative" (26).

In sum, Espín believes that Latino/a popular Catholicism and Latino/a popular religious expression as a whole serve as a conveyor of a history suppressed by the dominant Anglo culture as well as a surreptitious medium for cultural resistance and hope. That is, Espín believes that the insistence on preserving these particular culturally embedded forms of Catholicism points to one of the ways that Hispanics in the United States have attempted both to maintain their marginalized cultural traditions and to defend, affirm, or reconstruct their unique identities in a hopeful manner. In these popular religious practices and devotions, he surmises, we find evidence of the creative defense of Latino/a cultures and identities among Hispanics in the United States.

To close my hermeneutical rendering of Espín's work I highlight the point that we witness in his interpretations of Latino/a popular religious expression an understanding of culture both as an identity marker and as a space or process of creative agency. In this sense Latino/a popular religion is represented as an element or component of Latino/a culture—one that provides a window onto Latino/a identity and agency.

Charting New Paths for the Use of Culture in Latino/a theology

My goal in offering interpretive excursions into the works of Virgilio Elizondo and Orlando Espín has been to bring us to a better comprehension of the commitment to the idea of culture found in Latino/a theology as well as to a better awareness of the usefulness of this commitment. In other words, I wanted to establish or demonstrate that the enthusiastic theorizations of *mestizaje* and popular religion found in the work of these scholars, and more broadly throughout Latino/a theology, give witness to an intellectual awareness of the role of culture. Moreover, I have suggested that the underlying pursuit of this turn to culture is at once a celebration, defense, and reconstruction of Latino/a cultural traditions and identities as well as of Latino/a agency. Latino/a theological scholarship as a whole is characterized by this turn to the idea and realm of culture in the interest of promoting cultural affirmation, positive self and group identity, and creative as well as oppositional agency among Latinos and Latinas in an unjust social and cultural setting in the United States. The recurrent references to mestizaje and popular religion, as well as the earnest attempts to theorize and theologize *lo cotidiano* (everyday Latino/a life), in the annals of Latino/a theology provide, I believe, ubiquitous examples of this strong disposition and focus.[28]

The emergence of culture as a recurrent theme or reflexive category in Latino/a theology is something to be appreciated, celebrated, and preserved. Given the historical realities and dynamics of cultural subjugation, ethnic prejudice, and negative stereotypes with which Latinos and Latinas have often had to contend, and the continued existence of strategies of cultural oppression within the United States, this turn to culture is an important and necessary strategy. It concurrently provides Latinos and Latinas with a conceptual basis to examine neglected elements of their cultures and histories; to highlight their creativity and distinctiveness; to celebrate, defend, and win recognition for their identities; to foster positive self-identity and collective cultural identity; and perhaps even to "protest the disguised particularisms—the masculinism, the white-Anglo ethnocentrism, the heterosexism—lurking behind what parades as universal."[29] By placing emphasis upon the realm of culture, Latino/a theologians have managed to make cultural study a project that is political as well as aesthetic and theological.

Although I am deeply appreciative of this turn toward culture in Latino/a theology in the United States, I am convinced that we Latino/a theologians are now in a favorable position within the evolution of our distinctive theological discourse to advance our mode of cultural theorizing. One of the ways in which we can enhance our theological treatment of culture is through an even greater level of immersion in Latino/a popular culture— that is, the texts, symbols, artistic creations, practices, and processes of the construction of meaning that distinctively mark Latino/a agency. As I see it, the basic purpose or intention of understanding culture is or should be to more fully engage in it. Yet apart from engaging with certain forms of Latino/a religious expression that may be called popular, and then more recently with examples of Latino/a literature, our theologies have not yet immersed themselves in the broader cultural productivity of Latinos and Latinas. Although Latino/a theologies have placed much emphasis upon the category of culture, they still have not made wide use of the cultural production—the literature, music, visual art, drama, dance, film, television shows, *telenovelas*, comedy, fashion, and food, for instance—generated by Latino/as in the United States, and as such they have thus far provided a limited depiction of Latino/a identities and agency.

I suggest that the possibility for a theology that is grounded in Latino/a history and everyday life, in the specificity of Latino/a experience, exists in just such a cultural immersion. Sustained engagement with Latino/a literature, music, dance, art, film, drama, comedy, food, fashion, and other such cultural expressions and practices could serve to proffer an existential historicity, a contextuality, a corporeality, and a palpable "Latinidad" to our theologies. Moreover, besides extending the possibility of a grounding specificity, further engagement with the matter of Latino/a cultural production could aid our development of distinctive Latino/a constructive theologies.[30]

A second way that we can further our mode of cultural theorizing is by scrutinizing the meanings of the term culture and exploring alternative understandings of it. Indeed, I think it is important to keep in mind that "culture" is a theoretical category, a concept, a construct, an idea. The temptation is often to treat the term as if it were a self-evident given, as an incontrovertible aspect of life that can be abstracted from the complex reality of human existence. Thus culture is often taken to stand for a certain, concrete, and bounded set of beliefs, conventions, practices, or characteristics assumed to "belong" to a society or to a social group. In this way culture, cultural production, and cultural agency are treated as ontological entities or as experiential or historical givens. Although there are certainly currents and developments within Latino/a theology that evidence movements toward different treatments and understandings of it, my sense is that this usage of "culture" still shows up from time to time in our Latino/a theologies.

I submit that such a usage of "culture," even if at times potentially propitious, can serve to hinder our attempts to apprehend and represent the disparateness, changeableness, and even disjointedness of human cultures. Rather than treating culture as self-enclosed, static, fixed, completely coherent, and impervious to challenge, we can treat it instead as a sphere of signification and practice shot through with at times willful and at other times indeliberate action, power relations, struggle, contradiction, transverseness, and change. Such a view and treatment of culture, I would suggest, could open up new vistas in our theologies, thereby allowing both for a more nuanced depiction of the variety and complexity of Latino/a agency and also a more critical handling of it.

I conclude by suggesting that a third way that we Latino/a theologians can deepen our work on culture is by connecting the study of cultural signification to a deeper and more critical analysis of institutions and social structures. Elsewhere I have scrutinized the tendency of Latino/a theology to restrict itself to the realm of what we may call "symbolic culture," as well as its general tendency to treat culture in abstraction from social relations and social structures, especially political economy.[31] Although I support the commitment to cultural theorizing and, concomitantly, to a cultural politics of identity and recognition, I suggest that the justice demands of our time call for the coupling of cultural theorizing and social theorizing and for a dialectic negotiation between a cultural politics of identity and recognition and a social politics of redistribution.

This discursive maneuver is especially at issue within Latino/a theology (perhaps particularly given the fact that it generally identifies with the paradigm and project of liberation theology) because Latino/as in the United States suffer injustices that are traceable not only to the denigration of their culture and identities but also to socioeconomic exploitation and inequity. Accordingly, I submit that Latino/a theologians must work toward a bivalent theoretical framework, giving equal scrutiny to socioeconomic injustice (which is rooted in the political-economic structuring of society) and cultural or symbolic injustice (which is rooted in social patterns of representation, interpretation, and communication). This involves granting the same attention to issues such as exploitation, economic marginalization, and deprivation that we have accorded to cultural domination, nonrecognition, and disrespect.[32]

This negotiation also involves addressing not merely how cultural identities and agency may be recognized and celebrated but also how they are produced and sustained within a deeply hierarchical and exploitative society. Cultural identity and agency always transpire within a larger web of shifting social, political, and economic relations that must be accounted for when theorizing on matters of culture.[33] Hence, matters of symbolic culture cannot be studied in abstraction from social, political, and economic structures or relations. Instead, these matters must be understood in relation to broader societal, political, and economic constituents that transcend the space of the self and the local and yet, nevertheless, influence everyday personal and local realities. To close, I submit that the prospect and hope that our theologies may be helpful toward and availing of both cultural liberation and socioeconomic liberation depend in good part on our willingness and readiness to work toward such a bivalent analytical framework.

Notes

Parts of this essay were previously published in my book *Mapping Public Theology: Beyond Culture, Identity, and Difference* (Harrisburg, Pa.: Trinity Press International, 2002).

1 Given this strong bent toward culture and the cultural in its theological and political project, I suggest that Latino/a theology can generally be defined as a culturally contextualized theology of liberation—that is, as a kind of theological undertaking that is generally concerned with injustice and suffering and the historical prospects of human-social liberation but one that has thus far—whether intentionally or unintentionally—given special attention to modes of cultural injustice (e.g., social patterns of representation, interpretation, and communication such as cultural domination, nonrecognition, the threatening or disregard of cultural traditions and identities, and disrespect). Although sufferings and injustices that are traceable to political economy have certainly been addressed in this theological tradition, these issues and concerns have not yet received the same rigorous analysis within Latino/a theology as have those concerning the defense of imperiled identities, the ending of cultural domination, and the attainment of recognition for Latino/a culture(s) and identities. This characteristic, however, extends beyond Latino/a theology and is found in most other expressions of liberation theology formulated within the United States.

2 Friedman, *Mappings*, 83.

3 Garcia-Rivera, *St. Martin de Porres*, 40.

4 For example, see Gibson, *Spain in America*, esp. 1–47, 112–35; Bethell, *The Cambridge History of Latin America*, esp. 1:149–388, 2:67–49; and Jiménez, Kanellos, and Esteva Fabregat, *Handbook of Hispanic Cultures in the United States*, vol. 2 , esp. 23–183.

5 For more on this topic, see Klein, *African Slavery in Latin America and the Caribbean*; and Bowser, "Colonial Spanish America."

6 I borrow these choice words from Fusco, *English Is Broken Here*, 33.

7 See especially Vasconcelos's 1925 essay "La raza cosmica" in *The Cosmic Race/La raza cosmica*.

8 Elizondo, *The Future Is Mestizo*, x.

9 Ibid., 21, 26.

10 I borrow these words from Friedman, *Mappings*, 97.

11 Anzaldúa, *Borderlands/La Frontera*, 4 (my translation).

12 Elizondo, *Galilean Journey*, 10.

13 Interestingly, shortly before 1983 when Elizondo published his work that connects Latino/a mestizaje to Jesus's own hybrid cultural identity as a Galilean Jew, the late Protestant Latino/a theologian Orlando E. Costas also called attention to Jesus's Galilean identity, and he too compared it to the sociocultural identity of Latino/as today. See, for example, Costas's "Evangelism from the Periphery: A Galilean Model" and "Evangelism from the Periphery: The Universality of Galilee." This same idea and connection is made by Costas in a lecture he presented at Southeastern Baptist Theological Seminary on October 5, 1982, titled "The Meaning of Christian Mission from the Periphery of History." Both of these Latino/a theologians, then, were making this connection in similar ways and contemporaneously. It is important to note, however, that Elizondo's *Galilean Journey* is based on his doctoral dissertation, "Mestissage, violence culturelle, annonce de l'evangile," which was presented at the Institut Catholique in Paris in 1978. This would seem to make Elizondo the first theologian to employ mestizaje as a starting point to interpret Latino/a cultural identity, and to make a connection between it and Jesus's Galilean identity. I am in debt to my brother Elieser Valentín who unearthed and provided for me the writings by Costas mentioned above.

14 Elizondo, *The Future Is Mestizo*, 77.

15 Elizondo, *Galilean Journey*, 49.

16 Ibid., 51.

17 Elizondo, *The Future Is Mestizo*, 77.

18 Ibid., 77.

19 Ibid., 80.

20 Elizondo, *Galilean Journey*, 53.

21 Elizondo, *The Future Is Mestizo*, 74.

22 Ibid., 77.

23 Elizondo, *Galilean Journey*, 100.

24 I must note that Elizondo's focus is particularly on the Mexican American situation. Nevertheless, I believe that his work clearly has bearing for other Latino/a subcultures. Elizondo himself implies or allows for this broader applicability in *The Future Is Mestizo*, esp. 87–111. I believe that a note is also called for here regarding Elizondo's claiming of the privileged space of hybridity for Mexican Americans, Latinos and Latinas, and other bicultural or culturally hybrid persons. Elizondo often tends to view mestizaje as something that is

unique to certain peoples or to some cultural groups. But one can instead view hybridity as an ordinary, ubiquitous, routine component of any cultural formation—as, in other words, the inevitable process of transculturation that all cultures experience in some way or another. Instead of uplifting unique cases of hybridity (i.e., hybridity versus purity), or instead of employing mestizaje and hybridity as a unique identity marker for a particular cultural and social group, this latter view would suggest that hybridity is an ongoing condition of all human cultures. For theories or treatments of hybridity that go in this direction, see García Canclini, *Hybrid Cultures*; Rosaldo, *Culture and Truth*; and Hall, "New Ethnicities," in *Stuart Hall*, 441–49.

25 Although Elizondo often does employ Latino/a mestizaje as a position of distinction between Latino/a selves and others, his ultimate aspiration, I believe, is to present Latino/a mestizaje as a fertile borderland and as a locus for personal and collective intermingling and interfusion. Thus, I suggest that from very early on Elizondo was able to convey or intimate two insights regarding identity generally and Latino/a identity specifically: first, that Latino/a cultural identity is perhaps best theorized as an intersection or a crossroads of multiply situated knowledges; and second, that Latino/a cultural identity can be theorized and practiced as a relational affair.

26 Although scholars of "popular religion" are not of one mind about what this term stands for, popular religion basically has to do with what ordinary people believe and practice and how they incorporate these into their own lives. The term most generally denotes those sets of religious beliefs and practices that are either distinct from or, rather, not fully the product of religious specialists or of an elaborate "official" ecclesiastical organizational framework.

27 Espín, *The Faith of the People*, 21. Note that all further cites from this work appear as parenthetical page numbers in the text.

28 Inquiry into the meanings and theological utility of the notions of mestizaje and popular religion is extensive in Latino/a theology. For some other examples on the theorizing of mestizaje within the historical development of Latino/a theology, see Guerrero, *A Chicano Theology*; Costas, "Hispanic Theology in North America," in *Struggles for Solidarity*, 63–74; Isasi-Diaz, *En La Lucha/In the Struggle*; González, *Santa Biblia*; and Isasi-Diaz, *Mujerista Theology*. For some other examples on the theorizing of "popular religion" within the historical development of Latino/a theology, see Isasi-Diaz, *En La Lucha/In the Struggle*, esp. 34–61; Rodriguez-Holguin, *Our Lady of Guadalupe*; Garcia-Rivera, *St. Martin de Porres*; Goizueta, *Caminemos con Jesus*; and Recinos, "Popular Religion, Political Identity, and Life-Story Testimony in an Hispanic Community." The most extensive and creative interpretation of the idea and significance of *lo cotidiano* (i.e., everyday life) to be tendered thus far within the annals of Latino/a theology is found in the work of Isasi-Diaz, especially *Mujerista Theology*, 59–85.

29 I borrow these choice words from Fraser, *Justice Interruptus*, 5.

30 What I specifically have in mind when I use the term "constructive theology" is a kind of theology or approach to theology that, first, allows for the human constructedness or constructive-historical dimension of the doctrines, symbols, and systems of meaning in a religious tradition, viewing these as imaginative geographies or maps of meaning created by humans for human orientation and, second, does not merely look to identify and describe but also to critically examine and reconstruct/revise/rethink/reinterpret the beliefs, doctrines, symbols, and systems of meaning found in a religious tradition, drawing on insights, values, and practices found within contemporary life and a particular lived local culture while doing so. For example, for Latino/a theologians who are of Christian orientation this would include reformulating or rethinking, from the vantage point of Latino/a life and agency, the meanings of doctrines or symbols such as God, creation, human being, Christ, the church, etc. This does not mean, however, that other sources, themes, symbols, and language, existing beyond the realm of a particular religious tradition such as Christianity, cannot also be explored and used by the theologian for the purposes of evaluating and constructing forms of religious signification.

31 See my *Mapping Public Theology*, especially chapters 2 and 4.

32 My distinction between cultural and socioeconomic understandings of injustice draws upon the critical social theory of Nancy Fraser, set forth especially in *Justice Interruptus*.

33 I work here under the influence of a framework that distinguishes between several realms of social life: the economic, the political, the social, and the cultural. Thus, the economic can be defined as having to do with how people get their living. The political can be understood as having to do with the distribution of power—that is, how "winners" and "losers" in a society are determined. The social can be conceived as having to do with the relationships between people, groups, and institutions that both derive from and help reproduce political, economic, and cultural forms. The cultural, in turn, can be deemed as the sphere devoted to the production, circulation, and use of meanings and identities, as well as to the valuational structure of society. In reality or everyday life, of course, these realms are intertwined. Hence, this is an analytical distinction, fruitful insofar as it allows one to theorize how these realms interact with each other and structure each other to produce the totality of a society. Although this is a theoretical framework I prefer, and although it is in fact one that many theorists turn to, another possibility in the theorizing of culture is that of extending the meaning of culture, understanding it as a total way of life that is inclusive of processes of signification, aesthetic creativity, and representation as well as those of power or material relations, class interests, and distributive practices. In this grander rendering of culture one might speak of "symbolic culture" and "material culture."

Anthony B. Pinn

回

RESPONSE TO THE ESSAY BY BENJAMÍN VALENTÍN

While many of the sights and sounds of Latino/a self-understanding and interaction may differ from those related to African Americans involved in the same ontological and existential activities, there is a shared understanding of culture as the signs, symbols, behaviors, and attitudes that frame and define human existence. What is more, this thick understanding of culture renders "sacred" and "secular" divisions of human thought and life unimportant in that cultural developments and expression inform all dimensions of life. As Paul Tillich remarked, and Valentín would agree, religion is the substance of culture, and culture is the form of religion. And as the discussion of religious matters, Latino/a theology employs the signs, symbols, grammar and vocabulary of culture to frame and detail its work. The same, as I hope my essay suggests, can be said of black and womanist theologies.

Such a connection is understandable when we consider the nature of racial oppression in the United States, the manner in which it makes use of objective modalities of authority (e.g., laws) as well as subjective modes of authority that serve to justify the former. That is, both Latinos and Latinas and African Americans have experienced discrimination arranged vis-à-vis sociopolitical and economic inequality and rendered normative through the workings of culture and cultural production. Yet of greater importance than the modalities of discrimination is the fragile nature of discrimination and its logic shot-through with holes. Attacking the shortcomings of discrimination became the hallmark of progressive thought and endeavor for both African Americans and Latinos and Latinas. And in the realm of religion-based progressivism liberation (or constructive) theology provides the most recent attempt to use cultural resources to ground a religion-based attack against injustice. Culture is a tool for the theologian who is committed to the evaluation and transformation of life options for those who are suffering the ill effects of injustice. On this point Valentín and I agree, and in both of our essays such a connection is given analytical prominence.

What is less apparent, however, within Valentín's essay is the *substance*—the content of "culture" as found within the work of Latino/a theologians. Most pressing is the failure to acknowledge and comment on the manner in which the cultural terrain is in significant ways marked by the bodies that Latinos and Latinas (and African Americans) carry through the world. Both communities speak of embodied theology, and this is vital in that the sociocultural rendering of race and racism as natural and necessary was justified through the visual representation of "blackness" and "brownness" as inferior and aesthetically questionable. Ramifications of the physical raced body as ugly were played out in the arena of social interaction in ways consistent with Mary Douglas's noting in *Natural Symbols* of the body as both physical presence and symbol of the social system. It is true that culture is not restricted to aesthetics but is also political. Yet this pronouncement should not negate the significance of the body, the construction of the body made manifest through cultural forms, for the framing of both oppression and liberation. In other words, if Latino/a theologies (as is the case with African American theologies) are embodied theologies, what is the significance of this embodiment for the doing of theology and in this instance the understanding of culture's tone and texture? Where is the body in this? How does the body figure into the use of culture? Valentín suggests that culture is the ground upon which the political battle is waged. Yet this assertion, while true to some extent, fails to recognize the political construction, placement, and use of human bodies. That is, political inequality is justified and fortified through a ranking of bodies vis-à-vis sensory-based indicators of inferiority. Valentín's project urges an underlying or foundational question as follows: What is the significance of the "brown" body for theological inquiry that is sensitive to culture?

When taken as a whole, the work that Valentín and I seek to accomplish points to the importance of hemispheric considerations for the doing of liberation theology and for the type of dialogue we seek to nurture through this project and an earlier one. The effort to speak theologically (or in any other modalities of investigation) of meaning and identity in our racialized context must involve attention to more than the nation-state as the space and place of ontological and existential formation. The identity and meaning of black and brown bodies involves attention to a North-South arrangement of encounters and exchanges whereby cultural developments in the Caribbean or South America have profound bearing on what it means to "be" brown or black in the context of North America.

Implicit in this work on the religious significance of culture, particularly as it relates to a sense of hybridity or mestizaje, is the recognition of the need for liberation theologies in our two communities to take on the challenges and frameworks of the growing intellectual trend toward hemispheric studies. Interdisciplinary work that moves beyond analysis of any one nation in isolation and that places urgent intellectual questions in the larger matrix of the Americas as a hemisphere promises new opportunities for dialogical advancement through a more complex and thick understanding of what it means to carry a brown or black body through the world. Such a thickly textured comparative study might serve further to promote creative, original insights into the full complexities of life and thought in African American and Latino/a communities. For example, attention to a thicker geographic arrangement for understanding the construction and use of "brown" and "black" bodies offers a more vibrant sense of the interactions that comprised the "New World" and allows for a greater sense of solidarity and sustained synergy between these two communities. Furthermore, on a fundamental level the nature and meaning of life (the texture of individual and communal identity) in this section of the globe is brought into sharper focus through a hemispheric approach by giving greater attention to the complexity of human construction—namely, the dynamics at work and the terrain covered during the construction of the human body (as a symbol of social arrangements).

Borders (in thought and practice) are challenged in this regard, and theological inquiry, for instance, takes on a fluidity of expression and resource recognition. A hemispheric shift also affords an important theoretical (and methodological) challenge to both African American theologians and Latino/a theologians. When considered beyond particular nations (and their dominant religious sensibilities), questions emerge such as the nature and meaning of religion. Thus when Valentín refers to "popular religion" in this context, does it entail shorthand for less doctrinally defined Christianity? Or does it entail recognition of and appreciation for the rich variety of religious traditions alive in both communities? That is, in short, a hemispheric approach to the theologizing of both communities exposes and renders problematic Christian imperialism as yet another modality of oppressive ideology. It also reframes theological inquiry by highlighting the theoretical and methodological significance of embodiment as the character of our liberation theologies. Theologies of liberation (or construction) are altered by engagement within an existential and ontological geography that is expansive in scope and thick in nature.

PART TWO ▣ CONSTRUCTING BODIES AND REPRESENTATION

Mayra Rivera

回

MEMORY OF THE FLESH: THEOLOGICAL

REFLECTIONS ON WORD AND FLESH

And the Word became Flesh and lived among us,
And we have seen its glory.—John 1:13

To reflect theologically about the body is to be thrown into a zone of great ambivalence. On the one hand, Christian theology rightly claims to be a theology of incarnation in which a human body is placed at the center of salvation. John's statement "the Word became Flesh" is paradigmatic of hopes of incarnation. But have we seen its glory, the glory of the flesh? While celebrating the desire of God to take flesh, the statement's cosmology seems to advocate precisely the opposite: from the flesh toward a disembodied universality invariably represented in male terms. For the aim of the divine Logos is most often interpreted as the rescue of men from the particularity of the flesh and the offer of a birth "not of blood or of the will of flesh or the will of man, but of God" (John 1:13). Thus, Jesus's role is defined as one of bringing back, of rescuing creation from its creatureliness—from the original water, blood, and flesh. If Logos was born in the flesh, it is assumed, it was to erase once and for all a more pervasive origin of the whole humanity in the womb: "It is the Spirit that gives life; the flesh is useless" (John 6:63).

This depiction, however, hardly exhausts Christian attitudes toward the body. From its early days Christianity declared as heretical all attempts to separate word from flesh. Yet the flesh-denying interpretations of the Christian message continue to influence theology—as well as the popular reactions against it. The enormous success of Dan Brown's *The Da Vinci Code*, which represents Christianity as pathologically revolting against the flesh to the point of conspiring to hide aspects of Jesus's life, demonstrates how compelling such a characterization still is and how scandalous Jesus's sexuality can be. In our popular imaginary as in our theologies, word and flesh are still in conflict.

The Christian ambivalence toward the body only intensifies when we attempt to reflect theologically on the no less conflictive "Latina" body. I confess to have been paralyzed by the audacity (or naiveté?) of such an endeavor. This was not because such a signifier is unheard of; indeed, our culture is overpopulated by images that purport to represent Latina bodies. My hesitation derives from the ambiguous status of bodies as both flesh and image. Bodies are concrete and irreducible persons, but they are also elusive signifiers as key pieces in the social battles for authorization and value. And we are caught in those battles. Because we are simultaneously spectators and characters in these social performances, the effort to think critically about bodies and of ourselves as bodies induces a kind of disorienting double vision. On the one hand the representations of "our" bodies—these signs (and their logos)—are often alien, and yet they are so powerful that they seem simply to replace our bodies. The image becomes the body.[1] And yet the most threatening aspect of these cultural representations is that those images are never merely outside ourselves. Our bodies are signs within semiotic systems, and inasmuch as they affect how others react to us (how they "read" our bodies) we are also shaped by those images. Whether we find these representations repulsive or alluring—as we combat them, or mimic them, or both—we are affected by them. Thus the boundaries between bodies and representations, between word and flesh, are revealed as unstable and elusive.

Representations of bodies have been at the center of the social imaginaries that have historically justified the subordination of women, people of color, and especially women of color. Indeed, subordinated bodies are frequently imagined as wholly flesh. As we attempt to break loose of the grip of these cultural constructions, to distance ourselves from the images that supplant us in ongoing social performances, it might be tempting to seek another birth: a birth not of blood or of flesh, or the will of man, or of woman. We might be seduced by the illusion of overcoming the flesh and to create ourselves—just like the God of many dominant Christian traditions—out of nothing.

However, to write about black and Latina bodies theologically is precisely to refuse to accept the deception of a birth that disavows blood and flesh. But to turn our attention to our bodies—to ourselves as bodies—is hardly to escape the realm of representation. After all, I am writing—and writing in the hope that my words might contribute to the overcoming of oppression—in the flesh. Tellingly, the bodies I most identify with and as, "Latina bodies," are named (and thus inscribed) by language. Latin, the language of the first Christian empire, now signifies the language of the Spanish empire under the power of which these "types of bodies" were (literally) born.[2] The imperial word became flesh. Today the imperial language names bodies, even of those who have never spoken it or are no longer able to do so. The linguistic label is, however, insufficient for erasing the carnality of that colonial history. Words cannot perfectly obliterate (or reveal) the "memory of the flesh."[3]

My theological reflections about the body do not attempt to solve the ambivalence from which they spring. Quite to the contrary, my hope is to intensify the ambivalence. This is perhaps the best way to capture what I think is distinctive about the contemporary Latina sources with which I am in dialogue: namely, attentiveness to the uncertainties and ambivalence of the meanings of their own bodies—both flesh and word. In this essay I identify two conceptual splits that affect cultural and theological ideas about embodiment: the fracture between divinity and flesh and the concomitant one between nature and culture. I argue that these problematic dichotomies tend to become inscribed in the common uses of categories of race and ethnicity—just as in those of sex and gender. Constructive theologies of the body that are critical of the stigmatization of colored bodies and attentive to the concerns of Latinas and Latinos and African Americans must question the implicit dualisms of these common categories. In placing these constructions against the backdrop of colonial ideologies on the one hand, and contemporary Chicana/o literature on the other, I look at the particular dilemmas that affect the definition of Latina/o bodies as "mixed race." I hope to complicate the claims that *mestizaje* (cultural hybridity) is necessarily apolitical and that it reflects an attempt to deny the African or indigenous heritage of Latinas and Latinos. The criticism and longings drawn from the sources presented in this essay inspire my closing suggestions for imagining the body in its embodied transcendence.

Flesh and Spirit

The dualism of flesh and spirit has especially preoccupied feminist and ecofeminist theologians, for they have long recognized that the suspicion or even contempt against bodies lends support to the subordination of women.[4] This dualism is inscribed in and supported by the idea of a disembodied God. A view of God that emphasizes God's independence and separation from matter and flesh depends upon the disparagement of embodiment. In the words of Rosemary Radford Ruether, "The disembodied nature of the . . . divine . . . has served as a linchpin of the Western masculinist symbolic."[5] As an attribute of God, disembodiment becomes a supreme value that tends to orient the religious life away from the concerns of the body. Like the philosophical traditions with which it has always been in conversation, Christian theology has imagined the salvific trajectory of individuals as a movement away from the body and materiality.[6] Becoming more spiritual is imagined as entailing absolute control over the demands of the body.

Historically, the presumed ability to dominate the body has been unequally distributed. In this social imaginary, certain bodies are seen as more inextricable from materiality than are others. Bodies of women and those of darker complexion especially have been assigned the role of carrying the burden of materiality. The bodies of those who have performed the manual labor both inside and outside the home that society has consistently undervalued have been construed as the source of their inescapable fate. Patriarchy has described women as "naturally" inclined to (mostly physical and repetitive) domestic labor.[7] Similarly, colonial and enslaved subjects have been represented as rationally defective, perhaps even devoid of a soul, and thus incapable of controlling their "natural" (read "bodily") instincts.[8] They have been represented as wholly flesh.

Flesh and Words

In recognizing these representations of bodies as contributing to the legitimization of their oppression, feminist theorists' body talk has been marked by caution. This ambivalence is even more pronounced among women of color. As Karen Baker-Fletcher argues, historically the bodies of black women "have been forcefully displayed and spread for curiosity, amusement, observation, and consumption."[9] This gross objectification of women's bodies warns us of the dangers of any uncritical celebration of the body that would again place women on the side of a "natural" construed as that which resists spirit and culture.

Feminist deconstructions of patriarchal subordination have depended in large measure on challenging the appeals to the "natural" essence of womanhood typically tied to the body as the site of biological determinism. "One is not born a woman, one becomes a woman" was Simone de Beauvoir's famous statement of this stance.[10] Gender, as opposed to sex, became the name under which feminism struggled. The emphasis on identity as performed that characterizes the work of postmodern theorists like Judith Butler follows in that tradition.[11] One is certainly not born a Latina but rather becomes one in the context of political struggles through acts of identification. But if we affirm that indeed one becomes a woman and, in my case just recently, becomes a Latina, are we not joining John's gospel in asserting that the flesh is useless?[12]

Attention to the social construction of gender may still reproduce the nature/culture dichotomy. As Butler notes: "Originally intended to dispute the biology-is-destiny formulation, the distinction between sex and gender serves the argument that whatever biological intractability sex appears to have, gender is culturally constructed: hence, gender is neither the causal result of sex nor as seemingly fixed as sex."[13] On one hand, gender may seem to have no place for bodies. On the other hand, the split between gender and sex has seemed to imply that while gender is constructed, sex is "natural." A body gets conceptually fractured in its cultural and biological components.

A similar dilemma appears to be at work in discussions of ethnicity and race. Like gender, ethnicity emphasizes the social construction of identity through culture and custom. Ethnicity highlights the performative aspects of identity, which are most often conceived as freedom from the biological constraints of the body. Crudely stated, whatever biological intractability race appears to have, ethnicity is culturally constructed. When culture becomes the main focus, the effects of being bodies, and thus always already being signs that are read within defined semiotic systems, tend to fall out of sight. Ethnicity is at risk of losing the body altogether. The split between race and ethnicity, like that between sex and gender, risks reinscribing the construction of race as "natural"—and if natural also unconstructed, given, self-evident, and fixed.[14]

The use of categories of race and ethnicity frequently becomes a stumbling block in the discussions between African Americans and Latinas and Latinos on the subject of the body. Latinas and Latinos in the United States often waver between adopting "United States Latinas and Latinos" as a racial category, and define it instead as an ethnic one referring to culture, custom, and language. Those who opt for ethnicity often assume the racial definitions enforced by society in the United States. Some even call themselves "white women of color."[15] I must confess to be puzzled by such a description—it is one in which I sense an attempt to disown the indigenous and African foremothers without which "Latina heritage" loses all historical specificity. My personal response is perhaps best captured by a refrain I heard often during my childhood in Puerto Rico: "Y tu abuela a'onde e'tá?" (And your grandma, where is she?).[16] This well-known refrain, used colloquially as well as in music and poetry, is a recognizable shorthand for mocking claims to be "white," the implication being that the person is attempting to hide her or his ancestry. For historical reasons that I will touch upon below, light skin is not always considered equivalent to being "white"—whatever "white" means in the sense of the term as used in the United States. Surely, this personal account is not a description of how differences of skin color function in Puerto Rico; such a description is not my goal in this essay. Instead my comments are meant as a reminder, for the reader and for myself, of the multiple, shifting, and conflicting meanings of these categories: creating interpretative difficulties that are only intensified when the conversation crosses national boundaries, as it does when it involves Latinas and Latinos in the United States.

As an ethnic label Latina/o refers to a wide range of traits, some of which do not leave visible (or readable) marks on the body. Thus the emphasis on ethnicity foregrounds axes of oppression that do not neatly follow the black/white paradigms of racism in the United States. However, discussions about ethnicity too often neglect the body and, significantly, the primary meaning of skin color in the United States. Critiques of cultural imperialism shall thus be complemented by discussions of the racialization of bodies foregrounding the inextricable links between culture and flesh. These are complex issues that need to be addressed more deeply through honest dialogue, which the contributors to this volume intend to promote. I want to suggest that, as in the case of the discussions of gender versus sex, this requires not simply choosing between ethnicity and race but also looking more closely into the different worldviews from which our notions of embodiment emerge.

(In)Visible Ancestry

To say that society in the United States is organized around a black/white dichotomy has become almost tautological. The dominant culture conceives of race as discrete and binary.[17] Latinas and Latinos frequently observe that such a structure offers no space from which to claim their own collective identity, although the terms Hispanic or Latina/o often seem to function as a category comparable to black and white. However, the dilemmas that Latina bodies introduce to the system of representation in the United States cannot be addressed simply in terms of inclusion or exclusion from the existing social structures but rather requires a critical look at the ideological frameworks that inform our categories of analysis.

Robert Young in his study of the intersections between desire and race in colonialism observes that while "today's racial politics work through a relative polarization between white and black," colonialism worked also through systems of "degrees of deviance." That is, the position of people in the social hierarchy was reflected by their degree of deviance from the norm represented by those who embodied the image of the colonizer. Because of their attention to the outcomes of sexual encounters between rulers and subjects, systems of degrees of deviance linked racial difference with social and sexual deviance. As a result, "none was so demonized as those of mixed race."[18] Indeed the very idea of a "mixed" race is only meaningful within ideologies that assume the existence of discrete or "pure" races.[19] The territories under Spanish rule were considered the prime example of despised impurity. "Let any man turn his eyes to the Spanish American dominions, and behold what a vicious, brutal, and degenerate breed of mongrels has been there produced, between Spaniards, Blacks, Indians, and their mixed progenies," declared one Jamaican slaveowner.[20]

Complex systems of gradation according to inheritance and skin color were developed in Latin America and the Caribbean, including dozens of categories: mulatto, mestiza, chino, cuarteron, creole, quintero, zambo, and so forth. But despite the colonialists' sustained efforts to classify their subjects, "racial" inheritance would unavoidably become less readable from peoples' bodies, and sometimes it was altogether invisible. This unsettled relationship between biological inheritance and physiognomy has had lasting effects in the conceptions of race and blood, which cannot always be assumed to be visible.

It can be argued that colonialism is "the dominion of the eye."[21] The proclaimed inferiority of the colonized subjects must appear as natural and evident—an illusion that is accomplished by fixing visible physical traits in colonial discourses. The stereotype must acquire the status of "common knowledge" in colonial discourses.[22] Thus when mixed progenies threaten the supposed certainty of visible evidence (skin color, for instance), they become problematic for colonial rule.[23] The anxieties caused by the disruption of visual correlation can be seen in the following statement by Sir

William Lawrence: "Europeans and Tercerons produce Quarterons or Qua-droons (ochavons, octavones, or alvinos), which are not to be distinguished from whites; but they are not entitled, in Jamaica at least, to the same legal privileges as Europeans or the white Creoles, because there is still a con-tamination of dark blood, although *no longer visible*. It is said to betray itself sometimes in a relic of the peculiar strong *smell of the great-grandmother.*"[24] As blood slips away from the dominion of the eye, the slightest sign be-comes potentially important for the discriminating rulers—in this case even something as elusive as smell is constructed as evidence for colonial categorization. Since "contamination of dark blood" is not easily detected, all colonial subjects are under suspicion and become the object of obses-sive scrutiny.[25] All senses must be called upon to uncover the secrets of the other's body.

According to Young, from the 1840s onward the ideology of race "neces-sarily worked according to a double logic"; that is, "it both enforced and po-liced the difference between whites and non-whites, but at the same time fo-cused fetishistically upon the product of the contacts between them."[26] The so-called mixed races became the focus of the sexual fantasies—the "un-controllable sexual desire" and "limitless fertility" of the other—that drove racial theory. In short, mixed races were material evidence of illicit sex. As the emphasis on the distinctiveness of the races increased, so did the fan-tastic portrayal of mixed peoples as the incarnation of sexual degeneracy.

Although there are evident differences between the historical contexts described above and our own, important aspects of these racial ideologies still haunt us. People who fall outside the boundaries of visibly recogniz-able race categories are subject to the suspicious scrutiny of others; their bodies are searched for clues of their biological makeup and for anything that may clarify the question of origins—even if it is "a relic of the peculiar strong smell of the great-grandmother." The intensity of these investiga-tions betrays their link to concerns of sexual order and to fascination with its transgression.

Performing Bodies

Recognizing the common ideological roots of the ambivalence toward "mixed" peoples and of the belief in fixed classifiable races can help us more critically engage representations of black and Latina bodies in the United States imaginary and our attitudes toward them.[27] The traces of the ambivalence toward "mixed raced" bodies can be detected in contemporary discussions of mestizaje. Stephen Knadler in his essay "'Blanca from the Block': Whiteness and the Transnational Latina Body" challenges the claim of the mestiza as a "symbol of a liberating transnational and transracial identity." Knadler argues that despite the deployment by Latinas of the mestiza as an alternative to the racial paradigms in the United States, "many representations of the mestiza, even those coming from the margin, can preserve the strong normative function of whiteness and trivialize, if not completely erase, the mestiza's African diasporic history and culture."[28] For Knadler the mestiza has been constructed ideologically as a "blanca from the block"—a Latina identity that responds to the values of "white America" and thus reinforces their normativity. He traces this problem, for example, in two novels: the Dominican American Julia Álvarez's *In the Name of Salome* and the Cuban American Cristina García's *The Aguero Sisters*.

Knadler also sees this problematic tendency in the image of Jennifer Lopez—both in "JLo's" public persona and in the roles that she performs in movies. Knadler questions the "plasticity" of the representations of Lopez's body that allow her to represent and thus appeal to different groups: she appears as a Mexican woman, a Puerto Rican from el Barrio, and even an (almost) white woman. She presents "herself as a Latina and as a transracial American diva."[29] This kind of performative fluidity is "never some final transgressive *liberating crossing of borders*," as some Latinas claim. Quite to the contrary, it is "an on-going recombination, which changes as different social groups and economic and political forces try to shape this identity formation."[30]

The observation that fluidity does not necessarily result in the subversion of normative values is an important one, especially where hybridity becomes a central category of analysis, as it does in Latina theory and theology. But it is also dangerous to restate identity as delimited by clear borders that can be crossed in any final way, perhaps conveying the misleading impression that an adequate conception of identity is one that, unlike mestizaje, considers racial or ethnic categories as fixed, lacking "on-going recombination," not changing in response to "different social groups and economic and political forces." All identities are the product of ongoing recombination. To challenge the naturalization of racial constructs that support imperialist and racist discourses we should foreground the historical and cultural roots of all categories of identity. In other words, it is crucial to resist the split over nature versus culture operative in race and ethnicity discourses. We must further question the assumption that political alliances must be grounded on an assumed homogeneity or distinctiveness of race.

If we interpret racism in the United States exclusively as a self-other system of representation, mestizas would simply be considered others— that is, different from the norm. However, from the perspective of a social structure based on "degrees of deviance" we receive a more complex picture of social hierarchies in which bodies are judged not by their fit into discrete categories but by their degree of conformance to an imagined standard. Both systems of classification coexist in the context of the United States. In a framework based on degrees of deviance, the mestiza is placed on a comparative scale according to visible traits: more or less black (or white). This scale applies to all representations of bodies, and across a wider range of physical traits. For instance, poverty, obesity, and disability also function as markers of deviance, albeit in different ways, in relation to the privileged white norm. Attention to these other social markers allows us to see the dehumanizing representations of black and Latina bodies in their relationship with the broader cultural problems that affect women.[31]

That the in-betweenness of representations of Latina bodies can be co-opted in the struggles of racial authorization is hardly in question. Indeed, there are many instances in which Latina/o self-representations mirror that of the dominant culture in the United States. And yet mestizaje/mulatez might be the only alternative available in order for some Latinas to claim precisely what Knadler worries they might deny: their "African diasporic history and culture."[32] The problematics of Latina representation that Knadler detects are perhaps not the result of embracing mestizaje but of understanding mestizaje as a place between two purely and contrastingly defined groups: black and white. Such a conception places Latinas at the site of racial and political confrontation between two groups that are construed as opposite poles. As we observed above, the cultural paradigms of racial segregation and of fetishistic fixation with the "mixed race" have a common origin and intent that we must be attentive to as we evaluate representations and attitudes that pit black and Latina bodies against each other. Latina/o bodies can hardly be imagined much less accepted and loved in the richness of their ancestry without grappling with the tensions of their symbolical association with racial and sexual betrayal.

Given the colonial sexualization of mestizaje discussed above, it is hardly surprising that the discussion of just how "black" JLo really is carries sexual undertones. As Knadler observes, the media attention to Lopez's ample derriere "can provoke a primitivist fetishization." Replaying centuries-old colonial sexual fantasies, the (desired) derriere becomes a metonym for blackness. "In this fascination with the otherness of the Latina's possibly inherited black body, we see the struggle of mainstream society in the United States to define and regulate just how *black* the mestiza can be before she is no longer a *'white* woman of color.'"[33] This intense concern to define the amount of "blackness" seems to replay the scene of a colonizer trying to detect the smell of a great-grandmother, and thus accurately place the colonized subject in the social hierarchy. And once again we find an intense preoccupation for defining, detecting, and decoding the marks of the flesh to link bodies to stereotypical representations—a concern inscribed by sexual fantasy.

The "Latina" bodies that Jennifer Lopez performs are not quite de-Africanized. They represent no obliteration of racial impurity but instead, quite to the contrary, the haunting of denied fantasies of sexual and racial transgression that still provoke fear and fascination. It is no accident that Latinas are so frequently portrayed as the muse and temptress of "white" men. Consider Lopez's role in *Shall We Dance?*, in which she threatens the otherwise strong marriage of a "white" man and woman. Consider another example, this one involving the actress Paz Vega. In *Spanglish* Vega plays the part of a Latina maid, whose role as potential supplanter of a white wife is accentuated by the role of her daughter as the potential usurper of the love of the white mother for her white daughter. In the latter case, the movie portrays a competition between two not-so-white potential daughters: the young Latina and an "overweight" white girl. Being overweight is temporarily ruled a worst deviance than being Latina. Represented as a threat to society, the mestiza becomes the heir of the deviled women both blamed for and symbolic of communal betrayal and defilement.[34] It is always tempting for spectators to join the crowd in accusing such women of the humiliations to which their communities are subject, and this is perhaps the goal of these accusatory representations—that is, to shift the blame away from the patriarchal systems that continue to view women as objects of exchange.

The hopeful, or even celebratory, aspects of the body of literature that advocates the embrace of mestizaje are often discussed and questioned. But reducing the ambiguity of mestizaje in order to place it neatly within the dominant United States symbolic structure prematurely dismisses what might become productive tension between competing views of the world and the body and, further, may reify racist paradigms. Here I would like to focus on the potential of the writings of self-proclaimed mestizas and mestizos to highlight the peculiarity of the seemingly self-evident categories with which we think about our "ethnosexual" selves, to "identify otherwise outlawed epistemologies and ontologies" and perhaps even inspire us to imagine new ones.[35]

Reconciliation of the Flesh

The works of the Chicana writers Gloria Anzaldúa and Cherríe Moraga and of the Chicano Richard Rodriguez are each starkly different in ideological stance, style, and strategy. Richard Rodriguez's *Brown: The Last Discovery of America* especially stands out for its problematic stance in almost every key political issue regarding minorities in the United States, but the sentiments expressed by his frequently provocative statements offer windows into paradoxes that affect the topic I address in this essay. Furthermore, the social imaginary from which these writers speak—who in addition to being Chicana/o are queer—is also in contrast with my own. These named distinctions certainly do not exhaust the differences between these writers and me—or those touching Latina/o lives. But I call upon these categorized differences to stand symbolically as guardians to protect us from the illusions of being capable of representing a coherent cultural stance.

Despite the stabilizing effect of Latina/o as a label of identity, the starting point of these authors is not one of certainty but of puzzlement. *Brown* recurrently foregrounds the question of the meaning of the author's own color. From the world described in the writings of white Americans ("the part of America where I felt least certain about the meaning of my brown skin") to an interview with Malcolm X (where "I felt invisible, as anonymous, as safe as I have ever felt") brownness is a sign that invites and resists being deciphered.[36] While these examples pertain to public sociopolitical identification, Moraga takes this questioning of the meaning of her skin color to the intimacy of her familiar home. Pained by the awareness that her own light skin has given her privileges that are denied to her own mother, Moraga calls attention to the unreliable grounds of social identification.

> *See this face?*
>   Wearing it like an accident
> Of birth
>   It was a scar sealing up
> A woman . . . [37]

Moraga describes her experience of having her body read in the United States: a complex heritage reduced to the visage, to the visible. Skin for

Moraga is not necessarily the mark of her ancestry, but it is also and simultaneously its denial. An accident and a scar that separates her from the mother, or unites her with her oppressor. Although as Knadler points out a lighter skin can easily lead to powerful participation in a system of clearly demarcated fields of power, it is often also a source of estrangement. For Moraga this estrangement is felt viscerally, for "the object of oppression is not only someone *outside* my skin, but the someone *inside* my skin."[38] The ambiguity is inescapable. "Both strains contributed to their bodies, to their waking spirits. I am the same distance from the conquistador as from the Indian," explains Rodriguez, and he draws the crucial implication that "righteousness should not come easily to any of us."[39] Ambiguity is directed toward self-scrutiny.

It is not only the complexity and irreducible multiplicity of biological inheritance that these writers scrutinize as they ask, in Anzaldúa's words, "Just what did she inherit from her ancestors? . . . Which is the baggage from the Indian mother, which is the baggage from the Spanish father?"[40] They also highlight the almost comical implications of the differentiations between race, ethnicity, and social ideology: "Pero es difícil differentiating between lo heredado, lo adquirido, lo impuesto,"[41] Anzaldúa ponders. In contrast with the apparent clarity and stability of the theoretical categories that are used to describe it, self-identity is evidently conflictive and puzzling. In highlighting the perplexity of her own attempts of self-representation, Anzaldúa calls into question the compartmentalization of identity produced by the reification of categories of analysis.

Thus representation and embodiment are drawn closer together—a development that is offered as a challenge to the "illusion of precision about race categories."[42] Rodriguez's *Brown* is as much a celebration of the racial impurity associated with Latinas and Latinos as it is a critique of—and invitation to move beyond—the cult of (imagined) purity in United States culture, where there is "no seem to seeming; no nurture to naturalness."[43] At the heart of United States culture's privilege of purity, Rodriguez argues, is a repression of a male erotic fantasy and an enforced silence around the history of race in the United States: "When mulatto was the issue of white male desire, mulatto was unspoken, invisible, impossible."[44] And brown bodies find themselves at the terrible site of the unnamed desires of the American symbolic—a madness that is most often not their own. But the goal of these Chicana/o authors is to turn that anxiety into a provocation that may lead to a deeper questioning of the very foundations of society in the United States. Brown thus becomes a category of analysis: "Brown made Americans mindful of tunnels within their bodies, about which they did not speak; about their ties to one another, about which they did not speak. This undermining brown motif, the erotic tunnel, was the private history and making of America."[45] And the return of that which has been suppressed causes violent anxiety.[46]

The challenge to acknowledge and perhaps even embrace impurity entails an epistemological shift to recognize "the ability of language to express two or several things at once, the ability of bodies to experience two or several things at once."[47] And this affirmation of multiplicity is also a sexual challenge. For the privilege of oneness over multiplicity is part of what the French feminist Luce Irigaray terms phallocentrism—that is, patterns of thought founded on the privilege of the male organ and therefore bear the marks of masculine morphology. Phallocentric thought patterns share "the values promulgated by patriarchal society and culture, values inscribed in the philosophical corpus: property, production, order, form, unity, visibility . . . and erection." And, further, "the value granted to the only definable form"—that of the male organ—not only excludes female eroticism, but generates a "systematics of representation and desire" that confers the highest values to the "*one* form, of the individual, of the (male) sexual organ, of the proper name, of the proper meaning."[48] Irigaray turns to female morphology—"*neither one nor two*," a nearness that does not long for becoming one—to provide an alternative vision for overcoming the phallic economy of the one. But she never pursues the potential of this multiplicity for articulating the complex intertwining of race, ethnicity, and sexuality in a single body—which is *not one*.

Moraga may, like Irigaray, imagine a sex which is *not one*. But in writing from the conflicted space of racial and sexual wars Moraga represents the social constitution of bodies through figures of not only multiple but also partial or wounded forms of embodiment. For instance, a woman's skin appears as the site of memories of the touch of the maternal dwelling, as it does in Irigaray's work. But skin is also the site of painful and guilt-ridden separation: Moraga's light skin is a sign of her distance from her brown mother and thus a reminder of her complicity with a racist society. Her skin is a "scar sealing up a woman." From another perspective, however, Moraga is brown. In United States society, she is "darkened" by her desire of women; Moraga's sex, she observes, is "brown."[49] As we observed above, the standards of whiteness include a wide range of "biopolitical" traits.[50] "By incorporating pain, difficulty, and failure in the re-imagining of a sexual and social world, [Moraga] represents a non-redemptive vision that obliges the reader or spectator to account for the conflictive social and cultural contexts providing the arena for sexual experience."[51] She imagines bodies that are not yet whole, which are portrayed in her plays as dismembered bodies. These disjointed bodies dramatize the internal wars that afflict them and their yearning to be reborn as one—or at least as a multiplicity capable of lovingly touching itself. For these bodies, the promise of caressing their own multiplicity (as Irigaray's woman does) is yet to be fulfilled.

"Can what love has bound together as flesh be reconciled?"[52] This question by Rodriguez looms large for these authors. While Moraga's depictions are characterized in the passage above as "nonredemptive," the works by Anzaldúa and by Rodriguez do offer visions of embodiment that may allow these bodies to lovingly caress their multiplicity—without having to become one. Anzaldúa calls for the development of a "mestiza consciousness" that moves beyond a "counterstance" toward a new way of life. Rodriguez dreams of the liberation of the flesh from the burden of the demands of purity.[53]

Rodriguez's and Anzaldúa's transformative visions entail not only accepting the heritage that has thus far formed Latin American self-conception but also embracing the open-endedness of identity: "Brown, not in the sense of pigment, necessarily, but brown because mixed, confused, lumped, impure, unpasteurized, as motives are mixed, and the fluids of generation are mixed and emotions are unclear, and the tally of human progress and failure in every generation is mixed, and unaccounted for, missing in plain sight."[54] Given the particular colonial history of Latinas and Latinos—which is the history of their becoming bodies—it is hardly surprising that much of their self-representation is characterized by a strong destabilizing, disseminating, perhaps deconstructive impulse.

This taste for uncertainty might sometimes seem at odds with the demands for clarity of political struggle. But the processes of self-definition—speaking from and about our bodies, for instance—are best served by cycles of construction, questioning, deconstruction, reconstruction. The dialogue between black and Latina/o theologies might offer a context in which our differences lead to a healthy appreciation of the openings and closures that are coupled within our bodies and our words.[55]

Transcendence in the Flesh

Creating theological visions appropriate for the redemption of bodies is a crucial step toward liberation. This endeavor is consonant with the commitments at the heart of black, womanist, and Latina/o theologies. Positioning the acceptance and love of black and brown bodies as a central demand of God-talk challenges Christian theology to face the implications of an incarnational faith: divine word has taken flesh. Through their analysis of oppressive words and their effects on bodies, black, womanist, and Latina/o theologies have recognized and confronted the ambivalent power of words by refusing their objectifying power and reclaiming the authority to redefine the meaning of words such as black, woman, Latina/o, and mestiza/o. A theology of the body that is attentive to the historical realities of those who have been represented as wholly flesh cannot dream of any simple return to the flesh, just as it cannot continue to reduce bodies to their sociopolitical and economic placement. Instead, it must find ways to reconcile *word* and *flesh*—as well as spirit and matter, transformation and memory.

The split between these aspects of existence is inscribed in the theological ideas of immanence and transcendence. Immanence is associated with that which is inside creation, in the flesh. Unfortunately, creation, and thus immanence, is often conceived as a self-contained system locked within the boundaries of what is already given. Transcendence, on the other hand, is associated with the freedom of the spirit—beyond, pure, unlimited by materiality. Articulating the "theological weight" of physical bodies requires a challenge to this dualism, for the dualism conceives materiality, and thus bodies, in mechanistic and deterministic ways that always need an external principle to enliven them.[56]

In Marcella Althaus-Reid's interpretation, the deconstruction of the dualism of immanence and transcendence is implicit in Latin American liberation theology, which "is based on the search for the materiality of transcendence." Attending to the transcending aspect of the material world, liberation theology "knows how God is to be found in the presence of the untouchables."[57] This transcendence is not conceived as an ability to escape physical limitations but as openness to transformation beyond what has already been received and beyond the self. As the Latin American liberation theologian Ignacio Ellacuría notes, we can see "transcendence as something that transcends *in* and not as something that transcends *away* from; as something that physically impels to more but not by taking out of; as something that *pushes* forward, but at the same time *retains*."[58] The very life of creatures and their transformations are signs of divine transcendence.

At an individual level this notion of transcendence may help us resist the ideologies that objectify our bodies by reducing them to the dominion of the eye, or to the assumed determinations of narrowly defined notions of "race" or "sex" within the paradigms of nature as opposed to culture or spirit. Instead, we may conceive of transcendence as a force that impels us to "create ourselves," but not in the fashion of an external god that has no use for matter or for the past. Instead of dreaming of abandoning our bodies to create ourselves in absolute freedom from the past, we can see the process of self-creation as driven by a force that impels us to more and that pushes us forward at the same time that it retains us. Creating ourselves through our relationships with others and with the divine is perhaps best imagined as rebirth, where the transcendence of the new is always already taking flesh. Rebirth reminds us of our own beginning in the flesh and in the womb, and it invites us to new embodied beginnings and to incarnate transcendence.

Reimaging transcendence in the flesh entails overcoming the objectifying tendencies that affect descriptions of others and ourselves. Bodies are visible signs within semiotic systems but not only that. As incarnations of transcendence, bodies exceed the limits of representation. Even if signs are always already written on the flesh, no word or image can fully grasp the mystery of creatures. That mystery, however, is inextricable from the names and categories through which we represent our bodies. A theology of the body must recover the transcendent dimension of the body, but that transcendent dimension must not be detached from the realm of the social and the world of representation. The incarnation is always "casting iridescence over nominal triumphs of the word, and flesh . . . always carries the word inscribed on its inmost parts."[59]

Latina/o theological anthropologies have attempted to reconcile the sociopolitical body and divine word by emphasizing a sacramental understanding of reality. In the words of Miguel Diaz, the common element in these anthropologies is a commitment "to underscore very specific social, gender, cultural, and political experience for encountering grace."[60] However, we need not only to bring these elements together but also to foreground their inextricability. The transcendence of bodies entails not only the linkages of bodies with the divine but also (and simultaneously) the relationality of bodies with their own pasts and with other people.

Rather than seeing individuals as self-contained entities that can be placed in discrete categories, we can learn to see the ways in which we are connected to others through the ties in which one life extends in time as well as in space. Although the societies that we live in put us into categories and those categories affect who we might become, we are not reducible to such categories. No name or category can possibly describe all that a person is. This is not because we are absolutely unaffected by social structures or one another, instead it is a result of the complex and infinite relationality of creatures. The transcendence of the person is that which exceeds all representation. It is neither abstract nor otherworldly but rather is openness at the heart of relations.

Each aspect of a person's identity develops in relation to realities that transcend her or his particularity but also in which she or he transcends: community, race, gender, sexual identity, and so on. For instance, the realities of my own community—its history, its language, the geography in which I feel most at home—all embrace me not only as *past* realities but as things that I continue to relate to, be transformed by, and transform. And yet I never grasp them, just as they never completely define me. These transcending realities exist only in particular persons. That is, they are never fully present, as such, and never appear in isolation from other aspects of a person's life. In each person, different realities meet and transform one other in unique ways. Our encounter with others touches and is touched by realities that transcend us both. In each encounter these realities elaborate themselves by "acquiring an internal richness, writing its *exegesis* on the bodies named."[61] In each encounter with others, with our past and our heritage, we open ourselves to new incarnations of transcendence—that is, to new births of blood and flesh, and the will of woman and man, *in* God.

Notes

1 See Norton, *Bloodrites of the Post-Structuralists.*
2 Derrida has coined the term "Globalatinization" to refer to the universalization of the religion of Rome. See Derrida and Vattimo, eds., *Religion.*
3 I borrow the phrase "memory of the flesh" from Luce Irigaray.
4 This has been amply argued in feminist scholarship. For a founding feminist text that addresses this issue, see Ruether, *Sexism and God-Talk.*
5 Ibid., 269.
6 For one account of the philosophical tendency to imagine human development as a journey away from the body, see Irigaray, "Each Transcendent to the Other" in *To Be Two.*
7 The identification of women with materiality and the body is well documented in feminist theory. See Spelman, "Woman as Body."
8 The ontological status of the inhabitants of the Americas was a central issue in the legal debates concerning Spanish colonization, as exemplified by the famous disputation between Bartolomé de las Casas and Juan Ginés de

Sepúlveda. At issue was the question of whether the natives could be defined by the Aristotelian category of "natural slaves." See Arias, *Retórica, historia y polémica*; and Hanke, *All Mankind Is One*.

9 Baker-Fletcher, "The Erotic in Contemporary Black Women's Writing," 208.

10 Simone De Beauvoir, *The Second Sex*, 281.

11 See Butler, *Gender Trouble*.

12 Of course, this is a simplistic statement that does justice neither to John's gospel nor to feminist theory. My purpose here is only to highlight the challenges of foregrounding the material specificity of bodies while revolting against social constructions of particular bodies.

13 Butler, *Gender Trouble*, 10.

14 "Race is just as much a political concept as economic class. . . . Neither ethnicity nor skin color determine race; race is determined politically by collective struggle" (Hardt and Negri, *Empire*, 104).

15 Knadler, " 'Blanca from the Block,' " 3.

16 The phrase comes from a poem by the Puerto Rican writer Fortunato Vizcarrondo entitled "Y tu agüela ¿aónde está?"

17 A parallel tendency can be observed in conceptions of sex that lend normativity to heterosexuality. See Butler, *Gender Trouble*.

18 Young, *Colonial Desire*, 180.

19 To signal the dependence of the concept of a "mixed race" on the very ideology that I am seeking to challenge I place the term mixed in quotation marks.

20 Young, *Colonial Desire*, 175. Similarly, the United States missionary Robert McLean declared the following about Puerto Rico: "The Spaniards did not draw the color line very closely, consequently the population was decidedly mixed both as to color and to blood. *This mixture was bound to cause many complications*" (Robert McLean and Grace P. Williams, *Old Spain in New America* [New York: Association Press, 1913], 106; italics added).

21 Norton, *Bloodrites of the Post-Structuralists*, 33.

22 See Bhabha, *The Location of Culture*, especially 66–84.

23 Norton, *Bloodrites of the Post-Structuralists*, 33.

24 Sir William Lawrence, *Lectures on Physiology, Zoology, and the Natural History of Man, Delivered to the Royal College of Surgeons* (1819), quoted in Young, *Colonial Desire*, 177 (italics added).

25 In fact, revolutions in South America would be blamed on the detrimental effects of racial mixture on people's character.

26 Young, *Colonial Desire*, 180.

27 The question of the relationship between these and the ideologies of multiculturalism remains to be explored.

28 Knadler, " 'Blanca from the Block,' " 1.

29 Ibid., 3.

30 Ibid., 2 (italics added).

31 For an analysis of the relationship between the colonial devaluing of some bodies and representations of disabled bodies (even in liberation theologies) see Betcher, "Monstrosities, Miracles, and Mission."

32 Knadler, " 'Blanca from the Block,' " 1.

33 Ibid., 2 (italics added).

34 Young describes the twisted logic that managed to accuse "half-breeds" in the United States South of provoking miscegenation: it was argued that "the effect of philandering with mixed-raced servants is that the white Southerner male increasingly acquires a taste for pure black women" (*Colonial Desire*, 149).

35 Aldama, *Brown on Brown*, 24. We must also be mindful of our tendencies to interpret racial discourses in other countries—especially Latin American countries—using United States paradigms. Although no doubt there are hierarchies of body types, we shall not lose sight of the particularity of racial systems in the United States, even while attending to the exportation of such ideology around the globe.

36 Rodriguez, *Brown*, 15.

37 Moraga, "It Got Her Over," in *Loving in the War Years*, 64.

38 Ibid., 46.

39 Rodriguez, *Brown*, 228.

40 Anzaldúa, *Borderlands/La Frontera*, 104.

41 Translation: "But it is difficult differentiating between the inherited, the acquired, and the imposed."

42 I borrow this phrase from Matsuoka, *The Color of Faith*.

43 Rodriguez, *Brown*, 136.

44 Ibid., 133.

45 Ibid.

46 For a discussion of the parallel projections of "guilty imagination" onto black bodies, see Hopkins, "The Construction of the Black Male Body."

47 Rodriguez, *Brown*, xi.

48 Irigaray, *This Sex Which Is Not One*, 86, 26.

49 Yarbro-Bejarano, *The Wounded Heart*, 19.

50 I borrow the term "biopolitical" from Hardt and Negri, *Multitude*.

51 Yarbro-Bejarano, *The Wounded Heart*, 92.

52 Rodriguez, *Brown*, 226.

53 I see this longing expressed in the song entitled "Raza pura" ("Pure Race"). In evident mockery of the demands for purity, it states: "I am from a pure race / pure and rebellious / I am from a pure race which has had nails in its hands / and scars in its knees." The implicit similarities between Jesus' crucifixion and slavery is followed by a redefinition of the claimed purity: "I am Borincano / black and gipsy / I am taíno / I am tears and also pain / for all that I've lived / for all that I've suffered / I am of a pure race / pure and rebellious" (my translation). The hard-won "purity" is irreducibly multiple.

54 Rodriguez, *Brown*, 197.
55 Norton, *Bloodrites of the Post-Structuralists*, 2.
56 The term "theological weight" is taken from Pinn, "Cartography and the Children of the 'Americas.'"
57 Althaus-Reid, "El Tocado (Le Toucher)," 394.
58 Ellacuría, "The Historicity of Christian Salvation," 254 (italics added).
59 Norton, *Bloodrites of the Post-Structuralists*, 2.
60 Díaz, *On Being Human*, 56.
61 Norton, *Bloodrites of the Post-Structuralists*, 20.

Traci C. West

◉

RESPONSE TO THE ESSAY BY MAYRA RIVERA

Dear Mayra,

I am writing this response in the format of a letter addressed directly to you because this format allows for a more personal (embodied?) encounter than the neutral (disembodied?) tone of a response written in the third person. Your work in "Memory of the Flesh" persuades me of the necessity to recognize its actual, flesh-bound author together with its intangible, theological creativity. Your work also beckons me to draft a response that explicitly involves risks, uncertainties, and an embrace of ambiguities. As I explore differences and similarities in the views offered in our essays, I want to discover the possibilities and impediments that they reveal for solidarity between us. In my projections about the kind of continued dialogue that would be helpful, I consider what might be encompassed by our combined theo-ethical vision of flesh-spirit wholeness and liberation from subjugating cultural norms.

Your essay attends to history in a way that mine does not. I am grateful for your reminder of how racial categories for colonized subjects were created in this hemisphere and of how Latinas embody that legacy today. In particular, you remind us of how in the nineteenth century "mixed races were material evidence of illicit sex." This labeling of Latino and Latina bodies reflects society's concern with sexual order and fascination with its transgression. The whole notion of racially categorizing bodies is a chosen or willed activity that is largely driven by the impulse to dominate and exploit. Yet, as you also point out, Latino and Latina bodies represent the crossing of boundaries that protect racial categories. Latino and Latina bodies could therefore be considered human artifacts of cultural ambivalence about maintaining racial boundaries. This is a history of mixed messages about race and sexuality that produces the category of "mixed" peoples and uncertainty about the definition of racial identity and the acceptability of sexual desire for the other.

Because I think of eighteenth-century and nineteenth-century black history as pivoting on the issue of slavery, it would probably not occur to me to describe interracial sexual intercourse during this time in terms of "illicit sex." Instead, my interpretation would more than likely focus on the rapes that occurred. These were incidents where there was little uncertainty about the politics of the encounter or about racial identity. Sexual intercourse between black women and white men was usually a matter of sexual exploitation. Further, according to the rule in much of the United States any children produced from these assaults were considered black, as was all progeny carrying "one drop of blood" of African ancestry. Far from illicit, the sexual exploitation of slave women was considered to be a right of their white male owners. Intercourse between black men and white women was also considered rape in all circumstances, and when it was discovered or even falsely invoked it could cost the black man his life.

Although I have addressed the point in my essay, I suspect that the absence of an emphasis on rape and violence in your historical summary could be an impediment to building solidarity between us. Stories of sexual coercion, including the rape of black women slaves and free black women domestic workers are for me an essential part of any retelling of the history of interracial heterosexual sex in the Americas and the Caribbean. Especially since we share parts of this colonial history and black ancestry, this difference in our views might possibly foster tensions that could lead to distrust. I am not backhandedly lobbing some false and hackneyed accusation at you about denying the existence of your black foremothers, but I do want to understand how you incorporate the suffering and unjust treatment of raped black slave women and servants into your view of the transgression of racial categories that interracial sex represents. I am assuming that these women are included in your focus on historical, boundary-crossing heterosexual sex and the symbolic meaning of the bodies that resulted from it. If my assumption is correct, your conceptualization represents their experiences of violation (and that of Indian women as well) in a manner that is too benign. I find it troubling, for instance, to accept Richard Rodriguez's language characterizing the significance of brown bodies in American history in terms of an "erotic tunnel." The violence against black and Indian women that exists in that history seems to be enfolded into a morally relativist framework about eroticism and male fantasy.

I also do not understand why Rodriguez's assertion that his "distance from" (relationship to?) the conquistador and the Indian are the same and therefore forces him into a morally ambiguous position. Rather than reading one's body as a sign of complicity in the violent act that the conquistador commits against the Indian woman because of the ancestral ties to him, and equally a victim of oppression because of his ancestral ties to her, I would plead for a different interpretive choice. Instead, by acknowledging oneself as the product of a violent act, why not view oneself as a bodily reminder that his violence must be denounced and that her suffering must not be forgotten? I am in disagreement with the reinscription of racialist criteria for morality that seems to be assumed by Rodriguez (and perhaps Anzaldúa) that morality is transmitted through blood lines. I would caution against finding moral lessons in blood ties to ancestors in favor of, instead, drawing them from the practices of ancestors.

You have incorporated an awareness of national border crossing and varied combinations of Indian, European, and African ancestry for the Latino and Latinas you describe. I tend to focus a race-sex historical inquiry on the violence and politics surrounding peoples of African and European ancestry, or Indian and European ancestry, with a method based more on the United States. But besides my questions for you about your approach, the emphases in your essay that I've noted here also generate very personal reflections for me.

I am reminded of stories I grew up hearing about my mother's family history. Her family was located in Florida, where she was born. The stories describe one side of her family as stemming from an eighteenth-century German white woman who ran off and married her black slave. Their "elicit sex" resulted in creating a family with several children, and they remained together until her brothers lynched the black husband. The children of these black children later married into the Indian side of the family. My mother described to us her memories of her elderly Creek-Seminole great-grandparents (her words) and how she was afraid of them because they seemed so "ancient and wrinkled" to her as a small child.

I do not claim this "mixed" ancestry or even try to find out if it is all true. There is no political pressure related to detecting the smell of these great-grandmothers. I am black. This is my unavoidable, unambiguous sociopolitical reality, as is the historical fact that all African Americans have "mixed" ancestry. But is the categorization of one's racial and ethnic identity and heritage purely socially imposed? Is there any degree of choice or participation in their social construction? Is it politically viable to try to participate in "creating ourselves"?

Finally, an insistence on interrogating how the policing of racial categories informs issues of sexuality is clearly important for both of us. My Christian ethics questions about how this policing occurs in contemporary public practices in the media are different from yet complementary to your Christian theological questions about how this policing is performed and resisted in the culture. You inquire about the constructive theological task of imaging bodies, while I probe the limits and expansion of our moral imaging of women's sexuality. How my exclusive focus on women and your inclusion of a male perspective shapes our differing views and the contrasts between them is a topic we could explore further in the future.

You find in the queer space of selected gay and lesbian Chicano and Chicana writers a place to explore and equip your theology. These sources provide analysis of how common racial and ethnic meanings are inscribed on Latino and Latina bodies and impact identity formation and self-understanding. In contrast I have claimed the repressive space of the government-sponsored promotion of heterosexual marriage and church attendance for African American welfare recipients. It is a useful cultural site to explore and challenge my liberative Christian ethics. In the midst of repressive societal notions that label one's identity, the Chicano/a writers offer personal witness to the painful alienation, creative adaptation, and profound questioning that can emerge. You allow their actual voices to be heard and self-representations to be aired, while I allow the details of specific repressive practices to be seen. Fortunately, solidarity does not emerge simply from agreement and sameness. These differences form a sturdy basis for building solidarity; they strengthen the possibility of developing a transformative vision and social practice.

Our homophobic society, especially in the Christian tradition and churches, reduces queer identities to shameful sexual acts. Lesbians, gay men, bisexuals, and transgendered persons are seen as merely bodies that have the wrong kind of sex and sexual desire. From the thoughts produced by brown, queer bodies you gather paradigms for a destabilizing Christian theological vision of reconciled materiality and spirit. In a differing but parallel social process, compulsory heterosexuality is enforced in marriage-promotion ideology that shames black women and Latinas for their sexual reproduction while they are poor, single, and seeking economic assistance from the state. From the public policies that view these mothers as merely undisciplined, sexually reproducing bodies that need to be controlled by Christian religion and by a husband, I have gathered a social change agenda that requires a Christian ethical response. An affirming recognition of brown, queer socio-autobiographical reflections on identity as a strategic resource could be joined together with a repudiation of practices that compel heterosexual marriage for black and brown poor women. Working in these differing directions could be a concerted effort that forms liberative body/sex sensibilities and contributes to the alleviation of marginalizing conditions because they centrally involve those at varying social margins of our communities.

In addition, the tensions that any differences in our perspectives bring should not be ignored for the sake of a unified, combined analysis. In my Christian ethics approach I want to emphasize learning from practices in a way that may conflict with the part of your embodiment theology about learning ambiguity from ambiguous ancestral legacies. We need to discuss this issue further. But in conflict and in concert with one another we still build solidarity if we are able to find noncompetitive ways of seeing each other and remain focused on spiritually fed materialist political struggle. Tasks like resisting that unrelenting white supremacist standard telling us that brownness and blackness are inferior parts of our identity entails scrutinizing our self-definitions and our public practices. Decolonized, liberative Christian theology and ethics requires notions of embodied transcendence and immanence as well as notions of truth telling that defy subjugating public fictions and practices.

Thank you for the deeply inspiring challenge of your work.

Sincerely,

Traci

Traci C. West

USING WOMEN: RACIST REPRESENTATIONS

AND CROSS-RACIAL ETHICS

Images of women's sexuality in popular culture in the United States contain persuasive messages about morality. These images influence women's self-understanding and generally inform the public's moral imagination about women's worth. We should make conscious choices about accepting or rejecting the moral lessons taught by the media, but how do we do so? How do we come to our own conclusions about whether or not, for example, the depiction of a female character's sexuality in a Hollywood movie affects her capacity to be seen as an appealing heroine? Similarly, how do we judge if it is right or wrong to agree with a newspaper's laudatory description of a government policy that focuses on the sexual and marital choices of women who are poor? If in the former instance the movie character was a white woman, or in the latter case the poor women in the news story were identified as white, the sexual and moral presuppositions we would take into consideration would likely be different from what they would be if the women were identified as African American or Latina.

Religion should be a moral resource that aids in this kind of discernment. For Christians there ought to be some distinctively Christian understandings available to function as a lens for helping to identify truthful representations of women's lives in popular culture. Unfortunately, within history and culture in the United States, the competing moral influences of racial and ethnic prejudices supportive of white dominance are often welded to Christian beliefs. I want to encourage liberative Christian social ethics that nurture constructive, communal social values by confronting racist attitudes rather than adapting them to fit under Christian rubrics. But when I, a black feminist ethicist, publicly assert the need to sort out racist values from Christian moral values to assess media images of women, certain racial expectations are likely to be automatically assumed by my audience. There is usually an expectation that I will give primary focus to racial and ethnic prejudices impacting "my own" African American group. But this approach does not seem adequate. So many of the images of women's sexuality that need critique include instances of racist victimization that are shared across marginalized racial and ethnic groups or involve competition between them about that victimization.

Though the task of identifying constructive communal values is already formidable when I limit my analysis of white supremacy to its peculiar historical relationship to African Americans, it seems overwhelming when I also try to integrate a discussion of the historic impact of white supremacy upon Latinos and Latinas, Asian Americans, or Native Americans. Yet I bear some responsibility for considering this shared social and political reality in my ethics, do I not? The racial formulations that I want to criticize often not only involve interracial relationships between racially devalued groups but also repressive social policies that impact individuals across these groups.

Support for more multicultural analyses of racism might even be found in unlikely places like the insights from struggles and studies of progressive social change movements within black communities. The regard by black feminist scholars and activists for the sexist treatment of black women has repeatedly shown the perils of a simplistic formula that presumes a singular, homogeneous racial and ethnic group experience as the mandatory, primary category for analysis of white supremacy. An insistence upon uniformity results in the neglect of too many dehumanizing conditions and moral norms that must be addressed in order to create change. They include conditions such as male sexual harassment of and assault on women, and norms such as uncritical deference to patriarchal power in religion. Analyses of racism that insist upon a homogeneous cultural group experience of victimization can therefore impede an accurate political assessment of American popular culture and hinder an appreciation of how racist political manipulation and domination are maintained through multiple ambassadors. Liberative public ethics should incorporate a critique of racism that mediates the moral and political terrain between the justifiable self-interested claims of individual victimized groups and mutual, cooperative understandings across such groups.[1]

Certain representations of women's human worth projected in the news and entertainment media and encoded in government public policy provide venues for scrutinizing popular, culturally generated moral norms that are loaded with racial assumptions. These examples also offer the opportunity to study sites of interracial and ethnic encounter where women's personhood has been usefully employed in the merger of Christian principles and demeaning social values. Christian ideas are not always explicitly stated in the instances cited below. But many of these sites of popular culture still reveal the usefulness of assaults on women's personhood for perpetuating unjust social practices, about which there should be a Christian critique.

To identify possibilities for the role of a liberative Christian ethic in interracial and ethnic public representations, I focus upon two specific case studies: representations of Hispanics and Latinas as popular movie characters in interracial relationships and representations of black women in the language used in the government public policy for marriage promotion aimed at black and Latina single mothers applying for welfare benefits. In these examples, particular women's bodies and lives are used as symbols for communicating moral values in ways that may add to racial tensions or mitigate them in United States culture, but they consistently teach restrictive moral lessons about gender and sexuality. I am concerned with the public lessons on morality that these examples offer about the permeable boundaries between fiction and fact, truths and falsehoods, and Latina personhood and black women personhood.

It should be possible to foster public morality that supports women's moral worth and well-being by marginalizing reductionist ideas about women in popular culture that are intolerably one-dimensional, objectifying of their bodies, and politically subjugating. As the contemporary moral philosopher Seyla Benhabib states, "A coherent sense of self is attained with the successful integration of autonomy and solidarity, or with the right mix of justice and care."[2] The likelihood of this needed coherence being achieved by and about women will be greatly diminished without a critical examination of public representations of them, such as those in the mass media images of Hollywood movies or on government Web sites. Further, the possibilities for the development of a coherent self and respectful communal relations are enhanced when we learn more about the role of religion in shaping those understandings. Hopefully we can locate progressive articulations of religious values related to sexuality that bring a critique to repressive cultural ones.

Image Making

It is difficult to overstate how powerful a role the media plays in shaping our moral imaginations. It is almost impossible to comment on racialized depictions of women in popular culture without at least a minimal tribute to the contributions of the Hollywood film industry.[3] Sadly, for the vast majority of people in the United States, Hollywood and television are the primary resources for acquiring the moral categories, boundaries, and aesthetic sensibilities needed to imagine virtuous human character traits and behavior. Furthermore, my inclusion of Hollywood as a reference point for considering images of women in popular culture can serve as a reminder of the pervasiveness of the consumer market mentality for the widely ranging elements of public discourse in the United States. Depictions of black women and Latinas that are presented to the public—whether they are created by the entertainment industry, articulated through government policy and politicians, or featured in a news broadcast about a local incident—are driven by this same mentality. The categories used by media ratings systems, political pollsters, and shareholder reports for the owners of news media conglomerates map the scope of the mass public's moral and political universe. And the assumptions underlying these categories are captive to a capitalist market mentality obsessed with the singular goal of figuring out what sells the best.

Hollywood images can therefore be a barometer of those racial and ethnic images deemed most tolerable to the broader public (what they are willing to consume) and in what forms the crossing of racial and ethnic borderlines is welcomed. Also, since these fictional depictions are by design intended to provoke emotional and occasionally even thoughtful reactions, our experience of watching movies teaches us what to feel and think about women. Enhancing our recognition of the meanings embedded in mass-produced Hollywood images can provide practice for any public venue where representations of blacks and Hispanics and Latinas occur. By reflecting on the content of movies, we can practice the effort required to become self-conscious about what "buttons are being pushed" by certain depictions and why.

Angharad N. Valdivia argues that Latinas "are portrayed in a limited number of roles. Some of these, such as the maid and welfare mother, overlap with African American female images. We also get the virgin/whore opposition that women in general experience . . . in contrast to the rosary-praying maids or devoted mothers, we get the sexually out of control and utterly colorful spitfire, an image quite specific to Latinas."[4] This virgin/whore opposition is a reference to how the Virgin Mary, mother of Jesus, is seen as representative of ideal womanhood, and how as such she stands in contrast to the Christian legends that cast Mary Magdalene as a prostitute—that is, as the quintessential (female?) sinner. Valdivia rightly points out the constraints for women set up by this formula based upon Christian gospel legends. A rigid moral dichotomy is reproduced over and over again by media images offering this limited range for imagining women's sexual expression and establishing a competitive dynamic between women.

The role of Christianity may be subtle for consumers of these images. Its defining presence is so normalized in the cultural assumptions behind women's sexual expression depicted in movies (and even in feminist cultural critiques of those depictions) that the religious origins of those assumptions are probably imperceptible. Nevertheless, peculiar Christian traditions help to undergird this dichotomous and competitive moral valuing of women. Religion provides the material for cultural straitjackets of certain racial and ethnic as well as gendered images projected in the mass media, just as it has for the actual historical experiences of women.

This competitive and oppositional relationship of the virgin/whore dichotomy has historically contributed to racist hierarchies in the attitudes about and treatment of women. The Victorian notions stressing the virtuousness of bourgeois white womanhood and the need to protect them from any form of sexual violation by male strangers stood in contrast to the acceptance of the wanton sexual exploitation of black women by white slave masters and later by many white male employers of black domestics.[5] This black-white moral dualism is reflected in the proliferation of roles created by the white-owned entertainment industry that portrays white women as innocent and vulnerable victims of stalking, rape, and murder, while depicting black women as hardened prostitutes.

And yet Valdivia's comment about the limited roles assigned to black and Latina actors calls attention to the relationship of these two groups to *each other* and makes a comparison. When I reflect upon how she points out the overlapping depictions of black women and Latinas as the maid or the welfare mother and then makes specific distinctions, I wonder about what drives the need to distinguish the racially based barriers that Latinas face from those faced by blacks. Valdivia isolates the images of "rosary-praying maids or devoted mothers" and "sexually out of control and utterly colorful spitfire" that are specific to Latinas. Such distinctions are essential for clarifying the cultural patterns that can fracture and distort one's self-image, and thus impede women's development of a coherent self. But how are such distinctions maintained in ways that also build solidarity rather than competition between Latinas and African American women? This issue may be especially difficult because to be seen—that is, to be politically recognized—Latinas and black women are most often in contention for the same desirable location of being positioned in relation to white women.

In her essay analyzing the character portrayed by the Puerto Rican actress Rosie Perez in the movie *Fearless*, Silvia Tandeciarz writes about the racial dynamics in the storyline that place Perez's character (Carla) in opposition to a white woman character, but with the husband of the white woman between them. Tandeciarz stresses the ways in which Carla is needed by Jeff Bridges's character (Max) to be cured of his guilt and trauma after they both survive an airplane crash.[6] In this movie almost all of the passengers are killed in the crash, including Carla's little boy who was sitting next to her. Max spends a considerable amount of time talking with Carla and building a posttrauma bond with her that he does not have with his wife. He and Carla share their survivor's guilt as well as a somewhat dazed and fearless state (exemplified by their deliberate automobile crash into a wall while Max is driving at a high speed). Carla is the "devoted mother" preoccupied with grief over the loss of her child. She provides an opportunity for an intense, nonsexual relationship for Max, as well as a useful point of focus for him as he tries to cope with his own emotionally needy state.

Tandeciarz notes the film's pitting of "colored Carla vs. white European wife played by Isabella Rossellini" and how it shows that in such a competition it is the wife, "the face of Lancôme," who wins.[7] For it is his wife who saves Max at the end of the movie when he has a severe allergic reaction to a strawberry and falls to the floor choking in their living room. Max hears his wife's scream and her fear saves him. In a provocative commentary about the political significance of these images in the film, Tandeciarz explains that it is his wife, "the legitimate, socially sanctified partner[,] who must secure for Max his old identity and save him. She is the signifier par excellence of that bourgeois basis of dominance, it being white, upper middle-class American power under siege. . . . As he returns to his wife and child, Max is freed from his guilt about the hundreds of people he has not been able to save, [and] this family triumphs over a social discourse of responsibility that demands we look beyond our homes to our communities and the power dynamics that shape our lives."[8] The movie's conclusion reassures its audience with the depiction of a stabilized, white, heterosexual marriage bond (with their male child in the background). This stability has been achieved with the use of Carla's friendship: available to Max when he needed a distraction and dissolved when the wife decides it's time for her to go away and tells her so.

I catch myself thinking that of course I recognize the image of "colored Carla" who is available for this anxious white man while he maintains a strained relationship with his wife. This is a variation on a black "mammy" character, one who freely provides nonsexual, emotional triage that helps keep white families together. At the same time, I am uncomfortable with my desire to fit Carla into one of "my own" familiar categories of black female stereotyped roles. It is as if I am seeking recognition, as if *I* must be recognizable in an interpretation of how this Latina character, her losses, and the others she may represent are rendered invisible. My recognition of the reductive imaging of Latinas seems to emerge most fully when I can see something familiar there that is reflective of representations of me.[9] Most disturbingly, as a consequence of being narrowly focused upon what is familiar to me, I avoid contact with the difference that is manifested in how Latinas are represented. I may even be guilty of mimicking white supremacist strategies when I use the Latina other to lead me back to a way of promoting my self-interest. (But I am seeking recognition of the oppressive stereotyped images that entrap my own black womanhood, not trying to preserve racist superiority.) I am also seeking solidarity. Yet perhaps solidarity cannot be built from a focus upon the recognition of oppression. Solidarity may need to be rooted in a responsible communal relationship that requires a genuine encounter with difference. This is not to be confused with popular entertainment's media representations of such encounters.

Hollywood images of an encounter with racial difference may be seen in the casting of Latina actresses in what are sometimes called "bridge" character roles. For example, Rosie Perez's characters are often romantically paired with non-Latinos (e.g., *It Could Happen to You* with Nicholas Cage and *Somebody to Love* with Harvey Keitel). But when she is paired with non-Latinos Perez serves as a bridge between whites and blacks, such as in *White Men Can't Jump* (between Woody Harrelson and Wesley Snipes) and in Spike Lee's *Do the Right Thing* (where she was also featured as a dancer during the opening credits).[10] Similarly, the Puerto Rican actress Jennifer Lopez has also portrayed bridge characters romantically paired with white actors (e.g., *Maid in Manhattan* with Ralph Fiennes and *The Wedding Planner* with Matthew McConaughey) and as a bridge between black and white male buddies such as in *Money Train* (between Woody Harrelson and Wesley Snipes).[11] Referring to Lopez as the "ideal bridge," Valdivia even includes Lopez's real-life celebrity romances where she is seen as "the woman who can date P-Diddy or Ben Affleck."[12] The role played by the Mexican-born Selma Hayek in *Wild, Wild West* (between Will Smith and Kenneth Branagh) could be another example of this kind of bridge role for Latinas.

Like the lighter-skinned African American actresses such as Halle Berry,[13] the Latina actresses noted above have earned recognition for their "crossover" appeal, which can be seen in their success in bridge roles. The hybridity in how their heterosexual sex/gender identity is raced has proven to be marketable to a mass audience. Perhaps one of the most sensational examples of the usefulness of this racial hybridity can be found in the publicity about Lopez's "crossover butt." This sensation was captured in news headlines such as *USA Today*'s "Jennifer Lopez: She's Proud of Her 'Bottom Line'" or the *Chicago Tribune*'s "Booty Boon: Jennifer Lopez' Backside Makes an Impression on the Nation's Cultural Landscape."[14] Discussions in the popular entertainment news about how Jennifer Lopez's body type, specifically her buttocks, had crossover appeal may indicate some breakthrough in the public's imagination of racial norms. Lopez defies standards of beauty that identify the thin, flat, and narrow body types of idealized white women as most sexually desirable, while remaining enormously popular in the romantic lead opposite white males in high-grossing Hollywood films.[15] Is this image transgressive or a reenactment of an old sexually objectifying stereotype?[16]

Crossover appeal is a problematic litmus test for measuring breakthroughs in racist racial norms. It usually refers only to the tastes of white audiences, thereby indicating that whites are able to cross over and find certain Latino/a or black entertainers appealing instead of just members of "their own" white group. One hardly ever sees entertainment news discussions of the crossover appeal of white celebrities such as Sandra Bullock and Jennifer Aniston for black or Latino/a audiences.

I am suspicious of the celebrations of Latinas for their success in bridge roles and the resulting capacity for crossover appeal. This focus seems to celebrate possibilities for being linked to whiteness, and thus it provides the familiar result of marginalizing and exoticizing blackness (starting with the blackness of Lopez and Perez). The phenomena of crossover appeal also exemplifies how the business of generating images in the entertainment industry can create yet another means for valuing the capacity to be seen by whites as desirable. This is a desirability that imbues social status while deepening racist pathology. The moral framing of this desirability includes either chaste or sexually suggestive images of bridge characters, thereby harkening back to the virgin/whore options with whiteness as the god one must please.

An expansive ability to imagine ourselves and our moral relations within society is essential fuel for the creativity and moral agency needed to transform racist pathology. As bell hooks explains, claiming subjectivity means insisting "that we must determine how we will be and not rely on colonizing responses to determine our legitimacy."[17] A struggle is required to control the damaging impact that can result from popular images mass produced by Hollywood and others. It is a struggle for the freedom to legitimate one's own moral self-evaluations and judgments. Yet how much freedom from control is really possible, and for whom?

Disciplining with Images

The potential consequences generated by Hollywood's stereotyped images of black women and Latinas overlap and yet differ significantly from the effect of the state's controlling images of black women and Latinas that are used to legitimate socioeconomic policy. The nature of the political struggle intensifies. The direct consequences for women mushroom when the government pronounces certain representations of poor women as fact and regulates their lives by establishing material consequences—punishments and rewards—in accord with those representations.

The entertainment industry and the state (in its regulation of the poor) do share some similar methods. That is, they both creatively provide certain images of women that feed the public's moral imagination. Industry executives are the arbiters of those images of fictional female characters designed by Hollywood studios. Political officials are arbiters of those images of females in certain problem populations that are encoded in public policy. Both select certain ideas about women's identities that they wish to convey with those images and place them on display for the public to consume. While the precise social effects that can be directly attributed to Hollywood's constructed images are hard to pinpoint, the government's creatively edited images are explicitly linked to a national policy that is enforced on a daily basis by the state.

The Internet is a relatively new media outlet for disseminating state-sanctioned, politically constructed, images and serves as a resource explaining the federal government's welfare reform policy.[18] This was the case with the Bush administration's Healthy Marriage Initiative ($1.5 billion), a program administered by the U.S. Department of Health and Human Services (HHS). Welfare reform policies regulate access to programs that are relied upon by socioeconomically poor people seeking emergency assistance, and the HHS Healthy Marriage Initiative Web site includes a specific focus on black and Latino communities. Below, I discuss the messages about morality and poor women that were found on the Healthy Marriage Initiative Web site during George W. Bush's second term (2004–8).

I must note at the outset of this discussion of the Healthy Marriage Initiative that the HHS Web site acknowledged that the promotion of healthy marriages does not "immediately lift all families out of poverty."[19] Yet even this qualification clearly suggested that the initiative was able to lift some families out of poverty, or that it could eventually lift some families out of poverty. An unanswered question remains about precisely how heterosexual marriage helped those women who are poor and seeking public assistance to meet their needs for food, health care, child care, affordable and safe housing, educational opportunities, employment opportunities, and cash. This initiative apparently included an unstated but crucial proviso that these women were not to marry men who were either as desperately poor as they were or even worse off. Furthermore, the Web site's disclaimer about the ability of the Healthy Marriage Initiative to actually lift families out of poverty sounded like a disingenuous political equivocation, since the initiative was slated to spend over a billion dollars of funds from the only federal program whose primary function was to assist people facing immediate crises of poverty.

The Healthy Marriage Initiative stems from the Personal Responsibility and Work Opportunity Reconciliation Act of 1996 (PRWORA), which was signed by President Clinton and accomplished a radical moral shift in the United States.[20] The Healthy Marriage Initiative was built on the grounding moral assertion of the 1996 law that "marriage is the foundation of society." The 1996 law shifted government policy from an understanding of poverty as a problem related to economic conditions that require a coordinated national response to an understanding of poverty as an individually generated problem that requires a state-by-state approach for disciplining individuals whose poverty was caused by their failure to adequately take personal responsibility for their lives.

In addition to the HHS Web site there were many other sources that disseminate the agenda of marriage promotion agenda, notably black newspapers. For example, the *Broward Times* featured an article entitled "The Most Effective Anti-Poverty Program Ever Created: Marriage," and an editorial from the Washington, D.C. *Afro-American* decried the problem of too many children born to unwed mothers in the black community and then touted the African American Healthy Marriage Initiative of HHS as a "blessing."[21] Nevertheless, although the Healthy Marriage Initiative Web site that I have chosen as my focal point is not the only vehicle for spreading this agenda, it does illustrate a unique and far-reaching means for communicating it.

The design of the government's Healthy Marriage Initiative Web site under the Bush administration serves as a case study in racialized moral disciplining. The site's home page was designed to lay out the core components of this program, for which it singled out two groups: Hispanics and African Americans.[22] The top three pieces on the first page of the site were conveyed as follows: "What is the HHMI [Health and Human Services Marriage Initiative]?" "What is the Hispanic HHMI?" and "What is the African American HHMI?" The home page also gave additional details about the program and provided information on how an individual could get involved with the initiative and receive some of its funds. The first page also featured a photograph of two white men with warm smiles: Dr. Wade Horn (an assistant secretary of HHS who served as a principal innovator and director of this program) and President George W. Bush.[23] When the Healthy Marriage Initiative's major emphases were listed on the site, whites were unnamed. Why? Were there no poor white people who received public assistance?[24] Assuming there were, would not poor whites also have benefited from strengthened heterosexual marriages? Or perhaps whites were not named because the public must be taught that white interests could not be crudely lumped together under the heading "white" initiative. The absence of poor whites from this initial page targeting African Americans and Hispanics taught the public that whites were not to be seen (politically recognized) as the problem population with regard to poverty. Instead, whites were to be seen as entitled to make individual, private decisions about their heterosexual marriages.

Representations of black women and Latinas found on the HHS site placed an official understanding of what matters for insuring their well-being on exhibit to the world (at least, the world of millions of Internet users). The HHS site on marriage sanctioned an intrusive public surveillance of their lives. It represented these women not only by lumping them together under a heterosexual, racial, and ethnic group identity but also by making very personal choices related to their romantic and sexual lives a matter for public discussion. The Web site helped to establish their lack of an entitlement to privacy and the public's lack of respect for their individuality with regard to sexual/romantic choices.

Since religion was so centrally concerned with defining parameters for moral relations, it was no accident that from its inception the PRWORA legislation of 1996 included a focus on religion.[25] The Bush administration extended this focus with direct references to it within its welfare reform programs, which this HHS Web site on marriage exemplifies. When one clicked on the African American pages of the site, one of the five featured "fact sheets" discussed a topic titled "Religion and Marriage among African Americans in Urban America." Although not evident in the title, women were the focus of this section. The "Religion and Marriage" fact sheet presented charts and graphs about black urban mothers' heterosexual marital status, sexual reproduction of children, and participation in Christian organized religion. As one part explained:

Compared to African American mothers who attend church infrequently:

Churchgoing African American women are seventy-three percent more likely to be married at the birth of their child.

Churchgoing African American married mothers are thirty-one percent more likely to report that they have excellent relationships with their husbands.

Compared to African American unmarried mothers who attend church infrequently:

Churchgoing African American unmarried mothers are one hundred-forty-eight times more likely to marry after the nonmarital birth.

Churchgoing African American unmarried mothers are sixty-two percent more likely to rate their relationships with the fathers of their children as very good/excellent.[26]

Through this Web site, the state advocated church attendance for black women who lived in urban America. The patronizing moral message offered to and about these women was quite explicit here. It includes the following: a bad African American woman is one who does not attend church on a frequent basis. (Urban black women who are Muslim were rendered either invisible or inherently bad.) Further, when urban black women do not go to church they are likely to exhibit bad behavior that was identified here as having a child without being married to a man and having a bad relationship with their husbands or with the fathers of their children if they are unmarried. Married black women who face battering husbands and unmarried black women who are emotionally or physically abused by the fathers of their children were egregiously provided with yet another reason to blame themselves for their abusers' behavior—the insufficient frequency of their church attendance.

Those who looked at this site on the Internet received a carefully crafted moral view of black women that was verified by the United States federal government as the sponsor of the site, as well as by those experts who produced the presentation of this information and whose university training was prominently listed at the beginning. African American churches were also implicated by virtue of the shameless promotion they receive on the site. (The study concluded that the "Black church is the bulwark of marriage in urban America.") This group of authoritative and official sources seemed to collectively agree that what urban black women and their children needed most for their well-being was for these women to be married to men, which was likely to occur if they frequently attended church.[27] Since poverty was not mentioned, it is not clear whether it was assumed to be synonymous with urban black women or if all urban black women, regardless of class background, were supposedly in need of this marital-Christian remedy.

Remember that this overall formula of a correlation between church attendance and "nonmarital births" must be interrogated. Correlations such as this one on the HHS Web site should not be automatically viewed as causations. For instance, suppose I could demonstrate that young black women in the military are 75 percent less likely to have "nonmarital births" than those not in the military. Using the faulty logic of this material on the HHS Web site, I would then conclude that all black women over the age of eighteen should be drafted into the military to prevent "nonmarital births," and I would proclaim that army enrollment helps to create moral black communities. The presentation of statistics associating church attendance and "nonmarital births" deceptively suggested causation. It left the consumer of this information with the false perception that "nonmarital births" were caused by failure to attend church frequently. In this way it taught a fictitious narrative of these women's lives.

Whites *were* named in this section of the Web site that concentrated on the African American Initiative. Two of the charts at the beginning of the

so-called fact sheets on church attendance and marriage offered comparative analysis of black women, white women, and Hispanic women. On the
first graph measuring their sexual reproduction, black unmarried women
with babies represented the worst statistic (70 percent) when compared
to white unmarried women with babies (18 percent) and to Hispanic unmarried women with babies (40 percent). As Hispanics were shown to
be much closer to the white standard than were the black women, one of
the racial messages seemed to be that Hispanic mothers were the other
others (i.e., problem population), and they were useful for highlighting
the inadequacy of blacks. "But Church Attendance is High among African
American Mothers" the very next title reassured, and it was accompanied
by a bar graph demonstrating how black mothers who frequently attend
church won out over the other two groups when it came to religion. The
next graph measured frequency of church attendance and showed that
blacks had the highest percentage points for church attendance relative to
both their white and Hispanic counterparts in the categories both of married and unmarried mothers.

In this section of the document the women were not only assumed to
be in a competitive and oppositional relationship with one another, but
their segregation by racial and ethnic group also appeared to be quite natural for the boundaries of this competition. At the same time, all three of
the racially separated groups of women do share in having the conditions
of their lives measured in terms of their sexual reproduction of children,
marital attachment to men, and Christian religious expression of faith.
After the cross-racial comparison about church attendance, the rest of the
fact sheet on marriage and church attendance was dedicated solely to black
women.

The conclusion of this section asserted the importance of "the black
church" in marriage promotion. This leads one to wonder if the intent
of this entire fact sheet was to promote church attendance at exclusively
black churches. What about black women who attend predominantly
white churches? Or multiracial churches? Are these churches as effective
in bringing about the desired result of marriage? Multiracial and interracial religious contexts are ignored as well as interracial identities. Black
Hispanics and Latinas are not accounted for in this study.

Competitive comparisons were included in several other places on the
site. The Hispanic Healthy Marriage Initiative pages on the HHS site, for
instance, were filled with comparative statistics that included whites and
blacks. In the initial introduction of the Hispanic Healthy Marriage Initia-

tive fact sheets, a competitive perhaps even antagonistic relationship was fostered with comments such as "There has been a relative lack of research on Hispanic and Latino families, particularly in comparison to the volume of research examining African American families."[28] In addition to the competitive dynamic, this assertion also cultivated the questionable assumption that Hispanic and Latino/a families ought to have a desire to be research subjects in the same way that African Americans have been.

When reading through all of the pages of the Web site for the HHS Healthy Marriage Initiative the struggle for inclusion that blacks and Latino/as face in other influential public forums is not the problem they faced here. Black women and Latinas are undeniably politically recognized populations in welfare reform policy. The abundance of direct references, statistics, and graphs about them on the fact sheets of the Web site indicate the extent to which they are seen as useful for shaping public views. The images of black women and Latinas that were communicated in the Web site reinforced the idea that they lacked moral discipline. The narrative constructed about the women, their families, and communities conveyed an emphatic message about the need for discipline. Of course, a very specific form of discipline—marriage to a man—was recommended for them. Most importantly, the narrative constructed about the women on these fact sheets attempted to discipline the mind of the viewer, who was probably not one of the women seeking public assistance. Most poor women in need of welfare assistance are not likely to be surfing the Web on their home computers in order to read about this program. The audience for this site may have been a government social worker who was receiving an orientation, or perhaps the staff of a faith-based community organization in search of funds. And it definitely included segments of the general public.

The need to morally and spiritually discipline unmarried, sexually reproductive, socioeconomically poor black women and Latinas is a moral message that evidently sells well to the general public. A moral message about how blacks need to do better than Hispanics and Latino/as in morally and spiritually disciplining their unmarried and sexually reproductive, socioeconomically poor women no doubt also sells well to the black general public, especially the segments of it that are not poor.

After viewing these fact sheets on the HHS Web site it is almost impossible to imagine an alternative communal (national) goal for serving the needs of these economically impoverished citizens that does not include some scrutiny of their sexual reproduction. One cannot imagine what it would mean to create national initiatives that foster solidarity and support among poor women instead of competition. It is almost inconceivable that there could be an initiative that would lead to a more just distribution of the power and resources of the socioeconomically advantaged, rather than intrusive, paternalistic shaming of those with the least power and socio-economic resources. One cannot even begin to envision an overarching societal consensus on the goal of treating women who are poor in a way that fosters such solidarity and justice, nor conceive of how the realization of such a goal might occur.

Who knows what policy could be formulated by listening to the needs named by mothers *across* racial groupings who seek childcare options, whose families reside in unsafe, inadequate housing, or who have chronic health conditions and inadequate healthcare. It seems impossible to imagine a state policy for addressing the economic crisis of a woman that is not concerned with limiting her consensual adult sexual and marital choices, whether they include a desire for complete independence from her husband (or her wife) or building a safe and nurturing household with her wife or female intimate partner or with a male intimate partner. Our inability to summon any of these requisite images for an alternative to the Healthy Marriage Initiative approach is not because we have no imaginations.

The public's moral imagination has been trained by too many constraining images. For instance, when the ending of the movie *Fearless* depicts a stabilized white, heterosexual marriage bond between the Jeff Bridges character and the beautiful Isabella Rossellini character in their lovely bourgeois home (their son in the background), it is comforting. Perhaps the repetition of facts about mothers of color in the popular news media, such as those offered on the HHS Healthy Marriage Initiative Web site, contribute to this comforting feeling. Such routine, allegedly factual representations of black women and Latinas as social problems help to evoke the moviegoer's recognition of a truly promising vision of love and happiness in the depiction of the couple in the conclusion of *Fearless*.

On the other hand, perhaps the repetition of popular movie endings with a white heterosexually married couple, such as the one in the conclusion of *Fearless*, disciplines the news media consumer's imagination. Because of repeated exposure to such movie images that are presented as the resolution of turmoil and ambiguity, the supposed facts in the news media about poor women of color, such as those presented on the the Healthy Marriage Initiative Web site, appear to offer a truly promising vision of American moral and religious goals. I'm not certain which of these influences is more successful in shriveling the expansive moral imagination that is needed to revolt against subjugating practices aimed at poor black women and Latinas. They are mutually reinforcing representations.

For Christians, I wonder if certain countercultural images in scripture could aid them in breaking out of their accepted role of reinforcing popular cultural narratives of woman-as-useful-object and of providing religious legitimation for state regulations. I wonder if Christians could be inspired to revolt against this legitimating role by the characters in the Christian gospel story where a pregnant, unmarried young Jewish woman who goes to see her older married cousin who has also just become pregnant, neither of them with the assistance of a man. In that story, these two pregnant women, one married and the other unmarried, joyously and empathetically talk with one another. One of them, the unwed pregnant one, starts prophesying in the midst of this supportive moment of woman-bonding. In thankful response to God for the miracle of her unwed pregnancy, she prophesies about the rich being sent away empty and the powerful being brought down from their thrones. Studying this scripture requires a faith-filled, cross-cultural encounter between Jewish ancient eastern Mediterranean female characters and twenty-first-century United States Christians. An expansive, imaginative spiritual awakening to truth could be stimulated by this gospel scripture where wed and unwed, pregnant, low-status women supporting one another evolves into prophesy. It could, perhaps, teach contemporary Christians about the kind of interference with subjugating cultural norms that God expects them to recognize as just.

Notes

1 I am employing the conceptualization by Benhabib in *Situating the Self,* 48.
2 Ibid., 198.
3 "Hollywood" is a shorthand reference to the massive film industry based in the United States that produces films shown on home and automobile VCRs and DVDs; on network, cable, and satellite television; and in movie theaters all around the world.
4 Angharad N. Valdivia, "Stereotype or Transgression?" 395.
5 See the discussion of controlling images in Hill Collins, *Black Feminist Thought,* 69–96.
6 Tandeciarz, "Some Notes on Racial Trauma in Peter Weir's *Fearless,*" 60.
7 Ibid., 64.

8 Ibid., 64–65.

9 This discussion of recognition is based upon the work of Kelly Oliver in *Witnessing*, 9.

10 Valdivia, "Stereotype or Transgression?" 401.

11 Mary C. Beltrán, "The Hollywood Latina Body as Site of Social Struggle," 74. Lopez was also featured as a "Fly Girl" dancer in Damon Wayans's *In Living Color*, a program to which Rosie Perez also contributed choreography for the "Fly Birls."

12 Valdivia, "Stereotype or Transgression?" 14.

13 For example, in her academy award winning performance in the movie *Monster's Ball*, Berry's character is the wife of a black death-row inmate, and she becomes the intimate romantic partner of his white jailer after he is executed.

14 Teresa Wiltz, "Booty Boon: Jennifer Lopez' Backside Makes an Impression on the Nation's Cultural Landscape," *Chicago Tribune*, October 15, 1998, 1.

15 For a detailed discussion of the significance of this phenomena, see Beltrán, "The Hollywood Latina Body as a Site of Social Struggle"; and Collins, *Black Sexual Politics*, 27–30.

16 I am borrowing Valdivia's terminology from the title of her essay "Stereotype or Transgression: Rosie Perez in Hollywood Film."

17 hooks, *Yearning*, 22.

18 The U.S. Department of Health and Human Services (HHS) oversees the welfare reform program Temporary Assistance for Needy Families (TANF) and its explanation can be found on the HHS Web site, http://www.acf.hhs .gov/recovery/programs/tanf/tanf-overview.html. The HHS site explains that "the Deficit Reduction Act of 2005 reauthorized the TANF program through fiscal year (FY) 2010 with a renewed focus on work, program integrity, and strengthening families through healthy marriage promotion and responsible fatherhood." Although my analysis focuses upon the Healthy Marriage Initiative during the Bush administration, the initiative and the same basic design of the Healthy Marriage Initiative Web site (http://www.acf.hhs.gov/healthy marriage/index.html) discussed in this chapter continued under the Obama administration.

19 See http://www.acf.hhs.gov/healthymarriage/ (site visited in October 2005).

20 See my extensive discussion of the origins of this program in *Disruptive Christian Ethics*, 75–111.

21 Joseph C. Phillips, "The Most Effective Anti-Poverty Program Ever Created: Marriage," *Broward Times*, October 14–20, 2005, 5; Editorial, *Washington Afro-American*, December 3–9, 2005, A12.

22 The racial focus on this Web site has continued to expand. The bulk of my research and analysis of this Web site was based upon its presentation through January 31, 2006. A Native American Healthy Marriage Initiative and Asian

and Pacific Islander Healthy Marriage Initiative have since been added to the site.

23 Under the Obama administration, a photograph was added of *both* Michelle and President Barack Obama, along with their two children.

24 A total of 954,000 whites, 480,000 blacks, and 368,000 Hispanics received TANF/Welfare (AFDC) according to the U.S. Department of Commerce, *Statistical Abstract of the United States: 2004–2005, National Data Book*, 124th edition, October 2004, 345.

25 In the "Charitable Choice Provision" of the 1996 PRWORA, historic legislation for federally funded entitlement programs was created with a provision to expand the role of religion as service providers.

26 W. Branford Wilcox and Nicholas H. Wolfinger, "Religion and Marriage among African Americans in Urban America," HHS, Administration for Children and Families, http://www.acf.hhs.gov/healthymarriage/ (site visited on October 11, 2005).

27 The page indicates that the data is from "The Fragile Families and Child Well-being Study."

28 HHS, Administration for Children and Families, http://www.acf.hhs.gov/healthymarriage/ (site visited in October 2005).

Mayra Rivera

回

RESPONSE TO THE ESSAY BY TRACI C. WEST

Thinking ethically about the body shall not be done with an exclusive focus on the group to which one belongs. This basic principle of Tracy West's essay calls for a response—one that is more than a reply to an extended dialogue beyond the limits of the pages and the writers in this volume. A sense of the urgent need for such dialogue connects West's essay and my own, which are in my view already "turned toward each other." Both of our essays try to think about the body as always already in relations that need to be foregrounded, critically analyzed, and transformed.

Relationships with the dominant group (the colonizers of the past and the white supremacists of the present) and with other "racially devalued groups" form a complex web from which our understandings (and feelings) about our own bodies and those of others emerge. Both of our essays are thus alert to the inscriptions of representations of racially or ethnically marked bodies on our own personhood and their effects in our emotional reactions. They look at the body as both sign and person. In the case of West's essay these explorations emerge from an insightful look at what is arguably the most exemplary site of representation and materiality in the United States: Hollywood as an image-making machine, on the one hand, and a tool of socioeconomic policy on the other. Image making is shown to materialize in economic sustenance: the image and the body are intertwined.

My essay also explores that interrelation. However, this thematic convergence reveals also significant differences, not all necessarily traceable along the lines of African American and Latina identities. First, there are evident methodological differences related to our disciplines: West is a

Christian social ethicist and I am a Christian constructive theologian. These different scholarly arenas influence the strategies that we adopt for our work. However, as I read West's essay I am less interested in simply noting the difference than in pondering how her work in social ethics can affect my own theological work more deeply. I am especially challenged by West's commitment to keep her theoretical work as close as possible to real lives and specific bodies. Inasmuch as theology proposes visions of the world, it aims at broad, even "universal" images. But I agree with West as she notes in her *Disruptive Christian Ethics* that the dichotomy between the universal and the particular is an unnecessarily restrictive one, indeed a false one. Thus I ask myself how a theology of the body can consistently highlight the interrelation between concepts such as "the human body," "Latina bodies," "African American bodies," and specific bodies in its commitment to constructive theological production.

"The human body" as a theological concept is crucial for making normative theological and ethical claims. But these are certainly constructed concepts that must be continually analyzed as such, lest we lose sight of the contingency of the meanings that present themselves as self-evident—not only for the dominant groups but also for ourselves. A dialogue between Latinas and Latinos and African Americans on the cultural histories that have influenced our self-understandings would help us uncover *specific* constructs that silently hinder our efforts to build solidarity. As these essays have shown, current categories of analysis (e.g., mestiza) frequently mask complex and conflictive meanings that need to be explored in their contextual specificity. In addition to investigating the historical paths of cultural production, liberative theologies of the body would draw from specific articulations of the experiences of the body in relation to sociohistorical contexts, but without subsuming their specificity under named identities or perspective. West accomplishes this by referring to singular women's stories (a strategy that she develops more fully in *Disruptive Christian Ethics*). It is similarly as singular stories—not as communal representation—that I have read the Latinas and Latinos I discuss in my essay. In their singularity they can question and transform our more general (or "universal") concepts. Our challenge is to develop methodologies that move between the specificities of these stories, broad historical questions, and normative theological and ethical claims without obscuring the interdependence and tensions between them.

Their definition of the contexts of their work is another important difference between our essays. This difference cannot be defined simply as responding to the differences between the histories of African Americans and Latinas. While West's work is grounded in the analyses of racial dynamics in the United States, I find myself drawing both from the theoretical resources that focus on the United States and those that attend to the histories of Latina/o identities outside of the United States. The use of postcolonial sources demands attention to the specificity of the Caribbean background that I claim and to the distinctive self-understanding of Caribbean peoples in relationship to African Americans in the United States. Because the self-understanding of Caribbean peoples is distinctly constructed as shaped by their African ancestry, further dialogue between African Americans and Latinas about the body would benefit from closer attention to the differences between racial understandings developed in different areas in Latin America and how they affect racial relationships in the United States, including the welcomed "forms of crossing of racial and ethnic borderlines" explored in these essays.

The ways to solidarity between Latinas and African Americans in the United States requires our constant critical evaluation of our constructions of ourselves as much as those of others. Thus both essays challenge the oppositional understandings of the relationship between differently racialized women by foregrounding how those oppositions, which serve the interests of the dominant groups, are internalized. The ambivalent position of the bodies of Latinas in relation to white supremacy as both its victim and its potential tool reveals the urgency of developing dialogic methodologies for liberative theologies and ethics, a methodology that explores differences (and its categories of analysis) in their sociopolitical and historical contexts. This scholarly aspect of a much needed "responsible communal relationship" might stimulate an "imaginative-spiritual awakening to truth."

PART THREE　　▣　　LITERATURE AND RELIGION

James H. Evans Jr.

◻

THIS DAY IN PARADISE: THE SEARCH FOR HUMAN

FULFILLMENT IN TONI MORRISON'S *PARADISE*

Toni Morrison's *Paradise* (1997) is the final part of a trilogy of historical novels. The first book in the series, *Beloved* (1987), explored the effects of slavery—especially the Fugitive Slave Law of 1850—within the African American experience. The second book, *Jazz* (1992), examined the period of the Harlem Renaissance and the emergence of a distinctively African American creative genius. *Paradise*, which the author originally titled *War*, is an imaginative exploration of the historical search of the progeny of enslaved Africans for a place of their own. Morrison skillfully weaves the threads of the stories and legends of the founding and failure of all black towns in the nineteenth century and presents a cultural, psychological, and spiritual tapestry of African American life. She uncovers, celebrates, and critiques these stories, and in the process she raises unavoidable questions of hidden pain and tragedy. In this richly textured tale we find one of the key motifs in the African American search for fulfillment.

The central issue I address in this essay is how the notion of paradise within African American experience is construed in Morrison's novel. I argue that there are two fundamental structural components to Morrison's portrayal of this slice of African American life. The first is the puritan myth with its emphasis on progress, manifest destiny, and exceptionalism. I will briefly examine this myth and its contribution to the tenor and tone of the novel. The second component, which I am asserting is greatly under-appreciated in most contemporary assessments of this novel, is what I am calling the "back to Africa" motif. This motif carries connotations of a return to origins, collective identity, and communalism. Both of these foundational myths address issues of place, power, and purpose in the quest of that form of human fulfillment that we call paradise. The difference between the myths corresponds roughly to the two major forms of nationalism that, historically, have captured the African American imagination. The nationalism of Booker T. Washington, with its puritan emphasis on hard work, a stern morality, and even personal hygiene, focuses on the task of building a nation *ex nihilo*. The essence of this nationalism is the creation of a new order. The nationalism of Marcus Garvey, with its Africentric emphasis on cultural giftedness, a celebratory religion, and personal relationships, focuses on the task of rebuilding a nation. The essence of this nationalism is the retrieval of a preexisting order.[1] However, because these myths arise out of two distinctive historical realities, their manifestation in African American experience is the result of the powerfully creative and adaptive capabilities of the souls of black folk. It is my hope that the exploration of these themes will enrich our understanding of the African American quest for human fulfillment.

Paradise as the Search for Place

Anna Maria Fraile-Marcos, in her fine essay "Hybridizing the 'City Set upon a Hill' in Toni Morrison's *Paradise*," argues that a major key in understanding the thematic structure of Morrison's book is the puritan mythical construct of "a city set upon a hill." Fraile-Marcos examines the construction of a national identity in a country as diverse as the United States. She notes that this national identity was based on several key unifying myths: "One of those shared unifying myths is that of America as an earthly paradise. John Winthrop, the first governor of the Massachusetts Bay Colony, not only legitimated the Puritan venture in 1630 with his 'Model of Christian Charity,' but his sermon created the foundational fiction of America as 'a City upon a Hill.'"[2] This fiction was the fertile seedbed for the growth of America's myth of origins. It is the acceptance of this myth as historical fact that cements national identity from generation to generation. African Americans did not share the historical context that gave rise to these powerful national myths. They did not flee Europe but rather were forcibly kidnapped from Africa. The ideas of freedom and destiny that fueled the Puritan imagination did not include African Americans. Yet, the power of these myths lies in their capacity to garner allegiance from diverse populations. Thus, while African Americans may not have been the focus of these myths, to the extent that they identified them-selves as African *Americans* their identity was profoundly shaped by them. One of the keys to understanding Morrison's *Paradise* is to see the "Old Fathers" as types of "founding fathers." Like the puritan fathers, Morri-son's patriarchs are determined to respond to the desire of their followers to have a place of their own. While the puritan settlers' sojourn to the New World was a bold statement and an act of agency, Morrison's patriarchs are responding to a more tragic historical series of events. The community described in the novel is reeling from a forced removal and dispersal—a "scattering" if you will. This displacement is the root of continual attempts at replacement. The historical rectification of this removal, dispersal, and displacement is not only the seeking out of new territory as envisioned by the puritans but also a return to origins, or a return to Africa. Here the "back to Africa" motif addresses the distorted economy of a racist society. The etymology of the word *economy* is the Greek word *oikos*.[3] In its secular context the word refers to the arrangement of a household, including the proper distribution of resources necessary for the sustenance of the occu-pants of that household. In its Christian theological context the word also refers to "the family of God" as a trope for the church. The displacement of Africans represented a corruption of the "household arrangement" of this world. That is, the Atlantic slave trade displaced Africans in what we might call "the world house." This dynamic of displacement and replace-ment is a response and an attempt to restore the economic dimension of not just African American experience but the experience of all Americans. Morrison's patriarchs are in search of a place that they can call their own. However, this search becomes tragic because their understanding of that ideal place is limited by the narrow perspective of the puritan vision. That is, in mimicking the puritan worldview of a controlled and coercively uni-fied community they actually impede the possibility of the creation of true community. As a result, their search for a place is continuously frustrated by the limitation of their vision. A key limitation in this respect is the ex-clusive focus on the future as redemptive as well as an inability to see that the return to African origins is just as crucial to their collective identity. Of course, the "back to Africa" motif does not necessarily result in a historical movement of people to the African continent, although that is the root of the motif. This motif has a life of its own because it provides a language for the missing pieces in the identity formation of African Americans.

A key element in the evolution of this motif is that the journey back can be experienced as an internal journey. This is one of the primary functions of the place in Morrison's novel called the Convent. Unlike the tightly structured and coercively unified community envisioned by Morrison's patriarchs, the Convent is a liminal space. It is a space where human diversity is not only tolerated but celebrated. It is not paradise itself but rather a space where one might find one's place. Morrison's description of the Convent recalls the ancient Jewish community described by the first-century historian Philo in his essay *On the Contemplative Life*.[4] This community, called the Therapeutics, is composed of men and women devoted to a lifestyle focused on the presence of God. There are several features of the life of this community that bear mentioning in this context. First, as their name suggests, they were devoted to the practice of healing both the body and the soul. Second, they were absolutely opposed to the ownership or employment of slaves or servants because they believed that nature had made all men and women free. Third, while there were monastic elements to their common life they were not a monastery. A monastery, as the name suggests, is focused on an eremitic (or desert) existence. That is, the monastery elevates the model of the hermit. The convent, as the name suggests, is focused on a common existence and a coming together of individuals. The convent promotes a life that is, in the words of John Dominic Crossan, "*coenobitic* (from the Latin word *coena* for common 'meal'): [a place where] individuals live in total human community, with everyone praying, working, studying, and worshipping together."[5]

Morrison's description of the Convent reflects these features. The women celebrate their common life together and they center their lives around the work of healing. Further, the women come together around a common meal. Indeed, the preparation of food appears to be almost a constant activity of the Convent. But one more feature needs to be noted of the community of Therapeutics described by Philo. The image of this community and its continuing impact on religious life led later Christian scholars to claim that it was merely a prefiguration of later Christian monastic movements. Early Christian leaders found it difficult to believe that such a powerful and effective community could flourish outside of an explicit, institutionalized Christian context. Likewise, the opponents of Morrison's Convent, noting that its residents "never step foot in church . . . they don't need men and they don't need God," are more afraid of the extra-Christian religious practices taking place there.[6] The women in the Convent refuse to dichotomize God. They reverence earth, air, and water but not apart from God. The women are instructed not to "separate God from His elements. He created it all. You stuck on dividing Him from His works. Don't unbalance His world" (244). These insights and perspectives suggest, perhaps, that this community embodies the indigenous values of traditional African religions and Native American religions.

The women who occupy the Convent are displaced and misplaced persons. Yet they are also women who are in the process of rediscovering their place. This rediscovery has the character of both an inward journey toward origins and an outward journey toward destiny. The Convent was a stark reminder to the patriarchs of Morrison's novel that there was trouble in their paradise—a paradise based on a utopian ideal that asserted that an idyllic existence free from external interference was possible. However, utopian communities have historically faced a critical choice: they could either eschew the acquisition of material power and become separatist colonies, or they could embrace material power and become empires. The first choice leaves a community vulnerable and at risk of conquest. The second choice leaves a community exposed to demonic distortions of humane communal values. The leaders of Morrison's paradise chose to risk demonic distortion rather than vulnerability, and with it they inherited certain imperial tendencies. The Convent, by its very existence, was a critique of the choice made by the patriarchs of paradise. Therefore, like any anti-imperial presence, the Convent had to be destroyed.

Paradise as the Search for Power

The search for a place is only one part of the quest for paradise. The puritan myth described above sought to create a national identity. A fundamental aspect of this identity was participation in the creation of a new state. This participation was a sign of citizenship. This new state was understood in the puritan imagination as the Promised Land and the New Jerusalem. This new state was a symbol of political power. The desire of Morrison's patriarchs for a new political reality found concrete expression in the establishment of a town called Haven. This community, like the puritan Promised Land, is centered on a foundational narrative. The narrative employed by the patriarchs of paradise was, as Morrison writes, "a story that explained why neither of the founders of Haven nor their descendants could tolerate anybody but themselves. On the journey from Mississippi and two Louisiana parishes to Oklahoma, the one hundred and fifty-eight freedmen were unwelcome on each grain of soil from Yazoo to Fort Smith. Turned away by rich Choctaw and poor whites, chased by yard dogs, jeered at by camp prostitutes and their children, they were nevertheless unprepared for the aggressive discouragement they received from the Negro towns already being built" (13).

This group for a time successfully established themselves in a "promised land." This place, which they called Haven, was settled by a mixed and motley group that like the ancient Israelites was comprised of intact families as well as orphans, strangers, and stragglers. However, this original community was difficult to sustain: "From Haven, a dreamtown in Oklahoma Territory, to Haven, a ghost town in Oklahoma State. Freedmen who stood tall in 1889 dropped to their knees in 1934 and were stomach-crawling by 1948" (5). On the crushed hopes of the "Old Fathers," their descendants, ex-soldiers and veterans of the Second World War, the "New Fathers" attempted to replicate the journey and resurrect the dream of their forebears. They built Ruby, "a town justifiably pleased with itself. It neither had nor needed a jail. No criminals had ever come from this town. And the one or two people who acted up, humiliated their families or threatened the town's view of itself were taken good care of. Certainly there wasn't a slack or sloven woman anywhere in town and the reasons . . . were clear. From the beginning its people were free and protected. A sleepless woman could always rise from her bed, wrap a shawl around her shoulders and sit on the steps in the moonlight. And if she felt like it she could walk out the yard and down the road. No lamp and no fear . . . Nothing for ninety miles around thought she was prey" (8). The attempts of Morrison's patriarchs to establish a political reality must also be understood in the context of a corrupted *polis*.[7] The word *polis* in its original context refers to one's native city or a place where one might exercise the rights of citizenship. In its later theological context the word refers to the "New Jerusalem." While the puritan quest focused (accurately or not) on the establishment of a radically new political order, for African Americans this new political reality was corrupted by the denial of the full rights of citizenship to them. In response to this corrupted polis, Morrison's patriarchs sought to establish their own political reality. Thus the establishment of Haven and Ruby were not just imitations of puritan settlements but rather were concrete protests against them.

The attempt of both the Old Fathers and the New Fathers to construct a paradise out of the rubble and ruin of slavery and segregation is in some ways a counterpart of the utopian and communitarian movements of the eighteenth, nineteenth, and twentieth centuries. That is, they were driven by a conviction of the universal principle of human equality. In this case, however, the continued rejection of their claim to equality led to the creation of a mythos based on racial superiority. Morrison skillfully sets this search for community against the historical canopy of the establishment of all black towns in the United States in the late nineteenth century and the early twentieth. Morrison writes that in looking for a pattern for the establishment of their earthly paradise, the Old Fathers sent one of their representatives "to examine, review and judge other Colored towns. They planned to visit two outside Oklahoma and five within: Boley, Langston City, Rentiesville, Taft, Clearview, Mound Bayou, Nicodemus" (108). This tour led the Fathers to emulate the successes and avoid the mistakes of these other towns. Thus even racist acts of terrorism or the financial collapse of 1929 could not, in their opinion, destroy what their sheer dogged strength had built:

> Eleven years later Tulsa was bombed, and several of the towns [they] had visited were gone. But against all odds, in 1932 Haven was thriving. The crash had not touched it: personal savings were substantial . . . and families shared everything, made sure no one was short. Cotton crop ruined? The sorghum growers split their profit with the cotton growers. A barn burned? The pine sappers made sure lumber "accidentally" rolled off wagons at certain places to be picked up later that night. Pigs rooted up a neighbor's patch? The neighbor was offered replacements by everybody and was assured ham at slaughter. The man whose hand was healing from a chopping block mistake would not get to the second clean bandage before a fresh cord was finished and stacked. Having been refused by the world in 1890 in their journey to Oklahoma, Haven residents refused each other nothing, were vigilant to any need or shortage. (108)

This community was not one based on a sense of nationalism or cultural pride. The ethos of the community was one that knew little of and cared less about Africa. For Soane, a character typical of the community, "all she knew about Africa was the seventy-five cents she gave to the missionary society collection. She had the same level of interest in Africans as they had in her: none" (104). Even when the interest of some of the younger members turned to the Black Power movement, it was summarily rejected as "some African-type thing full of new words, new color combinations and new haircuts" (104). This rejection of "African things" is paradoxical in that many of the towns upon which Haven and Ruby were modeled were referred to as "Little Africa." That is, they were approximations of the freedom and integrity that attended to a kind of African idealism. In this instance the search for paradise was a quest for a community without dissent. The return to Africa in this instance could not be a return to a formal political reality known as Africa. The return to Africa could only finally be a return to an essential form of existence.

The Convent provided a way back to that essential form of existence. The power dynamics within the Convent were based in ritual and not in coercion. It was through ritual and not the rights-based activities of the corrupted polis that the residents of the Convent were empowered. Ritual allowed the potential conflicts and differences between people to be transformed into mutual respect and acceptance. As such, the Convent was a stark reminder to the patriarchs of Morrison's novel that there was trouble in their paradise. Therefore, as noted above, the Convent had to be destroyed.

Paradise as the Search for Purpose

The wanderers and pilgrims of Morrison's paradise became a people because of the historical trauma of what they called the "first Disallowal." This rejection by people who looked like them was the cement that held them together: "Afterwards the people were no longer nine families and some more. They became a tight band of wayfarers bound by the enormity of what had happened to them. Their horror of whites was convulsive but abstract. They saved the clarity of their hatred for the men who had insulted them in ways too confounding for language" (189). The identity of this group was confirmed by the sign 8-R, which was "an abbreviation for eight-rock, a deep, deep level in the coal mines. Blue-black people, tall and graceful, whose clear, wide eyes gave no sign of what they really felt about those who weren't 8-rock like them" (193). But it was that mark of identity that led to what they called "the second Disallowal." After the end of Reconstruction they discovered that the battle lines for the children of Africa had been redrawn: "For ten generations they had believed the division they fought to close was free against slave and rich against poor. Usually, but not always, white against black. Oh, they knew there was a difference in the minds of whites, but it had not struck them before that it was of consequence, serious consequence, to Negroes themselves . . . The sign of racial purity they had taken for granted had become a stain . . . [This] Disallowing came from fair-skinned colored men. Blue-eyed, gray-eyed yellowmen in good suits" (194–95). Now they saw a new separation: light-skinned African Americans and darker skinned African Americans.

The concrete symbol through which these pilgrims confirmed their hope and staved off humiliation was the Oven. Like the Ark for the ancient Israelites, the Oven was a constant reminder of what held them together as a people. The Oven, part council rock and part shrine, was a reflection of their determination to resist the dehumanizing forces of slavery and oppression. When the New Fathers decided to move again in the face of the second Disallowal they took the Oven with them: "They took it apart, carrying the bricks, the hearthstone and its iron plate two hundred and forty miles west . . . An Oven. Round as a head, deep as desire. Living in or near their wagons, boiling meal in the open, cutting sod and mesquite for shelter, the Old Fathers did that first: put most of their strength into constructing the huge, flawlessly designed Oven that both nourished them and monumentalized what they had done" (6). The Oven was the center of community life. It embodied the freedom and integrity that the Old Fathers envisioned as they stood in the middle of unconquered territory. Unlike the Ark of Israel which symbolized God's covenant with the chosen people, the Oven was the quintessential emblem of the robust covenant among hearty men who "believed the rape of women who worked in white kitchens was if not a certainty a distinct possibility—neither of which they could bear to contemplate. So they exchanged that danger for the relative safety of brutal work. It was that thinking that made a community 'kitchen' so agreeable" (99). Morrison's patriarchs understood their fundamental purpose to be the accomplishment of this thin but durable objective: survival. This was their calling. This is the ecclesial dimension of their quest. In its original context the *ekklesia* was a group of people who were called out for a particular purpose. In its later theological context it referred to those who constituted the church. In the puritan imagination, the community was the company of the elect—those who were called out. African Americans were not called out, they were taken out. And as such any rectification of this dimension of their existence had to attend to this matter. For African Americans, any notion of paradise had to include not only those who were called out but also those who have been called back.

As noted above, the Old Fathers constructed a paradise based on the model of those all-black towns—many of which, ironically, were referred to as "Little Africa." It was ironic because they sought to replicate the economy (*oikos*) of Africa as a means of resisting external interference from the white world, and to imitate the politics (*polis*) of Africa as a means of suppressing internal conflict in the community, but to have a truncated *ekklesia* of Africa as a means of rejecting eternal judgment. Even in the attempt to replicate an African economy the African connection was not recognized. (Tulsa and other towns proudly wore the title "Black Wall Street.") In this regard the problem with Haven and with Ruby was that the economics of separatism were not able to ultimately resist the twins of predatory capitalism and virulent racism. This was a community that eschewed the politics of the civil rights movement. Even after the death of the most visible symbol of that movement, "in their view Booker T. solutions trumped DuBois problems every time" (212). The trouble with their insular politics was that it focused on independence without integrity. Separatist politics ignores a fundamental feature of human existence. This feature is not a neurotic desire to be accepted by those who despise you, rather it is a claim to full humanity in all of its physical and spiritual dimensions.

Undergirding the structural flaws of this paradise is the concomitant rejection of the religious dimensions of black life. The residents of this paradise had the form of religion but were lacking in the power thereof. They subscribed to a functional faith that simply confirmed their sense of destiny. The Old Fathers bristle at a sermon delivered on the subject of love. The preacher declares that God is love and then goes on to conclude that God "is interested only in Himself which is to say He is interested only in love . . . God is not interested in you. He is interested in love and the bliss it brings to those who understand and share that interest" (142). This God, whose aseity is paramount, cannot be the deity that confirms a community whose raison d'être is historical pain and anger. That pain and anger had morphed into a claim of racial purity. This community was comprised of generations that were "not only racially untampered with but free of adultery too . . . That was their purity. That was their holiness" (217). It was a community that claimed racial purity without cultural integrity.

The following dialogue between a minister and a parishioner reveals the deep cultural ambivalence and even rejection that characterizes this community.

> "If you cut yourself off from the roots, you'll wither."
> "Roots that ignore the branches turn into termite dust."
> "Pat," he said with mild surprise. "You despise Africa."
> "No, I don't. It just doesn't mean anything to me."
> "What does, Pat? What does mean something to you?"
> "The periodic chart of elements and valences."
> "Sad," he said. "Sad and cold." . . .
> "I am not sad or cold."

"I meant the chart, not you. Limiting your faith to molecules as if—"

"I don't limit anything. I just don't believe some stupid devotion to a foreign country—and Africa is a foreign country, in fact it's fifty foreign countries—is a solution for these kids."

"I'm not really interested, Richard. You want some foreign Negroes to identify with, why not South America? Or Germany, for that matter. They have some brown babies over there you could have a good time with. Or is it just some kind of past with no slavery in it you're looking for?"

"Why not?" There was a whole lot of life before slavery. And we ought to know what it is. If we're going to get rid of the slave mentality, that is."

"You're wrong, and if that's your field you're plowing wet. Slavery *is* our past. Nothing can change that, certainly not Africa." (210)

The notion of "back to Africa" can have a double meaning. One can either attempt to get back to Africa or one can turn one's back to Africa. Both meanings have currency in African American cultural discourse. Neither meaning can be fully appreciated if Africa is viewed solely through the sad, cold scientific lens of politics or economics. The dialogue quoted above concludes with a reflection on the deeper meaning of Africa in this context, that is, home.

"But can't you imagine what it must feel like to have a true home? I don't mean heaven. I mean a real earthly home. Not some fortress you bought and built up and have to keep everybody locked in or out. A real home. Not some place you went to and invaded and slaughtered people to get. Not some place you claimed, snatched because you got the guns. Not some place you stole from the people living there, but your own home, where if you go back past your great-great-grandparents, past theirs, and theirs, past the whole of Western history, past the beginning of organized knowledge, past pyramids and poison bows, on back to when rain was new, before plants forgot they could sing and birds thought they were fish, back when God said Good! Good!—there, right there where you know your own people were born and lived and died. Imagine that, Pat. That place. Who was God talking to if not to my people living in my home?" (213)

Only when the deeper cultural and religious meaning of Africa in African American experience is explored can we determine whether the "back to Africa" motif can provide an image of community that can support the quest for human fulfillment. Morrison's tale suggests that a self-imposed isolation is a justifiable response to rejection but is a poor substitute for true solidarity. Racial chauvinism is a justifiable response to color prejudice but is a poor substitute for true integrity. Yet this search for a place of one's own, this nearly universal quest and insatiable thirst for home is an important theme in African American literature. In this context the search is for a place where the promise of a future heaven can be glimpsed in the here and now. Paradise is here understood as related to all three dimensions of temporality. Paradise is built upon the past, yet it is not a return to the past but instead the bringing of the past into the present. It is more than nostalgia. Paradise is built on the future, but a future that funds the present. It is more than a fantasy. It must have relevance for contemporary living. Perhaps what holds the key for us today are the words that a condemned and despised, but ultimately victorious, first-century Palestinian Jew at the point of death uttered to two dying thieves: "This day, you will be with me in Paradise."

Conclusion

Some of the most powerful, substantive, and enduring notions of human fulfillment in the United States experience over the last two centuries have come out of the African American context. The most poignant expressions of hope have, ironically, come from persons whose situations have been most hopeless. On many occasions these expressions of hope have come from social, political, and religious leaders like Dr. Martin Luther King Jr., Malcolm X, and Shirley Chisholm. Yet it has been more often the case that creative writers, novelists, and poets—whose business it is to work with images—have stirred our imaginations and motivated our will. Frederick Douglass, Linda Brent, Booker T. Washington, W. E. B. Du Bois, Ann Petry, Richard Wright, Ralph Ellison, Maya Angelou, and others have struggled to portray a future on which a community of people might build their hopes. Sometimes this portrayal was so apparently pessimistic that it provided a wobbly scaffold for collective optimism. Such was the case in the grim and realistic writings of Richard Wright (*Native Son* and *Black Boy*) and Ann Petry (*The Street*). On other occasions, writers presented a triumphant staircase for the ascension of hope. Such was the case with Maya Angelou (*I Know Why the Caged Bird Sings*) and Frederick Douglass (*Narrative of the Life of Frederick Douglass*). Yet, whether apparently pessimistic or optimistic, none of these writers could escape the demand to present some picture of reality that captured the pain of the past as well as the promise of the future.

The question of why one should hope and what one should hope for could scarcely be answered directly. Centuries of cultural caution on the part of African Americans as well as a finely developed sense of the complexity of things meant that apt symbolic expressions had to be found to give voice to this deep-seated quest for human fulfillment.

In this essay I have sought to examine, though certainly in not all of its richness, the notion of human fulfillment as paradise in a single textual component of the African American literary tradition. Further, my focus in this essay has been the "back to Africa" motif as one dimension of human fulfillment. The idea of paradise has a rich history in the European literary tradition. Dante's epic work depicts paradise as the culmination of an intellectual and theological quest that ultimately ends in an encounter with the mysteries of the Holy Trinity and the Incarnation. Milton's work on paradise is a saga of loss and restoration. Each writer is working with a different understanding of history and place. Dante's work suggests that time is cumulative and progressive and that, consequently, a place once left can never be recovered. Thus paradise is not where we are from but where we are headed. Indeed, like the Israelites in the story of the Exodus, we leave behind a sad estate as we seek a better place. Milton's work, on the other hand, suggests that time is cyclical, and as a consequence a place once lost can (and perhaps must) be recovered. Paradise, then, is a place of return. Like the story of the Israelites in the story of the Exodus, we are sojourners in a strange land and contentment will not be ours until we are repatriated.

Within the African American literary tradition the notion of paradise has developed distinctive nuances and dimensions because of the experiential matrix out of which it was birthed. In particular, the historical, cultural, and spiritual repercussions of the Atlantic slave trade, and especially the institution of slavery in the United States, have and continue to mold this idea. Nowhere is this fact more evident than in Toni Morrison's novel *Paradise*.

Notes

1 For an excellent study on black nationalism, see Dawson, *Black Visions*.
2 Fraile-Marcos, "Hybridizing the 'City Set upon a Hill' in Toni Morrison's *Paradise*," 3.

3 The following definition of *oikos* is taken from the New Testament Greek lexicon offered by Crosswalk.com:

> 1. a house; a. an inhabited house, home; b. any building whatever: 1. of a palace, 2. the house of God, the tabernacle; c. any dwelling place: 1. of the human body as the abode of demons that possess it, 2. of tents, and huts, and later, of the nests, stalls, lairs, of animals; 3. the place where one has fixed his residence, one's settled abode, domicile
> 2. the inmates of a house, all the persons forming one family, a household; a. the family of God, of the Christian Church, of the church of the Old and New Testaments
> 3. stock, family, descendants of one

4 This community is described in detail in Crossan, *God and Empire*, 38–40.

5 Ibid., 40.

6 Morrison, *Paradise*, 276. All further cites from this work appear as parenthetical page numbers in the text.

7 The following definition of *polis* is taken from the New Testament Greek lexicon offered by Crosswalk.com:

> 1. a city; a. one's native city, the city in which one lives; b. the heavenly Jerusalem: 1. the abode of the blessed in heaven, 2. of the visible capital in the heavenly kingdom, to come down to, 3. earth after the renovation of the world by fire; c. the inhabitants of a city

Teresa Delgado

RESPONSE TO THE ESSAY BY JAMES H. EVANS JR.

In James Evans's essay on Toni Morrison's *Paradise* he illuminates the quest for place, power, and purpose on which Morrison's characters embark in their search for a space of their own making and choosing. Through Evans's description of the story and its underlying message about the futility and necessity of the journey toward paradise, I was reminded of the story of Eduardo, the protagonist of Pedro Juan Soto's *Hot Land, Cold Season*, who journeys back to Puerto Rico in search of a "paradise lost" that is anything but the streets of New York City. And yet when he arrives in his hometown of Caramillo he finds only polluted water, corrugated tin houses, and resigned citizens. To his dismay, the paradise Eduardo sought existed only in his mind as a figment of his imaginative longing for the past that never was.

The experience of the Puerto Rican diaspora depicted by Soto in *Hot Land, Cold Season* and other stories in no way compares in magnitude, scope, horror, or loss to the mid-Atlantic slave trade, whose progeny inhabit the pages of each of the three novels of Morrison's trilogy. But Puerto Ricans are nonetheless descendents of that same theft of humanity and as such are heirs to the same longing for a place that the initial displacement provokes. This legacy is that of which Aurora Levins Morales speaks when she claims and celebrates her own hybridity in her poem "Child of the Americas":

I am a child of the Americas,
A light skinned mestiza of the Caribbean,
A child of many a diaspora, born into this continent at a crossroads . . .
I am not African. Africa is in me but I cannot return . . .[1]

In that same collection, coauthored by Levins Morales and her mother Rosario Morales, the latter offers this reflection on Africa:

> Africa waters the roots of my tree,
>   Pulses in my sap,
>   Seeps through my heartwood.
> Though my roots reach into the soils of two Americas,
>   Africa waters my tree.[2]

Another Puerto Rican poet, Sandra Maria Esteves, speaks to this longing for a reconnection with the lost remnants of Africa in her poem "It Is Raining Today":

> Each droplet contains a message
> Soaks my clothing·
> The earth is crying . . .
> *La lluvia* contains our history
> In the space of each tear Cacique valleys and hills
> Taino, Arawak, Carib, Ife, Congo, Angola, Mesa
> Mandinko, Dahome, Amer, African priest tribes
> Of the past
> Murdered ancestors
> Today, voices in the mist
> Where is our history?
> I pray to the rain
> Give me back my rituals
> Give back truth
> Return the remnants of my identity. . . .[3]

So where can paradise be found? Is it simply a utopian vision that can never be realized, or is it a long-lost memory embellished by nostalgia? Evans suggests that neither of these responses reflects the nuance of the African American story as told by Morrison; her fictional town of Haven falls a bit short of "heaven," literally and metaphorically, and the "return to Africa" movement never quite reaches its existential ideal. In the same way, these Puerto Rican poets reflect the sentiment that Puerto Ricans cannot simply "go back" to a preconquest Puerto Rico. As a product of slavery and conquest Puerto Ricans would have to erase history, and in so doing erase their very selves from their own creation story.

It seems to me that Evans is asking us to consider whether we, as African Americans and Puerto Ricans, can ever recover the Garden of Eden of our respective cultural identities and homelands—the original garden where God has said to us, after surveying the creation, "This is good." This consideration suggests that we as a people require such divine affirmation; that is, we need to know our existential starting point as a human community set in a particular context if we are ever to know where we are headed or if we are to experience our sense of human fulfillment. However, our existential or theological starting point cannot be equated with our sociohistorical starting point: the continent of Africa and the island of Puerto Rico can hardly be seen as the Garden of Eden, then or now. Paradise does not exist for Morrison's "patriarchs" or for Soto's "Eduardo," and neither does it exist for us on this earth—at least in the way that paradise has been used as a literary device to invoke a pure, uncorrupted original state of being.

Yet, Morrison's skill as a writer offers us a glimpse into what I believe is a new way of envisioning "paradise" that rejects its Dantian or Miltonian definition, or even her own "patriarchal" one (via the Old Fathers and the New Fathers). She gives us the space of the Convent, a haven in its own right for Roman Catholic and other Christian women who, for one reason or another, have rejected the normative societal role of "woman in relation to man." Is this not a rejection of the normative order as prescribed in that original Garden of Eden, where God fashions a woman to be man's companion and helpmeet? The Convent is a woman-only space, and one that is, as Evans describes, a liminal or in-between space—a space of ambiguity and unconventional boundaries: "It is a space where human diversity is not only tolerated but celebrated. It is not paradise itself."

Why not? Why isn't this the paradise that Morrison is alluding to? Why isn't the process of rediscovering one's place, an "inward journey to origins and an outward journey toward destiny," an occasion of paradise itself? Is it because it is not final and fixed or institutionalized and structured as a progressive endpoint, like the destination that the explorer expects to find when embarking on a quest? Is it because it is a space of women only, and that is not what paradise is supposed to be? The first two books of Morrison's trilogy have placed women's story at the heart of the African American experience; through the lens of her vision, the drama of the human community is played out. I believe the Convent provides a clue to paradise as a search for place, power, and purpose that is markedly different from any of the models presented thus far. Paradise, Morrison suggests, is an overturning of the normative sociohistorical and therefore male-centered notions of place, power, and purpose. I do not think it is an accident that the "patriarchs" of Morrison's tale use the "Oven" to keep themselves together as a people. This vessel for nourishment is nothing less than a male attempt to re-create a "womb" in their midst, an oven "that both nourished them and monumentalized what they had done."[4] The oven is another occasion for women's experience and lives to be put on a pedestal, as a monument and as means of nourishment for others but not lived on our own terms. The Convent, however, did allow women to live on their own terms, and this is the model that I believe Morrison is setting forth as the better alternative for those who live on to tell the story of our collective humanity.

Thus, our happiness or fulfillment as human beings is contingent upon not modeling the ideals of paradise that have been set before us via the biblical narrative (Genesis) or the literary narrative (Dante, Milton). Rather, our human fulfillment as African Americans and Puerto Ricans rests on our ability to be at peace with the journey, the movement, and the dynamism of our own human ambiguity; in other words, the journey is home.

Near the end of his essay Evans states: "Paradise is built on a future, but a future that funds the present." This is nothing short of an eschatological hope—a vision of the "ought" that informs and animates the present, the "is" of our existence. For both African Americans and Puerto Ricans there are very few if any models from which we can fashion a vision of that future. The earthly city can never duplicate the city of God, and yet we must find a way to embrace one without rejecting the other. To do so would be to cut off a part of ourselves, even if that is the part that bears the scar and the pain. Morrison has shown this to us quite vividly through her character Sethe in the novel *Beloved*; as Paul D runs his hands and mouth down the scars of her back, scars she endured by way of the slave master's cowhide—so severe they formed the shape of a chokecherry tree, "the roots of it, its wide trunk and intricate branches"—Sethe begins to feel and cry, even though "her back skin had been dead for years."[5] Perhaps our present is funded by a vision of paradise that embraces the paradise stolen, lost, or sought after that has been part of our journey; and with this we recognize that

> History made us
> We will not eat ourselves up inside anymore.
> And we are whole.[6]

Notes

1 Levins Morales, "Child of the Americas," in *Getting Home Alive* by Levins Morales and Morales, 50.
2 Morales, "Africa," in ibid., 55.
3 Sandra Maria Esteves, "It Is Raining Today," 188.
4 Morrison, *Paradise*, 6.
5 Ibid., 16–17, 18.
6 Levins Morales, *Getting Home Alive*, 213.

Teresa Delgado

▣

FREEDOM IS OUR OWN: TOWARD A

PUERTO RICAN EMANCIPATION THEOLOGY

In this essay I begin to construct a framework for the development of an emancipatory Puerto Rican theology that emerges from the Puerto Rican literature of Esmeralda Santiago, Pedro Juan Soto, and Rosario Ferré and takes seriously the history and present reality of oppression of Puerto Rican people.[1] I utilize the fictional works of creative writers because I believe that their stories lift up the voices of those silenced; we must hear these stories in order to lift out the theologically relevant categories that emerge from our particular Puerto Rican experience. I cite the categories of identity, suffering, and hope as central themes through the reading of the stories themselves. While this information could be gleaned from other methodologies (i.e., sociological survey, oral history, etc.) I believe that the stories themselves reflect the larger panorama of our community and experience. In addition, the process of storytelling has been a deeply ingrained mode of transmitting tradition within the Puerto Rican community. It is a legacy of Puerto Rican culture.

In this essay I also demonstrate how Puerto Rican writers through their literary production articulate a prophetic vision of emancipation for Puerto Ricans. To demonstrate this matter I pay attention to these writers' usage of literary devices to communicate a subversion of the status quo, namely the ongoing colonial relationship with the United States. I show how these writers maintain the critical consciousness of the people by undercutting the seduction for Puerto Ricans of the "American dream"; they illustrate through story an alternative interpretation of Puerto Rican experience that invokes an anti-colonial desire for freedom.[2]

The story of Puerto Rican people, when witnessed through the lens of freedom, demonstrates both the lack of freedom and the simultaneous desire for it. In addition, the legacy of creative freedom within the literary tradition makes the stories an appropriate source for a developing theology of emancipation as they confirm the sociohistorical data of multiple layers of oppression.

This essay is organized around three questions: "Who am I?" "Why is this happening?" and "Where do we go from here?" These three questions point toward three themes that emerge from the literature: identity, suffering, and hope. These themes have emerged from a Puerto Rican context that, while not exclusive to the Puerto Rican experience, provide the contextual basis for a relevant theological response as they refer to the doctrines of anthropology, soteriology, and eschatology, respectively.

Who We Are: Toward a Puerto Rican Anthropology

LITERARY ANALYSIS: "WHO AM I?" AND THE THEME OF IDENTITY

The writings of Esmeralda Santiago, particularly her novel *América's Dream* and her second memoir *Almost a Woman,* communicate a prophetic call for emancipation on many levels, including the personal, relational, and national, by summoning her reader to question and challenge the assumptions behind the prescribed identities of the characters she presents. In other words, Santiago's work asks the reader to ponder the question of what it means to be a woman in general and a Puerto Rican woman in particular.

Santiago's first publication, an autobiographical account titled *When I Was Puerto Rican,* details her youth in rural Puerto Rico, the culture shock of moving to New York, and her coming of age amid the difficulty of straddling two cultures—only to find herself graduating with high honors from Harvard University.[3] Her autobiography props up the myth of the American dream: a poor immigrant country girl overcomes all odds and climbs the ladder of societal success to the highest rung. Her story sets itself up in support of the myth of meritocracy: if you work hard and sacrifice enough in American society, you will certainly succeed. The element of myth, according to John Dominic Crossan, leaves us feeling at ease with our conscience assuaged, because "what myth does is not just to attempt the mediation in story of what is sensed as irreconcilable, but in, by and through this attempt it establishes the possibility of reconciliation."[4] For Santiago, the myth of the American dream is made reality for her through the telling of her life story . . . or so it seems.

The title of Santiago's second publication, *América's Dream*, plays into this American mythology; but now the dream is pursued by America with a Spanish accent. The protagonist is América González, a single mother working as a maid at the only hotel on Vieques.[5] The novel begins with the words, "It's her life, and she's in the middle of it"; and to be sure América's life is centered on her suffering. The story opens with the occasion of América's fourteen-year-old daughter Rosalinda (beautiful rose-flower) running away with a young man. Her daughter's impulsive action stands in the tradition of similar conduct taken earlier by América and América's mother Ester (star); indeed, Rosalinda is but the latest in a long line of fatherless illegitimate daughters of a mother maid.

América is abused, physically and otherwise, by Rosalinda's father Correa (belt/strap) who, at ten years her senior, impregnated but refused to marry her when she, too, was fourteen. Although he is married to another woman with whom he has three children, Correa continues to possess and oppress América; she is not permitted to be with or even speak to other men since Correa must know her whereabouts at all times. Even the slightest provocation, interpreted as such through his chauvinistic paranoia, could lead Correa to beat América. But he always does his penance. Ester's house (where América and Rosalinda live) is full of his penitential offerings: "Electronics typically mean he knows he's really hurt her, but chocolates always mean she deserved it. . . . A coffee brewer for a split lip. A toaster oven for a black eye. A rocking chair for a broken rib that kept her out of work for a week."[6] Correa, with all his charm and good looks, is the quintessential abuser; América is the archetype of the battered woman.[7]

So as not to give away the entire story I will jump to its ending, which appears all too familiar. Now living with Rosalinda in New York and working as a maid in an exclusive Midtown hotel, América takes a moment to stand in front of a mirror to examine her reflection: "It's a reminder of who she is now, and who she was then. Correa's woman was unscarred, but América González wears the scars he left behind the way a navy lieutenant wears his stripes. They're there to remind her that she fought for her life, and that, no matter how others may interpret it, she has the right to live that life as she chooses. It is, after all, her life, and she's the one in the middle of it."[8]

The story thus seems to end as it begins; despite all that happens to América—"freedom" from Correa, relocating to New York City, claiming her daughter back—she remains in the same psychological state.[9] There is no transformation or reconciliation in the story itself. *América's Dream* is no myth; rather, it is a parable. "Parable is always a somewhat unnerving experience," Crossan says, "You can usually recognize a parable because your immediate reaction will be self-contradictory: 'I don't know what you mean by that story but I'm certain I don't like it.' "[10] While myth mediates reconciliation, or at least its possibility, parable undercuts reconciliation showing that it, too, is a myth of our own making. Again, Crossan's definition is useful: "The surface function of parable is to create contradiction within a given situation of complacent security but, even more unnervingly, to challenge the fundamental principle of reconciliation by making us aware of the fact that we made up the reconciliation . . . You have built a lovely home, myth assures us; but, whispers parable, you are right above an earthquake fault."[11]

I believe that this story is a parable about and for the Puerto Rican people. To state it in the biblical formula: "Puerto Rico and Puerto Ricans are like a battered woman." Puerto Ricans are, the story suggests, victim, survivor, and accomplice of their current condition. From the character names alone we can understand the parallel that Santiago makes with the history of Puerto Rico—the "shining star of the Caribbean" (Ester),[12] the island paradise in full bloom (Rosalinda), America with a Spanish accent (América)—and América's story shared with her mother (past) and daughter (future). Correa is the (Operation Boot) strap that binds and thereby cuts off circulation and squeezes out the breath of life. When pulled up by the bootstrap, so to speak, América finds herself in target range of being struck down again.

How América and Puerto Rico and Puerto Ricans have been victimized is clear from reading the story and knowing the history. The fact that Puerto Ricans have continued to live to tell the story has been a formidable task given the continuous oppression and annihilation; it is evidence of their determination to survive. But to say that América, and Puerto Ricans, act as accomplices to their own victimization and struggle to survive is something else. This is not what Puerto Ricans are prepared, nor wish, to hear. But Puerto Ricans must hear precisely this message if they are to have an authentic response to the prophetic imagination of the author. This prophetic message for freedom jolts their complacent consciousness and makes them think about their condition in a new way; yet the messenger/author refuses to prescribe an easy solution. The statement that Puerto Ricans are accomplices in their continued captivity is, at the very least, an acknowledgment of the theft of their spirit and, more importantly, the recognition of their inner collective power to get it back.[13]

In an essay entitled "Island of Lost Causes," published in the *New York Times* on November 14, 1993, the day of the plebiscite to *recommend* independence, statehood, or commonwealth status for Puerto Rico,[14] Santiago wrote:

> We are taken for granted by the U.S., and that sharpens in us a stubborn nationalist streak—yet we don't demonstrate it at the ballot box. In our hearts, we want to believe independence is the right choice, but our history forces us to see it as a lost cause. Still, we are not willing to give up so completely as to vote for statehood. It would be the ultimate statement of our surrender.
>
> This is why so many Puerto Ricans will vote for the status quo. It fosters the illusion of choosing a destiny, neither capitulating nor fighting. But it continues to evade the question of who we are as a people.
>
> An elusive cultural identity lies at the heart of our unwillingness to declare ourselves either a nation or a state. A vote for the commonwealth insures that we don't have to commit one way or the other.
>
> Ironically, neither violent insurrection nor the democratic process seems able to solve that question. . . . We need to look at ourselves hard and stop hiding behind the status quo. It is not a choice. It is a refusal to choose.[15]

The refusal to make a choice is, as América's story reveals, as deadly as choosing the path of life and emancipation. Her story illustrates how the silence that envelops such a refusal slowly but certainly leads to greater isolation and alienation. América hardly communicates her inner thoughts and feelings to her mother or her daughter; she is resentful and suspicious even of them, thus severing all possibility of mutual wisdom gained from relationship. Her involvement in any meaningful community is nonexistent; she listens to the sermons of the Pentecostal preacher from the rocking chair on her own porch as they are broadcast to the neighborhood on a Saturday night. When América comes to New York to work as an au pair for a wealthy white family in Bedford, she is cautious of the other *empleadas* (nannies) she meets at the playground. While they share the same childcare and housekeeping tasks, they are different, she reasons, since they are Latin American and she is American. Like Puerto Rico in relation

to Latin America, América fears having a relationship because it will somehow break the silence of her true condition of oppression and domination—a condition that she has escaped only temporarily and superficially.

América's silence and self-perpetuated isolation, fueled by justifiable
fear, puts not only herself at risk but also those for whom she is responsible: the children she cares for and her own daughter. Without a support
system, a community of solidarity, she becomes an island unto herself
("It's my life and I'm in the middle of it") without recognizing that her life
includes the lives of those with whom she is in relation and who will come
after; she is still responsible for their well-being. While it may be true that
"it is all uphill from *Esperanza* (Hope) to *Destino* (Destiny),"[16] the two need
not be exclusive of each other when the path is paved with the wisdom of
community. By walking away from hope and identifying herself as a victim
whose life is caught in a cycle of dependency, América puts her daughter
into a situation that will be difficult to change—to break a cycle of a destiny
without hope.

Santiago conveys the incredible hardship of breaking such a cycle given
the history of oppression. Yet the author allows us to catch glimpses of revelatory moments in América's life: for five days a month, when she takes
her blue placebo birth control pills, she is in tune with her natural hor-
monal cycle and true emotions. She is reflective of her situation; she cries
tears of "hurt and anger, fear and frustration."[17] But on the sixth day she
goes back to her usual self: humming and singing, sedated from her reality, numbed. In these bursts of revelation, América talks to herself more
and seems assured to make some change; she even fights for her daughter
to stay when Correa has made plans to take her away. These moments,
however short lived, carry the seed of transformation; they are nonetheless
ineffective because they are not witnessed by or testified to others to hear
and participate with her in the transformative process that will lead her
toward freedom. They are like seeds that fall onto rocky ground; without
the nourishment of a community of solidarity, they do not take root and
flourish.

Santiago's second memoir, entitled *Almost a Woman*, chronicles her
life after coming to live in New York City at the age of thirteen. It is a tale
of adolescence and, more important, it is a tale about choices. While her
first memoir can be seen as a myth of the American dream, and her novel
as a parable of the same, this memoir can be likened to a quest, a coming-
of-age tale, the hero's journey. We are not privy to the actual arrival at her
destination—womanhood—but we know that she has in fact arrived by

the telling of the story itself. We can see that the choices she makes along the way have as much to do with her desire to attain "womanhood" as with not wanting to be the same kind of woman she considers her mother to be. In this sense Santiago tells us more about the negative choices (what she chooses against, or rejects) than the positive ones (what she affirms and claims as her own). In either case Santiago tells the story of her adolescent quest for freedom through her maturity into womanhood; she ends up telling us more about her desire to achieve freedom *from* the most influential and controlling force in her life—her mother: "To become a woman . . . I must rebel against my own mother."[18]

How does this coming-of-age story, a recollection of memory in the service of the quest for womanhood and identity, function in the broader picture of Santiago's work taken as a whole? Further, how does that purpose inform us of her perspective regarding the plight of Puerto Rico and Puerto Ricans? By asking these questions I am making the assumption that Santiago is, in fact, making a statement regarding Puerto Rico by using her life and memory as a parallel to the life and memory of the island and her people. Her life and memory demonstrate, above all else, that often we know what we *do not* want in our lives before we discover what we actually want in our lives. The *via negativa* is more clear to us than the path our life's journey is bound to take.

In this sense the protagonist of *Almost a Woman*, Negi, is very clear about the reasons she chose not to be in relationship with the various suitors in her life. She is less clear, however, about the reasons for choosing to be with Ulvi, the man whose destiny she chose to accompany. She wanted to be with Ulvi for reasons she could not explain except that his life was the antidote to her own: ordered, planned, without expectations, quiet, and suspended in time and space. When asked by her best friend, Shoshana, why she chose him, Negi could not answer the question: "No, he wasn't as handsome as Neftali, Otto, Avery Lee or Jurgen. In the week we'd been together he hadn't taken me to any restaurants, the theater, not even the movies. He'd spent no money on me. He hadn't asked me to be his girlfriend, his mistress, his wife. He'd made no promises whatsoever. He seemed to have no expectations except that I show up at his apartment at the agreed time . . . In his arms, I didn't have to think, didn't have to plan, didn't have to do anything but respond to his caresses. When he held me, I didn't question or challenge him, because I knew nothing" (275–77).

Negi does not realize in the same way that Santiago the writer acknowledges by the inclusion of this affair in the story that the two lives—with her mother and with Ulvi—are strikingly similar in their opposition. Both try to mold her into the woman they believe that she should become: how to dress, walk, listen, speak, eat, and so forth. The fact that Negi allows herself to be molded, assimilated, and appropriated in such ways demonstrates that she is not yet a fully matured woman on the inside, despite her chronological age of twenty-one at the end of the memoir. Her movement toward Ulvi comes at a time when her mother begins to let go by easing up on the restraints that have been placed on Negi for so long. Once freed from that grasp, Negi is drawn immediately into the grasp of another who aims to control her as much as her mother did if not more: "He needed a disciple; I needed to be led. I felt myself submerge into his need like a pebble into a pond, with no resistance, no trace I'd ever been anywhere, or anyone without him. With Ulvi I wasn't Negi, daughter of an absent father, oldest of eleven children, role model for ten siblings, translator for my mother. I wasn't Esmeralda, failed actress/dancer/secretary. My head against Ulvi's chest, my arms around his neck, I was what I stopped being the day I climbed into a propeller plane in Isla Verde, to emerge into the rainy night of Brooklyn. After seven years in the United States, I had become what I stopped being the day I left Puerto Rico. I had become Chiquita—small, little one. Little girl" (306).

Just as Santiago uses the story of a battered woman to tell the story of Puerto Rico, she is similarly using her memory of her coming of age to tell the story of Puerto Rico's coming of age in the twentieth century, a process that has yet to reach maturity even after more than one hundred years. She seems to be saying that, like herself, Puerto Rico has made a choice to align itself with the American way of life (Ulvi) with the promise that Puerto Rico will be molded into the shape and form that America deems is best for Puerto Rico. Even before she meets Ulvi, Negi is fearful of the telltale signs of age through her physical appearance. In the context of applying makeup for a class on theater, Santiago reveals her fear of "getting old" and of becoming the old woman she sees reflected back to her in the mirror—a face that bears striking resemblance to her grandmothers Tata and Abuela (82–83). This can be seen as a parallel of the fear of Puerto Rico maturing as a community and a nation—of being almost but not quite a full-fledged adult, politically and otherwise.

Negi values the relationship she has with Ulvi because it allows her to maintain her youthfulness and her childlike persona in a seemingly adult relationship. All this is done under the guise of stewardship, but the relationship is far from equal or reciprocal. On the contrary, the relationship

of Negi/Puerto Rico and Ulvi/United States is based on the imbalance of
power, where the terms of the relationship are not mutually agreed upon
but rather are based on the best interest of the powerful. The striking reality that Santiago is trying to convey through her memoir is that for all the
calm, quiet, ordered facade of "liberty in law," there is a sinister erasure of
all that has come before that has shaped the identity of the Puerto Rican
to this day. It is as if Puerto Ricans are now an empty slate with no history, upon which a future that is amenable to American interest can be
designed. And yet the relationship has many benefits like those bestowed
by the parent upon the perennial child: to be taken care of, directed, and
molded into the form that makes the parent proud, but never to be in the
position of the parent itself: arrested development at its finest.

There are moments—epiphanies of sorts—when Negi is aware of her
stifled growth. The first comes when at the onset of her mother's ninth
pregnancy a social worker pays a visit to their home: "I seethed but I had
no outlet for my rage, for the feeling that so long as I lived protected by
Mami, my destiny lay in the hands of others whose power was absolute.
If not hers, then the welfare departments . . . It was not funny anymore
to laugh at ourselves or at people who held our fate in their hands. It was
pathetic" (136–37).

The second epiphany comes at the point of her final high school performance as the Virgin Mary. Her role is danced Martha Graham style in
a costume, which unbeknownst to Negi is transparent. Despite the rave
reviews for her performance, her mother and grandmother are aghast.
And yet Negi is proud of herself while feeling "pulled by Mami, Don Carlos, and my siblings in one direction, while my peers and teachers towed
me in another. Immobile, I stood between them both, unable to choose,
hoping the party wouldn't move one inch away from me and that my family would stay solidly where they were. In the end, I stood alone between
both" (145).

The third epiphany comes at the point of her graduation from Performing Arts, as she celebrates her accomplishment without knowing about or
planning for her immediate future. Negi realizes that she embodies three
distinct realities within her, and that she would have to find some way to
negotiate these allegiances, often conflicting, in order to be a success on
her terms: "I'd have to learn to straddle all of them, a rider on three horses,
each one headed in a different direction" (153).

Thus Negi's coming of age can be understood in terms of the coming
of age of Puerto Rico itself: trying to assert its own identity and power

only to be pulled back by the power more absolute and encompassing that is the United States: "The home that had been a refuge from the city's danger was now a prison I longed to escape . . . I was tired of the constant tug between the life I wanted and the life I had . . . I wanted to become La Sorda, deaf to my family's voices, their contradictory messages, their expectations. I longed to cup my hand to my mouth, the way singers did, and listen to myself. To hear one voice, my own, even if it was filled with fear and uncertainty. Even if it were to lead me where I ought not to go" (210).

We are left at the end of the memoir without knowing for sure whether Negi chooses to follow Ulvi to Florida or stay with her mother and siblings in New York. It is at the onset of the memoir that we discover, upon second reading, that Negi made the choice to leave her mother and the life she shared with her family for twenty-one years: "To begin my own journey from one city to another" (2). We are left wondering how she finally lives into her own womanhood, hoping for a glimpse of how that transformation can be translated to the process for Puerto Rican political maturity and, in fact, Puerto Rican identity. All in all, we are left the same way we began each of Santiago's works: not having clear answers but rather more questions regarding the nature of identity and personhood, of community and nationhood. As a good writer, Santiago leaves that constructive work to the reader.

A PUERTO RICAN ANTHROPOLOGY

As Christopher Morse states: "In God's eyes, no life story is ever without promise."[19] This is the true nature of humanity viewed from the divine perspective. We are justified not because of how we know God or what we know of God. We are justified in our very human existence because God knows us and, with all of our flaws, sins, and failings, loves us: "What is proclaimed to justify our right to be as God has created us is that God acts to claim us for love and freedom precisely where we have suffered from the rejection of love and freedom, and does so in such a way that we are brought home to the uniqueness of who we are as God's own."[20] This understanding of our selves as humans takes on a profound significance when considered from a Puerto Rican perspective. In other words, God claims the Puerto Rican community for love and freedom because it has suffered from the rejection of love and freedom, and he does so in such a way that Puerto Ricans are restored to the uniqueness of who they are—their identity as God's own children.

Santiago's literature reflects the theme of identity as a central preoccupation of Puerto Rican life. Yet, how can Puerto Ricans see themselves
in that divine image, as God's own children, when they have been defined
for so long through the lens of socioeconomic factors that wrap up our
identity into lawlessness, violence, out-of-wedlock births, illiteracy, substance abuse, domestic violence, child abuse, and so on? How can Puerto
Ricans say that God chooses them precisely because of these conditions in
order to restore them to their own true selves? And what is our own true
identity when the vision of such has only been but a glimpse overarched by
their depressing reality? Accordingly, what clues does the literature offer
in their self-understanding and their identity, circumscribed by the overwhelming reality of colonization, that can speak to their relationship as a
particular people with their God?

First, I believe that the reality of colonization lays bare the dream of the
end of colonization; the colonized do not wish to remain so, deep in their
souls. They dream of freedom, if only as a dream, and maintain that dream
at all costs. The title of Santiago's novel implies as much, although her protagonist's dream falls short of reality. The colonized know that it is better
to be free from colonization than to be governed by it, just as those who are
enslaved know that the absence of slavery is better than its perpetuation.
Even while maintaining the dream of the demise of colonialism, the colonized learn much from that same system: subversive tactics, trickery, and
even silence, which masks pain and vulnerability. It also teaches survival
tactics of creativity, adaptability, compromise, resilience, and acceptance of
the "other" within one's own identity.[21]

Puerto Rican identity is a precarious term, one that has been and continues to be debated by many scholars. Yet these scholars agree that Puerto
Rican identity is both fixed and fluid, static and dynamic, the same as it
has been yet ever changing. Even the title of Jorge Duany's book *The Puerto
Rican Nation on the Move: Identities on the Island and in the United States*
suggests a notion of nationhood that is neither geographically bound nor
comprised of one definition of its identity. In an "uneasy" coexistence
of colonialism, nationalism, and transnationalism, Duany suggests that
Puerto Rican national identity is both fluid and tenacious "across many
kinds of borders, both territorial and symbolic."[22]

Thus the reality of colonization, as a starting point for a Puerto Rican
theological anthropology, suggests the discomfort of living in a liminal
space—an in-between state on the boundaries of existence that are not
concrete. It is certainly an uneasy existence when an entire people have

no sense of where they belong in relation to themselves or others: it would be a far happier situation to know exactly what one's identity consists of—its fundamental markers and attributes including language, culture, geography, and so on. But the comfort of a certain identity can lead to complacency and an acceptance of the status quo, as well as to the lack of questioning or critical perspective that brings about change. In light of this I propose that the discomfort or uneasiness of what it means to be Puerto Rican is a desirable place because it is a catalyst for creativity, not complacency; it highlights the contradictions of one's reality rather than status quo acceptance; and it challenges the existing reality by asserting a critical perspective. In fact what emerges out of a place of dis-ease is the voice of the prophet, which can motivate a people to change that which is seemingly unchangeable. The prophetic call is a voice from God giving the words that the prophet must speak "to uproot and to pull down, to destroy and to overthrow, to build and to plant" (Jeremiah 1:10).

If we understand the identity of Jesus as the oppressed one (e.g., James Cone), as the mestizo (e.g., Virgilio Elizondo), and as the divine/human "other" (e.g., Fernando Segovia), we can also see him, from a Puerto Rican perspective, as the colonized Jew in a land ruled by the Romans. As a colonized Jew from Galilee, Jesus's own identity is ambiguous and highlights the ambiguity of our own Puerto Rican identity—the main attribute of which is our collective colonization. Yet that same ambiguity, the belonging to all and nothing, is also a place of fruitfulness; in fact, it is the place that was chosen by God as the location of his incarnation, precisely for its ambiguity, as if to say that no one in their exclusive particularity can claim Jesus's life as salvific exclusively for themselves. On the contrary, everyone in his or her exclusive particularity can claim his or her life as salvific. That is the promise of Jesus's identity that we come to know through his life, death, and resurrection.

Why We Suffer: Toward a Puerto Rican Soteriology

LITERARY ANALYSIS: "WHY IS THIS HAPPENING TO ME?"
AND THE THEME OF SUFFERING

Pedro Juan Soto's novel *Hot Land, Cold Season* is a story that begins neither on the island of Manhattan in New York nor on the island of Puerto Rico. It begins in flight, ambiguously in the middle of nowhere: not belonging to either Manhattan or Puerto Rico but also not disassociated from them.[23] Eduardo Marín is flying back to Puerto Rico; it is only his second time on a plane, the first being the trip his entire family made when they moved from the Puerto Rican coastal town of Caramillo to the ghettos of East Harlem. He was eight years old then, and now, ten years later, he and his fellow Puerto Ricans in flight were like "prodigal sons returning home."[24]

Eduardo is reminded of his own father, a desperate alcoholic, when he helps an old man to his feet—a man who, as he emerged from the plane, bowed to kiss the ground, his beloved *tierra*. Eduardo imagined that it was not a "stranger's hand he was holding but his own father's: a man returning to his homeland with his son after countless defeats and endless years in captivity" (18). To Eduardo, hope for the future is associated with *la naturaleza* (nature and wilderness): the openness of the land, the vastness of the sky, the colors and spaces as the language of the earth (24, 25). Through the character of Eduardo the author suggests that one feels most free when in touch with the natural world. Eduardo begins to associate his own coming of age into adulthood with the openness and freedom he feels in Puerto Rico. Upon his arrival, Eduardo immediately associates Puerto Rico with all things positive and New York City with all things negative, including the notion of captivity. He does not want to meet the same fate as his best friend Lefty Fernández who, like Eduardo, wanted to become an engineer but died at too young an age. Lefty was a "free spirit" who hitchhiked his way around the country every summer in search of "wide open spaces, peace, natural beauty" rather than work a "normal" job like Eduardo in the local supermarket or pizza joint (97). But when a neighborhood thug sexually abused Lefty's sister, Lefty took justice into his own hands and stabbed the perpetrator to death. After outrunning the police he was finally cornered on a rooftop, and he made the fateful choice to jump to his death rather than be arrested and face life in prison.

Eduardo decides that he will not go back to New York but stay in Puerto Rico to attend the university for a degree in engineering. He has visions of becoming an engineer in order to help his hometown of Caramillo with new buildings, roads, and the like. He sees himself volunteering his time and efforts to improve the infrastructure while he lives as a hermit with ragged clothes and bare feet like a missionary. The true goal of his philanthropy is to prove to the people of his town that he has not forgotten them, that he is not a "sell-out," and that he is not an American (94). His efforts proved unsuccessful, however, as those in the town continue to refer to him as a "gringo Americano."

"The loneliness of feeling unwanted in his own country" was the worst kind of loneliness that he had ever experienced. Eduardo dreamed of combating the loneliness by putting himself in a stupor of liquor, sex, drugs, and repressed anger; he would never be at peace again (177). When he meets an old friend, Foron, the epileptic with whom he used to play as a child, Eduardo realizes that the world is full of malicious people who say and do hurtful things without any regard for feelings. He realizes that he had come back to Caramillo looking for something and yet had found nothing; and that the nothingness included him: "I am nothing."

The sense of nothingness is personified by acquaintances who Eduardo and Jacinto (Eduardo's older brother) call "the others," a group of quite colorful characters in and of themselves. The group meets in an old building in the heart of Old San Juan where the old Spanish style and that of modern America meet—a broken and incongruous city with drug dealers and prostitutes on every corner.

Eduardo, feverish and ill from his evening with "the others," begins to lose the naive nostalgia that had brought him back to Caramillo in the first place. Eduardo remembers the science notes he took as a child in school in Puerto Rico in which he wrote about the characteristics of elephants: "The elephant has a prodigious memory. His ivory tusks are very valuable. The elephant also has the longest life span of any mammal on earth. He knows at an early age where the elephant graveyard is. He is a peace-loving animal who attacks only in self-defense. His diet consists of fruit and plants. The jungle is his home. When he feels death approaching, he heads for the elephant graveyard, lies down and dies" (192). He remembers these characteristics because he begins to see his hometown, the place of his birth, Caramillo, as a graveyard and a place of death. He realizes that the place of his birth holds nothing more for him at this point in his life other than disappointment and disillusionment. He likens himself to the elephant as one who remembers too much; he also reveres the elephant for its ability to live in the jungle freely and for which memory is not the curse that it has become for himself.

Eduardo also remembers the story of the lilies in Don Eulogio's fields—a story that few others seem to recall. The lilies were originally planted as a memorial for the twenty soldiers from Caramillo who had died in service of the United States military in a war "on foreign soil." Now the lily fields were shared by squatters who were fighting eviction from the landowner, a man who at one time had welcomed them for their cheap labor. The lilies, which had been planted as a loving marker for the sacrifice of Caramillo, were now only as valuable as their market price. Don Eulogio's name proved quite fitting for him: in fighting the squatters for the rights to the land, he was eulogizing the memory of the past—a death that could not be brought back to life. The lilies, usually associated with death and rebirth, endings and beginnings, purity and spring (the classic flower of Easter), is representative of both death and life, just like the elephant.

With his clothes tattered and soaked from rain, and his body burning from fever after an evening with the "others," Eduardo feels as if he is going to die. His birthplace, he contemplates, will become his deathbed as well. There can be no healing in this place, Eduardo concludes, as there was in the past. While something did die—his illusions of Puerto Rico and the people of Caramillo—something else is born that day. Eduardo leaves with a new awakening that while not easy for him to bear is necessary nonetheless. He awakes to the idea that there is no dichotomy of good Puerto Rico and bad New York, and that there is a "both/and" quality to being Puerto Rican that is at the same time ambiguous and freeing. Whereas he had come to Puerto Rico initially to look for flowers and wide-open spaces as did his deceased friend Lefty, Eduardo now goes back to New York City for the same; that is, to a place where such things—flowers and wide-open spaces—would seem to be a rare find. We are left with the image of Eduardo going back to the same physical place but in a different spiritual place from within as a result of his experiences. His story informs us that, like Eduardo, we cannot run away from our pain but rather we must live through it wherever we are and seek healing even in the place of most pain and vulnerability.

In Soto's collection of short stories and vignettes, *Spiks*, he addresses themes similar to those in his novel, but the setting is the barrio of New York. As a literary technique Soto utilizes what he calls a "miniature" as a prelude to the larger story. In each miniature, there is at least one character who also appears in the larger story; this character's setting or environment is glimpsed in the miniature and gives the reader a clearer sense of what life must be like for that character. As such, the relationship of each miniature to the larger story is that of microcosm and macrocosm, where the relevant issues of pain, struggle, and desperation remain the same in both.

In the story "Captive" the seventeen-year-old protagonist Fernanda is in love with her sister's husband. In order to maintain all parties at a proper distance, Fernanda's mother decides to send her to Puerto Rico to live with a brother who will keep a watchful eye on her. The only one in the story who is named is Fernanda; her brother-in-law/lover and mother are not named, even though they wield a great deal of power. In a sense, the story itself and Fernanda's preoccupation with her man of choice is about her and no one else. Like Santiago's character América González, "it's [Fernanda's] life and she's in the middle of it."

The vignette "Miniature One" and its subsequent and related short story, "Scribbles," tells the tale of Rosendo, an unemployed artist with two children and a wife expecting their third child. He has no real financial avenue for making money with his art but he maintains it as the passion of his life. On Christmas Eve he decides to draw a mural in the bathroom of their small tenement apartment; his vision for the mural would be a depiction of the beauty of his love for his wife, Graciela. By the next day Graciela has erased all of it, down to the very last detail. Upon hearing what his wife had done, Rosendo reacted in this way: "When he rose from the chair, he felt all of him emptying out through his feet. All of him had been wiped out by a wet rag and her hands had squeezed him out of the world . . . The wall was no more than the wide and clear gravestone of his dreams."[25]

The story entitled "The Innocents" depicts a Puerto Rican family living in the barrio with only limited resources available to deal with a host of emotional, physical, and psychological issues. Hortensia is Pipe's sister, who is trying to convince her mother to have Pipe placed in a home for the mentally disturbed. Despite the numerous scars that Pipe has left on her from his violent tirades, Mami cannot face the possibility of turning her back on her son when he is in such need, even if it means sacrificing her very life for it. For Mami, the most intense natural disaster could not be worse than the tragedy of her daily life: "Facing the immense clarity of a June midday, she longed for hurricanes, eclipses and snowstorms" (47).

In "Miniature Six" an unnamed woman who is pregnant and unmarried goes to a fortuneteller to find out if the son she is carrying in her womb will love her in the future. We meet this woman by her name, Nena, in the next story "God in Harlem." Nena (which means little girl) is a prostitute who has tried to get out of the business, only to find herself at the service of one man only, Microbio (or microbe), the father of her unborn child. As his name suggests, Microbio is a minor figure in the world at large, but he has an incredible impact and influence on those he "infects" with his deceit, manipulation, and violence, namely Nena. She is lured into thinking that he is changing his ways as a result of the pregnancy, but she continues to mistrust him in the midst of her longing for him and for a better life for all three of them: "God is watching over all three of them" (81).

Nena is lured as well by suggestive fliers that rain down from the sky from an anonymous source. With its headlines "Await ye the Lord" and "The Lord is Nigh" Nena is drawn to the revival advertised on the fliers. It is at this revival where, in the end, she hears the words that allow her to begin to heal after having lost the baby at the hands of the drunken Microbio: "I am the door. He who passes through me will be saved." She comes to the understanding that, in God, all will be protected and there is no room for fear: "She knew neither pain, nor hate, nor bitterness. She was being born" (92).

How can Nena feel saved? How does she, as well as all of the characters we meet in Soto's collection, experience God in the midst of lives wrought with pain, deceit, degradation, and loneliness? Nena tries to confront the destruction in her way and on her time, only to realize that she cannot do it alone. She makes a positive step to move into a new way of being; she is not stuck in her circumstances. I believe that Soto is illustrating that Puerto Ricans as a whole are able to move, despite any difficult economic, emotional, physical, or psychological circumstances and despite the sociopolitical ambiguity in which the Puerto Rican people live. With a dead baby in her belly, Nena desires to be born again into herself. Even when there seems to be no salvation from the anguish of her life, salvation does exist and is present to her in her moment of greatest pain. That fact alone is enough to sustain her. In other words, God as the source of salvation is in Harlem, the source or location of suffering, in the present tense and not in the future. The eschatological vision is a vision of the present moment, a radical vision given that the present moment holds seemingly little to be hopeful for in the Puerto Rican context.

A PUERTO RICAN SOTERIOLOGY

Soto's literature reflects the theme of suffering as a constitutive element of Puerto Rican life. The overwhelming existence of suffering lends itself toward a soteriology—doctrine of salvation—that is articulated from a distinctly Puerto Rican perspective. What can Puerto Rican theology say about the suffering endured by its people when the starting point is the collective colonization of the people? Similarly, how does this suffering lead to a new understanding of salvation that is both particular to the Puerto Rican context and universal in its Christian foundations? These are especially difficult questions for me to answer, on so many different levels. I have always been stumped by the question of salvation, which has been posed personally from one too many inquisitors asking "Are you saved?" or collectively in its relationship to freedom and justice: "What constitutes salvation here on this earth?" What does it mean to be saved as a community of individuals in relation to one another? How does the Puerto Rican community extract from that definition meaning that makes it relevant to a daily life of struggle?

We cannot get to the heart of the meaning of salvation for the Puerto Rican community without changing the terms of the question itself. That is, the relevant soteriological question for Puerto Ricans is not "Are you saved?" but "What do you believe about Jesus Christ?" I can only approach an answer to this question by disclosing the ways Jesus has been presented that I, as a Puerto Rican woman, have refused to believe. First, I refuse to believe in a Jesus whose maleness is normative for salvation. As a Roman Catholic Puerto Rican woman, I refuse to believe that Jesus's maleness made him more authentically divine and therefore more reflective of God's image. If I believed in Jesus on these terms, I would be, in essence, submitting myself as one needing salvation not only through Jesus but also through every male person with whom I am in relationship. In addition, to believe in Jesus's maleness as normative supports the perpetuation of maleness as normative for apostolic succession and the priesthood in Roman Catholicism. I refuse to believe in this type of Jesus as salvific.

Second, I refuse to believe in a Jesus whose whiteness is normative for salvation. While Jesus's ethnicity and color has been affirmed by numerous scholars as other than white, he is still projected as a white man on the consciousness of many people, including many Puerto Ricans who display icons and illustrations of the Sacred Heart of Jesus as man with fair skin and hair and blue eyes. I do not reject the way in which Jesus is portrayed anthropologically—as a white, black, brown, red, or yellow man. On the contrary, I refuse to believe that any one depiction and understanding of Jesus's particularity excludes any other from his saving grace.

Third, I refuse to believe in a Jesus whose salvation is ushered in on the heels of conquest. This refusal is, for me, the most difficult because it discloses my suspicion toward my own church in relation to the way that Christianity, in its Roman Catholic and Protestant forms, came to Puerto Rico and to Puerto Ricans. The gift came with a high price tag; I refuse to believe in a Jesus whose salvation comes at the expense of all other manifestations of divine love and freedom.

The Puerto Rican community has maintained a tradition during the Lenten season that communicates our understanding of salvation through Jesus, which is quite different from the refusals disclosed above. During Holy Week on both the island and the mainland, we can witness a reenactment of the Passion of Christ in all its detail and pageantry. This is what we witness during these Passion plays: suffering at its very depth. To the outsider, it might look like Puerto Ricans experience a perverse pleasure in watching and participating in such a gruesome execution. Yet, the glorification of the suffering is not the emphasis in the Passion play nor in our soteriological understanding as it relates to Jesus's suffering. While it is true that the death of Jesus makes soteriological sense only in relation to his resurrection (as "Good Friday without Easter Sunday is senseless"),[26] the miracle and glory of the resurrection cannot be appreciated fully without comprehending, as best as humanly possible, the immense chasm that such a miracle has traversed. In the cross, we acknowledge "a very radical acceptance of life as it is, even in its most painful moments, [that] there is already the beginning of an experience of resurrection."[27] Our salvation is tied to our ability to accept our suffering insofar as we believe in its overcoming. The chasm of our suffering is deep and great; the miracle of our salvation by our belief in suffering's demise is greater and more profound. When we believe that God has the power to overcome all suffering, we are inspired to work as God's agents on earth toward that end.

Although we may have maintained rituals such as those relating to the crucifixion and resurrection, and perhaps we hang onto them when all else has failed, I believe that Puerto Rican Christians on the mainland have to their detriment adopted an understanding of salvation as personal and pietistic. The Puerto Rican Methodist pastor and theologian Hal Recinos suggests the same in both of his books.[28] Through his experience working with Puerto Ricans on the Lower East Side of Manhattan Recinos witnessed a level of resignation regarding the experience of suffering that was combined with an "otherworldly" understanding of salvation. At the onset of his ministry with a church on the Lower East Side, Recinos observed that "many people thought the Church of all Nations was a place to get away from the frustrations of daily life. They believed spirituality had nothing to do with the dynamics of racism, classism and sexism. In their eyes, the pulpit was not to be used to promote an understanding of social, political, economic and cultural problems. Prayer and the devotional life were the marks of true discipleship."[29]

As Esmeralda Santiago stated in her essay in the *New York Times* cited above, our history has told us that the struggle for freedom is a "lost cause." The sentiment reflected by Recinos in relation to his congregants suggests the same with regard to the daily suffering of the Puerto Rican community. But I believe that the continuation of the ritual enactment of the Passion, as well as other rituals in our communities, attests to the subreptitious hope that we are never a lost cause in the eyes of God. If God can overcome the most horrendous and scandalous suffering, why can we not overcome our own?

A Puerto Rican soteriology thus affirms that our salvation is contingent upon not turning away from the struggles of those who suffer in the here and now on earth. In fact, our turning toward the suffering is evidence of God's saving grace already at work within us: we love because God loves us first. Our salvation is not just about modeling Jesus's behavior, although this is an important point of departure. Our salvation is about walking in solidarity and compassion with those who suffer and addressing the suffering in all its forms—whether caused by physical ailment, emotional pain, economic strife, or political conditions including colonialism. The enormity of the resurrection miracle makes sense to us, in all its mystery and glory, when we have first descended to the depths of despair. This is the meaning of the confession of faith articulated in Luke's Gospel and Paul's letter to the Romans: "You will be saved" . . . "for the Son of Man came to seek out and to save the lost." In Jesus's cross and resurrection, there is always hope for the lost causes.

Where Our Hope Is Found: Toward a Puerto Rican Eschatology

LITERARY ANALYSIS: "WHERE DO I GO FROM HERE?" AND THE THEME OF HOPE

Just as in the works of Esmeralda Santiago, Rosario Ferré's art cannot be separated from her politics of personal, relational, and national freedom. While I have chosen for the purpose of this study to examine one collection of Ferré's short stories and two novels, all of her stories convey desires for freedom and independence, for the assertion of self and group identity, and for self-determination. As a Puerto Rican woman Ferré attempts to illustrate the quest for self-preservation that can leave the seeker feeling nihilistic and empty of true selfhood. Her work is consistent with the postmodern dilemma of acute literary self-consciousness. As Robert Detweiler states in his article "Theological Trends of Postmodern Literature,"

> Novelists are writing stories about novelists writing stories; characters watch themselves intently; images of mirrors, reflections, echoes, doubles abound. But they do so precisely because the concept of the self is fading. The eagerness to portray the self indicates a sense and fear of its immanent loss. This compulsive and anxious self-consciousness expresses itself in a vigorous "historicizing" effort, because if the self can

identify itself historically, in factual time and space, it can reinforce its reality. At the same time, this . . . effort also encourages the self toward group-hood, for in locating oneself historically one also places oneself in the context of others.[30]

Ferré's novel *The House on the Lagoon* follows this description accurately. It is the story of a woman, Isabel Monfort Antonsanti, who is writing the recollected family stories of her and her husband, Quintín Mendizabal, that they shared with each other before their marriage. In the text Isabel describes her aim in doing this as a way to

> examine carefully the origins of anger in each of our families as if it were a disease, and in this way avoid, during the life we were to share together, the mistakes our forebears had made. The rest of that summer, we spent many afternoons together, holding hands on the veranda and telling each other our family histories. . . .
>
> Years later, when I was living in the house on the lagoon, I began to write down some of those stories. My original purpose was to interweave the woof of my memories with the warp of Quintín's recollections, but what I finally wrote was something very different.[31]

Ferré presents to us the finished product of Isabel's creation: an interweaving of her storytelling, her first-person voice as commentary, and Quintín's third-person commentary as notes on the margin. We are thrown on waves that vacillate between fact (Quintín is a historian) and fiction (Isabel is a novelist), and we are left to wonder whether either distinction makes any difference to the true purpose of the story: the emancipation of the self, as individual and in relation to a community. For Ferré, the assertion of the self is a life or death mandate for women; through the story of a woman she, like Santiago, makes that claim for Puerto Rico as well. The issue of the Puerto Rican woman's identity does not arise in opposition to that of national and cultural identity; rather, Ferré's novel illustrates that both must be integrated in order to experience emancipation for Puerto Rican people.[32]

All of Ferré's stories, without exception, illustrate the need for our lives to be in balance; that is, we cannot live fully if we are split or cut off from our own spirit. This split is particularly deadly, and more commonplace, for women. In an oppressive environment that tries to maintain itself through the bifurcation of life and spirit, women who assert a balance between the lives they lead on the surface and the journey of their inner spirit are usually severed, maimed, or tricked—physically and otherwise—into perpetuating the status quo of alienation.

Ferré's collection of short stories, *The Youngest Doll*, abounds with examples of the severance, maiming, and trickery associated with a lack of harmony and balance as well as a series of dichotomies. In the short story (and fairy tale) bearing the same name, the leg of an unnamed aunt is infected by and now the permanent habitat of an angry river prawn. The doctor betrays her healing trust as he leaves the prawn in place so that he is able to send his son to medical school "up north" with the fees garnished from weekly visits. Eventually the youngest niece marries the doctor's son and receives a beautiful doll made by the aunt as a wedding gift; the gift of the doll becomes the revenge sought against the doctor and his insatiable greed.

Ferré's novel, *The House on the Lagoon*, is replete with cases as well. Early in the story, told within the context of Puerto Rican slave history, we meet Barnabé, whose name means "son of prophecy"; he had been a chieftain of his tribe when he was stolen from Angola, "a spiritual leader whose duty was to look out for [his] people."[33] He maintained his native language and by virtue of it was able to organize a rebellion with other slaves without the dutiful and docile *criollo* (mixed) slaves discovering the plans. After the insurrection was aborted, Barnabé was sentenced to a special punishment: his tongue was cut off. "One's tongue," Isabel tells us when speaking of Barnabé's language, Bantu, "was so deeply ingrained, more so even than one's religion or tribal pride; it was like a root that went deep into one's body and no one knew exactly where it ended. It was attached to one's throat, to one's neck, to one's stomach, even to one's heart."[34]

William Mendizabal, son of Quintín and Carmelina (Petra Avilés's granddaughter) and adopted by Isabel, survives the loss of vision in his left eye but lives to tell about it. In a violent clash between police and *independentistas* in front of the house on the lagoon, led by Quintín and Isabel's eldest son Manuel, Willie is brutally beaten by police in a case of mistaken identity. His maiming causes justifiable anguish; as a painter Willie questions whether he will ever be able to practice his craft again. But as one who had often met the face of death in life as a result of epileptic fits, Willie learns to see the loss of sight as a pathway to a renewed life.

As Jean Franco notes, "the repressed in Ferré's stories always return with violence."[35] The physical and psychological severance, maiming, and trickery against the spirit that chooses to live out in the open is thus forced into a subterranean and subversive life; it, too, can reemerge violently in an attempt to emancipate (or seek revenge for) itself, as these examples from the stories reflect. But emancipation from injustice encompasses a deeper meaning here. Ferré wages a fierce critique at the members of the upper classes of Puerto Rican society who in the unfair privilege of class usually reserved for the lightest skinned and purest bred Puerto Ricans fail to do justice for and with the poor working-class Puerto Ricans of more obvious African descent.[36] Her stories and their attention to the history and current reality of black and mulatto Puerto Ricans break the silence and invisibility that has characterized the official history of the island. Ferré suggests that it is those on the margins of society, in this case blacks, who understand deeply the issue of whether the outward living of one's life is in harmony with one's spirit. This is not to say that those of darker skin automatically live out the balance that Ferré seems to advocate. Rather, societal racism—in its overt and covert expressions—has not afforded darker-skinned Puerto Ricans the same "opportunities" to be lured into the seduction of a split life in a socioeconomic sense. The alienation has come via other means—substance abuse, gang violence, and disease—that plague the poorest communities on the island and mainland.

Still, Ferré's work continues to hold those of African descent in high esteem, and they constitute the spiritual foundation throughout her stories. This is nowhere more obvious than in *The House on the Lagoon*, where Petra Avilés (the *santera* [priestess or devotee of Santería] or *curandera* [female folk healer]) is the rock upon which the story is built. She lives in the dirt-floor cellar with the other domestic laborers who access the lower level of the house via the lagoon. Ferré's attention to the character of Petra, her function in the family and her spirituality, constitutes one way in which Ferré's authorship is prophetic; that is, she is questioning and challenging the validity, the assumed security, upon which the house, as the archetype of the condition of one's psyche, relationships, and nation, has been built. The formidable piece of architectural mastery that is the Mendizabal home is built on a swamp; but only those who enter via the swamp (the servants) are fully aware of this issue. The water is the true foundation, for it remains long after the house is gone. It is no mere postscript that the house was built originally over an underground spring; indeed, this fact is central to understanding that what is on the surface is illusory and that which is closer to the water is more authentic to our intended humanity. Petra lives on the level of the spring; her subterraneous existence is closer to our original source of life. Those who avail themselves of her wisdom, who enter the underground cell where the spring resides, come closer to mending the wounds of life-long maiming and scarring. Those who pay attention to their healing processes can then bring that wisdom to the surface; the wisdom cannot remain underground if it is to change the world order.

Rosario Ferré's *Eccentric Neighborhoods* is somewhat of an autobiographical novel that draws from the author's personal experiences with her father as an industrialist who later becomes governor of Puerto Rico.[37] Whereas *The House on the Lagoon* was a dualistic struggle between fact and fiction, *Eccentric Neighborhoods* is an intermingling of fact and fiction such that the facts become all but believable and the fictional becomes convincingly true. There are no distinctions; the truth is what is believed.

Ferré presents a dialectic relationship between the forces of industrialization and the forces of nature. The industrial overrides the natural but the natural remains in some way in spite of the industrialization. For example, the first half of the book is about the members of the Rivas de Santillana family who own a sugar plantation and maintain their ties to the land at all costs. They are a family deeply connected to *la naturaleza*, and they have a keen sense of the aesthetic and beautiful—a sensitivity that is influenced by the lush and breathtaking environment of Emajaguas.

The second half of the book is about the Vernet family. Their story chronicles the rise of industrialization (a cement factory) and creates a link with the economic structures of the United States. Star Cement is the company owned by the four Vernet brothers and their father, Santiago, in the town of La Concordia. The company begins to flourish during the time of the Second World War, when equipment and military products were desperately needed, as well as after the inauguration of Operation Bootstrap. The brothers are sophisticated in their dealings with the United States, in part because of their university education there. The brothers reject their Catholic roots and embrace Freemasonry as their religion. Theirs is a life of practicality and decisiveness, unhampered by concerns with nature or beauty and focused on the transformation and industrial growth of the island.

Freemasonry is a strong presence and influence in La Concordia; its values of humanity, fraternity, and harmony are also names of streets in the town. As such, Freemasons such as the Vernets aligned themselves with the position of statehood for Puerto Rico in the belief that the connection with the American way of democracy—"with liberty and justice for all"—would be of great benefit to Puerto Rico. This perspective was very different from that of the Rivas de Santillana family; the spirit of Emajaguas was a spirit of self-sufficiency, strong nationalism, and independence. Those who espoused other political opinions, including anyone who advocated statehood, were not fully welcomed into the Rivas de Santillana fold. This would prove to be quite a challenge for Clarissa Rivas de Santillana and Aurelio Vernet, whose daughter Elvira weaves the tales of each family as she is heir to both.

At the helm of the family cement business Aurelio was the negotiator and deal maker, the one who maintained the connections with businesses and governmental agencies in the United States. This was a role that later would serve him well as he won the governorship of Puerto Rico in 1968. For Aurelio politics, particularly the quest for statehood, was a primary motivation in his life. This motivation often placed him at odds with his wife, Clarissa, who as a Rivas de Santillana had less confidence in the dealings of men (politics) and more confidence in the dealings of the natural order (God). Still, Aurelio was the patriarch of the family, and as such Clarissa stood by her husband in his journey into business and politics. Their two children, Elvira and Alvaro, were afforded all the luxuries of the day as heirs of an industrialist. But their wealth and access did not change this one fact in Elvira's mind, which she finally realized after nine years of her own marriage to a man who wanted to keep her in a cage: "First I had belonged to Father and now I was Ricardo's. That's why women understood the politics of colonialism so well: if you treat them well, feed them, clothe them, and buy them a nice house, they won't rebel. Except that hatred keeps smoldering inside them."[38]

Unlike her daughter, Clarissa subordinated herself to her husband's dreams and aspirations by putting the needs and desires of her children and husband over her own. She was a Rivas de Santillana through and through, with a keen sense of aesthetics without the pretense of a *nuevo riche*. She was the product of the sugar plantation, a way of life that was steadily on the decline with the ascendancy of industry. Clarissa experienced the stark cultural shock of moving from the coastal richness of Emajaguas (a name that evokes the Taino language) to La Concordia (a name that is firmly grounded in Spanish tradition).

Although Clarissa's own personal dreams of working outside the home, attending a university, and maintaining financial independence were thwarted by the patriarchal culture upheld by her spouse and supported in the society, she would never imagine divorcing her husband. Her strong Catholic roots combined with her sense that all things tend toward unity and harmony precluded any attempt of severing that connection. In her final conversation with Elvira before her death, Clarissa confirms this belief:

"Nature, the positive current of the universe where everything is intercon-nected, is what really matters. Our duty is to partake of that unity, not of its differences. To try to understand ourselves and, by the way, to find God. That's why getting a divorce from Ricardo in order to live like an indepen-dent woman won't do you any good. You have to be independent in your own soul" (334). Clarissa's death is a reflection of her life: a sacrifice from within that is not visible from the outside until something is stirred. While her deathbed seems almost pristine, Clarissa is able to put forth one last act in death that speaks volumes of her life: After breathing her last breath, an assistant turns her on her side to bathe her in preparation for burial; when she does, fresh blood spills from Clarissa's mouth: "The sacrifice had taken place after all" (338).

Elvira is the narrator of the story that spans over one hundred years of her maternal Rivas de Santillana ancestry and paternal Vernet. She weaves the stories of her family in and out of each other, overlapping some and distinguishing others; in every case she tells the stories of their lives in the context of the environment around them. The setting of the stories is essential to understanding the inner meaning of the story itself; Ferré is quite intentional when she uses the following quote by Octavio Paz as a point of departure to the novel: "Geographies can be symbolic: physical spaces determine the archetype and become forms that emit symbols."[39]

Ferré opens the autobiographical novel with a description of the Crazy River (el Rio Loco) that the family had to cross by car without a bridge in order to get from La Concordia to Emajaguas. From the voice of Elvira we are told that the river reminds her of her own mother, that they share the same temperament and are never to be fully understood, controlled, or dammed: "Rio Loco got its name because it was so temperamental. When it rained in the valley and other rivers stampeded toward the sea like run-away horses, Rio Loco was dry. But when the sun was nailed to the sky like a hot coal, charring the cane fields and forcing the scorpions out of their burrows to look for water, it reared up like a muddy demon and tumbled this way and that over the dusty plain, enraged at everything that stood in its way. The river's source was far away in the mountains, and when it rained the floods rose, even when there was fair weather in the valley" (3). Elvira grows up believing that she and her mother are in stiff competition with each other for her father's love. It is not until she is a wife herself that she understands that in her father's eyes she and her mother are two parts of the same entity, both to be managed and protected. As a result of such competition, Elvira believes her mother is unnecessarily harsh and strict with her; she runs to her father on every possible occasion for sympathy and refuge. Underneath the surface Elvira is trying to reconcile herself with her separate yet intricately connected family histories; through the telling of her story, Elvira is trying to come to a conclusion about loyalty to either, or neither, side.

The reconciliation that Elvira tries to negotiate within herself parallels the dualisms in conflict in and around her: cement versus roses, statehood versus independence, father versus mother, Protestant versus Catholic, American versus Puerto Rican, and so forth. She desperately wishes to be an independent person and is faced with the reality that such independence must come at a high price—namely her mother's life.

Elvira's last dream of her mother is a telling one: it describes not only the struggles of the many women who had lived before her but also tells the story of women of privilege and status. It demonstrates the difficulty of giving up the benefits of patriarchy (or colonialism for that matter) and of the promise of a man rescuing the damsel in distress when the only alternative to such a coddled life is to swim against the strength of the current. It is a choice that comes with a price, one that is significantly higher than the dollar Clarissa waves from the safety of the car:

> I dreamed about Mother one last time. We were crossing Rio Loco and the family's temperamental Pontiac had stalled on us again. The river was rushing past, but instead of dogs, pigs, and goats being pulled along the murky rapids I saw Abuela Valeria, Abuela Adela, Tia Lakhme, Tia Dido, Tia Artemisa, Tia Amparo, all swimming desperately against the current. Clarissa and I sat safely inside the Pontiac, dressed in our Sunday best. She took a dollar out of her purse, rolled down the window just enough so she could wave the bill at the men on the riverbank, who soon came and pulled us out. And as we drove away I could hear through the open window the voices of those I could no longer see, but whose stories I could not have dreamed. (340)

Ferre's stories reflect a hope for the future in a number of ways. First, the main characters of her works demonstrate that we must understand our past and history in order to reconstruct the silences and create a new voice. Second, they demonstrate that when we are attentive to the wisdom of those who have suffered most we are able to move into a future with the tools to face such suffering. Third, the stories themselves illustrate the necessity of reconciliation with the conflicting parts of one's own being to move into a future with hope. Finally, the stories articulate the dialectic of death and life; something must die in order for hope to be made new and a new future restored in the present moment.

A PUERTO RICAN ESCHATOLOGY

Paul's letter to the Hebrews tells us that "faith is being sure of what we hope for and certain of what we do not see" (11:1). Where is such hope and promise found for Puerto Ricans and for Puerto Rico? Where can we catch a glimpse of a new tomorrow that is but a faint glimmer today? Our stories and our histories demonstrate that the hope and promise of a renewed future is not often found in the churches or places of worship of our respective traditions. Our stories and histories illustrate that we have had to use a lot of creativity to maintain the life-giving and life-sustaining aspects of our identity. These same stories and histories have reminded us that some things must die in order for others to grow, thereby making way for a new creation.

I believe that the fiesta as an embodiment of the renewal of relationships among family, friends, and community is one place where hope can be found for Puerto Rican people. I affirm all that has been said regarding the profound significance of the fiesta for the Latino and Latina community in general (e.g., in the work of Roberto Goizueta and Virgilio Elizondo). The Puerto Rican experience tells me that our understanding of *la tierra*—the earth, our homeland—is connected to the celebration of life in a particularly Puerto Rican way; that is, it is manifested in what has been called the revolving-door migration pattern attributed to the Puerto Rican community since 1964.[40]

For many Puerto Ricans, going back and forth from island to mainland is at the very least an annual event. In the course of the event, family and friends are reunited, meals and laughter are shared, memories are exchanged, relationships are renewed, and plans are made. These *visitas* (visits) are not a matter of luxury but rather a necessity of maintaining a connection to the people and the country in defiance of a dominant culture of assimilation that seeks to break it down. The revolving door is nothing less than a sacred passageway of hope and promise, where the scenery is the same upon return but the travelers are not. In other words, the journey into the sacred space of communion with the other side transforms and renews. The revolving door is an eschatological bridge of hope and promise that one day the journey between the two worlds will not be so long and arduous or so expensive and difficult. Instead it will be effortless and joyful as the fiesta.

The process of traveling across the eschatological bridge of hope and promise that is the revolving door of Puerto Rican migration presumes a foundation of reconciliation. Forgiveness and peacemaking are the supports that maintain the bridge's strength and function. It can be quite an effort that is less than joyful to journey back to the places and people of the past when one has not made peace with one's story. It seems much easier to block out the harsh memories and difficult experiences associated with a life's journey. Yet we can reconcile these painful elements of our past, and indeed our present, in the promise that there is no pain so great to undo God's love for us, and the face of Jesus in the "coming cloud" affirms this. Thus the revolving door of Puerto Rican migration is evidence, in the present, of our eschatological hope in the future made manifest. It is evidence that amid suffering and despair we can journey into joy with hope. While we may not feel secure in who we are or who we are becoming, we explore the possibilities of a new identity that goes back and forth in wholeness. The water over which the jetliner crosses from New York to San Juan is boundary and access once again.

This notion of reconciliation is quite different from that articulated by liberation theologians in the United States, particularly James Cone, in relation to oppressed communities. Speaking from the African American experience of oppression in its many forms, Cone warns that we must not fall too quickly into a desire for reconciliation between whites and blacks before the full implications of such reconciliation are expressed and exposed freely. His concern for his people compels him to be wary of any efforts to reconcile with whites at the expense of the liberation of his oppressed community or any other: "Black people must be aware of the extreme dangers of speaking too lightly of reconciliation with whites. Just because we work with them and sometimes worship alongside them should be no reason to claim that they are truly Christians and thus a part of our struggle . . . That is why liberation *must* be expressed in uncompromising language and actions, for only then can the conditions be created for reconciliation."[41]

Cone continues by stating that the liberation struggle must be focused less on the process of superficial reconciliation with white people and more on the gift of reconciliation among and within oppressed communities themselves. With the emphasis on the latter, he states: "We find that reconciliation is not a theological idea but a human struggle, a fight to create dignity in an inhumane situation. Reconciliation is not sitting down with white liberals and radicals, assuring them that we don't have any hard feelings toward them. Rather, it is a vision of God's presence in our lives that lets us know that the world will be changed only through our blood, sweat and tears. . . . From the experience of divine truth in our social existence, we now know that reconciliation must start *first* with black brothers and sisters who have suffered the pain of a broken community. . . . Reconciliation, like love, must begin at home before it can spread abroad."[42]

I am deeply indebted to Cone's theological interpretation of reconciliation, particularly his unapologetic stance for the primacy of liberation on behalf of the African American community, which was in many ways the prophetic voice that called me to question the conditions of my own Puerto Rican community. His analysis of reconciliation in relation to liberation also helped me to understand more clearly the dynamics of both at work for Puerto Ricans, and their significance for a Puerto Rican eschatology. Cone positions "black" and "white" on two opposite poles, and he clearly addresses the meaning of reconciliation and liberation. He asserts that reconciliation within the black community is a priority and a precondition for lasting liberation. Achieving reconciliation between black and white people, while an important task, should never be attempted at the expense of the hopes and dreams of liberation for black people. While Cone is not against black and white solidarity, particularly when that solidarity is created on black terms, he still articulates his vision of reconciliation in "us/ black" and "them/white" categories.

This is where the uniqueness of the Puerto Rican experience diverges from that of the African American theological analysis of reconciliation and liberation. While we share many common experiences of oppression in the United States, our relationship to the "other" is not an "us/them" relationship and thus it is less distinct. The "other" is within ourselves; that is, as Puerto Ricans we are both self and other simultaneously. Therefore, the process of reconciliation in relation to liberation cannot occur "at home before it can spread abroad"; the process is authentic only when it addresses the multiple and often conflicting relationships we embody at once: island/mainland, Puerto Rican/American, Spanish/English, Catholic/Protestant, and so forth.

Thus the eschatological vision of hope and promise in a future presupposes a foundation of reconciliation embodied in the process of the revolving door. This door is not a one-way exit or entrance but rather a constant process of change and transformation that connects the past with the present, and both with the future. It demonstrates that as Puerto Ricans we are no longer afraid to travel in the blurred boundaries of "either/or" but consider that space to be sacred in itself. The revolving door marks the fluid passage between the tomorrow we work toward achieving and the today in which we live with hope.

Even with the categories of Latino/a theology, the Puerto Rican experience demonstrates greater complexity and possibilities with regard to racial and ethnic understanding and reconciliation. Elizondo speaks of *mestizaje* as a theological category that parallels the lifespan of Jesus of Galilee, thereby creating an opportunity for Mexican Americans to understand their own mestizaje, the racial and cultural encounter between Spaniard and Indian, as a place of reconciliation. Other Latino theologians have spoken of mulataje in similar fashion, which recognizes the racial and cultural encounter between Spaniard and African as a source and locus of theologizing. The Puerto Rican experience demonstrates that neither one of these categories adequately captures their unique cultural makeup, nor do they offer an authentically Puerto Rican opportunity for reconciliation and liberation. We need to speak a new word that captures the multidimensional quality of our racial, ethnic, and cultural identity that reflects it honestly and points beyond it prophetically. The hope and promise for a renewed Puerto Rican tomorrow is embodied in the resurrection of our body and the world—our transformed *mulatizaje*—that rejects all that denies the love and freedom of our collective body.[43]

But to understand such hope in a way that helps to bring it to bear upon a suffering reality, Puerto Rican theology seeks to bring forth a radical conversion of its very community: a radical conversion to the message of the Gospel in order to respond to the call of living toward a true and full identity, of participating in the work of salvation, and of ushering into the present the vision of an eschatological future of hope. This means that Puerto Ricans need to start questioning critically those powers that undermine their quest for identity, their efforts to end suffering, and their vision of a future lived in freedom, even if those powers exist from within our own community and within ourselves.

Puerto Rican theology requires that one experience a deep and radical conversion within one's community in relationships of solidarity. This is the task of true Christian discipleship in relation to the poor. When Jesus said, "Leave all that you own and follow me," he is mandating our conversion, of leaving our comfort zone so to speak, to take on his way of life dedicated to the oppressed. His mandate is about getting our hearts rightly aligned to a way of life that focuses less on what J. Lo's latest love interest is as the emblem of Puerto Rican importance, or whether Ms. Puerto Rico will win the Ms. Universe pageant, or whether salsa is better than meren-gue or reggaeton is better than both. A Puerto Rican theological perspec-tive on eschatology—the "end of things"—offers a way of living into a state of emancipated hearts, and of not waiting for that honor to be bestowed by others but claiming it in the now for ourselves because it is already promised by God. Our hearts will only be emancipated if we begin with the internal task of reconciliation between the oppressors and oppressed—our mulatizaje—which we embody within our selves.

The nature of a Puerto Rican theology of emancipation informed by identity, suffering, and hope and grounded in the life, death, and resur-rection of Christ is a powerful theology because it says that Puerto Ricans themselves dare to live, right now, as a people who are called by name and who know who they are and the nature of their purpose. It is a powerful theology because it says that Puerto Ricans dare to experience their suf-fering as salvific in itself; that is, not for the purpose of glorifying that suffering but to say that the suffering need not diminish to experience salvation. Puerto Ricans are saved because God has saved them here and now through free and unconditional love. It is a powerful theology because it says that Puerto Ricans can, will, and do hope, not just in the future but in the present even in the midst of despairing situations. This hope is emancipatory because it rejects the belief that despair is one's lot in life. For Puerto Ricans there is a promise that has already been made but has yet to be claimed. Freedom is truly their own.

Notes

1 I have examined Esmeralda Santiago's novels *América's Dream* (1996) and *Almost a Woman* (1999); Pedro Juan Soto's novel *Hot Land, Cold Season* (1973) (originally published in Spanish in 1961 under the title *Ardiente Suelo, Fria Estación*) as well as his collection of short stories titled *Spiks* (1973) (originally published in Spanish in 1970 under the title *Spiks*); and Rosario Ferré's novels *The House on the Lagoon* (1995) and *Eccentric Neighborhoods* (1998) and short story collection *The Youngest Doll* [*Papeles de Pandora*] (1991).

2 There are a number of assumptions implied in the term "American dream." While it is beyond the scope of this project to analyze all of the meanings here, the authors challenge the notion of the American dream as an ideal achieved by individual hard work, meritocracy, and a fair and even playing field. In general terms, the authors suggest that the notion of the dream is but a myth, whereas the reality for the majority of Puerto Ricans shows that hard work doesn't always win the prize; that in more cases than not one does not merit

what is deserved; and that the playing field is very uneven with the rules of the game changing all the time.

3 Santiago received some criticism for the title of this work because, based on the use of the past tense, it suggests that she does not consider herself to be Puerto Rican any longer. However, I believe her use of such a title highlights the dichotomy and tension that exists between the island Puerto Ricans and the mainland Puerto Ricans, with each claiming an identity to be more authentically Puerto Rican. I believe Santiago is intentional in her choice of such an ambiguous title, as it emphasizes the ambiguity of Puerto Rican identity itself.

4 Crossan, *The Dark Interval*, 32. Crossan makes a distinction between myth (as a perpetuation and support structure of the status quo) and parable (as a subversion or undermining of the status quo).

5 The name América is quite common among Spanish-speaking peoples. In Santiago's novel the name has a number of layers of meaning and reference, including for the protagonist herself, as well as a metaphor for Puerto Rico (America with a Spanish accent), and for the United States of America. I believe the author is deliberate about the ambiguity of the reference as a literary tool for illustrating the ambiguous nature of Puerto Rico's relationship with the United States and vice versa.

6 Santiago, *América's Dream*, 91.

7 "Archetypes: content of the collective unconscious; meaning original model after which other similar things are patterned; synonym: prototype; birth rebirth death hero child demon trees wind fire rings weapons trickster . . . ; not to be regarded as fully developed picture in the mind but as a negative that must be developed by experience; persona, anima, animus, shadow, self: important archetypes for Jungian psychology; archetypes can form combinations and interact with each other; archetypes are universal; everyone inherits the same basic archetypal images (i.e., infant with mother archetype); archetype functions as a magnet attracting relevant experiences to form a complex; in this way the archetype gains consciousness on the surface." See Hall and Nordby, *A Primer of Jungian Psychology*, 41–53.

8 Santiago, *América's Dream*, 325.

9 "Freedom from Correa" in this instance refers to América's physical freedom from her abuser who will never hurt her or her daughter directly again.

10 Crossan, *The Dark Interval*, 39.

11 Ibid., 40.

12 For many years, Puerto Rico was portrayed in tourism advertisements as the shining star of the Caribbean. The name Ester is a derivative of the word *estrella*, meaning star.

13 Throughout the writing of this essay I have been nurtured, sustained, and brought back by Clarissa Pinkola Estés's *Women Who Run with the Wolves*. The notions of capture, theft, and returning to the self that resonate through-

out her work are brought into sharper focus in her chapter "Homing: Returning to Oneself," 255–96.

14 I emphasize the word *recommend* because in truth the plebiscite had no real power of persuasion for those in whose hands lie the power to change Puerto Rican status, namely the United States Congress and the Executive Office of the President. The plebiscite is also questionable because it was conducted by the colonial power and not by an independent party, as would be required by United Nations standards for a legitimate vote.

15 Santiago, *Boricuas*, 24.

16 Santiago, *América's Dream*, 19. Esperanza and Destino are two actual towns on the island of Vieques; in the novel, América physically walks away from the former (hope) to the latter (destiny).

17 Santiago, *América's Dream*, 78–79. The motif of the birth control pill is significant for the Puerto Rican woman since reproductive rights have been exploited through forced sterilization and unethical "experiments" with birth control pills on Puerto Rican women by pharmaceuticals in the United States. See Acosta-Belen, *The Puerto Rican Woman*; and García Coll and Mattei, *The Psychosocial Development of Puerto Rican Women*, 147–48, 217.

18 Santiago, *Almost a Woman*, 283. Note that all further cites from this work appear as parenthetical page numbers in the text.

19 Morse, *Not Every Spirit*, 271.

20 Ibid., 270–71.

21 This is what Elizondo calls the "gift" of mestizo identity—that we can do and be both. Fernando Segovia in "Two Places and No Place on Which to Stand" confirms this perspective from a biblical vantage point.

22 Duany, *The Puerto Rican Nation on the Move*, 284, 285.

23 The notion of ambiguous middle ground is one with a great deal of biblical resonance and richness.

24 Soto, *Hot Land, Cold Season*, 16, 17. All further cites from this work appear as parenthetical page numbers in the text.

25 Soto, *Spiks*, 39. All further cites from this work appear as parenthetical page numbers in the text.

26 Elizondo, *A God of Incredible Surprises*, 101.

27 Ibid.

28 See Recinos's *Hear the Cry! A Latino Pastor Challenges the Church* and *Jesus Weeps: Global Encounters on our Doorstep*, as well as his essay "Mission: A Latino Pastoral Theology," in *Mestizo Christianity*.

29 Recinos, *Hear the Cry!* 111.

30 Detweiler, "Theological Trends of Postmodern Fiction," 225.

31 Ferré, *The House on the Lagoon*, 5–6.

32 René Marqués in his essay "The Docile Puerto Rican" claimed that machismo was the last (and necessary) cultural bulwark to resist United States imperialism and Puerto Rican docility. These authors challenge assumptions that the

self-determination of women and Puerto Rico are mutually exclusive; and that to critique Puerto Rican sexism is to negate Puerto Rican culture. See Vélez, "Cultural Constructions of Women by Contemporary Puerto Rican Women Authors."

33 Ferré, *The House on the Lagoon*, 59.

34 Ibid., 60. The word "Bantu" means "people" in the Tshiluba language of the Luba peoples of Angola and the Congo, whereas the term "Bantu bafika" means "black people."

35 Franco, foreword to *The Youngest Doll*, xiii.

36 I say "more obvious" here because I believe that all Puerto Ricans have African blood running through their veins, regardless of whether their physical features reflect this fact in a lesser degree. Puerto Rico's slave history, as well as the forced and consensual interrelationships that have marked our history since, bears witness to this reality.

37 The author's use of the term "neighborhoods" in the title of her work suggests a community and a terrain that have the ability to transform or shift with the comings and goings of successive generations. Neighborhoods do not always remain the same; they can experience their own process of life, deterioration, restoration, and so forth, just as do those who inhabit them. In the realm of archetypal symbols the neighborhood can be a transitional place.

38 Ferré, *Eccentric Neighborhoods*, 331. All further cites from this work appear as parenthetical page numbers in the text.

39 Paz, *Postdata*, quoted in *Eccentric Neighborhoods*, 1.

40 See Díaz-Stevens's *Oxcart Catholicism on Fifth Avenue* for a complete explanation of the notion of revolving-door migration.

41 Cone, *God of the Oppressed*, 243.

42 Ibid., 245.

43 I recognize that *mulatizaje* is not a "real" word in Spanish. I coin it here to make the point that reconciliation for Puerto Ricans means, in part, that they mend the parts of themselves that have served to split their identity and their allegiances into parts without embracing the fullness of their multidimensional humanity, inclusive of the African, Taíno, and Spanish cultures, as well as a myriad of other heritages that have become a unique mixture in contemporary Puerto Rican life.

James H. Evans Jr.

RESPONSE TO THE ESSAY BY TERESA DELGADO

First I want to thank Teresa Delgado for her signal contribution to contemporary theological debate. Her passion and creativity are evident throughout her presentation, and I am honored to be able to offer this brief but hopefully suggestive response. My response is an attempt to relate to the struggles, insights, and development of a Puerto Rican theology from an African American perspective, and as such it is based on my interest in the compelling story that the author tells and how that story might be connected to my own.

In her essay Delgado outlines the distinctive parameters of a Puerto Rican theology by drawing from the rich store of Puerto Rican literature. The historical development of the Puerto Rican literary tradition holds great promise as a source of theological insight. Key texts and moments in this history include, among others, the publication of Manuel Zeno Gandia's novel *La Charca* in 1894; Antonio S. Pedreira's *Insularismo* (published in English as *Insularism* in 2005); and the appearance of a distinctive body known as Nuyorican literature. Within these texts and moments are elements of creative resistance and alternative views of reality that can aid meaningful theological discourse. *La Charca* (The stagnant pool) is a text that resists the distorted romantic views of Puerto Rico that preceded and followed the Spanish American War. Its realistic portrayal of life on the island was an important part of the foundation upon which subsequent literary works were built. *Insularismo* paints a picture of the reality of life in Puerto Rico after thirty-five years of United States rule. In some ways it is reminiscent of W. E. B. Du Bois's pioneering sociological narratives on the true condition of African Americans in the decades immediately following the end of chattel slavery. The emergence of Nuyorican literature finds its roots in the early-twentieth-century contributions of Puerto Ricans following the Spanish American War, and the mass migration of people from the island in the years following the Second World War. These movements resulted in the need for Puerto Ricans to redefine their reality in a new place. Here the early Nuyorican writers and the writers of the Harlem Renaissance shared in the heady optimism that a new world order was possible. The later Nuyorican writers and the writers of the Black Arts movement shared an aesthetic and political passion to construct a new identity, to demystify historical pain, and to articulate a new future. Delgado's essay seeks precisely to address these issues of identity, suffering, and hope as foundational to a Puerto Rican theology.

Delgado argues that the basic question of identity in Puerto Rican life is shaped by a history of victimization and the collective communal ambiguity symbolized by the nation vs. state debate. Drawing on the works of Esmeralda Santiago, Delgado draws out the implications of that history and ambiguity for theology. Particularly striking is her claim that the story *América's Dream* is, despite its title, neither dream nor myth but rather parable, and as such it is multidimensional in its depiction of identity. In this sense, we are reminded of the observation by one of Zora Neale Hurston's characters that "the Black woman is the mule of the world," or Richard Wright's poignant insight that "the Negro is America's metaphor." In all of these cases true identity is contested and distorted. The reclamation and reconstruction of identity under these conditions require a rejection of victimization as the basis of one's personhood. The second key to identity in Delgado's work is the nation vs. state debate. The question of whether Puerto Rico should pursue statehood or nationhood is less a conversation about political options and more about the meaning of being Puerto Rican. It is a conversation about the fundamental human need for both inclusion and recognition. In a different contextual setting, this conversation is structurally similar to the historic "integration" vs. "separatist" conversation in the African American community. Of course, the underlying issue is whether or not one was or is an American. Delgado argues that rather than being an existential limbo this liminal condition can be a profoundly creative place. Just as African American thinkers have found Du Bois's concept of "twoness" as a place to begin a conversation on African American identity, so too does the recognition that the fundamental feature of Puerto Rican reality is neither nationhood nor statehood but colonization provide the basis for a Puerto Rican theological anthropology.

The second theme addressed by Delgado is that of suffering. She mines the rich repository of insight found in the writings of Pedro Juan Soto, especially his novel *Hot Land, Cold Season*. In this work, Delgado finds that the main character, Eduardo, encounters a kind of suffering that seems to attend to his very being. The context of that suffering is the tension between *la naturaleza* (nature or wilderness) associated with the island of Puerto Rico, and the cold, manufactured existence that is associated with life in New York City. The island is associated with freedom and life and the city is associated with captivity and death. Eduardo comes to the realization that the essential tension is within him. He also comes to understand that this tension is or can be a place of spiritual strength. This notion of living in the tension between the natural and manufactured worlds is one that has occupied the imagination of African American writers. Richard Wright's pictorial essay *Twelve Million Black Voices* and Ralph Ellison's *Invisible Man* address this same reality. The suffering that manifests itself politically, socially, and economically has its roots deep within the self.

This theme of suffering, which Delgado posits is "constitutive of Puerto Rican life," is what she uses as the foundation of a distinctively Puerto Rican soteriology. However, she makes a critical shift in perspective from the question "Are you saved?" to the question "What do you believe about Jesus?" In making this shift, Delgado does not get caught up in the tautological snare of having to explain why the saved suffer, and why are not all who suffer saved. Instead, by focusing on the relationship between the sufferer and Jesus, soteriology is redirected toward a focus on love. Indeed, the real question is "Under what conditions and circumstances is the love of God in Christ apparent as saving love?" Delgado provides an eloquent answer to this question: "A Puerto Rican soteriology thus affirms that our salvation is contingent upon not turning away from the struggles of those who suffer in the here and now on earth. In fact, our turning toward the suffering is evidence of God's saving grace already at work within us: we love because God loves us first." African American theologians have wrestled with the question of the meaning of suffering in depth. The works of Anthony Pinn, David Goatley, and especially the pioneering work of William R. Jones are examples of this struggle. The relationship between suffering, love, and salvation is an apt point of departure for further conversation and joint witness between African American and Puerto Rican theologians.

The third theme addressed by Delgado is that of hope. Here she analyzes the stories and novels of Rosario Ferré, whose artistic vision of hope is multidimensional and richly textured. Delgado deftly probes this vision and successfully uncovers themes of theological significance. She argues that this literature suggests that a genuine Puerto Rican notion of hope requires an understanding of the collective past and history so that those voices so long silenced might be lifted up and re-created. This notion of hope would also require attention to the wisdom and insight of those who have suffered, and the recognition that within that wisdom are the tools of resistance. This notion of suffering would highlight the necessity of reconciliation of the warring dichotomies within the Puerto Rican experience. Finally, this notion of hope would accept "the dialectic of death and life"—that is, a somber embrace of the fact that for something new to be born something old may die. Delgado lifts up a number of insights from the writings of Ferré, but the one that I believe holds the most promise for advancing a conversation between African American and Puerto Rican theologians is Ferré's attention to the particular plight of Puerto Ricans of obvious African descent. Certainly the dynamics of race and class make up important elements of Puerto Rican reality, but Ferré presents a revolutionary portrayal of "black/mulatto Puerto Ricans" that can be a significant point of departure for dialogue.

Delgado concludes that a Puerto Rican eschatology must recognize that "our stories and our histories demonstrate that the hope and promise of a renewed future is not often found in the churches or places of worship of our respective traditions." Here Delgado presents what to me seems her most potent suggestion. As she writes: "I believe that the fiesta as an embodiment of the renewal of the relationships among family, friends, community is one place where hope can be found for Puerto Rican people." Delgado notes that the fiesta is an opportunity for Puerto Ricans who live on the mainland to return to their ancestral *tierra*, or homeland. It is a joyful opportunity for reconciliation, forgiveness, and reconnection across space and time. I would argue that what the fiesta is and does for the Puerto Rican community, the family reunion is and does for the African American community. Like the fiesta, the family reunion often involves the return to the ancestral home, usually in the South. It is the occasion for reinforcing familial ties and passing down family stories and traditions. Indeed, even an event such as the commercial success of Tyler Perry's film *Madea's Family Reunion* serves as a belated response to the importance of this ritual. Here is the exciting possibility that African American and Puerto Rican theologians might profitably converse about the relationship between the fiesta and the family reunion as critical rituals of hope.

Delgado has provided an important starting point for a potentially revolutionary discussion. As I consider what the content and context of such a discussion might be, three tasks come readily to mind. First, we might work on redefining our collective identity. How is the Puerto Rican struggle with nationhood, statehood, and colonization related to the African American struggle with integration, segregation, and political and cultural nationalism? Second, we might explore our distinctive but interrelated literary traditions as the loci of critical and creative ideas. How is the emergence of Nuyorican literature connected and related to contemporary African American literature? Third, we might partner in a project of the recovery of submerged theological discourses in an imperial context. What can our histories of enslavement, colonization, oppression, and marginalization teach us about listening to the whispers of those who suffer? Although it is not possible within the context of this brief response to exhaust the suggestions elicited by Delgado's essay, doors have been opened and invitations extended. Let the conversation begin.

PART FOUR MUSIC AND RELIGION

Alex Nava

回

THE BROWNING OF THEOLOGICAL THOUGHT

IN THE HIP-HOP GENERATION

I was raised on hip-hop. Some of my earliest memories of music con-
jure up the sights and sounds of hip-hop, from the rhythm and flow of a
rapper's voice to the bodily movements and contortions of a break dancer.
Among many of those in my generation and especially of my hood, hip-
hop was too alluring and "fresh" to resist. Before we were able to recite a
Bible verse or a classic literary text we could recite by heart the lyrics of
"Rapper's Delight" by the Sugarhill Gang or "The Message" by Grandmaster Flash. I vividly remember an incident in my childhood that started
in a conversation with a suburban kid from a private school in town. I
don't exactly remember the nature of our dialogue, but I do remember
him (proudly if not pretentiously) quoting to me a verse of Shakespeare. I
wasn't sure what he meant or who he was referring to, but without thinking I came back to him with something familiar to me, a couple of lines
from "Sucker MCs" by Run D.M.C.

> Youse a sucker MC and you're my fan
> You try to bite lines, but rhymes are mine
> Youse a sucker MC in a pair of Calvin Klein
> Comin from the wackest part of town
> Tryin to rap up but you can't get down.[1]

Without speaking for everyone of the post–civil rights generation, hip-hop
became a part of my identity growing up in Tucson, Arizona. While this
was clearly not the only factor that influenced the person that I am today,

it was not an insignificant influence in the formation of my personal identity. Hip-hop is a part of my autobiographical story.

My interest in intellectual life developed later than my love of hip-hop. It was not until well into my college years at the University of Arizona that I developed my interest in philosophy and theology. It was only in college that I was exposed to the classic literary and philosophical texts that the private school kid from my childhood encounter must have had at a very early age. Late in college Plato and Kierkegaard, Shakespeare and Cervantes, and Joyce and Borges became soul mates for me as much as Tupac was. As Tupac rapped about making change, my mind and soul underwent a profound change: I became captivated by the world of ideas. It was nothing short of a shock of recognition. Something profound resonated within my spirit that awoke in me a sense of wonder, a love of learning, and a desire for intellectual exploration. I recognized something important that I had been missing in my life. It was this awakening that eventually led me to the University of Chicago to pursue graduate studies in religion.

My growing interest in intellectual life, however, never entirely eclipsed my connection with hip-hop. In fact, my youthful love of this music and subculture influenced some of the choices I would make in academic life. My background in hip-hop was a catalyst for my burgeoning academic interests pertaining to race, culture, class, and even gender. And hip-hop surely led me to my interest in African American history, literature, and theology. To borrow a notion developed by Richard Rodriguez, hip-hop has, in effect, led to the "browning" of my theology.

For Rodriguez, brown is a metaphor used to describe Hispanic cultures, and yet not in an exclusive manner. Instead it is a metaphor for all of us—for human culture itself. If brown is a color then it is one produced by wild mixtures of blood, language, religion, culture. It is a dirty, impure color.

> Brown as impurity. I write of a color that is not a singular color, not a strict recipe, not an expected result, but a color produced by careless desire, even by accident . . . I write of blood that is blended. I write of brown as complete freedom of substance and narrative. I extol impurity. I eulogize a literature that is suffused with brown, with allusion, irony, paradox—ha!—pleasure. . . . Brown bleeds through the straight line, unstaunchable—the line separating black from white, for example. Brown confuses. Brown forms at the border of contradiction (the ability of language to express two or several things at once, the ability of bodies to experience two or several things at once).[2]

While brownness for Rodriguez can describe the human condition per se, it is a color not inappropriately associated with Latin Americans and Hispanics in the United States—cultures that are often described as brown. It was the strange and fantastic encounters of the "New World" that gave birth to these brown peoples. As an adjective, brown tries to capture the extraordinary richness and diversity of these new individuals and communities in the New World setting. Language falters in the face of it. The creation of new words appears to be the best strategy—short of silence—to name these new beings. Rodriguez notes that "Mexico has for centuries compiled a ravishing lexicon of brown because in Mexico race is capricious as history is capricious. From the colonial era, the verbal glamour of Mexico has been to entertain a spectrum of brown—of impurity—as rich and as wet as a Hollander palette: *mestizo, castizo, alvina, chino, negro torno atras, morisco, canbujo, albarrasado, tente en el aire, canpa mulatto, coyote, vosino, lobo.*"[3] "The Last Discovery of America," the subtitle to Rodriguez's work brownness, refers to this American sensibility—this erotic mixture of different bloods and traditions and this crossing of cultural, national, and religious borders.

As a North American I understand Rodriguez's celebration of brownness. I relate to his confession of belief: "By telling you these things, I do not betray 'my people.' I think of the nation entire—all Americans—as my people. Though I call myself Hispanic, I see myself within the history of African Americans and Irish Catholics and American Jews and the Chinese of California."[4] This passage resonates with me. I do not betray Latino theology to call it myopic and narrow at times. I see myself working within the field of Hispanic culture and theology as long as this designation is faithful and open to the plurality and diversity of the human condition, and as long as it is faithful to the universal God of the Jewish-Christian-Islamic traditions. After all, God-talk in these traditions becomes idolatry when one's loyalty is to the tribal gods before YHWH. The influence of hip-hop in my life, oddly enough, has made me aware of how brown my identity is, which is much more brown than that of my brothers and sisters south of the North American border.

For me the recognition of my own brownness describes the complex, heterogeneous elements and influences that have shaped my identity, from Mexican food, the Spanish language, and Catholicism to North American democracy and pluralism, Chinese martial arts, and the culture of hip-hop. I am brown because I refuse any simplistic reduction of my identity to a single unmixed or pure substance. With Rodriguez, I see myself within the history of many cultures and peoples (I claim W. E. B. Du Bois as my own mentor and ancestor as much as I claim Tupac as a brother). My theology is brown because I cannot subscribe to any form of theology that is narrowly and exclusively nationalistic or ethnocentric. A brown theology owes loyalty to the universal God and refuses worship of any tribal idols.

Although in this essay I have been a little slow in coming to a concrete thesis, let me be clear now in what I am saying: "Latino and Latina theology of the hip-hop generation is marked by brownness. The tone and purpose of the newer generation of Latino and Latina theologians is different from the first generation—from those inspired by the civil rights movement." In the case of the first generation, cultural nationalisms and cultural essentialisms prevailed in much of their language and ideas. As such the task of theology was to define and justify the uniqueness, beauty, and dignity of one's own cultural and religious tradition relative to the dominant cultures worked to deny this right and purpose. Not surprisingly, this often led to forms of cultural nationalism that bordered on ethnocentrism similar in appearance to the Eurocentrism that many cultural theologies sought to challenge. While these earlier forms of cultural theology have served important and valuable strategic purposes, they also prove to be unsatisfying to the hip-hop generation of theology. The brownness of theology in the hip-hop generation celebrates hybridity and contradiction, cultural miscegenation and cross-cultural contamination. There is no pure identity. While the persistent presence of injustice, prejudice, racism, and inequality in North America today makes cultural nationalisms still an appropriate and valuable option, I believe that the hip-hop generation of theologians needs to forge a theology of openness that is attuned to the diversity and multiplicity of any human individual and community.

To justify this position of a brown theology, I would like to explore in this essay some of the affinities and cross-cultural contaminations of black and Latino and Latina theologies. I will do so with a consideration of hip-hop as a movement that has influenced many black and Latino and Latina kids, especially those raised in the ghettos and barrios of North America.

Prophetic Elements in Theology and Hip-Hop

To explore some of the shared perspectives and projects in black and Latino and Latina theologies, I would like to begin with a consideration of the prophetic dimensions of these theologies. Without subjecting this term to an exhaustive analysis, let it suffice to say that I use the term prophetic to mean a tradition of thought and practice that begins with the biblical prophets and extends throughout Christian history to involve a passion for justice and, concomitantly, an anger at instances of injustice, inequality, and mistreatment of the poor, oppressed, and needy. The prophets of the scriptures proclaimed the word of God not as a sentimental and soothing message of consolation; instead, the word of God came to them as a violent, disruptive force that denounced the sins and injustices—and the apathy and indifference—of the people and society around them. No wonder the prophets are the least amiable of the biblical characters. Their aim to be intentionally disturbing made them targets of persecution, abuse, and death.

One clear example of the shared perspectives and projects among blacks and Latinos and Latinas is in the field of the prophetic movement known as liberation theology, which exploded onto the theological scene in the 1970s. James Cone's classic work *A Black Theology of Liberation* came out in 1970 just as Gustavo Gutiérrez was putting the finishing touches on his own classic, *A Theology of Liberation*. There are many points of affinity between these works, but what stands out for me is the general insistence that the voices and experiences of whole communities and traditions have been ignored, overlooked, and subjugated; that so many non-European traditions have been treated with indignity and dishonor; and that no theology that pretends to speak of God merits credibility when the God-talk of so many cultures is of marginal importance at best.

While hip-hop may lack the sophisticated level of philosophical and theological analysis evident in liberation theology, I think there is in fact a strong tradition of prophetic thought in hip-hop even if the tragic sensibility (as I will argue in the following section) is more pronounced. The prophetic element in hip-hop is especially prominent among those artists influenced by and in continuity with civil rights. Consider the origins of the civil rights movement. Hip-hop, not unlike reggae, emerged from the slums and ghettos. Hip-hop culture is the creation of urban youth. It is the voice of the poor and disenfranchised in the urban centers of North America. While rap music is indebted to aspects of African and Jamaican aesthetics and oral traditions, it is a North American invention (from the Bronx in New York) that expresses the views and concerns of young people in the urban centers of the United States during the period of late capitalism.[5] Rap music expresses a great range of human emotions including anger, frustration, despair, anguish, sexual desire, and joy. It is filled with so many ambiguities and contradictions that it is almost unfair to generalize a common theme.

There are some rappers who define their work in connection with civil rights. These artists have strong prophetic sensibilities. One notorious case is Public Enemy, a group that consistently appeals to the forebears of the hip-hop generation. The painful and anguished struggle for justice is noted by Public Enemy, but it is done in a tone of rage more obvious than that of the civil rights generation. Consider, for instance, the song "Prophets of Rage" (2005):

With vice I hold the mike device
With force I keep it away of course.
And I'm keeping you from sleepin'
And on stage I rage
And I'm rollin'
To the poor I pour it on in metaphors
Not bluffin,' it's nothin' that we ain't did before.
We played, you stayed
The points made
You considered it done
By the prophets of rage.

I rang ya bell
Can you tell I got feelin'?
Just peace at least
Cause I want it, want it so bad
That I'm starvin'
I'm like Garvey
So you can see B
It's like that, I'm like Nat[6]

For those who know Public Enemy, this piece is rather tame relative to many of their works. There are other songs that pack a more powerful punch and that target the government and the American people for the centuries of the mistreatment and subjugation of blacks in America.

Many other rap artists show this same anger. The artist KRS-One (an acronym for 'knowledge reigns supreme over nearly everyone') has been around since the early days of hip-hop. His anger is directed in different directions ranging from the injustices of American life to the betrayal (in his view) of much of hip-hop in the interest of money and power. What stands out in the following piece is his description of the true aim of rap: the description of the hoods of America. The demand to keep the music real, to remain faithful to the brothers and sisters in the ghettos, is always on the mind of many rappers, as it is for KRS-One in this piece titled "R.E.A.L.I.T.Y."

> These are the streets!
> Shit is real out here!
> This ain't no fuckin' joke!
>
> I lived in a spot called Millbrooke Projects
> The original Criminal Minded rap topic
> With twenty cents in my pocket I saw the light
> If you're young gifted and black, you got no rights . . .
> I wake up wonderin' who died last night
> Everyone and everything is at war
> Makin' my poetic expression hardcore
> I ain't afraid to say it, and many can't get with it
> At times in my life, I was a welfare recipient
> I ate the free cheese, while the church said believe . . .
> The city's a jungle, only the strong will survive . . .
>
> So when I kick a rhyme I represent how I feel
> The sacred art of keepin' it real.[7]

The classic work of two other New York rappers, NAS in his classic "Illmatic" and Jay-Z in "Reasonable Doubt," also invoke this strategy of "keepin' it real" and of representing the struggles and injustices of ghetto life. According to Todd Boyd, in "Illmatic" NAS gives us "some of the most poignant words ever to describe the postindustrial urban experience."[8] Indeed, on the topic of the hardships endured by blacks and Latinos and Latinas in urban America one can learn more from NAS than from most sociologists. Jay-Z, who is one of the best rappers alive today, also speaks with passion and frustration at the persistence of prejudice, police brutality, and violence in ghetto life. While Jay-Z's politics are subtle, his prophetic voice can be heard by those who listen closely. At one point in *The Black Album*, Jay-Z calls for the president of the United States to come and break bread with urban America so as to learn firsthand of the struggles and obstacles faced by so many poor Americans today.[9] As NAS and Jay-Z represent their East Coast hoods, there are others who speak for the West Coast. The most famous of these is NWA, a group that during its heyday described in unforgettable and angry language the circumstances of life in South Central Los Angeles, in Compton, and in other West Coast ghettos.

As their name suggests, The Geto Boys also speak to us of ghetto life, but in one song the ghetto comes to symbolize the poor and oppressed throughout the world. As such, it symbolizes the other:

> Let's take a journey to the other side
> Where many people learn to live with their handicaps
> While others die.
> Where muthafuckas had no money spots. . . .
> I'm from the ghetto so I'm used to that
> Look on your muthafuckin' map and find Texas
> And see where Houston's at.
>
> Five hundred niggas died in guerilla warfare
> In a village in Africa, but didn't nobody care.
> Don't nobody give a fuck about the poor
> It's double jeopardy if your black or Latino.[10]

The Latino rapper Fat Joe may be best known for his suggestion that gangsters don't dance, they "lean back," but there is plenty of social and political criticism in his work. In "Born in the Ghetto," for example, he expresses in no uncertain terms the anguish and struggles of life in the ghetto.

> I'm flirtin with uncertain death
> Lord I gotta be dyin, cause after all this cryin, how much hurtin's left?
> This depression and anxiety is gonna make me show another side of
>   me.
> My niggas ride with me cause I'm the truth . . .
> I'm bringin opportunity to my community
> Probably the only rapper that cares, but you still out to ruin me.
> Who you foolin' B? I'm for unity, Latins and Blacks.
> Could you fathom the strength . . .
> Born together, voted alike. These uncle charm politicians ain't holdin
>   us right
> How could the same nigga be 20 years in office
> When its clear the only thing rising is unemployment
> Abortion, little kids having kids.
> The school system is failing us, now ain't that some shit
> While the rich keep gettin richer, the poor keep dyin young

I could give many other examples but the point should already be clear: many of the best hip-hop artists offer us harsh but real, angry but truthful, descriptions of life in postmodern urban America. They speak from the margins of the United States, in locations where politicians and the mainstream media rarely travel. The best of these artists are prophets of our own times.

Tragic Reflections

Miguel de Unamuno in his classic work *The Tragic Sense of Life* celebrates the unique vision and passion of the Spanish soul vis-à-vis European thought and philosophy. Since modern times, Unamuno argues, European intellectual life has operated with a consistent and stubborn bias: European thought has marginalized, if not completely ignored, the cultural and intellectual achievements of Spain.[11] Unamuno contends that this prejudice stems from the hubris of the Enlightenment: only Europeans—outside of Spain, Portugal, and Italy—possess the light of science and logical, empirical methods of rationality as well as a rational economy based on capitalist enterprise. The rest of Europe—particularly the Catholic cultures—remain premodern and unenlightened.

A thorough study of Unamuno's work is beyond the scope of this essay, but I want to introduce his name if only to highlight one of his central points—namely, that a tragic sensibility is pervasive in Spanish cultures. He explores the tragic soul of Spain in his reflections on Catholicism, on the Spanish mystics, on the omnipresence of images and rituals of death in Spain, and finally, on the tragic story of Don Quixote de la Mancha.[12] Unamuno's reading of Spanish culture is consistent with many other great Spanish intellectuals and artists, ranging from Federico Garcia Lorca to Picasso and Goya. These figures all noted the black, plaintive, and death-obsessed tones and images of Spain. The terrifying creations of Goya's *Black Paintings* (painted toward the end of his life, after the Napoleonic Wars) or the black-and-white image of Picasso's *Guernica* (painted after the bombing of a Basque town) are representative of this tragic sensibility.

The vision of death and life in Spanish culture found its way to the cultures of the "New World." The preoccupation (or even obsession) with death survives and thrives in Mexico. Recall the famous words of Octavio Paz on how death is viewed in Mexico: "The word death is not pronounced in New York, in Paris, in London, because it burns the lips. The Mexican, in contrast, is familiar with death, jokes about it, caresses it, sleeps with it, celebrates it; it is one of his favorite toys and his most steadfast love. True there is perhaps as much fear in his attitude as in that of others, but at least death is not hidden away: he looks at it face to face, with impatience, disdain, or irony."[13] Anyone who has traveled south of the United States border can attest to the omnipresence of death in Mexican culture, from the bloody, tragic depictions of Christ in the churches to the celebrations of the Day of the Dead and other sacred and profane festivals in the Mexican calendar. The North American artist Robert Motherwell tells of the impact that the culture of Mexico had on his artistic vision.

> All my life I've been obsessed with death and [I] was profoundly moved by the continual presence of sudden death in Mexico. (I've never seen a race of people so heedless of life!) The presence everywhere of death iconography: coffins, black glass-enclosed horse-drawn hearses, sigao skulls, figures of death, corpses of priests in glass cases, lurid popular wood-cuts. Posada . . . and many other things . . . women in black, cypress trees in their cemeteries, burning candles, black-edged death notices and death announcements, calling cards and all of this contrasted with bright sunlight, white-garbed peasants, blue skies, orange trees, and everything you associated with life. All this seized my imagination.[14]

Richard Rodriguez speaks beautifully of the way this sense of mortality has made its way across the border to North America. As much as he cherishes the accomplishments of the American experiment—the comforts provided by science and technology, the optimism and celebration of newness—a Latin skepticism and sense of death define his worldview: "I believe in human advancement. I believe in medicine, in astrophysics, in washing machines. But my compass takes its cardinal point from tragedy. If I respond to the metaphor of spring, I nevertheless learned, years ago, from my Mexican father, from my Irish nuns, to count on winter. The point of Eden for me, for us, is not approach but expulsion."[15] This understanding of life as exile was central, Rodriguez tells us, to his education at the hands of Irish nuns. Religion class spoke to the young boy about sin, death, and life as a vale of tears: "The story of man was the story of sin, which could not be overcome with any such thing as a Declaration of Independence. Earth was clocks and bottles and heavy weights. Earth was wheels and rattles and sighs and death. We all must die. . . . The dagger in Mary's heart was pain for her Son's passion. The bleeding heart of Jesus was sorrow for man's sin."[16] While pieces of this description may register an unmistakably Catholic experience, the tragic sensibility crosses the boundaries of Catholicism. This sensibility resonates keenly with the African American experience, and it is pervasive in the music of hip-hop.

Death was all too familiar for Tupac Shakur. He saw the countenance of death everywhere in the ghettos of America, and he was haunted by the prospect of dying at an early age—a tragic prophecy that was soon to come true. It is not surprising that Tupac appealed to the theme of apocalypticism so often because life in the hood was best described by this term (his first major work is entitled *2Pacalypse Now* [1991]). The conditions and characteristics of apocalypticism—crisis, chaos, conflict, violence, injustice, poverty, the preponderance of death—were pervasive in the ghettos that he knew.

Because of these circumstances, Tupac's sensibility is more tragic than prophetic. As Michael Dyson has argued, Tupac gave up on many of the hopes and aspirations of his mother's civil rights generation. Tupac's mother, Afeni Shakur, had been involved with the Black Panthers and was imprisoned for being part of the "New York 21," a Black Panther group arrested and charged with conspiring to bomb New York department stores, police stations, and commuter railways.[17] As much as Afeni Shakur sacrificed for the civil rights and Black Power movements, the children of her generation saw little or no progress—at least Tupac didn't. Skepticism about any advancement and progress naturally sets in when dreams remain empty and unfulfilled. Dr. King's dream may have paved the way for countless Americans, but the hip-hop generation remains unsatisfied and angry, distrustful and rebellious. If the young people of the hip-hop generation, including Tupac and Biggie, are prophets, then they are tragic prophets of doom.

The omnipresence of the theme of death appears in various Latino hip-hop artists as well. One of the most recognized songs from the Los Angeles–based group Ozo Matli is entitled "Cumbia de los Muertos" (Cumbia of the dead). Besides the creative use of Latin song and dance (cumbia and salsa) mixed with hip-hop, the song is a musical rendition and celebration of the Mexican festival Dia de los Muertos. The song envisions a time and place where the dead return and there is no sadness but rather only joy, song, and dance (or what Tupac once called the "Thugz Mansion").

Aqui no existe la tristeza (Here sadness does not exist)
Solo existe las alegrias (Only joy)
el baile de los queridos (the dance of the loved ones)
de los queridos del pasado (of the past, or dead loved ones)
mira como baila mi mama (look at how she dances, my mother)

The Latino hip-hop group Orishas is another example of syncretism between Latin music (Cuban son and meringue in this case) and rap. The themes of exile, the struggle of Cuba, and the quest for freedom all ring loudly in the music of this very talented hip-hop group. The Orishas also add a unique dimension to their remaking of hip-hop—namely, a celebration of the indigenous deities of Cuba. The name Orishas refers to the gods or spirits worshipped by Yoruba tribesmen. The Orishas too, however, manifest a clear tragic sensibility with their vision drawn from the well of exile and from histories of oppression and subjugation. In one of their songs entitled "Desaparecidos" (The disappeared) they speak of victims of political violence and repression.

> Otro mas de los caidos (Another fallen one)
> Otra espina otro dolor (Another thorn, another pain)
> Otro madre sin un hijo (Another mother without a son)
> Arbol que fruta no dio (A tree that did not bear fruit).

The famous line from Ernst Käsemann, "When prophecy fails, apocalypticism takes over," illuminates this move from the prophetic to the tragic among the hip-hop generation.[18] I argued above that there is a prophetic dimension to the culture of hip-hop. This prophetic tone existed from the beginning of hip-hop and continues to the present. However, it is the note of apocalyptic crisis—of cries of anguish and anger, of tragedy in the face of unexplainable and unredeemable suffering—that is most prominent in the hip-hop generation. Disappointment and dissatisfaction are closer to the generation of ghetto and barrio kids than is any triumphalistic celebration of progress and achievement.

Thus the lyrics of Tupac and Biggie are saturated with dark, tragic themes, with hopelessness and despair, and with violence and death. They constantly question their existence on this earth. They recall for us the anguish of Job, Jeremiah, Hamlet, or Qoholeth. In Biggie's first album, *Ready to Die,* he describes his birth in a way that any of these figures would understand.

> Then came the worst date, May 21st
> 2:19, that's when my momma's water burst
> No spouse in the house so she rode herself
> To the hospital, to see if she could get a little help
> Umbilical cord's wrapped around my neck
> I'm seeing my death and I ain't even took my first step.[19]

This song echoes the tone of much of the work by Tupac. As much as Biggie or García Lorca, Tupac was obsessed with death. The difference between Tupac and Biggie is clear, however: Tupac is obsessed with God as much as death. This view is expressed in his song "Who Do You Believe In?" from the album *Better Dayz*:

Can't close my eyes cause all I see is terror.
I hate the man in the mirror
Cause his reflection makes the pain realer
Times of Armageddon
Murder in mass amounts
In this society where only getting the cash counts.
I started out as a beginner
Entered the criminal lifestyle and became a sinner.
I make money and vacate, evade prison
Went from the chosen one to outcast, unforgiven.
All the Hennessey and weed can't hide
The pain I feel inside.
You know it's like I'm living just to die.
I fall on my knees and beg for mercy
Not knowing if I'm worthy
Living life thinking no man can hurt me.
So I'm asking
Before I lay me down to sleep
Before you judge me, look at all the shit you did to me.
My misery.
Made it out of the flames
In my search for fame . . .
And I'm asking

Who do you believe in?
I put my faith in God
Blessed and still breathing
And even though it's hard
That's who I believe in . . . [20]

In another song from this album Tupac directs his anguish to God and wonders "if the Lord still cares, for us niggaz on welfare."[21] The tone of lament and protest continues in Tupac's piece "Only God Can Judge Me," in which he speaks of being trapped since birth, "cautious, cause I'm cursed . . . visions of a hearse. . . . Oh my Lord, tell me what I'm livin' for. Everybody's droppin' got me knockin' on heaven's door."[22] In the prelude to his rap "So Many Tears" he prays these lines: "I shall fear no man but God though I walk through the valley of death," and then he adds his own words, "I shed so many tears (if I should die before I wake) Please God walk with me (grab a nigga and take me to Heaven)." He continues with lines that are Job-like in their intensity:

> God can you feel me?
> Take me away from all the pressure and pain,
> Show me some happiness again. . . .
> Now I'm lost and I'm weary,
> So many tears, I'm suicidal,
> So don't stand near me.
> My every move is a calculated step,
> To bring me closer to embrace an early death. . . .
> Lord, I suffered through the years,
> And shed so many tears.
> Lord, I lost so many peers
> And shed so many tears.[23]

It is possible to read these passages from Tupac as indicating mental instability or at least severe depression and despair. However, such a psychological interpretation—even if partly true—is cheap, simplistic, and misses the point. I read Tupac as speaking from the deep wellspring of artistic creativity, and I see him as speaking and rapping through his *duende*. He is wrestling with the suffering of the world, with death, and with God. Life is conflict and this tragic sensibility influenced not only Tupac's social consciousness but his theology as well. Tupac's theology is a thug's theology, a theology that is rebellious and unconventional. It is a theology that is inextricably linked with theodicy and with an existential battle with the forces of evil and suffering in the universe.

Tupac is not alone in this tragic vision; indeed, this sensibility is pervasive among hip-hop artists. As I suggested earlier, this is one of the key differences between the hip-hop generation and the civil rights generation. If the latter has a prophetic tone, the former is less hopeful and more tragic. This is evident in so many artists. One of the most important songs in the history of hip-hop, "The Message" by Grandmaster Flash and Melle Mel, includes the famous hook, "It's like a jungle, sometimes it makes me wonder how I keep from going under." In speaking of the social conditions of life in the ghetto it describes the brutalizing effects of this environment on the young. It ends with a tragic note: "It was plain to see that your life was lost. You was cold and your body swung back and forth. But now your eyes sing the sad sad song of how you lived so fast and died so young."[24]

My final example is from the hip-hop group the Wu-Tang Clan. Widely considered to be one of the greatest groups in the history of hip-hop, their music is often a poignant, philosophical description of the hoods of the East Coast. In one of their most well-known pieces, "C.R.E.A.M.," they describe the allure of money for poverty-stricken ghetto youth and the long-term effects of incarceration on blacks in America.

> I went to jail at the age of 15.
> A young buck sellin' drugs and such, who never had much
> Trying to get a clutch at what I could not. . . . could not. . . .
> The court played me short, now I face incarceration
> Pacin'—goin' up-state's my destination
> Handcuffed in back of a bus, forty of us
> Life as a shorty shouldn't be so rough.
> But as the world turns I learned life is hell
> Living in the world no different from a cell.[25]

The apocalyptic and tragic tones of the hip-hop generation are unmistakable. What is at work here, argues Cornel West, is the threat of nihilism. With his admirable ability to think outside of conservative or liberal boundaries, West delves into "the murky waters of despair and dread that now flood the streets of black America. To talk about the depressing statistics of unemployment, infant mortality, incarceration, teenage pregnancy and violent crime is one thing. But to face up to the monumental eclipse of hope, the unprecedented collapse of meaning, the incredible disregard for human (especially black) life and property in much of black America is something else."[26] West argues that the effect of this nihilism (defined as the threat of meaninglessness, hopelessness, and lovelessness) is evident in a cold-hearted, mean-spirited, and callous disposition toward others.[27] This attitude is all too common in the culture of hip-hop.

What makes the threat of nihilism so dangerous in the hip-hop generation is the loss of the cultural and religious communities and traditions that provided protection and support to ward off the nihilistic threat. Relative to earlier generations the hip-hop generation is more vulnerable to nihilism. As West further notes: "The recent market-driven shattering of black civil society—black families, neighborhoods, schools, churches, mosques—leaves more and more black people vulnerable to daily lives endured with little sense of self and fragile existential moorings."[28]

Although I write of tragedy, I do not want to conclude on a tragic note. I have argued, in fact, that the tragic tones in music forms such as flamenco, the blues, and jazz are, as in hip-hop, life affirming and redeeming. These soulful meditations on death are art, after all, and they are beautiful. They shatter sentimental, naive, and triumphalistic versions of the human conditions and of human history. They are honest, lucid, creative, and prophetic. They are epitaphs of tragic beauty.

This essay is an experiment in working toward a brown theology. I believe that a brown theology is a resource that by nature of its heterogeneity holds together contradictory and pluralistic elements (prophecy and tragedy, for instance). A brown theology thinks outside of boxes, crosses borders, and transgresses boundaries. Methodologically, a brown theology is interdisciplinary and calls upon art and music, philosophy and literature, and religion and culture when the moment calls for it. A brown theology will always listen and learn from the other—both outside and within—and wear representations of diverse traditions such as black and Hispanic, Asian and Arab, and many others. Certainly many of us may identify more completely with one particular tradition and culture or religion over others, and thus we cannot always be what St. Paul admonishes—"All things to all people." Still, our common humanity is a theological dogma central to the Jewish, Christian, and Islamic traditions, if not to most of the world's religions. It is a dogma that must be protected and preserved when instances of prejudice and xenophobia, hatred and violence, threaten its survival. Cornel West begins his book *Race Matters* with this confession, and in doing so he highlights the major flaw of many cultural nationalisms: "To establish a new framework, we need to begin with a frank acknowledgement of the basic humanness and Americanness of each of us."[29]

The influence of hip-hop on my identity has made me realize the heterogeneous and complex nature of all racial categories (in my case Mexican American). I still embrace my own Latino and Latina cultural traditions and the religion of my parents and ancestors (Catholicism), but I am also profoundly American: a hybrid of everything from Jewish and Irish to black. Even this listing of identities cuts the list short: I am so much more than that. I owe as much to Run D.M.C. as I do to Shakespeare; they both taught me something profound about prophetic and tragic thought and about the common humanity that we all share. And they both taught me about the value of a brown vision of the world, one that occupies the liminal space in-between polar opposites.

If some of the cultural nationalistic theologies of the civil rights generation tended to draw clear and unmistakable boundaries between races and cultures (a black theology, a Latino and Latina theology, an Asian theology, a feminist theology, and so forth) then a brown theology confuses the boundaries, crosses the borders, and stands in-between the lines where dialogue is possible and where a recognition of our shared humanity reveals itself. This brown theology is not a Latino and Latina theology (although it draws from the wisdom of Latino and Latina traditions and cultures) and it is not a black theology (although it learns from black history and cultures) but rather something more syncretistic. A brown theology is closer to the colors, images, sites, and rituals of Brazilian carnival celebrations. It is a theology of hybridity, of a mosaic of fragments from the wide diversity of the human experience. Ultimately, a brown theology owes its primary loyalty to the universal God. All nations, Isaiah once prophesied, will stream to the mountain of the Lord. Only then, he wrote, "shall they beat their swords into plowshares, and their spears into pruning hooks; nation shall not lift up sword against nation, neither shall they learn war any more" (Isaiah 2:4). It seems to me that for all their anger and moments of hopelessness, the best of the hip-hop artists maintain a hope that goodness will prevail and that justice will be done. If not here on earth then perhaps in some ghetto heaven.

Notes

1 Run D.M.C., "Sucker MCs," *Run-D.M.C.*, Profile/Arista Records, 1984.

2 Rodriguez, *Brown*, xi.

3 Ibid., 132.

4 Ibid., 128.

5 See Pinn, ed., *Noise and Spirit*, 13. On rap music as a North American invention, see Perry, *Prophets of the Hood*.

6 Public Enemy, "Prophets of Rage," *Power to the People*, Def Jam, 2005.

7 KRS-One, "R.E.A.L.I.T.Y.," *KRS-One*, Jive Records, 1995.

8 Boyd, *The New H.N.I.C.*, 91.

9 See Jay-Z, "Justify My Thug," *The Black Album*, Roc-A-Fella/Def Jam, 2003.

10 The Geto Boys, "The World Is a Ghetto," *The Resurrection*, Virgin Records, 1996.

11 Unamuno, *The Tragic Sense of Life*, 301.

12 The horrors that Don Quixote endures through the novel—the shame and ridicule, the contempt and persecution—make this story one of the most tragic novels of Western literature. Quixote's struggle with time and death is a central theme. Harold Bloom in *Where Shall Wisdom Be Found?* concurs with Unamuno in seeing Cervantes's great novel as a tragedy.

13 Paz, *The Labyrinth of Solitude*, 57–58.

14 See Hirsch, *The Demon and the Angel*, 186.

15 Rodriguez, *Days of Obligation*, 29.

16 Ibid., 221.

17 See Dyson, *Holler if You Hear Me*, 24.

18 Käsemann, *The Testament of Jesus*, 45.

19 The Notorious BIG, "Respect," *Ready To Die*, Bad Boy, 1994.

20 Tupac Shakur, "Who Do You Believe In?" *Better Dayz: Book 2*, Interscope, 2002.

21 Tupac Shakur, "My Block," *Better Dayz: Book 2*.

22 Tupac Shakur, "Only God Can Judge Me," *All Eyez on Me: Book 1*, Koch Records, 1996.

23 Tupac Shakur, "So Many Tears," *Me Against the World*, Jive Records, 1995.

24 Grandmaster Flash, "The Message," *The Message*, Sugar Hill Records, 1982.

25 Wu-Tang Clan, "C.R.E.A.M.," *Enter the Wu-Tang, 36 Chambers*, RCA, 1993.

26 Cornel West, *Race Matters*, 19.

27 Ibid., 23.

28 Ibid., 24–25.

29 Ibid., 8.

Cheryl A. Kirk-Duggan

RESPONSE TO THE ESSAY BY ALEX NAVA

Duke Ellington, the phenomenal jazz artist and composer, created a symphonic suite titled "Black, Brown, and Beige" that involves his musical meditations on the evolution of African American history and on culture, and includes moving poetry, soaring gospel vocals, sparse haunting piano, booming horn-featured swing, and a symphonic unity par excellence.

Alex Nava's essay is an eloquent, symphonic-like autobiographical analysis of a Latino and Latina theology of the hip-hop generation. His development of a brown theology is from a vantage point different from that of the first generation of Latino and Latina and Hispanic liberation theologians, who were primarily inspired by the civil rights movement. Nava is trained in microbiology, chemistry, and religious studies, and it is in light of this background that he engages in a constructive work sensitive to sociocultural, historical, religious, and theological perspectives. He is well versed in the language, ethos, cosmology, and spectrum of hip-hop artists, and his reflections on them are engaging. My response to Nava's essay is a critique that addresses points of commonality and difference and also suggests options for further conversations between African Americans and Latinos and Latinas.

Based on an interdisciplinary poetic analysis, both Nava's essay and my own celebrate the contributions of hip-hop—notably as a culture that has provided a context for a rich diversity of music with prophetic messages and that proclaims a deep awareness of the impact of socioeconomic and political disparities, particularly those affecting brown and black communities. Our essays express appreciation for the tremendous contributions and gifts of Tupac Shakur as an iconoclast with a tremendous sense of honest social critique and as a prophetic voice amid a compassionate desperation to inform the public about the oppressions that disrupt the life of many in urban and impoverished communities. Our essays note within the world of hip-hop the themes of prophecy, religion, theology, and ethics, specifically as they relate to a focus on family, drugs, abuse, sorrows, pains, joys, the divine, and the importance of security. While in our essays we have similar commitments to appreciating the artistry, poetry, and sociopolitical critique of hip-hop, we also have differences in our approach, scope, and goals.

Nava has lived through the development of hip-hop as a participant observer. I come to hip-hop as a poet and a trained pianist and vocalist who has done primary research in the music genres of classical, jazz, blues, and the spirituals as well as in ethnomusicology. As such I come to hip-hop with intrigue and with a deep interest in and awareness of the musical background upon which hip-hop erects its existence. Methodologically, Nava's essay and my own use a liberative approach through brown theology and womanist theology respectively. Nava's view of brown theology as it interfaces with hip-hop is a post–civil rights reading that focuses on the tragic. My essay is a womanist reading that sees the nihilistic and violent amid some hope. I intentionally view hip-hop as a cultural matrix and rap music as a product of hip-hop culture. I support Nava's thought that Tupac's work hovers over the tragic forms of death and annihilation. I am convinced that Tupac's nihilism heightened and became suicidal after his stint in prison. His music, his associations, and his creative attitude speak death as if while he was incarcerated something so tragic and unforgivable happened to him—to his body, itself a living canvas—that he could no longer live with himself.

In contrast to Tupac's nihilism and total despondency, Lauryn Hill's persona adds themes of destiny, freedom, creation, authenticity, reality, relationships, and the importance of respecting one's self and the experience of sexual relations. Shakur and Hill both focus on conscientization and an embodied sense of God that presses us to change the way we see, think, believe, and act. Nava's essay and my own both listen to the hip-hop psalmists as they name the apocalyptic, prophetic tragedies and offer their social constructions, from which we weave the threads of their praxis, theology, and sometimes the condemnation presented as a wake-up call to those who hear their music. While Nava sees a distinct difference between the generation influenced by civil rights and the hip-hop generation, I offer some qualifiers to Nava's distinction.

Not all of those who participated in and lived during the civil rights era benefited from that experience. The vast majority of poor people did not benefit in major ways, for although access was a primary result of the nonviolent direct protest, if one does not have funds one still cannot access colleges, hotels, restaurants, vacations, and the like. With downsizing and outsourcing many jobs that baby boomers or those in the hip-hop generation might have had are no longer available. In many cases there are individuals who were active in the civil rights movement or invested in its outcome who are disillusioned, angry, and perhaps even nihilistic about the potential for transforming the systemic injustices that plague us in the United States and in Latin America. In addition, there is a music—the music of the blues—that held the anger and fire of protest during the civil rights era and before. The Black Power, feminist, gay rights, and Gray Panther movements all emerged from the energies of the 1960s civil rights movement, which affects the hip-hop generation. Neither I nor Nava reflect on those sociopolitical realities. My biographical, interdisciplinary approach honors the stories of the two artists, Tupac and Hill, and their music. Nava tells the story of hip-hop through the music of many artists, and as such the reader does not gain an in-depth sense of who the singers are and how the music relates intimately to their lives. By reading the biographies of Tupac and Hill, one can see the importance of their life experiences on their artistry and their artistry on their lives.

Reading the two essays in dialogue provides a rich experience in creativity and the sociopolitical, economic, and cultural experience of many peoples of color—those who are poor and those who the "have and have mores" often want to dismiss from the earth. We also have to remember that many of those who purchase the music of hip-hop culture are middle- and upper-class Euro-American, Black, Asian, and Latin youths who may or may not be a part of Nava's brown theology. A fascinating question is to reflect on the worldwide impact of the 1960s civil rights movement and hip-hop culture.

Our essays both serve as invitations to do much more work in the area of interdisciplinary analysis of cultural artifacts from a global perspective. Such work should aim toward helping those of us in the academy recognize the language of youth whereby we create theory toward praxis to move from nihilism to transformation, as a prelude to intergenerational dialogue. In short, our essays call for more global intergenerational dialogue. The members of each younger generation feel that the generation before them does not listen to their voices or understand their experiences.

To a certain extent these sensibilities are true but in other ways they are not. Some of the circumstances of maturing and growing up have changed regarding intensity, nomenclature, and certain subtleties, but the oppressions such as those that the 1960s civil rights activists worked against have not disappeared but rather are only less visible.

An interesting discourse could emerge by placing male and female hip-hop poets and musicians in conversation with blues and jazz musicians and perhaps the musical and other literary artists from the era of the Harlem Renaissance. What might we learn from the African American sculptors Warrick Fuller (1877–1968), Sargent Claude Johnson (1887–1967), Augusta Savage (1892–1962), and Richmond Barthe (1901–1989); the painters Palmer Hayden (1890–1973), Lois Mailou Jones (1905–1998), and Romare Bearden (1914–1988); and the photographer James Van Der Zee (1886–1983)? I include their dates to illustrate how many of them were active during the time of swing, rock and roll, and rhythm and blues. Some lived long enough to sense the oncoming wave of nihilism in culture and the world. Think about the kind of jam sessions and learning opportunities we might have if we brought together experts and aficionados of the music of Louis Armstrong, Josephine Baker, Edward Kennedy "Duke" Ellington, Dizzy Gillespie, Billie Holiday, and Charlie Parker with those who create, listen to, and purchase music from the hip-hop experience. What legacy do we engage when listening to the writings of Harlem Renaissance writers and poets like James Weldon Johnson, Claude McKay, Langston Hughes, Jessie Fauset, Paul Lawrence Dunbar, Gwendolyn Bennett, Countee Cullen, Georgia Douglas Johnson, Arna Bontemps, and Jean Toomer?

What magnificent exchange might occur if we put these black literary and musical artists in conversation with their brown sisters and brothers. What could we learn from authors and poets such as Nicanor Parra, Nicolás Guillén, Julio Cortázar, Carlos Drummond de Andrade, Carlos Pellicer, César Vallejo, Cecília Meireles, Mariano Azuela, Isabel Allende, Julia de Burgos, Haroldo Conti, Eduardo Galeano, Gabriela Mistral, Miguel Angel Asturias, Pablo Neruda, Gabriel García Márquez, Octavio Paz, Jorge Luis Borges, Silvina Ocampo, Alejo Carpentier, Marta Traba, Luisa Valenzuela, and Eraclio Zepeda, including their understanding of the impact of the Mexican revolution, the Cuban revolution, the 1968 Mexican student uprising, and the civil wars in El Salvador and Nicaragua? And the music, notably the Afro-Latin jazz music of Mario Bauza, Alberto Socarras, Nicholas Rodriguez, Juan Tizol; of the saxophonist David Sanchez, the pianist Edward Simon, and the trombonist William Cepeda? And what of the art of Diego Rivera, Frida Kahlo, Rafael Perez Barradas, Maria Izquierdo, and José Clemente Orozco?

These lists of artists are in no way complete but rather include only a sampling of artists, poets, and musicians from the twentieth century. When we know our historical legacies we can better engage each other, understand our true commonalities and differences, and celebrate both.

Black, brown, beige
And all in between
Creative, beautiful, magnificent
People, created by God
Let us celebrate ourselves
And love ourselves well enough
To dialogue, dance, and create with each other
Where artistry becomes a vehicle
For true engagement and liberation.

Cheryl A. Kirk-Duggan

THE THEO-POETIC THEOLOGICAL ETHICS

OF LAURYN HILL AND TUPAC SHAKUR

Hip-hop artists are wordsmiths in a way that is distinctive from those who use only the written word—that is, those in expressive culture. Hip-hop artists use powerful one-syllable words like love, war, and peace to relate literal, figurative, emotional, and realized life-and-death issues to the various people in their listening world. Indeed, many concepts, actions, and philosophies begin with ideas and then soon are concretized in the spoken and written word. Hip-hop artists design and articulate profound pictures and symbols in their patter-like rhythmic artistic word usage. Such usage has had a long history: earlier wordsmiths such as Gilbert and Sullivan in *The Mikado* and *Pirates of Penzance*, Stephen Sondheim in *Sweeney Todd*, Andrew Lloyd Webber and Tim Rice in *Jesus Christ, Superstar*, and Duke Ellington and Ella Fitzgerald in their jazz works engaged in rhythmic artistic word usage through vaudevillian patter songs and scat. Even some of the biblical psalms, when sung instead of being proclaimed in a dull monotone, seem to engage such rhythmic schematics. While these various types of music function in different ways, they share an ingenious and creative use of rhythm as a framework for rapid-fire word delivery.

In this essay I explore themes in the prophetic rap music of Lauryn Hill and Tupac Shakur and their contextual "hip-hop" development toward depicting their theo-poetic theological ethics. *Theos* is the Greek term for God, and *poetic* (from the ancient Greek ποιεω [poieo], which means "I create") pertains to an art form that employs human language for its aesthetic qualities. Theo-poetic theological ethics thus is a type of discourse where one creatively uses verse to reflect on realities of God and spirit in relation to humanity, and it addresses how individuals relate to each other or behave and embody value in light of their belief systems. In this essay I first provide an overview of the womanist methodology approach that I use in my analysis, and then I define terms related to hip-hop culture. Following this explanatory material I offer biographical sketches for Hill and for Shakur. Finally, I explore selected prophetic themes and other biblical subjects that occur in their work, while also discerning their theo-poetic theological ethics toward conscientization and embodied God consciousness.

Womanist Thought

Womanist theory calls for a revolution in ways of seeing, living, and being. By being involved in this effort we can appreciate stories about self and community and engage in radical listening and discerning. Such awareness recognizes and embodies the good and refutes and works against evil. We can experience a heightened epistemological sense that moves us to make a difference in the world via empathy and compassion. The term *womanist*, derived by Alice Walker from the word "womanish," refers to women of African descent who are audacious, outrageous, in charge, and responsible.[1] Womanist thought, as embodied theory and praxis, appreciates the importance of analytical and critical thinking, encourages holistic living, and offers tools that are critical in analyzing the work of artists such as Lauryn Hill and Tupac Shakur. Womanist theory is interdisciplinary and complex, and it builds on the varied texts and other modes of cultural production by women of the African diaspora. As a tool, womanist theory names, exposes, questions, and helps transform the oppression of women and of all people, particularly those who are daily affected by race, gender, and class domination. Womanists champion freedom. Since a personal God spoke the world into being, many womanists value language usage between the divine and the human and within human relationships and in culture. The politics of language, where words and expressions construct realities, is central to the analysis of hip-hop culture and of rap music. Womanists commit to listening to all and to the healing of all. Womanist theory frames womanist theological ethics.

Womanist theological ethics—the study or discipline of God-talk amid forms of human behavior and their related value systems—originates in the experience of the women of the African diaspora. This theory and praxis analyzes human individual and social behavior, and their related value systems, dialogically with the divine toward exposing injustice and the malaise due to multiple oppressions and the misuse of power. A womanist emancipatory theological ethics embraces mutuality and community and honors the incarnated Imago Dei in all individuals. Womanist theological ethics builds on the essential goodness of humanity and focuses on the transformation of personal, societal, and spiritual fragmentation. This way of seeing questions individual quality of life and stewardship, critiques decision making, and asks how these inquiries effect and are affected by the related socioeconomic, political, and cultural environment. My womanist analytical framework includes but is not limited to issues in theology (identity, sacrality, subjectivity, spirituality, power); biblical and other sacred texts (authority, characters, language, rituals, history); ethics (value, behavior, visibility, integrity, praxis); and context (authority, culture, aesthetics, ecology, community). These tools support a critical analysis of hip-hop culture and rap music.

Hip-Hop Culture: An Overview of Terms

"[Hip-hop] is a kindred spirit to bebop, the music that started [Quincy Jones on his] career. Hip-hop is reminiscent of the griots of ancient Africa, the praise-shouters, and the many other ways that cultures have communicated through the power of the drum. I [Quincy Jones] have included this powerful music in many of my creative endeavors. I love this music, . . . But I also know its history. The gangster lifestyle so often glorified and heralded in this music is not 'real.' It's fake, not even entertainment—it is a sad farce at best and a grim tragedy at worst."[2] The cultural movement known as hip-hop was developed in the 1970s by African Americans living in New York City. Today it is a global phenomenon. The cultural experience of hip-hop includes, among other elements, political activism, fashion, slang, double-dutch moves, and beatboxing. Double-dutch is the complicated variety of jump rope where the participants jump over and through two ropes that are swung in a crisscross manner by two turners. Beatboxing involves a machine that generates an electronic beat—the vocal percussion facet of hip-hop culture and music—and is focused on the art of creating beats, rhythms, and melodies using the human mouth. It also involves vocal scratching (the imitation of turntable skills), singing, and simulating a variety of musical instruments, including strings and horns, to replicate a wide spectrum of sound effects. Though some literature uses hip-hop as a synonym for rap music, I identify hip-hop as a cosmology, ethos, or cultural context and rap as a musical by-product of hip-hop.

Within the development of hip-hop culture its progenitors created various social structures and networks of crews or posses—the vehicles for expressing local connections and characteristics. Rap, hip-hop's vocal representation, is a revolutionary and emotional focus point of the performance. Its thematic and stylistic roots come from signifying, toasting, and dozens of other traditions from the United States and Jamaica, as well as from double-dutch chants and sing-song children's games. As Guthrie Ramsay notes, its roots can also be found in "black vernacular preaching styles; the jazz vocalese of King Pleasure, Eddie Jefferson, and Oscar Brown, Jr.; the on-the-air verbal virtuosity of Black DJs; scat singing; courtship rituals; the lovers' Raps of Isaac Hayes, Barry White, and Millie Jackson; the politicized story telling of Gil Scott-Heron and the Last Poets; and also the preacherly vocables of Ray Charles, James Brown, and George Clinton, among others."[3]

For some artists the ethos of hip-hop and the music of rap have become a platform for social commentary and prophetic speech: hip-hop and rap decry the ongoing malaise and degradation resulting from myriad forms of oppression and argue in favor of the poor and downtrodden. Clearly, all rap music is not concerned with social consciousness and empowerment. According to the cultural critic Michael Eric Dyson, rap music frequently contains excessive violence, recycles vicious stereotypes, focuses on non-black or lighter-skinned women, does not deal with politics, is inundated with references to sex, and has sold out to capitalism. Dyson claims that the sexism and misogyny is crude, disturbing, and destructive. Rap music and hip-hop culture are thus both indigenous art and highly capitalistic, commercialized, corporate venture. The music industry that popularized rap created a formula that determines how many times terms like hos, bitches, and so on must be used to be commercially viable. Hip-hop navigates between conflict and contradiction. It often appeals to suburban white kids, a pattern that follows many other discourses invented by black folk.[4]

Hip-hop is the cultural and attitudinal context for the development of rap music. The characteristics of this culture include attitude, dress, dance, language, and distinctive graffiti. A source of motivating pride and identity, rap as a musical vehicle for poor blacks in the United States in the 1980s mimicked what reggae did for Jamaicans in the 1970s. Rap music is an African American genre or type of music where performers rhyme lyrics as they sing, engage in speak-singing, and chant in time to a musical accompaniment of prerecorded sounds. Kool Herec, a Jamaican artist, is one of the catalysts for the mechanics of rap's musical technique, including beats or break beats. Other DJs who helped create the hip-hop style embodied in rap include Grandmaster Flash who combined sound technology and hard funk and worked with a beatbox, and Afrika Bambaataa who worked to inspire black gang members and street kids to embrace communal solidarity and a more constructive life experience by using rap music, hip-hop style, and dance to replace drugs and violence. With the evolution of break dancing came a push toward a casual, washable, and comfortable clothing style. The art form that emerged amid hip-hop culture was a kind of wild-style graffiti where artists scribbled their nicknames or "tags" on various flat surfaces. The key focus for hip-hop culture is vinyl LPs as a source for audio tape. Traditionally, the musical rap artists sampled vinyl recording for its basic parts and then remixed the samples on tape. While such sampling may have infringed copyright law, the artists argued that no one could have exclusive domain over a sound or a rhythm. This music was first heard on the radio from vinyl recording in 1979.[5] The origins of hip-hop, however, occur much earlier.

Rooted in a myriad of traditions ranging from ancient African oral practices to Bessie Smith, Pigmeat Markham, and Gil Scott-Heron, rap evolved and began to critique and analyze the socioeconomic and political issues that were catalysts for the development of heightened drug addiction, teen pregnancy, police brutality, and forms of material deprivation. Many thought rap was a flash in pan or a fad. Yet, Run D.M.C.'s success signaled a new place for rap as artistic expression. Many recognize Run D.M.C. as the progenitor of the modern genre of rap, and its creative use of different musical elements, social commentary, and cultural identification moved rap into the mainstream with an identifiable tradition. In the wake of its meteoric rise, rap involved several distinctive traits. Musically, the rap of Run D.M.C. combined rock music and the new music generated by hip-hop culture to produce a musical hybrid with a strong critique and passionate lyrics. Further, rap became a vehicle to address urban pain, racism, classism, and social neglect. Many mainstream blacks and whites argue that rap is a significant trigger for violent behavior, even though the music that many rappers perform is antiviolent. The issues of racism, sexism, classism, poverty, and the impact of politics aimed against the urban poor are illuminated in the world of rap music. Rappers often continue to align with one of their constituencies (namely the ghetto poor), maintaining their aesthetic. Rappers need to heighten their critique, not only of police brutality but of black-on-black crime and of the sexist, misogynistic lyrics that pervade much of rap music. A critical engagement between rappers who engage more so-called secular material and performers of Christian rap and hip-hop might bring a deeper awareness of communal complicity in crime, due to the loss of the village in supporting children, lower standards of expectation for the education of black children, and systemic oppression, including ludicrous acts like "No Child Left Behind" (which has indeed left many children behind, because they are taught to pass tests yet simultaneously are being crippled, for they are not taught how to think critically). Such challenges as these, along with the impact of religion when it engages mission and social justice (as compared to prosperity gospel ideologies), could bring the artists together where they would see that they are challenging the same things, although dressed in different garb.

Opportunities and challenges come with rap music and hip-hop culture. Many Rap singers participate in cooperative entrepreneurial transactions and experimentation in orality and literacy—a historic element of African American creative and educative communities, and a retrieval of movements, ideas, and figures in black history. Reconnecting with black history helps rappers and others to learn about their associations to the past. Two additional challenges of rap music pertain to an uncritical use of history and the grafting or use of music by others without giving acknowledgment or paying royalties. The uncritical use of history often leads to misunderstanding; the grafting of music by others permits the creative use of the work of others without their receiving retribution or payment. Perhaps both of these scenarios can change while people can continue to enjoy the sociocultural and musical creativity of the hip-hop genre of rap.[6]

Rap songs are musical compositions in which the words are the most important element. With their words, samples, and attitudes hip-hop wordsmiths engage in highly creative writing. Their goal is to create hip words that are more powerful than music and that loop back on the power of music so that the words say more than music can say by itself. A hip-hop song is, as Greg Tate notes, a "thematically coherent essay in rhyme form."[7] It may rhyme about love or it may rhyme about death and all other topics in-between.

It is a cruel irony that the survival, success, and transformation of hip-hop depends upon its capacity to sell death—namely black death. Celebrity, glamour, and hyped pictures of ghetto life have resulted from an embrace of ghetto life, guns, and gangsterism. Many rappers have countered ghetto life with corporate hip-hop and its carefully articulated, orchestrated message. At the same time hip-hop is new, vital, and creative; it remains largely undefined about the specifics of its identity, purpose, or destiny. Hip-hop continues to be quite self-critical yet also self-championing. Thus there is a great deal of tension in hip-hop, for despite its allure within pop culture and its economic success, hip-hop culture has not accomplished what many participants and aficionados believe is its most important task: the opportunity to shape and have a meaningful impact on the lives of young people. Does hip-hop really have that kind of impact? Rap and its progenitor, hip-hop, have not only a strong political force but also commercial dynamics that press them to both celebrated heights and lethal depths—involving everything from race, politics, and history to violence, generational divisions, and corporate power—that ultimately are bigger than hip-hop itself. Hip-hop culture and rap music have given inspiration and hope to many.[8] What are the results of that hope?

The conservative right argues that hip-hop culture pollutes family values and morality. Many liberals and middle-class blacks critique hip-hop because of its homophobia and misogyny. Some of the critique emerges out of a sense of culture and values concerning the ways that identity gets rooted in the middle of ideological and material spaces of racism, colonialism, and national identity. This identity interrogates authentic blackness as communities move between poverty and decadence. Questions arise regarding authentic blackness—the dimensions of imposed racial authenticity and that which emerges within authentic blackness—and frankness about sexualities; these questions offer a critique of nostalgia rhetoric, keeping it real, and examine issues of complicity with white patriarchal structures and the role of black popular culture. For example, the music of some black female rap stars has focused on embracing economic and sexual self-satisfaction. Others now see such alternative voices as deviant. In working to repress and regulate interpersonal and personal black conduct, a new black aesthetic in hip-hop is emerging that may shift the polarities of male/female, black/white, and authentic/commodified and possibly challenge hip-hop norms as an arena that can purify the impure. This aesthetic discredits the debate that the truest form can bring delinquent brothers and sisters who lack self-knowledge to their truest, authentic selves, as if any such claims of identity were ever stable. Often ideology trumps reality. Some hip-hop artists recognized that black politics can emerge within the practice of consumption. During the twentieth century, marginalized United States citizens across the board have used "gangsta" as a locus of socioeconomic mobility; the pimp or gangster's "hustle" or "game" is the vernacular of the culture industry. Hip-hop artists and other culture workers have aesthetically and commercially used the culture industry to create black institutions. Despite any growth, the basic critiques about gangsta rap pertain to drugs, sex, patriarchal masculinity, gunplay, and consumption habits. Positive or so-called conscious rap focuses on gatekeeping that chronicles who gets dubbed as authentically black.[9] Many black folk have rejected any notions of empowerment and change via hip-hop.

Many within the black musical media networks avoided rap and rejected hip-hop culture in the late 1980s and 1990s, just as many in earlier generations dismissed the blues as the devil's music and gospel as denigrating the spirituals. Generational tensions and the desire to maintain a respectability that would not damage relationships with white advertisers and their perception of black radio stations initially made it difficult for hip-hop to make any inroads. After a few DJs in New York began to play rap music during off-peak and late-night hours and the summer months to avoid losing advertising revenue and adult listeners, rap eventually gained a larger listening audience. This increased listening audience, together with changes in the radio broadcasting industry and shifts into niche marketing with increased segmentation and fragmentation, caused changes in programming based on age and genre. Many stations began to play rap to attract younger audiences.[10] Two artists, Lauryn Hill and Tupac Shakur, who were part of this change attracted their own followings for a variety of reasons; one remains larger than life in the flesh, the other remains larger than life from the grave.

Artists at a Glance: Lauryn Hill and Tupac Shakur

Lauryn Hill is an intelligent, articulate, spiritual young woman. She is a mother who writes and performs music antithetical to slick R&B sounds and to misogynistic rap. As an activist, writer, singer, arranger, performer, and actress Hill honors a closeness to God. She has gained a sense of self and has become established in her business, with her love for music stemming from the days when she first found her mother's collection of 45s.[11]

Soul music became Hill's classroom for studying music theory. She sang as a little girl and in middle school, and she showed tremendous social consciousness and compassion as she helped feed students who came to school without breakfast. Her relationship with God since childhood was and remains the locus of her courage and strength. In high school

Hill worked with various hip-hop groups and participated in numerous extracurricular activities including theater productions, and she founded her school's gospel choir. After high school Hill continued to work with the group Translator Crew with Wyclef (Clef) Jean and Prakazrel (Pras) Michel, both originally from Haiti. This group later changed its name to the Fugees. When embracing hip-hop culture they intentionally chose to celebrate life, not negativity, in their music. They sang about respect, love, and about being one's own person, and they avoided drugs. Hill began dating Rohan Marley and she was pregnant by 1996. The Fugees won Grammys in 1997 for best rap album and for best R&B performance by a duo or group. That same year the Fugees continued touring and did a benefit concert in Haiti, where they received the Haitian Medal of Freedom. As a hip-hop, rap, and R&B artist, Hill's lyrical themes include relationships, family, communal roles and responsibilities, and identity.[12]

In her first solo album, *The Miseducation of Lauryn Hill*, she strove to create a hip-hop collection with the roots, integrity, and sound of an old 78 rpm record. She wanted street youth to hear the hip-hop aspect and also experience solid musicality in order to understand that one element did not have to be sacrificed for the other. In using a variety of music forms, including doo-wop, R&B, hip-hop, and pop, *Miseducation* is a saga of Hill's life history, hopes, fears, and passions. She wrote, produced, and performed the album with several guest performers. In the process, she faced sexism and overcame those who doubted her ability because she was young and female. She overcame the doubts that gave people permission to make assumptions about her talent when in 1999 she received both Grammy and Soul Train awards for *Miseducation*.[13]

Miseducation's spectacular mastery of a combination of musical genres energized both rap and hip-hop. Hill's artistry and her gender made her achievements in a male-dominated arena even more important. Not intimidated by reality or her gifts, Hill embraces her sexual pleasure and power and transcends tight gender boundaries. Her wonderful arrangements, powerful lyrics, and inspiring lessons about relationships, community, and self-esteem are antithetical to an industry that usually demands that women accentuate their sexual rather than their musical selves.[14]

Dubbed the queen of hip-hop, Hill writes songs of spiritual uplift. As a middle-class woman who in the media is depicted as folksy and down to earth, Hill encourages this kind of persona. She sometimes seems to speak from a contrived "blacker-than-thou stance," however, as she seems to have realized the rhetoric of persecution without actually having lived

it.[15] In contrast, Tupac Shakur's life was riveted with the violence and persecution that formed the core of his music.

Many people are not aware of the complexity of Tupac Amaru Shakur.
He was a Renaissance man whose life and lyrics exuded violence. He was
a vociferous reader and a keen observer of life, and he listened to a variety
of music ranging from rap to classical. Shakur wrote plays at age six and
attended the Baltimore School of Arts as a professional child actor, where
he excelled. He also experienced rootlessness—by junior high school he
had lived in twenty different residences. Moving to California, he met difficulties as a nonathletic outsider who wrote poetry. He was targeted by
street gangs and secretly hated himself. He critiqued the expendability of
poor black children and the inadequacy and irrelevance of the educational
system as well as political policy and White House strategies. He read everything from classics, history, and feminist theory to poetry, mysticism,
philosophy, and cultural studies.[16]

Shakur grew up with a maternal dominatrix, Afeni Shakur. She was a
woman who at times could be both militaristic and political. As a former
New York Black Panther she was once arrested on conspiracy charges.
She was also an addict, and her escapades critically marked her son. The
family's destitute, homeless status and her devastating alcoholism and co-
caine addiction emerged in a climate of narcissism and social suffering,
gentrification, economic restructuring, and heightened gang warfare. As
a result Shakur had low self-esteem and insecurity because of his impov-
erishment, and he projected revenge on those that he sensed treated him
unfairly. Despite his later stardom, Shakur was never at peace. Locked into
his environment, he could not transcend the circumstances of his life.[17]

As a ghetto saint, workaholic, gifted poet, and musician, Shakur was a
complex individual. He embodied and emulated his thug image with its
strong sense of black masculinity and misogyny, and yet he also embodied
a keen intellect and forthrightness as an entrepreneur and as a prophetic,
charismatic, cultural icon who died prematurely. At the same time, in his
theology he was concerned for the downtrodden; he reflected on God, critiqued the church, and explored theodicy, which he often answered with
compassion.[18]

Like James Baldwin, Shakur confronted black suffering with moral ire.
That same conscience was problematic for Shakur's internal politics. He
destroyed himself internally with hedonistic behavior and materialistic
passions amid a race war via rap, while offering a valedictory expound-
ing the moral paucity of idealistic nationalism. Shakur's life mirrored the

conflicted symbolism of the hopes and failures of the Black Panther revolution. Yet it was this revolt that inspired him to focus on racial conflict within his art. Classically, he used his life story mixed with sociopolitical issues to highlight social injustice. While challenging authority, signifying morality, and exaggerating emotional injury to rationalize mutiny within popular culture, he transformed a common event to high drama: an exercise in self-respect and in respecting others. Shakur questioned everything, took risks, and was willing to fail; he embodied a revolutionary life, a commercial success story, and a thug existence.[19]

Shakur's thug life embraced a dialectic—a secular teleology emerging from a socio-location of disparate social relations with a subjective corrective that offends those seeking social justice, while undercutting the society the revolution seeks to change. This dialectic trapped him between defiant ambition and thug passion. His Panther revolutionary background served as both a burden and as a platform. The governmental harassment that conflicted Panther kids helped push Shakur into a thug life that mirrored the masculinization of the black freedom struggle. For Shakur the thug life was a mentality, a way of life, and a stage to go through. Euro-American and rich kids go to ROTC and put their energy in the armed forces. Poor kids of color release their energies in the street. The thug life is a rite of passage toward being a man where one embodies one's beliefs and responsibilities, regardless of political correctness. Related to thug life, an outlaw means that one is a minority and black. Shakur's acronym THUG LIFE is "The Hate U Gave Little Infants Fucks Everyone."[20]

Ironically, Shakur, the "ghetto's everyman,"[21] adapted a Machiavellian persona wherein he exhibited principles of behavior and conduct marked by cunning, duplicity, or bad faith. As an artist, he worked to convince the world that he was what he proclaimed on his CDs through his art, preaching, politics, and performance—arenas of self-definition and the communication of thought and ideas.[22] In naming these ideas, Shakur names pathologies and oppressions.

Shakur named hopelessness and rapped about death, dissonance, and revenge as he lamented the increased imprisonment of black youth. He continuously questioned himself and where he was headed. In offering a commentary on ghetto life Shakur saw the misery and testified to the same. He named perpetrators and victims of crimes in his lyrics, ever rapping about thugs: the characters who pleaded with God for guidance via explosive areas of self-destruction; those who posed the theodicy question while simultaneously causing others to suffer; and those who left and those who stayed in the ghetto. His quest for a theodicy is an attempt to systematize his belief in God with the perpetuation of evil and the vast suffering of those he held near and dear. Shakur's quest is not toward a traditional theist view of the problem of theodicy or moral evil; rather, his is more a confrontational, inclusive reality check that connects a street theism with humanism or human self-actualization. In his songs "Hail Mary" and "Blasphemy" evil is not an abstract theory, but instead a real presence—it lurks, it is human degradation and madness. Shakur and others on the street can be like phantoms or ghosts whose lives do not matter for larger society. Despite any negative actions he may take, Shakur still wants the solace of Mary. He pleas for help as prophetically he names the desperation and degradation all around him. In some respects a stoic, Shakur is quick to name the hypocrisy in society and the church. Further, the street experience, the thug life, is an experience of crucifixion, and too many people suffer there. In speaking of eschatology, heaven, and hell, Shakur notes a God who is female and taking her time. From this God, Shakur wants compassion and the gift of hope, for he sees himself as having a pure heart, as he argues against blasphemy.

Perhaps Shakur's faith is a vital yet profane and engaging belief system: ready for the grace, and no guilt about his wrongs. The violence that Shakur and other rappers romanticized usually paled in comparison to the violence of black youth that they themselves had experienced.[23] Shakur, as a rebel hero similar to Camus's rebel who tries to understand the times and sees the harm done when surrendering to ideologies that can destroy, expressed alienation and honesty. While many white youths assume a familiarity with the hip-hop of black culture, they tend to have a false sense of awareness of and familiarity with black people.[24] Most of these youths had no sense of the real Tupac Shakur, who amid his deep hurt and alienation often expressed profound religious sensibilities—a kind of street spirituality that invokes traditional faith categories across a spectrum ranging from irony and sarcasm to humility and sincerity, aware of the life and death issues that people face daily on the street. How do cultural expressions reflect the biblical and theological themes operative within our world?

Prophetic and Other Religious Themes

Shakur and Hill as hip-hop prophets speak through their lives and their rap music as they "deliver an appropriate word for a given situation."[25] The notion of a prophet connotes a reformer, an interpreter, and a proclaimer who speaks for God. In their music, in a variety of ways, both artists call for reform and speak spiritually about everyday situations. Prophetically, Shakur in his work cared deeply about family dynamics and about drugs, abuse, incest, and the related teen pregnancies and lost innocence, particularly when no one seemed to care or pay attention to those who suffered from these issues. Shakur named these destructive forces and offered a cautionary tale in his songs. Though he named the recklessness and the pain of losing friends and expressed a desire to change his life, in reality he did not really think he could escape negativity. Beyond awareness, actual spiritual growth came with listening to wake-up calls of life and connecting with a higher power.[26] For example, Shakur saw the possibility for new life experiences in his song "Changes," which called for making a new start and for treating each other better. As Alex Teter and John Gee argue: "Jesus did place the desire for change in Tupac's heart, despite his premature demise; and that the only real constant in life is change."[27] Despite his instability and emotional issues, Shakur honored his mother for her strength, inspiration, love, and commitment. In the end he finally realized that his mother had done a lot for him. Though he ran with gangs while he searched for love, which cost him dearly, the gangs did not provide true love to Shakur.

Prophetically, Hill helps us remember that we are who we are because of our past, and she never forgets her roots. She reminds us that our destiny is in each day that our experiences prepare us for. Destinies are designed by a higher power and accepted by us. In the process, Hill reminds women that some women and men only care about sex. Some pursue it for power, physical intimacy, image, or the adrenalin rush, but Hill assumes the role of prophet as she presses us to question cultural assumptions about sex. In her music Hill reminds us that there is something deep within that urges us to realize that we will be able to find something that will heal those broken facets of our lives; that is, success comes from looking, and getting better, from within.

Along with their prophetic themes both artists explore numerous other religious matters. The question of religion occurs within larger societal culture. Throughout this essay the discussion refers to the context of culture. Culture refers to the customs, mores, and civilization of a particular people or group. Thus what is the nature of the relationship between one's concept of God, spirit, or divine, and how does the expression of that relationship occur in humanly created artifacts like the music of Hill and Shakur? How do these artists provide us with religious meaning? In general, some would suggest that such questions help us define who we are, who made us, and why we are here. Pressing further, such questions and themes can tell us about what, why, and how we believe, and how this music affects our experience of truth, justice, knowledge, and authority. How does the music of Hill and Shakur help us contemplate issues like salvation, repentance, redemption, and love? How do these two artists signify messages of peace, compassion, service, nonviolence, and the witness of hope and possibility? How do cultural expressions of their music influence or critique our understanding of the role that spirituality and religion play amid our socioeconomic and political environment that is steeped in our particular history where sexism, racism, and classism have been and continue to be operative? An examination of three songs by each artist can help to provide some insight into the theo-poetics of Hill and Shakur.

Lauryn Hill's music evokes many themes around religious or spiritual behavior, which has an implicit and sometimes overt ethics. She sings about relationships, freedom, creation, options for choices, God's grace, being authentic, and respect for one's sexuality. In her title song from her award-winning album *The Miseducation of Lauryn Hill*, she contends that to transfer allegiance to anyone outside of one's own self denies and disregards the self, honors projection, and impairs greatness.[28] *Miseducation* produces pathologies; to reckon with *Miseducation* means that one must come to a point of awareness of reality and of God. With Hill's improvisatory, lush, lyrical singing over a pulsating bass and moving melody, her text shifts from a state of being aware to one of critical analysis and forthright engagement. Aware of a deep sense of Imago Dei, of being created in God's image, Hill posits that the answers lie within. Rather than focus on the external, she knows that one must look deeply within. Despite any forces pulling from the outside and its accompanying alienation, hope remains. From a womanist perspective, if one desires freedom one also needs to take responsibility, for in knowing and in seeing one constructs an anthropological theology where one knows the God within, the grace of personhood, and the call to embrace self-actualization. The response to *Miseducation* is to become aware of the divine and of the self so that one can take responsibility for personal destiny.[29] Hill presses this notion of authenticity when as a circumspect griot she challenges our understanding of fantasy versus reality.

In "Adam Lives in Theory" Hill uses a spare, rhythmic accompaniment in a pulse of two in order to signal to all humanity about the need to deal with reality instead of fantasy.[30] This commentary on Genesis 2 compels the audience to confront the nature of living an authentic life. As griot, Hill exposes matters of pretense, superiority complexes, idolatry, and being self-centered or in denial. Hill notes how denial triggers our downfall and how our use of technology can cause us to engage in lust and envy. Simultaneously, in viewing Adam as all humanity and naming Adam and Eve, she notes the tensions and struggles in relationships. When we give too much of ourselves, or are blinded by greed and pride, we come from a place of inauthenticity, confusion, co-optation, and bruised egos. In a sing-song recitative, Hill reveals that sexual relationships rooted in empty fornication result in sin and a loss of perception, perverted thinking and judgment, and a loss of true relationship. Such inauthenticity produces shame, distortion, deception, irresponsibility, and destruction. Theologically, she notes the existence of the Creator and implies a sense of original sin and the blanket guilt of humankind. All of humanity tends to love lies and hate the truth. She shifts from speaking of a general deity to that of a Christ crucified, as she talks about a crucified thief. In this vein she calls for justice, invites everyone to remain open and not entertain hopelessness, and names systemic oppression. She answers her own refrain of "What we gonna do now" and "Where we gonna go now, what we gonna say now" with a Christ figure who will teach us, who wants to be in relationship with us, and who questions how obedient we will be. This relationship requires love, and love that will be tested, and after being satisfied the Christ figure will tell us what to do, where to do it, and what to say.

Hill explicitly names the divine figure in her song that echoes Jesus's words of Luke 23:34a. The song "Forgive Them Father" incorporates the words of Jesus's utterances as he hung on a cross between the two thieves on the place called the Skull (Golgotha).[31] In a ballad-like fashion in a feeling of four, with mainly percussion and guitar accompaniment, Hill intones over and over, "Forgive them father for they know not what they do." The matter of not knowing what we do presses the need to be aware of danger and the false intentions of others. Hill reminds us of the need to work in community toward balance, and she questions why people need to be greedy and jealous. She invites people to avoid deception, pretense, and lies. One should not lie to others or to God. In naming dyads she sees the backstabbing and break of relationships in the stories of "Cain and Abel, Caesar and Brutus, Jesus and Judas." Three times she sings the chorus of forgiveness. Above all, in her songs Hill sings of life, freedom, relationships and wholeness.

Tupac Shakur, the poet of death, sings about the dynamics of life. With a heartbeat mimicked by the bass drum and the religious overtone cued by the chimes amid staccato rap in a triplet fashion, "Hail Mary" evokes a communal rosary that names the joys, sorrows, and pains of urban life.[32] Shakur adopts the moniker of Makaveli for his album *The Don Killuminati: The 7 Day Theory*. He plays off the Italian statesman, political philosopher, and theorist Niccolò Machiavelli, who in his book about Caesare Borgia, *The Prince* (1513), ignores classical theory and medieval theory: classical theory based the state on reasoned moral norms; medieval theory supports a theocracy. Ultimately, the goal of politics is to attain a safe and secure state. A safe and secure state was one of Shakur's desires, and it is a theme present in "Hail Mary." Shakur mingles the language of the prophetic and the profane as he makes a call to prayer in hopes that God listens, after proclaiming that revenge is as sweet as having sex. Equating Los Angeles with the killing fields of Cambodia, Shakur's rosary becomes a dirge of self-deprecation in one breath and a request for mother Mary to pull him toward safety. This chant is totally unmasked as Shakur names the violence of guns, corruption, prisons, alcoholism, insanity, and the commodification of the self. In fearless language, he tells about the thug life, a life of being "outlawz" on the street; a life of survival, a life that does not fear death; a life that often lacks clarity. Thugs include not only pimps and gangsters but preachers too. Regardless of one's circumstances one must survive, even if that means stealing out of need, dealing with destiny, or hoping that one can meet God at the heavenly gates. In singing "Hail Mary" one ultimately does not worry, because of freedom, while one cannot have any delusions about reality. One probably will not be delusional when faced daily with life and death, the antithesis of safety in Los Angeles.

"To Live and Die in LA" is a confrontational hymn by Shakur's Makaveli as he names the turmoil and frenetic life experience of those who hustle and try to make a living through hard times.[33] In this hectic life, death is a close confidante. In this litany Shakur blends his creativity and his particular woes dealing with the stress of plea bargains, being on bail, and the expense of freedom, all in the same breath that he sings of a comrade who died at the end of someone's gun. His story of Los Angeles, the "City of Angels," is one of constant drama. Los Angeles is a sensational place to be, for he loves being in California with its proliferation of thug life. Within the thug life, even if its members fight each other, they will ultimately band together and take charge of the same place that he adores. In the midst of gunfire blazing, he gets high as he deals with Los Angeles. As he ends the song, he salutes those who support him, who play his music and buy magazines that have articles about him.

In "Words of Wisdom" the hip-hop poet Shakur speaks of civil religion and religious themes.[34] In American civil religion, the term coined by Robert Bellah, we live out our civic lives in a religious manner as we share common religious characteristics expressed through beliefs, symbols, and rituals that provide a religious dimension to all aspects of life in the United States.[35] Shakur names the systemic oppression of racism as he confronts the reality that ghetto youth are dispensable, especially black ghetto youth. In a rocking beat of four with a consistent but not overbearing remix accompaniment, Shakur confronts the fact that black youth are being killed and that neither the black community nor the larger United States community is fighting back. He frequently uses the word nigga—a term normally viewed as derogatory in nonghetto society, though often used as an endearment by those in a particular thug life "in-crowd." It's meaning is at times transformed by this in-crowd, as in the case where it is shaped by the positive acronym "Never Ignorant Getting Goals Accomplished."[36]

"Words of Wisdom" offers a critique of classism, marginalization, and the disregard of human life. It is also a critique of the telos of the 1960s civil rights movement (the period when Shakur's mother was a Black Panther), which did not help really poor people—they were left out then and remain left outside today. He warns about having an allegiance to a system that both neglects blacks and with ridicule holds up the Emancipation Proclamation as another failed instrument. He wonders out loud how kids can successfully say no to drugs when the government allows them to be imported into the community. He indicts the government, society, and its legal document, the Constitution, for destroying unity, hindering children's education, and helping people remain crippled through poverty. In this song, from the album 2Pacalypse Now, Shakur plays off of the movie Apocalypse Now (which is based on Joseph Conrad's Heart of Darkness) and the essence of apocalyptic revelation, an unveiling of seven seals, and in this instance a call for the end of our social world milieu—namely the raping, assaulting, and murdering of Shakur's people. He calls for everyone to get out of denial, to cease the practice of racism, and to debunk the myth of an attainable American dream. In questioning the absence of Malcolm X and the appearance of Martin Luther King Jr. in textbooks that encourage turning the other cheek, Shakur says that things will not change until blacks sing the "words of wisdom." In naming colonialism, he says that he is America's nightmare, because America created him. Speaking prophetically and biblically, the indictment ends with naming the many kinds of nightmares and reminding us that we reap what we sow.

Theo-poetic Theological Ethics

The music of Hill and Shakur embodies a theo-poetics. The nature of their music and songs speaks to the connections between the divine and the human, both as individual and community. While Shakur's language is more of a street vernacular, it does not preclude the intent of his message. Not romanticizing the violence, Shakur is not a hypocrite because he names both his shortcomings and those he sees in the world. Both Hill and Shakur produce music that invites a new way of being that involves conscientization and embodied God-consciousness. The building of a pedagogy of the oppressed or a pedagogy of hope is central to this awareness and to the pedagogy of conscientization—developing consciousness, but one that is understood to have the power to transform reality.[37] To transform reality using the artistic renderings of Hill and Shakur invites us to change the way we see, think, believe, and act.

Both Hill and Shakur invite us to resist denial and fantasy and see reality—good, bad, and in-between. They want us to understand the importance of relationships, personal and beyond, particularly the lives of children and the poor who often have no one to advocate for them. The spirituality of Hill and of Shakur has universal appeal and is rooted in faith and freedom. Both artists call for us to be aware that our actions have consequences, intended and unintended. With life and the interaction in our families and societies, we have choices to make and service to give. Ultimately both Hill and Shakur press for nonviolence and being authentic and a true self. For Shakur, however, sometimes being authentic is a question of survival, and that survival may require violence. Life, for some, is all too short.

Both Hill and Shakur desire for us to know peace, compassion, and hope, without being hypocritical. As we see what is happening in the world, these artists invite us to think carefully about what we observe and to not get trapped by appearances. As one thinks one is better equipped to know what to believe. When we are clear about what we believe, we will know how to act. Action is privilege and is necessary for our own survival and for that of the world. We cannot be cavalier and only think of ourselves, instead we must remember that we live in community. Shakur and Hill are both charismatic, creative artists who have poured out their souls in their music and have dared to confront us about our denial, hypocrisy, and complicity in the many wrongs in our society. The question remains: are we really listening, and if so what are we going to do about it?

Gentle giants dropping
Sounds to aspire us with hope
Sounds of love renew.

Notes

1 See Walker, *In Search of Our Mothers' Gardens*, xi.
2 Quincy Jones, "Foreword" in Light, ed., *Tupac Amaru Shakur, 1971–1996*, 13.
3 Ramsey, *Race Music*, 165–66.
4 Dyson, *Holler If You Hear Me*, 109, 130, 137.
5 Hebdige, "Rap and Hip-Hop," 223–27.
6 Dyson, "The Culture of Hip-Hop," 61–67.
7 Tate, "Diatribe," 155.
8 Watkins, *Hip-Hop Matters*, 2–5.
9 Baldwin, "Black Empires, White Desires," 159–62.
10 Watkins, *Hip-Hop Matters*, 78–81.
11 Nickson, *Lauryn Hill*, 2, 5, 17.
12 Greene, *Lauryn Hill*, 7–8, 13, 21, 24–25, 31–43, 49–50.
13 Ibid., 54, 58–60.
14 Watkins, *Hip-Hop Matters*, 71–72.
15 Als, "No Respect: A Critic at Large," 209.
16 Dyson, *Holler If You Hear Me*, 70–83, 94–100. The remainder of my discussion of the life of Shakur is based largely on Dyson's work.
17 Ibid., 21–25, 31–43.
18 Ibid., 11, 13–16, 21.
19 Ibid., 47–62.
20 Ibid., 64–67, 112–15.
21 Ibid., 107.
22 Ibid., 107, 100, 117.
23 Ibid., 123, 128, 130.
24 Aaron, "What a White Boy Means When He Says Yo," 234.
25 Gee and Teter, *Jesus and the Hip-Hop Prophets*, 7.
26 Ibid., 25–26, 30, 43, 51, 57, 59, 64–65, 69, 78–79, 95.
27 Ibid., 100.
28 Lauryn Hill, "The Miseducation of Lauryn Hill," *The Miseducation of Lauryn Hill*, RuffHouse Records, 1998.
29 Kirk-Duggan, *Misbegotten Anguish*, 190–91.
30 "Adam Lives in Theory," in *MTV Unplugged No. 2.0*, Sony, 2002.

31 Hill, "Forgive Them Father," *The Miseducation of Lauryn Hill*, RuffHouse Records, 1998.

32 Makaveli (Tupac Shakur), "Hail Mary," *The Don Killuminati: The 7 Day Theory*, Interscope Records, 1996.

33 Makaveli (Tupac Shakur), "To Live and Die in LA," *The Don Killuminati: The 7 Day Theory*, Interscope Records, 1996.

34 Tupac Shakur, "Words of Wisdom," *2Pacalypse Now*, Jive, 1998.

35 See Bellah, *The Broken Covenant*.

36 Shakur, "Never Ignorant Getting Goals Accomplished," *2Pacalypse Now*, Jive, 1998.

37 See Taylor, *The Texts of Paulo Freire*.

Alex Nava

▣

RESPONSE TO THE ESSAY BY CHERYL A. KIRK-DUGGAN

I am grateful for the opportunity to respond to Cheryl Kirk-Duggan's essay on Lauryn Hill and Tupac Shakur. I found this essay to be an engaging and informative reflection on the history and significance of hip-hop. In addition to Kirk-Duggan's very fine exploration of the contributions of Lauryn Hill and Tupac, I found her remarks on womanist thought and her sketch of the history of hip-hop to be especially insightful. In many ways I share a vision and perspective on hip-hop that is similar to that of Kirk-Duggan. As I made clear in my own essay in this volume, hip-hop has spoken to my own generation and circle of friends—from African Americans and Latinos to white Americans—in a way that influenced our identity in the past and the present.

As Kirk-Duggan makes clear, hip-hop was a voice coming from the margins of society—from the disenfranchised and poor youths of the inner cities of North America. In many instances this voice became a stage for prophetic commentary on the social, cultural, economic, and political arenas of the United States in the late twentieth century. Hip-hop artists diagnosed and exposed the ills of American society. Artists such as KRS-One, Public Enemy, Grandmaster Flash, the Furious Five, Tupac, NAS, Jay-Z, and others described the feeling of alienation and estrangement from the American dream experienced by many poor urban youths. They described the anguish and hopelessness and the fears and anxieties felt by many minority communities in the United States.

I would maintain that we can learn more from the words of NAS in his classic "Illmatic" about the struggles, injustices, pressures, and tragedies of the poverty-stricken areas of urban America than we can from most sociological textbooks. The lyrics of NAS and those of the Wu-Tang Clan, for instance, describe the bleak and violent landscapes of life for many of the poor in New York. Not only are their words more creative and appealing than most academic treatments of poverty and social realities, but they speak from a firsthand experience of the issues involved. They are believable because so many hip-hop artists are deeply autobiographical. They give us descriptions that are deeply personal: the destruction of family life by the impact of drugs; the brutality of the police or of rival gangs; the uneven sentencing and incarceration of the poor; the intimate feelings of depression and hopelessness; the distrust and suspicion of love; the cold and heartless face of the urban jungle.

In confronting these conditions and experiences of urban American life some hip-hop artists have chosen the phenomenon of apocalypticism as a metaphor for life in the late twentieth century. If apocalypticism describes crisis and terror, the threat of chaos and violence, or the rule of unjust and demonic forces, then apocalypticism seems to be an appropriate description of the lives and social conditions rapped about in much of hip-hop (with Public Enemy's and Tupac's uses of apocalypticism being the most explicit). To those living in conditions of squalor and poverty with the signs of death everywhere, the time does seem to be "out of joint," to borrow the words of Shakespeare (quoted by NAS in "Illmatic"). If the civil rights generation responded and appropriated the great prophetic tradition, then the hip-hop generation is closer in tone to the apocalyptic tradition. To hip-hop artists tragedy is a more common theme and lament and anger a more common emotion than are the more hopeful words of the civil rights generation.

As I argued in my essay we need the efforts of both generations. It is sad and disturbing to note among many members of the hip-hop generation the lack of a memory and appreciation for civil rights leaders. If it is true that Tupac and Biggie have replaced the memory of Dr. King and Malcolm X for many of the hip-hop generation, then the condition of education among the youth of our time is in danger. This should alarm and trouble us.

The heritage of Tupac Shakur is a lesson in case. I fully agree with Cheryl Kirk-Duggan's analysis of Tupac. He was a creative, fascinating, and complex young man. The poetry and songs that Tupac wrote speak to the many different faces of his life. At times he is an innocent man struggling with his faith in God in a world of so much unjust suffering, or he is a prophet furious with the injustices and prejudices of the world. At other times, he is so much in the grip of depression that it is inconceivable that he might live to an old age. We might say that these dimensions of Tupac place him within the great civil rights traditions or, to speak biblically, with the great prophets. This is not all there was to Tupac, however. If he shows us many moments of vulnerability and fear, or of ethical-political anger, he also shows us moments of immaturity and cruelty. In his music and life, Tupac celebrated the excesses of materialism, glamorized and romanticized violence, used misogynistic and demeaning language toward women, and lived with great carelessness and arrogance. It is this face of Tupac that places him at a great distance from a Dr. King or Malcolm X.

The heritage characterized by Tupac is the one most common in popular culture today. Not long ago I saw a group of young kids (no more than twelve years of age) walking by dressed in hip-hop clothing. Two of the kids had T-shirts with large images of Tupac on their chests. The back of the T-shirts had images of money and guns. Whether we as defenders of hip-hop, and fans of Tupac like to admit it or not, these negative images are part of the legacy of Tupac Shakur.

For this reason we need the voices of the civil rights generation to inform and transform the legacy of the hip-hop generation. We need figures like Lauryn Hill to connect hip-hop to the great prophetic tradition of both the Bible and civil rights. Kirk-Duggan's choice of Lauryn Hill was wise for this reason. Lauryn Hill represents the very best qualities of the hip-hop artists. Her lyrics are at the same time deeply spiritual and deeply prophetic. They combine an extraordinary awareness of the needs and desires of the soul with a very alert and intelligent social consciousness. Hill is the artist par excellence who is talented and gifted enough to reconcile the accomplishments of the civil rights generation with the achievements of hip-hop.

As I argue in my essay I see a need for fostering the connection between generations. Equally important, however, is the objective set forth by this book project—namely the drawing together of the voices and experiences of African Americans and Latinos. I have suggested in my essay that one common experience, certainly related to the shared experience of marginalization, poverty, and injustice, is the role of hip-hop in the popular culture of blacks and Latinos in the United States. Hip-hop has been a point of unity and conversation for many young blacks and Latinos. It has brought together diverse communities and cultures, from the very beginnings of the movement until today. The expectations that I have for hip-hop rest with my hope that this movement will continue to mature and develop and yet never lose its edge and connection with the streets. Its own greatness has always been in its ability to express and describe the pains and sufferings and the joys and hopes of the disenfranchised and voiceless in American society. When it fails to do this, it would probably be best if it became another outdated fad left to die a quiet death by irrelevance.

PART FIVE ▣ TELEVISION AND RELIGION

Jonathan Walton

⊡

TV "PROFITS": THE ELECTRONIC CHURCH PHENOMENON

AND ITS IMPACT ON INTELLECTUAL ACTIVITY WITHIN

AFRICAN AMERICAN RELIGIOUS PRACTICES

Being in the pulpit was like being in the theatre: I was behind the scenes
and knew how the illusion worked.—James Baldwin, *The Fire Next Time*

Just over a century ago, the towering black intellectual of the twentieth
century, W. E. B. Du Bois, described the black preacher as "the most
unique personality developed by the Negro on American soil. A leader, a
politician, an orator, a boss, an intriguer, an idealist."[1] Yet in the dawning
of the twenty-first century, no longer are these unique and charismatic
characters trapped within the confines of local congregations or African
American communities. With the advent of satellite and cable broadcasting, all one has to do is turn on the television and channel surf from BET,
TBN, MBC to CBN to witness the oratorical artistry and infectious, rhetorical
tropes of these most engaging personalities.

One would be hard pressed today to enter into any African American
faith community—or the larger evangelical community for that matter—
and find someone who has not heard of the evangelical sensations such as
Bishop T. D. Jakes or Creflo Dollar. These figures, and many others like
them, have a seemingly ubiquitous presence in popular culture as a result
of their frequent television broadcasts, video distribution, Internet promo-
tions, ever-popular printed publications, and gospel stage plays and musical recordings. As walking marketing phenoms taking advantage of all

modern technological resources available, these industrious figures have greatly altered the landscape of American religious faith and practice.

To be sure, the best of these personalities—which in my opinion include preachers such as T. D. Jakes, Bishop Noel Jones, and even a white evangelical minister in Columbus, Ohio, named Rod Parsley—embody the rhythmic syncopation, kinetic orality, and emotional physicality of the African American preaching tradition. From the depths of their experience they are able to prime the fountains of their soul to evoke living waters of faith, hope and self-love. For this reason alone it makes sense that those who are dehydrated by the arid social conditions of doubt, despair, and dejection would flock en mass to baptize themselves in this transformative encounter. It is evident that those who are afforded the pleasure of participating in this experience—whether on Sunday morning in worship, via the viewing of video, or attending one of the oft-held mass events—are able to pierce through their existential angst to catch a glimpse of an alternate kingdom where the "first shall be last and the last shall be first."

If my preceding characterization is true, and I believe it is, already we can see why these figures would be particularly attractive to African American women. Living under what the womanist theologian Jacquelyn Grant has referred to as the "triple jeopardy" of racism, classism, and sexism in America, these women are able to transcend via their participation in the preaching moment the numerous mythical names of dominance projected upon black female bodies in America.[2] No longer are black women reduced to titles such as "single mother," "divorcee," "aunty," "ho," or "bitch" as they become "God's leading lady," "anointed woman of God," and "Daddy's little girl."[3] However, having acknowledged the strength of the preaching moment that creates affirmative images of possibilities within the heads of parishioners, to what extent are preachers held responsible to engage in the types of intellectual activity that both analyze and engage the very real conditions in which individuals live, move, and have their very being? In other words, is this aspect of the evangelical movement—which I refer to in this essay as the electronic church phenomenon—doing an equally effective job at offering an intellectual challenge to fossilized and emergent regimes of truth that petrify and reproduce structures of domination in American society? Further, what does it mean for participants within the African American community that the vast majority of these personalities are apolitical at best and covertly aligned with the religious right at worst? As I see it, these questions are of particular importance as select preachers are propelled by the winds of market forces to stratospheric levels of influence within the African American community, while wittingly and unwittingly contributing toward the truncating of other coeval intellectual voices.

A Dramatized Faith

When I speak of the electronic church phenomenon I am addressing two distinct areas of religious experience that have grown exponentially in the post–civil rights era: the electronic church and megachurch movements. The term electronic church is a broad-based designation employed to describe those who use electronic media as a primary tool of proselytization. This includes the teleministers, also known as televangelists, and the organizations from which these persons develop, package, and promote the many ministry-related products mentioned above. The organization can be the church where the teleministers serve or a separate entity established with the sole purpose of distributing the teleminister's message.[4]

In using the term *megachurch* I refer to congregations that claim memberships numbering into the thousands. Literature written on the megachurch movement has placed the membership bar at differing levels ranging from fifteen hundred to five thousand. Yet from the plethora of the largely African American congregations with memberships ranging from ten thousand to twenty-five thousand, these "established" numerical markers appear to be a moot point.[5] A further designation that supersedes, although is still dependent upon, membership totals is the quasi shopping-mall appeal of these congregations. Megachurches are characterized by colossal edifices that not only house sanctuaries that seat well into the thousands but also include childcare centers, gymnasiums, bookstores, and a host of other business ventures. There the seven-day-a-week, one-stop-shopping design has proven itself attractive to baby boomers, buppies, and "unchurched" populations.[6]

To be sure, the electronic church and megachurch movements are semi-mutually exclusive. It is true that being involved in teleministry does not mean that one must pastor a megachurch. However, I do agree with Quentin Schultze's determination that the megachurch can be regarded as the electronic church incarnate. This is, they employ TV-styled worship that includes replacing traditional pulpits with theater-like stages, installing movie screens in the front of the sanctuary that project both the words to the hymns and the pastor's preaching points, as well as utilizing popular musical genres with instrumentation that far surpass the traditional piano and organ.[7] For these reasons, among other shared characteristics that I address during the course of this essay, I include both the electronic church and the megachurch movements in the larger designation of the electronic church phenomenon.

Further, in speaking of the electronic church phenomenon, which is inclusive of teleministry and the megachurch, I am not saying that either the movement or its defining characteristics are new to the African American community. Indeed, C. Eric Lincoln and Lawrence Mamiya were correct in describing the black church as the "first black theatre."[8] Before there were Fred Price and Clarence McClendon there were Rev. Ike and C. L. Franklin; and before Greater St. Stephens, Trinity United Church of Christ, and West Angeles Church of God in Christ there were Wheat Street, Concord, and New Bethel Baptist churches. However, as a result of the technological advancements over the past few decades that have revolutionized the everyday practices of the majority of Americans, while limiting the divide between physical space and time, one can think of the electronic church as the traditional black church on steroids. Further, the combinations of charisma, technology, and money afford to a small but powerful contingent the opportunity not available to their progenitors—namely to transform their pulpits into satellites broadcasting instantaneously across the country. This places the local everyday African American preacher into a precarious position as he or she is measured daily against the ubiquitous images of a select few. In the words of one sister in response to her new pastor's initial sermon, "Pastor, you were excellent! I almost felt like we had Creflo Dollar here this morning."

So, how can we describe the electronic church phenomenon? Three overarching characteristics, I believe, adequately summarize the phenomenon in its entirety. First, the phenomenon is personality driven. The ministries are developed around the charismatic authority of a particular pastor, preacher, evangelist, or revivalist to the extent that the form and function of the ministry often wholly reflects the personal narrative—real or constructed—of its leader. This is observed in the ways that viewers and parishioners often reify the charismatic leader as the church or ministry. For example, often when particular congregations are mentioned it is not the names Temple of Deliverance, Crenshaw Christian Center, or New Birth Missionary Baptist that are mentioned but rather G. E. Patterson's church, Fred Price's church, or Bishop Long's church respectively.

Like movie stars, popular musicians, and athletes, these charismatic figures are in the minds of their fans transformed into living and breathing religious icons. Those who handle the publicity and marketing for the ministry are careful to repeatedly display the physical image of the leader so that their faces are indelibly etched upon the psyche of their followers. This creates a sense of comfort and familiarity as congregation members feel intimately connected to their "pastor." It goes without saying that this effort is somewhat ironic as the majority of those who purchase video series, books, and pack into cathedrals and arenas will never develop more than a one-sided relationship with these figures. However, consistent with the American fascination with celebrity and superstardom, wherein we are able to live vicariously through the perceived fabulous lives of those deemed as successful, the often heroic and inspiring personal testimonies of religious leaders impels adherents to follow the same "divine" formula.

Second, the electronic church phenomenon is crowd dependent. In the text above I employed Max Weber's designation of charismatic authority as representative of the phenomenon's leadership style. Weber defines charisma as "a certain quality of an individual personality by virtue of which he is set apart from ordinary men and treated as endowed with supernatural, superhuman, or at least specifically exceptional qualities."[9] Weber naturally situates the operational function of charisma in the societal context. In his view if a particular society is likened to a stage play the individual possessing the charisma is the captivating main character that by virtue of his or her presence drives the production. Nonetheless, a dynamic personality alone is insufficient: charisma also stems from the cooperation of the group population as much as it is projected by a particular personality. There is always a dialectical relationship between the gifted personality and the people with whom he or she seeks to engage. In other words, it is the members of the congregation that place the sacred stamp of approval on a particular personality, thereby validating whether the message conveyed is a gift of God's grace (χαρισματα) or of human origin.[10]

In addition, to put it bluntly, televangelism is expensive. There are ministries that spend millions of dollars per month, and for the most part financial support is derived from congregational support (if they have one), broadcast audience, and in some cases a handful of wealthy supporters.[11] Moreover, based upon my definition of what constitutes a megachurch, by quantity of members or quality of service, the life and vitality of the congregation is dependent upon mass attendance. The more individuals the ministry is able to attract, the better the financial contributions that can subsidize and expand the television ministry and expand the services provided throughout the week at the church. Moreover, we live in a culture in which "might is right." Thus, religious phenomenon is often measured quantitatively rather than qualitatively. This possibly explains why whenever preachers get together en mass the common response to the question "How is the church coming?" is commonly followed by a numerical figure.

The final characteristic of the electronic church phenomenon is its entertainment orientation. Whether people are sitting at home in a living room, in the sanctuary on Sunday morning, or packed in Madison Square Garden, they come to these places to be entertained. Worship services combine drama, amusement, and suspense, all of which is carefully orchestrated and premeditated in such a manner that congregation members actually witness their own lives being acted out upon the stage. T. D. Jakes is well known for having used trained actors to perform the parts of various biblical characters or other storylines during the delivery of his sermon. This effort coupled with the employment of physical props for visual effect assists viewers in identifying more readily with the enacted drama of the human condition. Further, the perfectly orchestrated sermonic soundtrack via the organ response adds to the aural sense of the experience throughout the delivery of the message. Like a movie storyline, a talented organist in collaboration with the preacher can help create tension, build suspense, and initiate celebration at the appropriate times. This tool is effective at spurring enthusiastic crowd participation.

Theological Consequences

Having set forth these three overarching characteristics of the electronic church phenomenon I would now like to offer what I believe to be three specific consequences of the convergence of religious practice and mass-mediated forms of communication. It is unequivocally clear—operating within the matrix of an American market-driven culture—that the electronic church phenomenon signifies religious faith and practice in such a way that representations of African American Christian experience have become increasingly sensationalized, superstitious, and insular.

Without a doubt the producers of the electronic church must follow the sensationalized suit of popular broadcasting because audiences desire eye-catching excitement, aural energy, and uncomplicated storylines. It is thus no surprise that the neofundamentalist forms of the Christian faith in general, and the African American strands of neo-Pentecostalism in particular, have come to dominate and define the phenomenon. With their dogmatic equivocations and histrionic celebratory style of worship, they offer the kinds of visual representations of joie de vivre that make for must-see TV. The biblical fundamentalist approach that appeals to the simplicity of "the word" offers clear-cut answers to life's perplexing ethi-cal questions while the seemingly extemporaneous preaching and sing-ing—though most events are usually well orchestrated—grab the attention of channel surfers.

Second, since sensationalism is a major characteristic of the electronic church phenomenon as a result of its power to aurally and visually capti-vate attention and appeal to emotion, it is safe to deduce that there is an intrinsic need to accentuate the magical and miraculous aspects of the Christian faith.[12] As a result the line dividing religious faith from popular superstition is blurred. Just as highly dramatized television commercials promote particular product brands as having the capacity to "instantly" al-leviate pain and anxiety while enhancing attractiveness and pleasure, faith is being displayed, packaged, and then subsequently consumed by parish-ioners as an omnipotent panacea. Just as a bottle of shampoo is marketed as an instant sexual gratifier or an automobile as a means to upward cor-porate mobility, God is represented as a sort of cosmic bellhop or vend-ing machine wherein all one has to do is "name it and claim it" to have their lives radically transformed. It is for these reasons that videotapes and books are touted as "being able to unleash divine favor in your life" or "not only bless you, but the lives of your children's children." Messages are en-coded in such a way to influence individuals to believe that there is some-thing inherently magical in the product itself. In this respect we could say that the modern video and audio series have replaced the blessed "prayer cloths" and "holy water" of the early televangelists.

Finally, because of the electronic church and megachurch phenomena, worship has been transformed from a communal exercise to an increas-ingly privatized activity. Although congregants believe themselves to be "joining the ranks of other like-minded disciples," they are in actuality rendered singular. Again, in following the trend of sensationalism that is indicative of a television-driven, dramatized society, the congregations of both the electronic church and the megachurch are reduced to audience members. What would be referred to as a congregation has now become a collection of believers loosely joined together within "imagined commu-nities" largely constructed upon their shared allegiance to a charismatic personality.

Remember that in both televangelism and the megachurch a screen takes the place of the pulpit, membership is designated by auxiliary orga-nizations such as "covenant" or "prayer partners," and commitment to the ministry is largely measured not by physical attendance or activity but by "sowing a financial seed."[13] Unlike authentic interpersonal relationships that require a level of transparency and commitment—a staple of more traditional congregational life—the electronic church and megachurch demand neither of these elements. Members have the options of showing up to church on Sunday in anonymity amid thousands of other parishioners, or they can access the divine by simply popping in a tape in the comfort, convenience, and privacy of one's own home. Yet the engaging personality and ubiquitous image of the televangelist or pastor, which is constantly transmitted over electronic mediums, gives the impression that parishioners are engaged in something larger than they are.

So it is for the three reasons outlined above that I make a final claim in this section. Due to the fact that the electronic church phenomenon has rendered religious faith as increasingly sensationalized, superstitious, and insular, it is no wonder that the drama, magic, and individualist perspective inherent to the prosperity gospel has become the dominant theological perspective for the majority of the movement. It is the hallucinogenic fumes of the health and wealth gospel that situates the attainment of material possessions as the telos of life while espousing the belief that economic prosperity or poverty, as well as physical health or illness, is wholly dependent upon the sovereignty of God. Liken unto the simplistic theology of Job's comrades, prosperity and health are the mark of spiritual devotion and fidelity to God, whereas poverty and illness are indicative of baleful behavior. All material and social conditions are reduced to one's personal faith, and as a result it is often the very victims of social injustice who are blamed for their own condition. Monthly in any given city mega sports complexes and convention centers are packed with African Americans gravitating to hear impassioned sermons that espouse traditional family values and individual pietistic morality as the key to personal prosperity as they simultaneously ignore larger social and political concerns. In these sermons America's social ills could be ameliorated if men would take their rightful place as the head of the family, women would live chaste lives until marriage, and the poor would accept Jesus Christ as their Lord and Savior. As I show in the concluding section, this aspect of the phenomenon alone could have grave implications within African American faith communities.

Intellectual Implications

In assessing the intellectual implications of the electronic church it is important to differentiate the concept of intelligence from that of intellect. I understand intelligence as the capacity to adjust, manipulate, and reconfigure oneself and one's conditions toward a particular telos. Intellect, however, is the by-product of purposeful mental engagement and activity. Unlike intelligence, intellect does not merely cause one to adjust or adopt based upon existential circumstances. Intellect cuts through the presentist problematic to critically evaluate the human condition from a panoramic perspective. Hence, intellect is contemplative, reflective, and in the final instance always creative.[14] To quote Edward Said, the intellectual—who for him is different from an intelligent professional—is not ashamed to "raise embarrassing questions, to confront orthodoxy and dogma 'rather than reproduce them,'" and one "who cannot easily be co-opted by governments or corporations."[15]

According to the aforementioned distinctions between intelligence and intellect, one can laud the producers of the electronic church phenomenon for their intelligence and professional ability not only as preachers but also business operators. To use a colloquial expression, "They ain't nobody's fools." It takes high levels of practical skill and business ingenuity to pastor a twenty-thousand-member congregation and oversee a multimillion dollar enterprise. Yet as I seek to demonstrate here, the overarching characteristics coupled with the resultant consequences of the electronic church phenomenon—which are wholly reflective of the larger cultural currents in American society—trump the sorts of intellectual production necessary to bring forth the prophetic discourse needed in this historical moment.

To examine the ways that the electronic church phenomenon impacts intellectual activity in the African American faith community we can begin by distinguishing between contemporary challenges and the anti-intellectual aspects of religious phenomena already examined within various areas of American religious history. For sure, the intellectual versus anti-intellectual debate, which is based upon varying forms of religious expression, antedates America as a nation. Nevertheless, the proliferation of the electronic church within the African American community has problematized conventional analytic discourse concerning intellectualism and religious expression as a result of, first, its embrace by the black middle-class and, second, the way that "otherworldly" enthusiasms commonly associated with evangelicalism have been transformed into "this-worldly" preoccupations.

First, the binary between rational and emotional religious expression can no longer be traced along class lines. The church versus sect typology (the former being rational and the latter being emotional) has been historically viewed as inherently divergent. That is, the socially dispossessed and unlearned sectarians defined themselves against the rationalized and formalized religion of the church. In responding to what they believed to be inaccessible liturgical formalism and cerebral, catechistic obligations, sectarians often vehemently rejected an emphasis upon "head knowledge" by opting instead for inner religious conversion evidenced through emotional response. While it may once have been sufficient to cite H. Richard Niebuhr's *The Social Sources of Denominationalism* or Max Weber's concept of "spiritual affinity" to locate one's religious affiliations (and thus intellectual acumen) based upon socioeconomic standing, the electronic church has rendered this type of analysis problematic. The electronic church has engulfed the black middle class in such a manner that overdetermined social analysis fails to consider the particular ways in which the electronic media has transformed sectarianism, evangelicalism, and even apocalyptic fundamentalism from a sectarian response of social outcasts to a means of social integration into mainstream cultural values.

Second, building upon the first point, we are forced to reconsider our outlook on the otherworldly versus this-worldly divide that has so informed our conceptions of religious faith and intellectual activity. Benjamin Elijah Mays's *The Negro's God as Reflected in His Literature* skillfully articulates the manner in which Jupiter Hammon, Phillis Wheatley, and Theodore Henry Shackelford's "otherworldly" compensatory conceptions of God, which advocate social adjustment, are in stark contrast to Benjamin Banneker, Olaudah Equiano, and David Walker's theologically supported claims of social rehabilitation and reconstruction in "this world."[16] Du Bois even provides us with a snapshot of this distinction in "The Coming of John," when he demonstrates the manner in which the same young man that is celebrated by his faith community for his academic accomplishments is in turn castigated for the intellectual challenges he poses to his congregation's "bye-and-bye" theology.

Modern-day evangelicalism, as largely signified by the electronic church, cannot be adequately measured along the otherworldly versus this worldly continuum. As representative of the health and wealth gospel, themes such as material wealth, entrepreneurial impulse, and personal relationships dominate the genre. Moreover, televangelists such as Creflo Dollar and Frederick Price who are particularly known for their health and wealth teachings take a heuristic approach that is characterized by a seemingly methodical examination of the biblical text. They tend to shun the extreme forms of histrionic preaching in favor of rationalized appeals to cognitive understanding that are premised upon faith in the "word." This style appears to have particular appeal among young African Americans moving into the middle class and away from the often-stereotyped "emotional and uneducated" representatives of the traditional black denominations.

Despite these differences I do assert that televangelism's very "worldly" discourse is anti-intellectually bound by the same types of compensatory theological rhetoric found in previous generations. As Mays articulates, compensatory conceptions of God impel individuals to adjust to their social conditions. Regardless of the "hell" that these individuals are catching in this world, an abiding faith in God will bring forth just rewards in heaven. Obedience, humility, passivity, and long-suffering are all seen as marks of Christ, and it is through the habituation of these spiritual gifts that God will compensate the believer.

Though theologically this-worldly, the compensatory conceptions of God that pervade the health and wealth gospel nurture the same dispositions toward the structures of American society. Themes such as submission and obedience—though ambiguously situated in the rhetoric to the extent that it is hard to distinguish whether it is toward God or the pastor—are promoted as a means to personal prosperity, thereby encouraging worshippers to abdicate responsibility to the sovereign will of God. When God is viewed as the sole source of one's financial future and overall social outlook, it is in vain to stand up against the systems that perpetuate injustice. Therefore, the same theological conclusions that influenced John Wesley Holloway to patiently "Wait on the Lawd" in the "bye and bye" is the same discursive move that propels T. D. Jakes to passively "Get ready, get ready" in the "here and now." Unfortunately, either way the inability of adherents to take responsibility toward cultivating the capacity to offer an inventive and critical challenge may cause followers both of Holloway and Jakes to passively adjust to their social conditions in the final instance.

In regard to new problems relating to the phenomenon, televangelists have spread their wings upon the winds of cultural and market forces, and as a result they have transcended the institutional structures of bureaucratized faith and denominationalism. As Stewart Hoover argues, "Broadcast production and distribution is a creative process. Art cannot be produced by 'committee' and neither can television. The democratically responsive biases of most denominations put them in a poor position to be able to develop a 'creative edge' and to be responsive to the interests and reaction of their audiences."[17] The producers of the electronic church must be able to conform their religious programming to the sensationalism of America's dramatized society and readily make the types of instantaneous decisions concerning creative adjustments. (For instance, T. D. Jakes did not have time to consult with a denomination representative concerning an official response to September 11, 2001, prior to erecting a wall-size American flag behind his pulpit and referring to Colin Powell as God's new Joshua heading to conquer Afghanistan. The mood of the country called for a timely and sensationalized response.) However, the types of institutional establishments such as those provided by denominations are conducive to intellectual activity. This is not to say that social and religious institutions do not have the capacity to stifle intellectual production; of course, in many instances they can and do. Nonetheless, denominations can be credited for being hospitable to reasoned, democratic exchange as well as fostering communicative networks that promote the types of discourse that challenge any one particular position. Too often, it seems, producers of the electronic church find themselves in a sectarian posture independent of the various spheres of society. From this paucity of communicative exchange, a rampant subjectivism is nurtured that can only be checked or countered by the unpredictable currents of market forces.

Once more, with so much emphasis placed upon aural and visual representation the notion of what it means to be an effective, "anointed" preacher is radically altered. Academic acumen and intellectual engagement are rendered impractical at best and antithetical to success at worst. All we have to do is to reflect upon why it is that many preachers spend more time and money on their wardrobes than on their personal libraries. (I have been inside of the offices of several prominent ministers who have walk-in closets full of "alternate outfits" in their personal quarters, while having only a row or two of books—often solely the various volumes of biblical commentaries—neatly situated behind their desks.) Or, is it not strange that homiletic emphasis is disproportionately placed upon proper timing and voice inflection as opposed to historical, sociological, or theological reflection? To be sure, these particular areas of ethical interrogation were present before the rise of the electronic church phenomenon in regard to the black preaching tradition. The autonomous nature of black congregational life, coupled with the emphasis placed upon the rhythmically spoken "word," has always been fertile soil to cultivate generation after generation of "jacklegs." However, it appears that the saturation of mass-mediated images exacerbates rather than ameliorates the negative aspects of African American Christian practices. Moreover, in a society wherein both educational training and intellectual activity are regarded as being in the service of the greater goal of personal advancement and pecuniary reward, merely looking and sounding the part can propel one further within the pulpits of the airwaves. Let's face it, this is what the fetishizing of images at the hands of mass-mediated society will do. That which is considered aesthetically impressive will have far greater value in the commercialized video age. In a society oriented toward MTV and BET it is better to look and dance like Beyonce and P. Diddy than to sing like Aretha or Luther.

In terms of the superstitious account of religious faith that is symptomatic of the phenomenon such as that described in Jeffrey Stout's account of contemporary forms of Black Nationalism, it seems that this miraculous rendering of the divine, particularly in the form of health and wealth theology, functions as a "gospel of velleities."[18] Those who face ostensibly insurmountable odds and immutable social conditions are able to find hope in this fantasized rhetoric of health and wealth. Despite the often ahistorical social analysis and theological concupiscence that renders God as a "sugar daddy," the cathartic release in the forms of visceral, joy-laden cries are socially understandable, if not theologically acceptable. The televangelists' clarity concerning the fight between good and evil, the scapegoating of social ills and injustices upon the cosmic forces of evil, and the bombastic declarations of God's ability to instantaneously "defeat and deliver" represent within evangelical circles what Stout refers to as a "rhetoric of excess."

Finally, it is around this rhetoric that the insular, imagined communities are formed.[19] We cannot help but imagine that this superstitious rhetoric of excess that pulls individuals into these imagined communities constructed upon theological velleities is deceitful at best and hegemonic at worst. Yet it is evident that this type of superstitious, mythic amplification of good and evil, not to mention the scapegoating of individuals and groups who are the victims of injustice themselves, truncates the types of intellectual and democratic discourse that is integral to societal transformation. Further, the revisionist, ahistorical, and contextualless social analysis that is essential to constructing a superstitious rhetoric of excess further codifies regimes of truth that are recalcitrant toward intellectual reflection.

Still, we are forced to wonder (aside from tapping into the patriarchal and homophobic sensibilities characteristic of black Christian practices) why this phenomenon—along with its theological ineptitude that has historically been associated with the religious right—has been welcomed with such a warm embrace by the new black middle class. Psychologically speaking, this religious phenomenon may appeal to the dual, paradoxical anxieties of avoidance and acceptance that have perennially plagued black people. The anxiety of avoidance, which can be interpreted as seeking to avoid conflict with the white dominant society, is consistent with both the accommodationist and nationalist approaches to white supremacy. Figures such as Booker T. Washington, Joseph H. Jackson, and Elijah Muhammad are classic examples of individuals and movements that would rather adjust to prevailing systems—either by acceptance or outright rejection—than offer a critical challenge to structures of injustice and inequality. The anxiety of acceptance has been demonstrated throughout the nineteenth and twentieth centuries as black people have fought relentlessly to be considered a part of American society—that is, as co-contributors toward a multiracial democracy. This profound desire of acceptance is witnessed in Du Bois's clarion call to "lift the veil," in Langston Hughes's "I, too, Sing America," in Baldwin's agape-laced *par'hesia* (bold, courageous speech), and Martin Luther King Jr.'s articulation of his dream.

In the case of this most recent religious phenomenon, I see in the black middle class the avoidance tendency at work among those who seek to transcend the social meaning of their minority status—that is, those who disassociate themselves from all signifiers that connote traditional "blackness." For these individuals who have moved up the social ladder surpassing their parents and grandparents, the seemingly antiquated organizations such as the NAACP and the local Baptist church are regarded as lifestyle relics of the "old Negro." However, insecurities abound among members of the black middle class concerning their fragile, delusive state, as often they are two paychecks away from bankruptcy or are living under the oppressive yoke of debt in order to finance their exorbitant lifestyles. Equally, these same individuals are insecure about their intellectual and professional credentials in relation to the dominant society. Anything too "black" is looked upon with disdain, while too "white" is viewed with fear and insecurity. As a result, like E. Franklin Frazier's characterization of the mythic black bourgeoisie, many of these individuals end up meandering spiritually within a lonely valley situated between two worlds that are both avoided.

This being the case, it is logical to conclude that contemporary forms of neoevangelicalism with their themes of racial reconciliation and, in some instances, racial effacement strike a harmonious chord with many members of the black middle class. We could even go so far as to say that within these neoevangelical circles, once solely occupied by the religious right, African Americans are a desired commodity due both to the talent and success of black religious leaders and to the fund-raising potential of their African American constituencies. Moreover, cultural nationalism, in the form of the theological sampling of the American dream and God-sanctioned upward mobility and economic prosperity, can also be viewed as particularly attractive to those needing to reconcile their diffidence in relation to their race, their uncertainty as it relates to their success, and their frustrations concerning their inability to live up to their idealized imagining of themselves as racially transcended Horatio Alger success stories in America.

Unfortunately, in too many instances, these latter frustrations are projected upon individuals who may possibly remind church members of the very things that they are not or do not possess. This projection takes place in the form of a "spiritual niggerization." It can be seen in the manner in which some church members theologically place the poor, homosexuals, and even women (read feminists) outside of the "will of God." Again, this often amounts to nothing more than the poor reminding the nouveau-riche that they are financially insecure and possibly in debt; gay men reminding black women that with every birthday her chances of marriage dwindle; or successful and independent women reminding black men in America of their insecure positioning. Yet, rather than call into question the hegemonic practices of the dominant society that contribute to each of the aforementioned examples of black disillusionment and despair, televangelists preach a message of spiritual passivity cloaked in aggressive phraseology that only serves to reproduce the very systems of repression and then the subsequent projections that will keep individuals attempting to "Watch this! Watch this!"[20]

A clear example of the reproduction of systems of repression can be found among the largest contingent within the African American faith community—the group that T. D. Jakes has had particular success in attracting. The reification of traditional family values with male authority figures resonates with African American women who have been reared to desire a "knight in shining armor." This espoused ideal, associated with biblical truth, offers a mental "carrot" of hope that they can chase until the day "their chance is gonna come." This constantly professed ideal, which for many is embodied in the person of their pastor, provides a psychological escape from the particular realities they face at home, including physical and psychological abuse, economic instability, and feelings of depression associated with loneliness.

Moreover, this offers additional reasons why African American women are particularly likely to accept fundamentalism's homophobic sensibilities. Black women often comment on how gay men are "just a shame" to the African American community. Yet, they are a "shame" for different reasons than Jerry Falwell or Pat Robertson might believe. Black women do not see a sinner as much as they see the loss of a potential mate. This holds true particularly in major metropolitan cities such as New York, Atlanta, and Los Angeles where gay black males comprise a disproportionate amount of the urban professional class, from which comes the oft-recited, frustrated declaration, "All the good men are either married or gay." Unfortunately, rather than black women fighting against their own "spiritual niggerization" under the oppressive yokes of patriarchal dominance, they cast their energies toward the niggerization of gay males. (Lesbians are rarely, if ever, brought up in African American evangelical communities.)

In sum, I believe that the resistance by the electronic church phenomenon to critical, reflective thought can be traced to its henotheistic roots. The phenomenon is constructed upon adherents who are able to place their trust in the dramatized, dogmatic equivocations of charismatic personalities. The "word," which is transmitted via technological mediums and embodied by the constructed narrative of the preacher, is held up as an absolute value from whence individuals in turn are able to find their own source of self-worth. Trust is placed in what is perceived as a center of value. Such passive trust is transformed into active loyalty toward a particular ministry, personality, or cultural worldview. As a result, adherents are unable to raise a viable critique against these systems that they have situated as their value center, because to do so is to challenge their own self-worth. Therefore, faith, as represented by the henotheistic cultural nationalism of the electronic church, becomes nothing more than a great lie that we cannot productively live within but fear that we cannot live without. In the words of Baldwin, faith becomes simply "a mask for hatred and self-hatred and despair."[21] For this reason it is time for those of us committed to the liberating power of the radical other in general, and the potency found within the freedom of black preaching in particular, to raise the stage curtains of mass-mediated faith. In doing so we can expose the smoke and mirrors that assist the ideological state apparatuses of America's illusions. If not, we will continue to produce intelligent profiteers who are masters of today while we intellectually abort the *par'hesian* prophets who can offer us a glimpse of a better tomorrow.

Notes

1 Du Bois, *The Souls of Black Folk*, 494.

2 See Grant, *White Women's Christ and Black Women's Jesus*.

3 For an important essay concerning the naming process of African American female bodies, see Spillers, "Mama's Baby, Papa's Maybe" in *Black, White*

and in Color. Further, I am being descriptive in this analysis as "God's lead-ing lady," "anointed woman of God," and "Daddy's little girl" are appellations commonly employed by T. D. Jakes (two of the three are titles of his books) to describe God's relationship with African American women. Obviously, seri-ous critique can be levied against the feminization of black women and the upholding of patriarchal systems of dominance that are inherent in Jakes's own designations. Unfortunately, I cannot adequately engage this problem in depth during the course of this essay.

4 For a comprehensive introduction to the electronic church phenomenon in America, see Hoover, *Mass Media Religion*; Horsfield, *Religious Television*; and Schultze, *Televangelism and American Culture*.

5 "The New Mega Churches," *Ebony*, December 2001.

6 Gustav Niebuhr, "Where Religion Gets a Big Dose of Shopping-Mall Culture," *New York Times*, April 16, 1995, 1:1.

7 Schultze, *Televangelism and American Culture*, 220.

8 Lincoln and Mamiya, *The Black Church in the African American Experience*, 6.

9 Weber, *The Theory of Social and Economic Organization*, 329.

10 My words here are in reference to Paul's personal defense directed toward the church in Galatia: "For I want you to know, brothers and sisters, that the gospel that was proclaimed by me is not of human origin; for I did not receive it from a human source, nor was I taught it, but I received it through a revela-tion of Jesus Christ" (Galatians 1:11–12).

11 Schultze, *Televangelism and American Culture*, 30.

12 To be sure, I understand that in many ways this is perfectly consistent with both Pentecostal and neo-Pentecostal practices. The argument could be made that these traditions situate better than other traditions with advanced forms of media.

13 Schultze, *Televangelism and American Culture*, 206.

14 Hofstadter, *Anti-Intellectualism in American Life*, 25.

15 Said, *Representations of the Intellectual*, 11.

16 Mays, *The Negro's God*, 97–161.

17 Hoover, *Mass Media Religion*, 238.

18 Stout, *Democracy and Tradition*, 52–53.

19 For instance, the oft-quoted scripture that undergirds the prosperity gospel movement is Proverbs 13:22: "The wealth of the sinner is laid up for the righ-teous." Obviously, this formulation begs the question of who can be defined as the righteous. The producers of the electronic church phenomenon provide a few answers. Often preachers via their prayers and sermons preface posi-tive declarations with phrases such as, "All those here under the sound of my voice." In essence, anyone who participates in the captivating power of the preaching moment is rendered as part of the righteous. Clearly, we can see the ways in which this would promote church attendance, the increased com-modification of sermon-related products, and overall fidelity to the ministry.

Another means, already alluded to, is through the financial investing in the ministry as a covenant partner. For example, "if you can stand to be blessed," T. D. Jakes invites individuals to become a member of the "Bishop's Circle" for an initial contribution of five hundred dollars and a subsequent contribution of a thousand dollars annually. Being part of this select group affords its members reserve seating at conferences and events as well as a monthly letter from Jakes "sharing his heart and updating you on how God is changing lives through television." Finally, one may become a part of the "righteous" by spiritually submitting oneself to the authority of a pastoral leader. In the words of Bishop Eddie L. Long, "You recognize who your DADDY is!"

20 The phrase "Watch this, Watch this," is a commonly employed trope of Bishop Eddie L. Long, senior pastor of the twenty-five-thousand-member New Birth Missionary Baptist Church in metropolitan Atlanta.

21 Baldwin, *The Fire Next Time*, 53.

Joseph De León

◙

RESPONSE TO THE ESSAY BY JONATHAN WALTON

The points of convergence or commonality that appear to predominate in the essay by Jonathan Walton and my own essay that follows tend to relate in general to the respective themes of communality, particularly to its structural and dynamic spirituality of interdependence and more generally to relationality as an ontological modality. For both African Americans and Latinos and Latinas this all-pervasive sense of communality occupies a specific place in their respective cosmologies; in point of fact it is for African Americans an existential verity. Pierre Erny, in *Childhood and Cosmos: The Social Psychology of the Black African Child*, says that for Africans the cosmos is "like a spider web: its least element cannot be touched without making the whole vibrate. Everything is connected, interdependent." Indeed, the quiddity of interconnectedness is not just a condition or mode of being but a life force or a vitality that pervades all of nature so that everything that exists does so by virtue of this constant oscillatory wave that flows through and unifies all things.

For Latinos and Latinas, and especially for Mexican American Catholics, the exploration of the importance of community is couched in a dialogical language that discusses a unique interpretation of the conundrum of the particular and the universal. It is in community that Latinos and Latinas understand, appreciate, and truly grasp what it means to be an individual. The horizontal border that is believed to exist at the junction between the immanent and the transcendent is seen as accessed through a peculiar Catholic understanding of an individual's relationship to the divine. The piercing of this "veil of Maya" is through what Catholics term "sacramentality"—a conceptualization of an at once metaphysical and physical experience that through an emphasis on the incarnational nature of one's relationship with the divine sees reality as either, or, and also both.

In Roberto Goizueta's work *Caminemos con Jesús* (We walk with Jesus) he shares a tender moment during an observation he made at the San Fernando Cathedral in San Antonio, Texas, during Holy Week. He describes the experience of how one devoted soul whose faith is a communally lived reality encounters God, Mary, and Jesus directly: "When at San Fernando, an elderly Mexican woman approaches the Crucified Jesus to plant a gentle kiss on his feet, or reaches to touch Mary's veil during a procession, there is little doubt that, for this elderly woman, Jesus and Mary are truly present here. These religious statues or figures are not mere representations of a reality completely external to them; rather they are the concrete embodiment, in time and space, of Jesus and Mary. These are, in short, sacramental images: natural, particular entities that mediate, embody, and reveal a supernatural, universal, absolute reality."[1]

Implicit in this definition of sacrament is the central notion of relationship—that is, communality. This is a relational inference of an aesthetical component, expressed within a construct of praxis, and it is indicative of the similarity of perspectives envisioned by Anglos and Latinos and Latinas alike. It is an inference that helps us to understand the sublime yet essential meaning of communality within the Latino cosmology.

To the extent that Latinos and Latinas participate in deep human relationships of love and caring, they also participate in and see the forms and rhythms of divine beauty in worship. Similarly, Latinos and Latinas use performance relatedness to understand and vivify human-to-human contact and relatedness and, like African Americans, to gain access to a more clearly perceived vision of God's experience and love of unity. In my essay I attempt to address the anagogical dynamics of a theology of relatedness and drama by arguing that at specific moments of the dramatic process we are drawn into a relational moment with the divine that is intrinsic and inheres to our undeniably communal nature as images of a triune, relational God. For both African Americans and Latinos and Latinas the sense of community is therefore the integrating linchpin that sustains and operates at a subliminal level to give rise to what Martin Buber called the I-Thou relationship, albeit for African Americans and Latinos and Latinas it is writ large as I, Thou, and We.

When envisaged from this particular point of view it is easy to understand why the elements of rhythm, physicality, and congregation play such a major role in the makeup and making of megachurches, as well as why the signatory orations of praise and worship are at the core of their services. These stylistically celebratory events appear to be driven by the powerful concept of flow and vitalism that is infused in the African American "soul" and is the substratum upon which charismatic individuals attempt to evoke the spirit of relationship and interconnection between the congregants and the divine. However, whether their efforts shatter the illusions of separateness and fuse their listeners into one community of believers appears to be very much in doubt, especially when the intent and essence of this unifying life force is to focus and thrive on true and authentic relationship and genuine interconnection. What also renders questionable this effort to engender true communality and dialogical relationship is the imposed emphasis and focus on materialism (the so-called health and wealth philosophy) against a communal and individual search for the spiritual gifts of grace and a recognition of the true relationship between creature and creator. Such an emphasis, it would appear, only serves to further erode the flow of moral authority based on indigenous kinship and stultifies the dynamic energy behind the concept of a unifying vitalism.

One particular point of difference (although it may be more of a sense of style) is how African Americans and Latinos and Latinas instantiate the notion of physicality within religious observances and celebrations—notably in liturgical praxis. It is true that whereas some evangelical Latinos and Latinas come very close to a form and praxis of faith belief that is similar in style and form to that of the African American megachurch and the oratorical style inherent therein, it is due more probably to mestizaje (cultural hybridity) or racial miscibility than to a particular cultural style or religious practice heritage. Within the Latino and Latina community those individuals who come from Puerto Rico, Cuba, or the Caribbean share a rich heritage with African Americans as well as some of the mainland indigenous peoples (albeit perhaps not to the same extent). Again, in addressing the issue from my particular perspective as a Mexican American Catholic male I perceive this difference in celebratory style as a liturgical praxis whose defining characteristic could be described as almost Asian in its expression—that is, as a preference and reverence for silence as opposed to the spoken word.

In my first reading of Walton's essay I felt that he was engaged in propounding the question of whether or not the current megachurch phenomena (characterized as charismatic, icon-driven, evangelistic theater) was properly fulfilling its historic role of theopoesis as opposed to mythopoesis: that is, the making of theological thought—the reflection upon the divine will so necessary before communal praxis—as opposed to the making of heroes to satisfy the spiritual and religious needs of a people still struggling for self-identity. I agree with him that both are necessary and that what we are witnessing is merely an adjustment—namely the development of a certain art form within a religious structure that in time will find its true purpose.

However, where the difference lies—and what may probably be a good point for future reflection and dialogue—is the question of when and where does the place for silence exist in the overall scheme of things. Pondering, as an attitude and an expression of faith, could properly be described as patiently and quietly holding something within one's soul, "complete with all the tension that it brings."[2] Pondering, and the notion of silent receptivity for receiving the word of God, should not be considered a passive state. Indeed, the proper attitude is expressed most clearly by the Virgin Mary, who is characterized by Hans Urs von Balthasar as fruitfully receptive, not passive, but representing "the highest act that a creature can perform in love of God, [a] firm, responsible readiness to accept the will of God with all its consequences."[3] Mary, especially in her representation as the Virgen de Guadalupe, typifies for Mexican American Catholics the very model of active passivity. We are, therefore, in obedient faith to be receptive to receiving the imprint of Christ in our hearts and the truth of God poured out upon us—filling us, molding us, and preparing us to be fruitful. It is not *apatheia* that we are to seek but rather true *kenosis* and the indwelling of the Holy Spirit—either in the celebration of joy within a community seeking first the will of God and the coming of the kingdom—or in the silence of the church at prayer.

Notes

1 Goizueta, *Caminemos con Jesús*, 65.
2 Roiheiser, *The Holy Longing*, 220.
3 Von Balthasar, *The Theology of Karl Barth*, 354.

Joseph De León

▣

TELENOVELAS AND TRANSCENDENCE:

SOCIAL DRAMAS AS THEOLOGICAL THEATER

Drama theory and religious experience are generally considered to be two existentially contrasting spheres of inquiry and insight. However, the fact remains that both drama and religion work to assist individuals to achieve a form of transcendence beyond the self to a vision of the divine or the mystical. In theological terms, for the practitioner of a religious faith this transportation into the realm of the ineffable may result in ecstasy, in an epiphany, or in a sense of apotheosis. For the playgoer, or in this case, for the viewer of telenovelas, these same psycho-emotional impacts, best understood within the Aristotelian category known as "catharsis," makes the theatrical experience practically indistinguishable from the theological experience of *cultus*, the system of religious performance.

This essay is a study of how the telenovela as a dramatic art form fosters, engenders, and supports a heterocentric community of mutual beneficence that is transported anagogically "into that spiritual realm where we behold mysterious and supernatural visions" by virtue of the medium of the theatrical performance.[1] In this project I address a unique anagogical dynamic using the rhetoric of a theology of relatedness and drama; that is, a theology of aesthetics that when combined with a contextual and hermeneutical approach reveals the notion that at specific moments of the dramatic process we are drawn into a relational moment with the divine that is intrinsic and inheres to our undeniably communal nature as images of a triune and relational God. In this inquiry I dwell briefly on the notion of interrelatedness, particularly as heterocentric community, and then I expand the scope to include an explication of the special sense of community relative to the Latino and Latina, with an emphasis on how this particular notion of relationship discloses a sense of belongingness that captures the essence of the perichoretic trinitarian unity. In so doing I conduct a brief, probative review of the dramaturgical, theological, and theo-dramatic elements that, within the complex of human interactions that is the telenovela, disclose a coherent vision of the absolute—a glint of light, reflecting off a darkened glass, that mirrors a faint image of the community "out of which it was born."[2]

The Telenovela as Drama

The noted film and media studies scholar Ana M. López defines the telenovela as "an essentially melodramatic narrative mode, with roots that can be traced back to prior (Latin American and international) melodramatic forms (in the theater, serial literature, etc.) and their re-inscription and recirculation by the mass media in the cinema and radio." She further notes that the form "ceaselessly offers its audience dramas of recognition and re-cognition by locating social and political issues in personal and familial terms and thus making sense of an increasingly complex world."[3] The telenovela is therefore a unique form of melodrama, one in which enumerable subplots move along at a brisk pace and various and sundry characters (usually poor or marginalized individuals) are able to persevere, and eventually triumph, in spite of obstacles such as social class, family ties, conflicts of interest, and so on. In all of them ultimately there is a happy ending (usually at the concluding chapters built up through agonizing months of situations that go back and forth) where everyone is reconciled, the good guys win and morality and goodness triumph, and the villains get punished. Whether filmed on location in an impoverished Mexico City neighborhood or amid the vast landscape of a wealthy and aristocratic Argentinean cattle ranch, telenovelas portray universal situations that provide for their viewers a feeling of identification with a story inspired by real life without being a carbon copy of it. The genre of the telenovela is not a Latin American invention as such; instead, it is merely the logical extension of the serial narrative that has existed in oral and written form since time immemorial, such as Homer's *Iliad* and *Odyssey*, the Icelandic *eddas*, the German *Niebelungenlied*, Charles Dickens's *A Tale of Two Cities*, Tolstoy's *War and Peace*, Gabriel García Márquez's *One Hundred Years of Solitude*, Isabel Allende's *House of the Spirits*, and the Bible.

The telenovela is unique, however, in that it is one of the most popular and resilient forms of storytelling ever devised. Indeed, quite literally at this very moment tens of millions of people are watching one form or another of a television serial drama.[4]

Around 1930 Colgate and Lever Brothers, the well-known makers of laundry detergents and other household cleaning products, discovered that serial narratives had the power to hold captive large numbers of housewives who listened assiduously to these episodic melodramas on their radios. The identification of these companies as major sponsors for the serial programs gave rise to the name "soap operas," a term that persisted even when televised serials were introduced in the 1950s. Not long thereafter the practices and technology for developing and disseminating serial narrative programs spread to Central and Latin America where, for various reasons, mainly economic, they became provincially innovative cultural art forms that ultimately surpassed in popularity, if not technical quality, the original creations from whence they sprang.

The telenovela today is an extremely popular and hugely successful artistic and commercial enterprise. As testament to its power to lure and captivate large numbers of viewing audiences, during Ramadan in January 2008 some of the mosques in Abidjan decided to bring forward their prayer time. This singularly unprecedented gesture saved thousands of the faithful from the painful dilemma of whether to do their religious duty or miss the latest episode of *Marimar*, a Mexican TV melodrama that had turned the whole country into telenovelas addicts. Meanwhile, on the other side of the planet, hundreds of thousands of Yugoslavs held their collective breath so as not to miss the tiniest detail of a Venezuelan soap opera entitled *Kassandra*. "We know Kassandra's innocent and we want her trial stopped," the townspeople of Kucevo in southeastern Serbia wrote to the Venezuelan government, with a copy also sent to Serbian President Slobodan Milosevic.

In Moscow following the broadcast of the final episode of *The Rich Also Cry*, a headline in the *Moscow Tribune* queried "Will *The Rich Also Cry* Beat the Congress?" The article went on to assert that "of all the schmaltzy soaps currently presented by Russian television, this one has been a *ne plus ultra* hit." Similarly, the *Moscow Times* contended that "when the film started, streets became desolate, crowds gathered in stores selling TV sets, tractors stopped in the fields and guns fell silent on the Azerbaijani-Armenian front."[5] In an article published by *Moskovsky Komsomoletz*, a hypothesis was voiced that the series had been more effective in increasing life expectancy in Russia than any health-promoting program because old people couldn't bear to die before they knew how the series ended.

And in the early 1980s, *La Esrava Isaura* (Isaura the slave), a Brazilian historical telenovela set in the colonial period with a vaguely abolitionist theme, was sold widely throughout Latin America (its Spanish-dubbed version even aired on Univisión in the United States), Europe, and Asia. In Poland it was named the best television program of the decade; it caused Cuban officials to reschedule meetings to avoid competing with it; and it resulted in a triumphant world tour for Lucelia Santos (the lead actress) who even in China was feted like royalty.[6]

Needless to say, in Latin America the telenovela is considered to be one of the most important—if not the most important—television program genres. As an enormously successful national and transnational cultural phenomenon, the telenovela has been the number-one catalyst for the successful development of the Latin American television industry, a status it achieved through years of successfully cross-breeding the latest in audio-visual technology with the stories, tales, and legends that form an integral part of the cultural life of the people of Latin America.

It is a given that telenovelas have had an enormous impact on the national economy of the states that generate them. In studies of the development of powerful TV-based conglomerates in Mexico and Brazil, for example, the popularity of telenovelas has played a crucial role in their history and continue to be a major factor in their establishment as global media power brokers. Beginning in the 1970s telenovelas were no longer considered to be, as López notes, "cheaply-produced filler material for day-time programming with content directly determined by advertisers and sponsors." Instead, they "began to successfully compete against the great US serials (like *Dallas*) for prime-time audiences. The telenovela (along-side the *show de auditorium*) proved that national productions were attractive to audiences and could replace prime-time canned US programs."[7]

Then in the late 1970s and through the 1980s the telenovela became prime export material. Within Latin America the trade in telenovelas has been controlled by Mexican, Argentine, and Venezuelan producers. In the 1990s, however, Telemundo, Univisión, and other producers challenged the status quo and began to establish their own international distribution networks. Thus in the 1990s it was not unusual to find as López notes, "Latin American telenovelas from nations (and television systems) as disparate as Brazil and Venezuela in the US (on the Spanish-language networks Univisión and Telemundo), Europe (especially in Spain, but also in

Italy, France, Great Britain, and eastern European countries), Asia (including China), and Africa."[8]

The reach of this unique art form has found millions of devotees around the world—all of them searching for and finding something fundamentally appealing in it. But what is it about the telenovela that is so addictive to a widely diverse viewing community that includes Russian cabinet members, Chinese street sweepers, Brazilian fishmongers, and Muslim grandmothers, uncles, children, and young couples? To what can we attribute this singular devotion to an art form that has been decried as so much pap by its detractors? I contend that the reason that telenovelas are so popular with such an eclectic range of audiences is that they function as a *locus theologicus* for entering into communion with the divine. The telenovela, like its mirror image religious ritual, serves to bring together into community those who seek to find order in a universe of ambiguities.

Community and melodrama are thus the twin driving forces—the human need for relating and relationality—that make and sustain the *telenovela* as the metaphorical portal for transcendence and transformation. As Jesús Martín-Barbero points out: "In Latin America, whether it be the form of *tango* or *bolero*, Mexican cinema, or soap opera, the melodrama speaks of a *primordial sociality*, whose metaphor continues to be the thick, censored plot of the tightly woven fabric of family relationships. In spite of its devaluation by the economy and politics, this sociality lives on culturally, and from its locus, people, by 'melodramatizing' everything, take their own form of revenge on the abstraction imposed by cultural dispossession and the commercialization of life."[9]

The community that figures so prominently in this discussion comes about because of the unique episodic form of the telenovela. Episodicity is the literary device whereby the imposition of institutionally controlled gaps in the narrative structure of the telenovela forces the viewer to anticipate what might happen next. This created indeterminacy, however, also serves to invite anticipatory public and private discourse, thus creating a community of expectant and concerned audience members who both collectively and individually review, share, and otherwise vicariously live through the sufferings and misfortunes of the characters and develop a true sense of complicity with them. Nora Mazziotti says that viewers faithfully follow the mishaps, injustices, dangers, and threats that the characters endure for months before "savoring with them the ultimate triumph of love and justice—observing that in the make-believe world, and maybe nowhere else, there really is justice—for all. That's something to be happy about."[10]

As a genre, soap operas can generally be categorized as either "open" or "closed" serial narratives. North American, British, and Australian serials are considered open in that, as Robert Allen notes, there is "no ultimate moment of resolution, there is no central indispensable character . . . to whose fate viewer interest is indissolubly linked. Instead there is a changing community of characters who move in and out of viewer attention and interest."[11] In open serials individuals may die or be removed from their role as a continuing part of the saga. Then at some point, conveniently enough, they may be resurrected (at times literally) either in the form of a plot device where the character may be brought back as in a flashback sequence or as someone who has been in an amnesiac fog but is now returned to his or her loved ones after many years of absence. The size of an open serial community along with the many complex relationships among its characters makes for a narrative indeterminacy that requires a specific device germane to the soap opera—the reiteration of important events. One program may be almost entirely devoted to the retelling of an important piece of narrative information; that is, where one character overhears someone telling someone else, who then tells another character, who telephones yet another with the news, and so forth. To infrequent viewers such reiteration does nothing to advance the story line and thus creates the impression that "nothing ever happens."

As Allen notes, however, to the informed and experienced devotee the business of "who tells whom is just as important as what is being related," since "each retelling affects relations among the community of characters."[12] Therefore the open serial requires that the plot line be carried forth not so much by action as by talk. The emphasis is on verbalizations, which makes important adjustments or possible alterations within each particular soap opera world. This is why so many of the characters have professions where dialogue is important (e.g., doctors, nurses, police officers, etc.) and where they are seen in locations where "talk" occurs (e.g., restaurants, hospitals, lawyer's or corporate offices, etc.). As a rule, in soaps in the United States most of these characters tend to be middle- to upper-middle-class individuals, while in Britain serial narratives represent the working-class social world where the rule of thumb is still dialogue, although in the British soap operas *Coronation Street* and *EastEnders* the most important location is the local pub.

The Latin American telenovela is structured as a closed form of serials—that is, they come to a terminus point, although reaching this point may not take place for several months or even two hundred episodes. The usual trajectory of the narrative plot can be divided into three parts, which according to Allen goes something like this: "The initial episodes introduce a variety of characters and open up a number of plot lines. In the next twenty or thirty episodes two or three major themes emerge, central characters are defined in greater detail, and the plot lines are further complicated. The final third of the telenovela is devoted to bringing the major plot lines to some form of resolution."[13]

The notion of closure, in addition to differentiating the Latin American telenovela from soap operas in the United States, allows the telenovela to also exploit personalization; that is, as López notes, "the individualization of the social world, as an epistemology."[14] This aspect of the telenovela works within the cultural context of how Latinos and Latinas perceive community and the high value that they place upon the issue of relationality. Telenovelas locate social and political issues and concerns within both a personal and a communal context, and they permit their viewers the privilege of looking back and revisiting—either individually or communally or both—the completed serial and to impose on it moral judgments and ideological order. This opportunity to recognize the completed text thus affords those who would be powerless otherwise to do so in today's increasingly complex and hegemonic world a chance to make sense of it. As a people who have been historically oppressed and marginalized, Latinos and Latinas can readily identify with those who are portrayed in like manner, thus insuring an almost guaranteed affinity with their plight and cosmological outlook. Anthropologically speaking, the indigenous mindset of the Latino and Latina searches for the "balanced" viewpoint—the signs and symbols that indicate that justice has been served, that wrongs have been righted, and that peace and harmony prevail. Moreover, these signs of harmony are further equated with a harmony that is collective; that is, humanity as a whole is in line with the harmony of the universe and the divine.

Telenovelas present a contrived reality where unexpected events such as meeting someone accidentally, a decision made without much thought, or an unprecedented bit of good luck or a meaningless tragedy all appear to be part of a larger pattern of some "hidden" moral order. This prompts the viewer to ask questions about each turn of events and to try to find the balanced outcome that is required to return to a harmonious world. However, because the narratives are presented in a controlled, episodic manner, there is ample time for the individual to ponder each twist of the plot and to enter into discourse with family members, neighbors, coworkers, or with the broader concept of community that is now made possible through the Internet. This wider cast of the intertextual dialogue now makes possible a wider range of interpretations and creates a community of dialogue where there was not one before. As a result telenovelas are today creating communities of interpretation on a global scale. The particular search for a balanced world—a world of peace—becomes universalized.

Telenovelas as Theological Theater

Theater brings people together by its very nature—that is, theater is communal. It is an interdisciplinary art and a collaboration of ideas and talents. A designer has vision. An actor speaks a playwright's words. The audience adds its own energy and rhythm . . . and then harmony. All of these elements intertwine together into a powerful shared experience. Theater is primarily about collaboration because it is the most communal art. Epistemologically, theater enables us to reach the universal by understanding the specific. We come to an understanding of the self in the language and space around us, and in that examination we find certain truths. Once we find those truths they become human truths. They are universal in that they speak to all of us. Therefore, it is the function of theater to present us with a grand view; to allow us to have an identity of place and to see the world and be part of it in a much bigger way without losing that sense of who we are and without feeling that we are made small by the greatness of that expanse.

From a theological viewpoint the telenovela as theatrical performance is refulgent with the power to metaphysically transform and translocate, and it invites those present, both performers and audience, to enter imaginatively into the drama and, coincidentally, into the lives of the other. The telenovela, therefore, has the unique ability to exist as both a variant of theological discourse and as religious experience—a phenomenological engagement that is made possible by the paradoxically ambiguous nature of drama itself. Drama works because it engages two realities simultaneously; the pretend world of the characters and the script and the everyday world beyond the stage from which the actors and the audience are fleetingly removed. Juxtaposed in this way, two realities cannot help but enter into dialogue. Thus different entities, viewpoints, worldviews, or cosmologies can coexist in dialectical relationship by virtue of the imaginative power of drama to hold two distinct realities in dynamic tension.

This is why I view a theological aesthetics as the proper approach for the resolution of this issue. Indeed, this method more than any other is capable of addressing theoretical issues concerning theology and the arts synthetically as opposed to analytically. As synthetic or relational this method privileges a language and point of view that is more applicable to discussing the ambiguity of the aesthetic, theological, and philosophical issues at hand. As such it is a procedure that more closely mirrors the intuitive sense of the human heart without necessarily eschewing the value and necessity of the analytical processes of the human intellect. It is the method that Alex García-Rivera utilizes to ask the defining question of what constitutes a theology of aesthetics, as noted in the following: "Asking the question, what moves the human heart?, I believe brings us closer to the mysterious experience of the truly beautiful, an experience that transcends geological space and prehistoric time, an experience that holds the most persuasive claim to being what has become an aporia in our day, the real universal."[15]

It is precisely this present-day sense of aporia, as evidenced in the multiple queries launched by the events of a telenovela, that move its viewers to enter into the profoundly communal experience of what can only be characterized as a life-affirming faith in the eudaimonia, the elated sense of happiness that comes from seeing restless hearts reunited, villainous plots foiled, goodness and justice triumphant, and love conquering all. The telenovela is about the paradox of goodness, truth, and beauty revealed and veiled at the same time. What better way to approach this mystery than with the inductive tools of the imagination; it is the imagination, as García-Rivera reminds us, that allows "mystery to be made manifest to our senses and our intellect" and to allow our "senses and intellect to respond to mystery. . . . In other words, the imagination is the prime mover and movement of the human heart. . . . The imagination allows apophatic Beauty and the kataphatic beautiful to have an organic connection within the human heart. Thus the imagination becomes the apogee of Glory's parabolic path as it emerges out of mystery, becomes appropriated by the human heart, and, then, returns to its source. Glory's *exitus* becomes praise *reditus* through the imagination which represents the human heart. . . . In other words, the imagination has organic affinity to what is known as the *imago Dei*, the image of God."[16]

Driven by an abiding need for meaning—to connect time and space, experience and event, body and spirit, intellect and emotion—the perceptive participants in the world of the telenovela, who in their commitment to the principles of mutual beneficence, harmony, and balance in the world, image the imago Dei even more clearly. They begin to work through a series of steps by which they aim to reach the highest level of spirituality and desire to commune with God, joyfully conspiring to gain this contemplative vision of goodness, truth, love, beauty, and justice.

But to do so demands that they achieve the subliminal state of existence known as community. During this inchoate-like stage of the process the telenovela exists in two dimensions—as a theatrical performance for a perceptive and open audience and as a creation to inform the viewer of its anagogical powers. In the anagogical experience of the telenovela, those who commit to the fullest sense of community experience the deepest sense of reality, cohesiveness, and relationality. The special community of the theatrical experience then becomes the heteronomic gift to themselves, linking hope to memory. It is in this that they reimagine collectively the heavenly image of "Original Giving and Gift"—a transformation that inspires courage, enriches their celebration, and makes their transcendence possible.[17]

The telenovela ultimately becomes the creative space where a theology of drama and a theology of interrelatedness can manifest with the greatest resonance; it functions both as model of and for a dynamic form of the dramatic religious ritual where a perceptive audience can partake in an alternative paradigm for experiencing truth, beauty, justice, and solidarity. The telenovela devotee in his or her own process of reception, in moving toward the stage of the emergent mestizoized community of committed love, reacts, grows, and transforms in particular ways according to his or her own experience and religious points of view.

To the extent that viewers of the telenovela can experience the love of relationality through the experience of theatrical performance, they gain a greater sense of belongingness and a deeper appreciation of relatedness. As a result of their transcendence as they are held in thrall by the desire to experience the beauty of perfect justice, they feel a sense of being cleansed with awe and their heightened understanding enables them to better care for every being, thus enabling them to fulfill their need to seek perfect goodness by loving and serving their neighbor.

David Mamet, one of America's leading playwrights, agrees that theater is a communal art form. When one attends a theatrical performance, he says, one has to be willing to say, "We are all here to undergo a communion, to find out what the hell is going on in this world.' If you are not willing to say that, what you get is entertainment instead of art, and poor entertainment at that."[18] First-rate theater for Mamet is therefore also anagogical, albeit in a secularized sense, because it satisfies the human hunger for ordering the world into a cause-and-effect conclusion—an embodied journey from lie to truth and from arrogance to wisdom. Or, in the parlance of the telenovela: What is going to happen next? Who will win or lose? How will everything work out?

Community, Mamet observes, is built by the commitment of audience members to suspend their disbelief—to go to the same place that the author goes to for his or her inspiration: "In suspending their disbelief—in suspending their reason, if you will—for a moment, the viewers were rewarded. They committed an act of faith, or of submission. And like those who rise refreshed from prayers, their prayers were answered. For the purpose of the prayer was not, finally, to bring about intercession in the material world, but to lay down, for the time of the prayer, one's confusion and rage and sorrow at one's powerlessness."[19] This simple act of trust begins a series of events that ultimately draws the orderly, affronted mind of the perceiver of the drama to confront the awesome and to discover the hidden structure of another reality. In this endeavor, the rational mind cannot help. This is the realm of theater and religion. So the purpose of the theater, according to Mamet, is not to fix the social fabric and not to incite the less perceptive to wake up to reality, not to preach to the converted about the delights (or the burdens) of a middle-class life. The purpose of theater, like magic and like religion, is also, as García-Rivera alludes, to inspire cleansing awe.

The Nature of Community

In this essay I have been referencing a specific sense of "community." It is one that conveys a certain state of interrelatedness that best describes the particular kind of human association that aims to recover a view of the person-in-relation, and that neither submerges the person under the domination of others nor allows an individualistic free for all.

John MacMurray in his study on community, *Persons in Relation*, claims that an ideal community is one in which each individual cares for all others.[20] This claim, besides being somewhat audacious and startling, also runs counter to the inherited wisdom of theologies of sin and of secular ideologies of realism, not to mention undermining the notion of the value of individuality. Josiah Royce considers this polemic to be a problem of resolving the dialectical tension that exists as an uneven equilibrium between two mutually opposing forces of the individual will and the collective will. The solution, he asserts, is to resolve the tension related not only to the moral burden of the individual but also to the moral burden of the collective—in other words, to embrace his definition of community as one that interprets events one to the other.[21]

Royce's approach is philosophically pragmatic and lays out his terms for understanding interrelatedness within the context of his own understanding of the Christian concept of loyalty to a cause. It is valuable in being able to discern how the individual and the community can interrelate and not become subsumed one into the other. However, it is Catherine Mowry LaCugna who provides us with the special vision of interrelatedness in community that describes a specific form of engagement necessary for achieving transcendence within and through the theatrical experience of the telenovela; an understanding that more closely approximates Latino and Latina theological thought.

LaCugna's vision of community, like that of the Latino and Latina, is a matter of love, family, and authentic relationships of mutual beneficence. The centrality of her claim resides in the concept of the person—both divine and human. Community, she says, requires persons in community. It exists for the "sake of friendship and presupposes relationships built on love. Friendship results from persons who are free, who do not relate out of fear of the other or fear for self . . . What distinguishes a community from a society is that a community is a group of persons united in a common life who actually form 'fellowship' with each other. A society might organize around a common purpose, but the individuals within it are defined in terms of their function or purpose. The basic structure of the community is heterocentric; the focus is the other, not oneself."[22] Community, for LaCugna, is the heterocentric relationship of persons; that is, a relationship of communality and interrelatedness that "neither dissolves personal identity in an organic pool in which all individual gifts and traits are washed away, nor defines one primarily in terms of one's 'role' or function within a subsuming organic whole." This particular model of personal relationships is also one in which "the unique gifts of each person are celebrated and nurtured, and in which the celebration and nurturing of others are the primary intentions of all the members."[23]

LaCugna was a trinitarianist who, along with Jurgen Moltmann, Wolfhart Pannenberg, Duane Larson, and Eberhard Jungel, believed that relationship is internal to God's life. As such she maintained that "the doctrine of the Trinity affirms that the 'essence' of God is relational, other-ward, that God exists as diverse persons united in a communion of freedom, love, and knowledge. The insistence on the correspondence between *theo-*

logia and *oikonomia* means that the focus of the doctrine of the Trinity is the communion between God and ourselves."[24] Thus God is not only relational but, as the origin of being, God also made relationship ontological—a trait that all of God's creation shares. The analogous character of the divine relationship of three persons in one God, and the authentic form of relationship for which we should strive to have with one another, she insists, is the true reality and our common goal. God is innately communal in nature and form, and through the many manifestations of this communality—the organized nature of the universe, the necessarily structured forms of life, even the notion of form and symmetry in art, science, and philosophy—God attempts to model and communicate this necessity of communality and interrelatedness to us.

To connote the innate sense of relationality inherent in her communal concept of God, LaCugna prefers to use the term *perichoresis*, the eighth-century word employed by John Damascene, to properly express this paradox of the many and the one united together. In describing the divine "dance" of perichoretic persons, LaCugna informs us that "each divine person is irresistibly drawn to the other, taking his/her existence from the other, containing the other in him/herself, while at the same time pouring self out into the other. . . . While there is no blurring of the individuality of each person, there is also no separation. There is only the communion of love in which each person comes to be (in the sense of *hyparxeos*) what he/she is, entirely with reference to the other."[25] Therefore, communion, community, and mutuality is the natural state of God, and as creation is made in the image of God so should we image our true likeness to God—as community living altruistically in communion with the stranger, the neighbor, the other. By joining with and becoming like the "other" of God, we become divinized ourselves and thus in effect become what we model. Or, as expressed in common parlance, like tends toward like. LaCugna cites St. Paul in his letter to the Ephesians (2:18–22) to explain it thus: "For through [Jesus Christ] (who was God who is Love), both of us have access in the one Spirit to the Father. So then you are no longer strangers and aliens but you are citizens with all the saints and also members of the household of God, built upon the foundation of the apostles and prophets with Christ Jesus himself as the main cornerstone. In him the whole structure is joined together and grows into a holy temple in the Lord; in whom you also are built together spiritually into a dwelling place for God."[26]

LaCugna's understanding of "heterocentrism," her forward thinking about community, and especially her notions on the communal nature of God as Trinity appear to be in many respects analogous to the Latino concept of *teología en conjunto* (the doing of theology cooperatively in an environment of mutual respect and support). Both of these concepts by virtue of their focus on mutual heterocentrism—that is, as Frank Kirkpatrick notes, the "manifestation of the mutual receipt and exercise of gifts in which all are fulfilled precisely because all are givers and receivers at the same time, though in different respects"—support the key existential concepts I advance in this essay.[27]

The experience of theater also brings about this sense of fulfillment when all of the participants in the performance willingly enter into a relationship of mutual beneficence and are thus brought anagogically to the verge of glimpsing at least preliminary answers to questions about meaning. This fulfillment is a precondition necessary for anagogical movement as occurs, I contend, during the viewing of a telenovela.

Generally speaking the overall meaning of community for Latinos and Latinas resides in the notion that all existence is interrelated—that is, that relationship is cosmic in its scope and function. Community for Latinos and Latinas, as for LaCugna, is ontologically universal and existentially necessary. The Latino theologian Roberto Goizueta goes even further in elaborating this thesis of the existential communal nature of human existence by arguing that "there is no such thing as an isolated individual," inasmuch as an isolated individual is understood as one "who is not intrinsically defined by his or her relationship to others."[28] Goizueta maintains that without a relationship to others and to a community, the individual would never appropriate his or her own sense of self—that is, awareness as a particular entity with individual identity. Community is therefore the place where the individual is defined and constituted because of the relationships effected therein.

For Goizueta, "the assertion that personal identity is intrinsically relational, or given by others from 'outside,' is thus the corollary of his sacramental worldview which asserts that the identity of every concrete, particular entity is relational, or given by an Other from "outside."[29] This sense of community is therefore all pervasive in defining the complete and universal interrelation of the entire cosmos—both heaven and earth into one interrelational reality where as in any living organism each unit is integrally and intrinsically related one to the other.

This sense of interrelatedness in the Hispanic sense of community is not, as Ada María Isasi-Díaz asserts, "something added on, but the web of relationships constitutive of who we are."[30] Martin Buber, in *I and Thou*, supports a similar thesis and likens it to the defining act of recognizing oneself as a self and as a person during the initial encounter of a newborn and his or her mother. Prior to this encounter, Buber suggests, the child has no personal identity and no idea of "self" apart from its immediate environment. In other words, the newborn experiences whoever is in the environment as an extension of itself and vice-versa. However, at the moment of recognizing the other as an "other," the sense of self-consciousness begins to emerge and thus the possibility of being able to relate to another beyond this "self," now perceived as separate from the newly conceptualized notion of the "other." Or, as Buber so eloquently puts it, "Man becomes an I through a You."[31]

Goizueta also sees this as an affirmation of the individual's own sense of particularity, and further, that in affirming one's relationship to another particular individual one is also able to understand one's relationship to oneself—a further affirmation of one's own particularity. This is of immense significance for Goizueta, who bases his understanding of the importance of solidarity for Catholic Christians on the sacramental issues inherent in a community experiencing communality cosmically. He argues, rightly, that "every human person is a concrete, particular, and unique mediation of the universal"—that is, each human is a mediation of the universal humanity, or universal creation, and "in the last analysis, a unique mediation of the Absolute."[32] This concept, which intersubjectively relates the twin poles of the particular and universal into one intercommunicating entity, is the core of his belief that "when someone encounters me, they also encounter my parents, relatives, friends, my people, my community, as well as the God who created me and the earth which nourishes me."[33]

Goizueta makes it quite clear that his interpretation of this interrelationship is not biased by any sentimentalist sense of community, since by its very nature sentimentality connotes a certain type of individualism. More to the point, intrinsic interrelatedness is seen as another type altogether—that is, of a constitutive notion of community. In light of this view Goizueta cites Michael Sandel's Liberalism and the Limits of Justice as follows: "For on the sentimental conception, the good of community was limited to the communitarian aims and sentiments of antecedently individuated subjects, while on the constitutive conception, the good of community was seen to penetrate the person more profoundly so as to describe not just his feelings but a mode of self-understanding partly constitutive of his identity, partly definitive of who he was."[34]

Goizueta's community, which is constitutive of the self, can exude and respond to the personal warmth of emotion and sentimentality. But this does not mean that the community is dependent upon the generation of these feelings as the basis for its existence. The community is more realistically defined by "its ability to partially constitute the very identity of each individual member."[35] Here the parallel to Royce's mystical blending of the individual selves into the community where all are preserved as individuals yet united to that which they love becomes apparent.

To the extent that we participate in deep human relationships of love and caring we also participate and see the forms and rhythms of divine beauty in theatrical performance. When we use performance-relatedness to understand and vivify human to human relatedness we can more clearly perceive God's vision of unity. In the anagogical dynamics of a theology of relatedness and drama, at those specific moments of the dramatic process we are drawn into a relational moment with the divine that is intrinsic and inheres to our undeniably communal nature as images of a triune, relational God. The border that exists at the junction between the immanent and the transcendent is accessible by the communal nature of the telenovela, in a manner that emphasizes the metaphysical nature of the community's relationship with the divine.

Conclusion

As a humanizing force the dramatic art form known as the telenovela asks its participants to enter imaginatively into the lives of others to experience their motivations, aspirations, and frustrations. Through our participation in the telenovela either as actors or audience we perceive ourselves in relation to others and confront our present and future lives. In a world that increasingly suffers from the spiritual mutation of violence, the value of understanding and empathizing with other humans cannot be overestimated.

The telenovela as a hybridized form of theatrical drama and religious ritual reflects the complexity of our reality and how we deal with it. Although it is perhaps better at illuminating questions than providing answers, its questioning spirit gives testimony to the seriousness with which it seeks to understand the past and the development of societies and cultures. Historically, humans have used drama and theater to describe, define, and deepen human experience. All people have an abiding need for meaning in order to connect time and space, experience and event, body and spirit, intellect and emotion. Therefore, theater is created to make these connections and to express the otherwise inexpressible. It is society's gift to itself by linking hope to memory, inspiring courage, enriching celebrations, and making tragedies bearable. Given that the telenovela functions as a creative space where a theology of drama and a theology of interrelatedness can manifest with the greatest resonance, it functions both as model of and for a dynamic form of redemptive religious ritual in which audiences and participants can experience an alternative paradigm for experiencing truth, beauty, and solidarity with a transcendent God.

To the extent that we can experience the love of relationality through the experience of theatrical performance that is the telenovela, we gain a greater sense of belongingness and a deeper appreciation of relatedness. This heightened understanding will allow us to better care for every being, thus enabling us to fulfill our need to seek God by loving and serving the neighbor. The telenovela thus is an activity that allows us to explore and access these deeper meanings of relationship and make them more apparent to us. It is this proposition of relationality and interconnectedness in the theatrical discourse that enables us to find our way to the realm of God's immanence. Within the complexity of the human interactions of this quintessential communal art it is possible to locate a coherent vision of true community because of the relationality and interconnectedness that together comprise a wholeness that enables us to grasp an even greater wholeness—a cosmic unity.

Notes

1 Florensky, *Iconostasis*, 66.
2 Goizueta, *Caminemos con Jesús*, 47–76.
3 López, "Our Welcomed Guests," 258, 261.
4 Allen, *To Be Continued*, 1.
5 Ibid., 3–4.
6 López, "Our Welcomed Guests," 272.
7 Ibid., 259.
8 Ibid.
9 Martín Barbero. "Memory and Form in the Latin American Soap Opera," 276.
10 Mazziotti, *La industria de la telenovela*, 275.
11 Allen, *To Be Continued*, 18.
12 Ibid., 20.
13 Ibid., 23.

14 López, "Our Welcomed Guests," 261.

15 García-Rivera, *St. Martín de Porres*, 9.

16 Ibid., 24–25.

17 Ibid., 25.

18 Mamet quoted in ibid., 19.

19 Ibid., 68–69.

20 John MacMurray, *Persons in Relation*, 159.

21 Royce, *The Problem of Christianity*, 152.

22 LaCugna, *God for Us*, 258.

23 Kirkpatrick, "The Logic of Mutual Heterocentrism," 357.

24 LaCugna, *God for Us*, 243.

25 Ibid., 271.

26 Ibid, 300.

27 Kirkpatrick, "The Logic of Mutual Heterocentrism," 360.

28 Goizueta, *Caminemos con Jesús*, 50.

29 Ibid.

30 Isasi-Díaz, *En la Lucha/In the Struggle*, 171.

31 Buber, *I and Thou*, 76–80.

32 Goizueta, *Caminemos con Jesús*, 50.

33 Ibid.

34 Ibid., 63.

35 Ibid.

Jonathan Walton

RESPONSE TO THE ESSAY BY JOSEPH DE LEÓN

My essay in this volume provided an assessment of the ways that the electronic church, most significantly televangelism, impacts the theological thought and intellectual activity of African American Protestant communities. In his essay De León examines the sacred dimensions of telenovelas and how they reflect and engender the perichoretic model within Latino and Latina communities. I believe that a significant place to begin a conversation between these two approaches is by engaging the intersections between religion and popular culture. As our essays both demonstrate, popular culture informs and reifies religious imagination in African American and Latino and Latina communities and thereby is an essential source for theological reflection.

It is important first to distinguish what I perceive to be De León's and my own appeals to popular culture from how the term "popular religion" is typically deployed by black and Latino and Latina theologians of liberation. I understand popular religion to connote the religious practices of nonelites and as privileging the experiences of ordinary black and brown folk. In black theology, for instance, slave narratives, spirituals, folktales, and other oral traditions are forms of popular religion. But popular culture refers to cultural forms that are expressed through mass media outlets such as radio, the Internet, magazines, movies, and most notably television. Why is such a distinction necessary? Because rather than describing religious orientation from below as the organic articulation of common folk sensibility, an examination of religion and popular culture must consider the political and economic power elites at the helm of the varying culture industries. It is only through keeping track of both the religious mores of everyday folk and the market forces that impinge on as well as structure a person's existence can African American and Latino and Latina theologians really interpret the ways that mass mediated representations of reality serve to project, influence, and reinforce religious subjectivity. "Popular" theological sources cannot be interpreted through the essentialist lenses of authentic cultural production. Whether examining televangelism or telenovelas, as forms of popular culture they must be situated within the larger context of a market-informed society. This includes those with the economic capital and political cache to construct, package, and promote cultural products en masse. In this regard it appears that De León and I both seek to build upon and move beyond the traditional methodological emphasis on what constitutes "the popular" in black and Latino and Latina theologies. Televangelism and telenovelas are both uniquely "ours" and "theirs."

The second critical point of intersection involves the relationship between mass-mediated melodrama and religious experience. By identifying telenovelas as theological theaters of transcendence, De León strikes a common theme for African American and Latino and Latina theologians. In my essay I argue that the black electronic church is a form of dramatized faith that allows individuals to pierce through their existential angst in order to encounter the transcendent. Worship services combine drama, amusement, and suspense in such a way that congregants are able to witness their lives being acted out on the stage. The black electronic church and telenovelas thus perform a similar spiritual function. To use De León's phrase, televangelism and telenovelas become a "metaphorical portal for transcendence and transformation." There is a performative dimension to both that carves out a space of spiritual potentiality. As viewers identify with and even vicariously live through the characters on screen, they are able to imagine identities that are in contrast to their material conditions.

Further, De León's theological method is valuable because he constructively reconceptualizes the ways that we can assess the religious dimensions of mass-mediated forms. A theology of aesthetics, which I understand to take into account the production of meaning from alternative locations and sensory perception, considers the ambiguous nature of *homo ludens*. As a ritual of play, the enacted drama of the human condition synthetically involves the otherwise paradoxical realms of the "real" and the "make believe." Therefore, Latino and Latina and African Americans who participate in the ritual of telenovelas and televangelism, respectively, eclipse the dividing line between the empirically real and imagined. Traditional theological methods that seek to evaluate analytically religious activity against traditional, systematized categories and doctrines do not appropriately assess the affective dimensions of religious life that inform self-perception and animate human behavior. In this regard as it relates to the intersections of religion and popular culture De León's proposed theological method subverts the privileging of written texts to locate theological reflection at the experiential level. Such an approach, I believe, exemplifies and augments black and Latino and Latina theologies in important ways.

Though De León and I concur on the theological significance of popular culture, the spiritual potentiality of telenovelas and televangelism, and the need to deprivilege logocentric theological sources, we come to different conclusions concerning the ultimate value of mass-mediated religious experience. In the final instance, my essay does not regard the dramatized faith dimensions of the black electronic church phenomenon as necessarily positive. I argue that as a result of the convergence of religious practice and mass-mediated forms of communication, representations of African American Christian experience have become increasingly sensationalized, superstitious, and insular. In order to conform to the stylistic conventions of popular broadcasting, the producers of the black electronic church must heighten the melodramatic dimensions of the faith to the extent that theological discourse is reduced to catchy soundbites, and hope in the unseen is replaced with highly edited images of the miraculous in action. The dramatized narratives of success, representations of prosperity, and testimonies of individuals miraculously rising to the top of the social ladder—which are true in varying ways among both the electronic church and telenovelas—obfuscates the material conditions of those living on the underside of societies structured in economic, racial, and gender injustice. In my opinion, mass-mediated forms of religious expression abate rather than accentuate communities of struggle and resistance

On the other hand, I understand De León to assert that telenovelas reflect and strengthen the Latino and Latina community. He states that through the anagogical dimensions of the telenovela and the ability of the Latino and Latina community to reimagine themselves according to the heteronomic relations of the triune God, individuals garner a greater sense of belonging to the community. This experience, according to De León, "enables them to better care for every being, thus enabling them to fulfill their need to seek perfect goodness by loving and serving their neighbor." De León understands telenovelas as a positive reflection of "the indigenous mindset of the Latino" that seeks justice and a collective harmony among community members.

What De León regards as a connection with ultimate reality through viewer participation in mass-mediated drama I interpret to be a somewhat illusory representation of nonreality for the majority of viewers. What I regard as imagined communities of insularity that rally around a common theme, De León interprets to be heterocentric communities of mutual beneficence. Therefore, a continued point of dialogue may involve the ways that our respective communities can take popular culture seriously as an expression of the spiritual strivings of black and brown folk while acknowledging the ideological implications of mass-produced religious representations. This takes me back to my original point concerning the inclusion of the perspectives of the ruling elite in our theological valuations of popular culture. African American and Latino and Latina theologians must continue to wrestle with how we can incorporate contemporary religious experiences that are increasingly being mediated through mass culture as authentic, yet that nonetheless are influenced by the ruling ideals of societies structured in injustice. I believe it would be beneficial for African American and Latino and Latina theologians to become candid conversation partners on this very topic. Such a mature dialogue takes seriously the ways that our respective theological sources are given to justice and injustice as well as community concern and individual gain. This, indeed, would be a dialogue of mutual beneficence.

PART SIX   □   VISUAL ARTS AND RELIGION

Suzanne E. Hoeferkamp Segovia

THEOLOGY AS IMAGINATIVE CONSTRUCTION:

AN ANALYSIS OF THE WORK OF THREE LATINA ARTISTS

The contemporary Latina artists who fall within the Guadalupe tradition of image making may be encouraged by the fact that through the controversial content of their icons they are making significant contributions to an understanding of theology as imaginative construction.[1] A close look at the different order of symbols that appear in the icons of Yolanda López, Ester Hernández, and Alma López is useful in developing a theological understanding of the creative act and the image as a means of transformation.

In this essay I trace the trajectory of the religious icon of Guadalupe from the time of its inception to its contemporary expression in the context of faith and Latin American culture. An overview of the historical development of the image of Guadalupe serves to illustrate the creative process of imaginative construction as it occurs at the crossroads of theology and art.

A Transnational Tradition

There is a tradition among Mexican American Latinas who since the 1970s have sought to transform and reclaim the Virgin of Guadalupe—the traditional postconquest religious icon that symbolizes the female face of God. As a feminine symbol of the divine presence, which in the sphere of daily existence is a great source of emotive power, the Virgin of Guadalupe continues to be perceived as an expression of God's unconditional love for her people. In the realm of culture she is a powerful symbol of Mexican and

Mexican American identity. In colonial times just as today she was identified as a native and depicted as a kind, loving, and forgiving mother. But she also functioned as the intercessor to God the father and his son Jesus Christ.

Latina feminist writers, theologians, and artists who have difficulty accepting a patriarchal God have appropriated and reconstructed the traditional colonial image of Mary, the mother of God. No longer perceived as an intercessor for her son, Guadalupe has been reenvisioned as the divinity in her own right. In contrast to the traditionally modest representation of the familiar image showing downcast eyes and a prayerful posture of folded hands, she has reappeared as a powerful symbol of liberation and emancipative action. Today Latina artists are actively unearthing the icon's potential as a symbol of self-actualization. As the great mother goddess, she continues to heal the wounds of the past.

The Virgin of Guadalupe

The Spanish conquest of Tenochtitlan, the hub of the Aztec empire originally located in what is now Mexico City, was effective in destroying an entire civilization and in abolishing the cult of Tonantzín along with an entire pantheon of divinities whose cult had been censored and whose temples had been destroyed.[2] In the aftermath of the conquest, Guadalupanismo (the veneration of Guadalupe) made its way into the soul of the indigenous population through a legend whose chief protagonist was the Lady of Tepeyac. In 1649 Luis Lasso de la Vega, the vicar of Guadalupe, published *Nican Mopohua* (Here It Is Written)—a textual account of the original Náhuatl version of the legend by Juan Diego and Antonio Valeriano.[3] According to this legend, which was based on a vision, a young mestizo woman appeared to the Indian Juan Diego on the hill of Tepeyac where Tonantzín's shrine was located: "On the very site where the feminine aspect of the one, all powerful, creative spirit had been previously venerated a new beginning was emerging" (88). The woman identified herself to him as "Mary, Mother of the true God through whom one lives, of the Creator of heaven and of earth" (76). Hector Elizondo offers an explanation of the idea of God that is embedded in this phrase that appears in *Nican Mopohua*: "Mother of the true God would be quite understandable for us today. What is of special interest is the phrase '*through whom one lives*,' since this was a very common Mexican way of referring to the supreme creative power which not only brought things into being but sus-

tained them in existence. By using this term, in effect, she identified herself with Ometéotl who was the supreme, invisible and creative power. It
was the god who was beyond the gods, beyond history, beyond mythology
and, therefore, without representation" (88).

The idea of God that appears in the phrase by which the woman identified herself includes the symbol of creation: "'Of the creator of heaven and
earth'": this again was a reference to the creative and creating presence of
the all-powerful invisible god whose thoughts brought forth existing reality. It was this god who brought everything which is into existence and
sustained all things which are in existence in time and space" (88). The
one who had come to usher in a new order identified herself in effect with
the great creative power. The Lady of Tepeyac continued to appear to Juan
Diego during the days between December 9 and 12. She requested through
him ("Tell the bishop") that a church be built in her name at the place of
her apparition on the hill of Tepeyac.

At this point in the story the audience begins to perceive a reversal of
the common order, which is a reversal of power. Elizondo interprets the
event as follows: "It was the Indian Lady who sent her Indian messenger to
tell the Spanish bishop what she wanted! It was the Indian Lady, the Mother
of the true God, through Whom one lives, who desired and demanded that
a temple be built on this site. The temple that the Lady asked for was the
LIVING Temple of the collective consciousness of 'La Nueva Raza'" (89).
Elizondo's imaginative interpretation of the symbols contributes to the
new reality of that event in the story, which is still in process.

The story continues as follows. When Archbishop Juan de Zumárraga
required proof from Diego, the Virgin did not delay. She told Juan Diego
to pick roses from the hillside nearby, to place them in his folded tilma
(cloak), and then take them to the bishop. When Diego unfolded the tilma
in the presence of the bishop the roses were released, and the Virgin's
image was fixed on the tilma. Elizondo comments on this point: "In an unexpected way, dialogue began. It was the powerless that went to the powerful with what would become the instrument of their dialogue: the image
of Tepeyac" (91). In this encounter between two cultures that represent the
powerful and the powerless, respectively, we witness the beginning of a
creative process of theology and art in dialogue. The result of this process,
which is also one of imaginative construction, is that the roles of the powerful and the powerless are reversed.

The veneration of Guadalupe had its origins in 1531 in what is today
Mexico City, after which it continued to spread throughout the Anahuac

Valley. To this day we are moved to consider the manifold aspects of the re-creative power that is embodied in the symbol of the Lady of Tepeyac. To tell her story is to participate in theology as imaginative construction. Elizondo's interpretation of the Guadalupe event serves to show how the telling of a story from the perspective of a people's liberation can enlarge our understanding of theology as imaginative construction. His idea of the divine reality frees the imagination to read the following passage from a perspective that applies to our own contemporary situation. "Now they were no longer alone. There was a new force, a new power at work in their world, brought about not by the conquistador or his religion or even by the conquered, but by the all powerful creating force of the invisible God. This new force was not some abstract principle . . . It was coming to them in the very visible, sensible, tangible form of a loving and compassionate mother—who would listen to and give remedy to all their needs" (89–90). Elizondo's reading offers a perspective that allows us to trace the creative process of theology as imaginative construction. His interpretation of the events in the story is based on a process of liberation, which adds depth, meaning, and insight to the story. His method serves as a key that allows us to participate in his construction of a particular idea of God, i.e., an idea that is also at work in us. Elizondo's reading of the symbol of Guadalupe embodies a new depth of meaning that is based on the originating context of the symbol's birth. Consequently, he asserts:

> The significance of Guadalupe, far from being a pacifier, is a dynamic call to action and a powerful symbol for the unification of a people. For a people whose tragic existence began with conquest and rape, the only real beginning could take place in an event which was of equal or greater magnitude than the trauma they had suffered. Only in an event which clearly originated in heaven could the conquest and rape of Mexico be revised, and a people truly proud of their new existence begin a "raza" who had been born not out of a violated person but out of a pure and inviolate mother. This compassionate mother would "remedy" the worst of all miseries, pains and lamentations caused by the conquest with its subsequent illegitimate birth. (90)

The reader can thus infer that in the context of the first postconquest sign of "La Nueva Raza" (the New Race) the redeeming qualities in this image were instrumental in effecting genuinely liberating perspectives among the conquered people of Tenochtitlan (Mexico). But among the feminist community of Latina artists now living in the United States, the traditional representation of this "pure and inviolate mother" has become ambiguous and sometimes even oppressive. In the context of the contemporary laissez-faire market-driven economy, this image is hard pressed to deliver a genuinely liberating message. Further on in this essay I will show how Guadalupe's original strength and power have been reclaimed from the familiar version of the symbol and transformed in ways that are genuinely liberating, notably in doing justice to Latina women in the contemporary contexts of their daily existence. We discover now that the revelatory power of symbols that effect the reversal of an existing order abides in the level of depth that their meaning communicates. At this level there is a call to action. Consequently: "*Tell the Bishop*—It is the conquered who now tells the 'conquistador' group, in the person of the bishop, what is to be done. The reversal of power was not done through military force or intellectual argumentation, but through the interpenetration of symbols whose core meaning is somewhat mutually understood. After years of struggle and prayer, human dialogue finally started. The two worlds would be able to dialogue through the medium of an audio-visual constellation . . . , which ingeniously combined the symbolism and mythologies of the two worlds" (91). The European icon of Mary, which has often been linked to the Roman Catholic doctrine of the Immaculate Conception, was altered in the icon of Guadalupe. In the familiar image, which prevails to this day, the skin became dark and the hair was straightened and darkened. The Virgin has an indigenous face, yet her dress is Judeo-Christian. These characteristics stood out in the imprint that appeared after her third encounter with Juan Diego, and they became the basis for the familiar image. Particular characteristics in the icon allude to the woman of the Apocalypse, "a woman clothed with the sun" (Revelation 12:1), and are also reminiscent of the expression "I am dark but I am lovely" (Song of Songs 6:10).

The image on Juan Diego's tilma personifies a complex amalgamation of religious symbols: stars on Guadalupe's mantle, a sliver of the moon, a body halo, cherubs, and an angel. The body halo, sun, moon, crown, and the angel at Guadalupe's feet are traditional European motifs. Prior to 1531 they were common in the religious arts of Europe and reflect two distinct ways of representing Mary. The first way renders Mary as the Virgin of the Immaculate Conception, without the baby Jesus.[4] The second way is rooted in the woman of the Apocalypse, which is depicted in Revelation 12:1: "A great sign appeared in the sky, a woman clothed with the sun, with the moon under her feet, and on her head a crown of twelve stars." Soon after Guadalupe's appearance her image was linked to the biblical symbol of the woman clothed with the sun. In the spiritual context of the encounter between the culture of Spain and the cultures of Mesoamerica this reading of the symbol was especially relevant for understanding the importance of Guadalupe as the one who blocked the pagan sun god. By eclipsing sun worship in Mesoamerica she was perceived to be "a great sign" that united Europe with the New World.[5]

Most art historians link Guadalupe's body halo, crown, and crescent moon with European Christian views that are based on interpretations of the woman of the Apocalypse as described in Revelation 12:1. But others choose a Mesoamerican basis for interpreting these symbols. They see Guadalupe as eclipsing the rays of the Aztec sun and war deity. And they see in the crescent moon a native female symbol, the moon goddess (also known as the goddess of the night) who was among the most sublime of the Indian deities.[6] But they find that Guadalupe was greater than this goddess because she did not destroy the moon but instead lay her feet upon it.[7]

Ten years prior to the conquest, native wise men had interpreted the presence of a comet—or a large group of stars that made their way across their skies—as a token of the end of their civilization. To the naked eye, it appeared to be a huge star with a trace of what looked like a tail. Just as stars had once signaled the end of a civilization, on Guadalupe's mantle they hailed the dawning of a new one.[8]

Another symbol that the natives interpreted as significant is the fact that an angel supports Guadalupe on its shoulders. Those who were carried on someone's shoulders or who when out and about were carried by others were either royalty or envoys of the deities. The symbol of support by celestial creatures meant to the native peoples that Guadalupe was not brought by the Spaniards but rather came to them on her own. Having experienced the death of their own civilization they regarded the arrival of Guadalupe as marking the dawning of a new era. Symbols of celestial support indicated to them that her presence pointed to the beginning of a new civilization.[9]

Although the chief god in the native pantheon was the sun god, Guadalupe became even more significant. The sunrays still shine, but now they serve to highlight the Lady's eminence. Her image blocks the sun but does not put it out.[10]

The figure of Guadalupe wears the black band of maternity tied around her waist. Its presence means that she is with child, and her offering to the peoples of this New World is her child. On close examination of the image, an Indian cross can be seen above her navel. In the Indian world the navel symbolized the center of the cosmic order.[11] The symbol of the cross, placed above the navel, marks the new center of the universe: the word made flesh, which the Lady carries in her womb. The Christian cross also appears on the brooch that the Lady wears on her collar. Clearly, this Lady—one of their own—has not only brought Christ to them but is also a follower of the Christ.[12]

The traditional European motifs common in the religious arts of Europe prior to 1531—the body halo, sun, moon, crown, and the angel at the Lady's feet—were reinterpreted for Guadalupe through the cosmic vision of the native peoples. A native interpretation of the symbols in her image rendered them meaningful. The Marian image of Guadalupe as one of the indigenous peoples offers a Christ-centered presentation of the incarnation in the land of the Americas.[13]

The new representation of the Virgin Mary had great significance for the native peoples. Rather than simply rendering a purely European deity it incorporated symbols that were linked with indigenous deities, such as the sun, the moon, and the stars. The symbols that characterize her borrow from both pre-Columbian and Christian imagery. The description above makes it evident that they embody a new source of power and meaning. As Virgilio Elizondo notes in considering the dialogue that followed the apparition of the image of Tepeyac:

> This marks the beginning of the "reconquista." A new power had erupted from the soil which would give a new identity and dignity to the conquered people. It enabled them to begin the counter-attack upon the violence of the conquest which had been reinforced and deepened by the efforts to wipe out the religion of the people. They would go to the very core of this inner violence: the bishop.
>
> The bishop had been asking for divine assistance. Now it came in a totally unsuspected way. There would not be a "purist" religion which would eliminate the ways and traditions of the people. There would be a new religion, but it would come through the temple of the people's meaningful expressions.[14]

Through "the temple of the people's meaningful expressions" the tradition of Guadalupe would continue to forge its way into the future, delivering one form or another of its liberating message, according to the social and historical context of its expression. In 1810, for example, Guadalupe's image began to acquire liberationist nuances when during the Mexican struggle for independence from Spain Father Miguel Hidalgo y Costilla led his troops with Guadalupe's icon on his standard. The troops carried it on reeds and poles, and even on their hats.[15]

It all began when Father Miguel Hidalgo, the Mexican criollo patriot, delivered his battle cry "Grito de Dolores" (Cry of Dolores) at the crack of dawn on September 16, 1810. The purpose of the battle cry was to incite fellow Mexicans to overthrow the Spaniards from power and free the homeland from foreign control, crippling taxes, and abusive governance.[16] The cry was convincing: "Mueran los gachupines! ¡Viva la Virgen de Guadalupe!" (Death to the Spaniards! Long live the Virgin of Guadalupe!).[17] The famous cry moved the people to wage the Mexican War of Independence from Spain. When the cry was first uttered, Guadalupe came forth as a native symbol of freedom and strength. She stepped forward, beyond the home altar, to become immersed in the struggles of her people.[18]

A century later, in 1911 during the Mexican Revolution, the dissidents Pancho Villa and Emiliano Zapata took Mexico City under the banner of Guadalupe. Zapata, an indigenous Mexican farm worker, was an outstanding leader whose battle cry called for the recovery of native lands and liberty for the oppressed. Carrying Guadalupe's image on banners into battle, he and his troops struggled for the recovery of Indian lands from the federal government.[19]

Time and again the symbol of Guadalupe has been relied on to overthrow oppressive conditions. An outstanding instance of this occurred during the struggles of César Chávez, a North American–born labor leader who organized the United Farm Workers movement in the 1960s and 1970s. Through his leadership and his movement's slogan—"Sí se puede" (Yes you can)—Mexican American migrant workers, field laborers, and grape pickers were successful in demonstrating against unfair labor practices in California.[20] When the United Farm Workers in California went on strike, César Chávez carried the image of Guadalupe when he marched with the strikers.

These and other movements have given rise to a new enthusiasm for cutting-edge icons of Guadalupe. In contemporary Mexico the popular appeal of the Guadalupe symbol has made its way through all sectors of Mexican society. There one finds her icon displayed not only in churches but also in buses, taxis, trucks, restaurants, and family home altars, as well as in amulets and tattoos. The image of the Virgin of Guadalupe also cuts through the public and cultural sector of the Mexican American community in the United States. She is painted on neighborhood walls and on car windows, tattooed on male and female bodies, and imprinted on T-shirts.

As a manifestation of the biblical Mary, the Virgin of Guadalupe is a symbolic presence that abounds in the religious expression of contemporary Latin American culture. As the oppressed celebrate her presence in the midst of their daily lives they also continue to plead for her intercession in the midst of their struggles.

But among Mexican American feminists the omnipresence of Guadalupe arouses ambivalent feelings. Although some accept her as *nuestra madrecita* ("our little mother," a term of endearment) and an ever-present guardian, others cannot help but see in her image the embodiment of a medieval and monastic concept of woman. This concept limits human understanding to simple binary categories of perception that classify women as falling under one of two categories: that of virgin or that of whore.[21] Far from representing the actual situation of women the concept reflects the values of the ecclesial entity that originally embodied them in its structures. These are values that do not regard the full humanity of women as they really are. A woman is either *la buena* (the good woman, or the virgin) or *la mala* (the bad woman, or the whore). This fundamental idea of women was originally brought to the American continent by the Spanish medieval monastic orders that Christianized the extent of the Americas that became Spanish speaking. One way or another the idea has become deeply embedded in the psyche of Latin American cultures through Marian images that were first introduced by the Roman Catholic Church in the medieval period.

Although the manifestation of the biblical Mary in the indigenous Lady of Guadalupe deeply humanized the perennial image of the Virgin Mary, the contemporary implications of her representation in the visual arts of the Roman Catholic Church are most obvious in the popular media of Mexican television soap operas. Appealing to the masses, such programs are a powerful and effective organ of socialization that endorses the prevailing social order and the religious status quo in Latin America. In the context of our contemporary religious situation it is fair to say that feminist Latina women who are activists in one way or another feel that Guadalupe's traditional or familiar representation—with her eyes cast down and with the appearance of humility—encourages an already ambiguous and conflicting perception of women. Whether perceived as la buena or la mala, a woman in this situation cannot expect to win. In a culture that embodies a deeply distorted perception of the female gender it is difficult for a woman to acquire a healthy amount of self-understanding unless through critical perception she is able to break through the distortions that are represented either in historical or contemporary images of the biblical Mary. No wonder Sandra Cisneros writes the following: "That was why I was angry every time I saw la Virgen de Guadalupe, my culture's role model for brown women like me. She was damn dangerous, an ideal so lofty and unrealistic it was laughable."[22]

An imaginatively constructed image of the Virgin that acquired liberationist nuances in the context of the Mexican struggle for independence from Spain proved to be effective in winning the support of a people whose foremost appeal centered on the national effort to emancipate themselves. In the midst of this situation, the image of Guadalupe emerged as a symbol of liberation. Her strength lay in her look of understanding and humility. With eyes cast down she looked on her people with compassion, to the extent that they reflected upon her eyes. Guadalupe thus emerged to liberate the native peoples from their own particular situation in history.

The Guadalupe that is emerging in the multidimensional contexts of today is evolving to meet the liberationist demands of our particular conditions in history. To meet these demands, the biblical Mary who manifests herself in the contemporary expressions of the Guadalupe tradition sheds her husk but keeps her kernel in the good news that the Lady brings. That good news is the new being that is emerging in the image of Guadalupe and in us.

The perception of a particular form is linked not only with its meaning in a certain tradition but also with the historical and social context in which the form is being received. A particular form may be perceived as liberating in one historical or social context but oppressive in another. For example, in the social context in which the familiar image of Guadalupe first appeared, her downcast eyes were perceived as a sign of genuine humility and were held in high regard—just as the look of compassion was honored in her face and in her entire demeanor. In the United States these qualities in the posture and in the gestures of the familiar image are interpreted according to the experience of women who are far removed from the originating context. Gospel values that intend to communicate genuine humility and compassion in the familiar image of Guadalupe have been perceived in the social context of culture in the United States as expressions of passiveness and submissiveness. In the social context of Mexico, on the other hand, the patriarchy of the Roman Catholic Church has done much to encourage an attitude of passiveness and submissiveness in women's relationship with men and with the Church. They point to Guadalupe whose humble demeanor reflects the submissive attitude that is to be expected in a woman. The consequences of this misreading of Gospel values—those that were intended to be communicated through the image and story of Guadalupe—are apparent in the common mistreatment of women in the home and in the workplace. This mistreatment has its roots in the male attitudes of machismo and in the general regard of women as creatures whose humanity is not equal to that of men.[23] The consequences of these attitudes are devastating, as can be seen in the general situation of women in Latin America. For example, contrary to general belief women in Latin America do not have truly equal access to higher education. This is because misogyny is practiced under institutional guises that work to limit women's roles in society, government, and the economy at large. Women live in the shadow of men and are valued more for their biological functions and procreative roles as wife and mother than for the exercise of any talents or intellectual gifts that might contribute to the improvement and well-being of the local community or nation or of church and society.

The iconographic tradition of Guadalupe entails a variety of implications for the liberation of Latina women. Foremost among these implications is the need to reconstruct an image of Guadalupe that resonates with our own historical situation by responding to our deepest needs with a message that is genuinely liberating. Faced with this truth, Mexican American feminists have used a variety of methods in their efforts to reconstruct the image of the Virgin of Guadalupe. Many have attempted to recover the indigenous features of her identity and to regard her as the contemporary incarnation of preconquest goddesses such as Tonantzín, the preconquest fertility deity; Coatlicue, the mother warrior deity; Tlazolteolt, the goddess of purity and impurity in the native pantheon; or Ometéotl, the highest creative power—supreme and invisible. In *Goddess of the Americas: Writings on the Virgen de Guadalupe* (1996), Ana Castillo together with Sandra Cisneros, Gloria Anzaldúa, Cherríe Moraga, and Pat Mora effectively use this strategy. They recognize the Virgin of Guadalupe as a syncretistic symbol—that is, a blending of indigenous and Spanish cultures that join Tonantzín with the Roman Catholic Virgin Mary.

In *Goddess of the Americas*, the Virgin of Guadalupe is a complex spiritual figure who awakens the pre-Hispanic cosmos. She is linked to African Orishas, along with other female deities. In the volume Guadalupe is reconstructed as the life-giving goddess who empowers women who search for the female face of God. As stated by Sandra Cisneros in her essay "Guadalupe the Sex Goddess": "She is a face for a god without a face, an indígena for a god without ethnicity, a female deity for a god who is genderless, but I also understand that for her to approach me, for me to finally open the door and accept her, she had to be a woman like me."[24] Like other statements throughout *Goddess of the Americas* this statement provides a brief example of genuine theological reflection—that is, a thinking process that develops into nothing less than "a fully critical and self-conscious constructive activity."[25] Like Cisneros, each of the feminist Latina authors who contributed to the reconstruction of the Virgin of Guadalupe has in her own way exercised "the proper business of theology," namely in "the analysis, criticism and reconstruction of the image/concept of God."[26]

Like their Latina colleagues in the literary arts, Latina visual artists, especially Mexican Americans, have made significant contributions to feminist reconstructions of la Virgen de Guadalupe. Inspired by the depth of meaning that is embodied in the mestiza holy mother, they have openly resisted, as Claire Tron de Bouchony notes, "the weight of tradition that immobilized woman as a mythic image and fixed her in the form of a statue, thus depriving her of any possibility of action or creative initiative."[27] They note that although the ancient indigenous goddess of creation was effaced from the surface of the supreme female deity, she re-emerged as the Christian Virgin of Guadalupe. They attach great significance to the fact that this ancient goddess was not completely banished but rather simply transformed. Lucy Lippard, who summarizes and synthesizes López's insights, comments as follows: "The Virgin of Guadalupe was the Americas' first syncretic figure . . . the pan-Mexican icon of motherhood and *mestizaje*, a transitional figure who emerged only fifteen years after the Conquest as the Christianized incarnation of the Aztec earth and fertility goddess Tonantzín and heiress to Coatlicue, the 'Lady of the Snaky Skirt,' in her role as blender of dualities."[28]

The tradition of Guadalupe has never altered the importance of its liberating message but only the form of its expression. This form is perceived according to the spiritual demand of the times as well as according to the context in which it appears. In keeping faithful to its liberating message, the image evolves only to the extent that this message requires—that is, in its ever-changing social context.

Contemporary Latina Artists in the Guadalupe Tradition

The seminal work of three leading Mexican American feminist artists has called attention to the transformations that are taking effect in contemporary representations of the Guadalupe icon. Along with renewing a general interest in the subject matter of Guadalupe, her reconstruction in a selection of the images by these artists has incited significant debate and controversy in the spheres of religion and culture. In the discussion that follows I address the multifaceted contributions of Ester Hernández, Yolanda López, and Alma López.

Ester Hernández was born in Northern California in 1944 to farm laborers with a family tradition in the arts. Her best-known work, *Sun Mad Raisins* (1981), is a satirical comment on a well-known logo, and as such it represents a forceful statement against the exploitation of farm laborers. Her woodblock print *La Virgen de Guadalupe Defendiendo los Derechos de los Xicanos* (1974; The Virgin of Guadalupe Defending the Rights of Chicanos) is quite compelling. In it the Virgin as a black-belt karate fighter steps out of her full-body *mandorla* (halo) to deliver a karate kick—thereby leaving behind the role of the passive mother that appears in the traditional icon. This Guadalupe is physically active, strong, and expert. Although the title of the image implies that she is devoted to serving her people by means of her skills and talent, it is also clear that she can defend herself. The female dignity portrayed in Hernández's print expresses an image of self-sufficient strength that reaches out to protect her children.

Yolanda M. López is a Chicana artist and social activist who was born in San Diego, California, in 1942. She is one of the best-known Latina artists in the United States. Among her most famous works is a pastel-on-paper series titled *Our Lady of Guadalupe*. This triptych includes a portrait of the artist as the Virgin of Guadalupe. The icons in this series are purposefully constructive. López uses her art as a means of stimulating change in the self-awareness of Chicanas. By breaking away from the kind of stereotyping that prevails in female icons that serve to bind women to oppressive ideologies, López's work seeks to construct genuinely liberating images on the basis of the religious tradition of Guadalupe. Her pioneering *Virgin of Guadalupe* series of paintings, drawings, and posters explores the possibilities of the Virgin of Guadalupe as an influential female icon. In this series, López has interpreted anew and reconstructed the traditional Roman Catholic icon as a relevant contemporary female role model. In so doing, she has transformed the "passive" and "submissive" colonial Guadalupe into a more powerful role model for Mexican American and Latina women. To symbolize contemporary cultural struggles López recast Guadalupe in a three-piece series titled *The Guadalupe Triptych* (1978). In this triptych, she effectively uses the streams of light associated with Guadalupe as a means of expressing a symbolic transformation.

In López's oil pastel series on paper (each approximately 28 x 32 inches), she celebrates the lives of ordinary mestiza women by transferring the symbols of Guadalupe's power and virtue onto their portraits. Amalia Mesa-Bains introduces and interprets *The Guadalupe Triptych* as follows:

> López restates the Virgin of Guadalupe by removing the traditional figure from the halo of rays and replacing it with powerful images of family and self. The traditional icon is customarily portrayed as a passive and submissive figure. López's Guadalupes are mobile, hardworking, assertive, working-class images of the abuela [grandmother] as a strong, solid nurturer, mother as a family-supporting seamstress, and daughter as a contemporary artist and powerful runner. This repositioning becomes both satire and provocation, while retaining the transfigurative liberation of the icon. . . . The art in this series does not simply reflect an existing ideology; it actively constructs a new one. It attests to the critique of traditional Mexican women's roles and religious oppression in a self-fashioning of new identities.[29]

In the first piece of the triptych, *Margaret F. Stewart: Our Lady of Guadalupe*, the figure of the artist's mother is depicted sitting at her sewing machine stitching the deep blue cape of stars that traditionally covers the Virgin. This portrayal reminds us of the underpaid labor of the invisible mestiza women who also sew our own clothes. As she sews, the mother pauses for a moment from her labor to regard the viewer who returns her gaze. A priestly cherub whose wings are striped with the colors of the Mexican flag emerges from beneath the cloak on the floor. Roses, an Aztec symbol of the divine presence, appear next to the cherub. A radiant body halo softly blazes as it casts its rays around the figure of the holy mother. López honors all working mothers through this icon. As she states: "I feel living, breathing women also deserve the respect and love lavished on Guadalupe. . . . It is a call to look at women, hard working, enduring and mundane, as the heroines of our daily routine. . . . We privately agonize and sometimes publicly speak out on the representation of us in the majority culture. But what about the portrayal of ourselves in our own culture? Who are our heroes, our role models? . . . It is dangerous for us to wait around for the dominant culture to define and validate what role models we should have."[30]

In the second portrait, *Victoria F. Franco: Our Lady of Guadalupe*, López represents her grandmother sitting on a stool that is draped with the Virgin's blue cape of stars. From behind a large halo of light surrounds her entire body. She regards the viewer with a straightforward, matter-of-fact expression. With her hands crossed on her lap she holds a snake skin in one hand and a knife in the other. Both symbols refer to her vital connection with the soil, which she nurtures in providing food for the family. The winged cherub emerges again from behind the cloak, carrying a garland of roses. Here the grandmother is honored as the embodiment of wisdom, power, and strength.

The third icon in the trilogy, *Portrait of the Artist: Our Lady of Guadalupe*, is a self-portrait. In sharp contrast to the sedentary figures of her mother and grandmother, the artist represents herself as a marathon runner who is La Virgen. With the muscular legs of a runner she seems to leap toward the viewer. She holds a live snake in one hand, while in the other hand she grasps a corner of the Virgin's blue cape of stars that billows over her shoulder. As a spirited and powerful runner she radiates the full-body halo, and her smile radiates confidence. And, as she leaps, she runs over the priestly cherub who has red, white, and green wings. López identifies the plump cherub as "a middle-aged agent of patriarchy."[31] *The Guadalupe Triptych* portrays symbols of a divine economy in the form of a trinitarian deity. In strength and humility, this trinitarian deity lifts up and honors its female expressions.

Like Ester Hernández and others after her, Yolanda López has relocated the Virgin of Guadalupe in a contemporary context that reflects her own experience. As feminist Latina artists respond to the new challenges they face in the portrayals of a contemporary image of divinity, they are forced to address the difference in the Virgin's appearance. As Alma López explains: "More than 20 years ago, artists Yolanda López and Ester Hernández were threatened and attacked for portraying the Virgen in a feminist and liberating perspective. In 1978 Yolanda López received bomb threats for her portrayal of the Virgen wearing low-heeled shoes. In this image the Virgen walks with her head bowed, hands clasped, wearing a dress below the knees. I think that people were upset because the Virgen was able to walk away, especially if she didn't care to listen to someone's prayers."[32]

Alma López is an innovative Latina artist and activist from Los Angeles. Born in Sinaloa, Mexico, and reared in East Los Angeles, López grew up revering the image of Our Lady of Guadalupe. One of her consistent aesthetic goals is to raise public awareness of the misrepresentation of Latinos and Latinas in mainstream American culture. In addition to her photo-based digital prints, López works in painting and video and also creates murals and installations. She is internationally recognized for her innovative digital images that place prominent icons and figures of significant women from Mexico in context with issues of race, gender, and sexuality.

Her art reflects the fact that she grew up honoring Our Lady of Guadalupe. She collects and creates digital photographic images from a large variety of sources and uses computer technology to alter, rearrange, and superimpose them in meaningful and constructive ways. From a feminist perspective that is deeply critical, her work is often perceived as powerfully subversive and yet beautiful. Influenced by the contemporary visual language of Latino pop artists living in Los Angeles, her images reflect the rich legacy of the East Los Angeles art scene. As she continues in the ongoing attempt to recover the indigenous origins of Guadalupe, her work portrays the Virgin as a contemporary apparition of Tonantzín-Coatlicue—that is, as the sacred guardian mother and goddess of the cosmos.

López's 1999 *Our Lady of Guadalupe*, which depicts a personal response to the familiar Mexican icon of the Virgin of Guadalupe, attracted a great deal of attention when in 2001 it was exhibited at the Museum of International Folk Art in Santa Fe, New Mexico. Perceived as a particularly controversial piece in the exhibition titled "Cyber Arte: Where Tradition Meets Technology," the work elicited an unexpected wave of reaction. It was featured along with other works by López in addition to three other contemporary Latina artists who combine recent computer technology with traditional folk elements. Richard Meyer comments on *Our Lady*, the most conspicuous piece in the exhibit, as follows: "Although López sought an updated but still beatified Guadalupe in *Our Lady*, its detractors saw just the opposite. José Villegas, a Catholic parishioner who helped spearhead the protest against *Our Lady*, said 'I see the devil, I don't see our Blessed Mother.'"[33] *Our Lady*, a digital photograph portraying the Virgin of Guadalupe, includes the familiar rays of light, the blue cape of stars, the crescent moon, the roses, and the angel. But instead of the composed, reserved, and modest Virgin with her head turned down, López presents a physically confident Latina who poses in a noble stance and with a direct and defiant gaze. Rather than join her hands in a gesture of worship, she places them firmly on her waist. And instead of covering her entire body in drapery, beneath her open *manta* (cape) the Virgin is dressed in a lively arrangement of roses.

The supreme creative power expressed itself among the Aztec people through song and roses. The Virgin in this image offers the viewer what the Aztecs considered to be the most exalted means of communication: roses. The roses in this image appear as more than a mere gesture of clothing; instead, they are the most powerful sign to her people. As a symbol of the resurrection they give the image an immediate atmosphere of divinity.

The divine presence calls forth new life in the blooming of roses. As López notes, "Roses were the proof of her apparition to Juan Diego" and she adds that "Our Lady not only wears flowers, but also the Coyolxauhqui robe of the pre-Columbian moon Goddess and warrior."[34] This robe (*manta*) is now imprinted with the astounding Aztec image of Coyolxauhqui.

A bare-breasted angel, the portrait of Raquel Gutiérrez, a friend of the artist, holds the crescent moon aloft where the Virgin stands. The angel's arms are outstretched with butterfly wings that extend from her shoulders and back. As López comments, "The butterfly angel represents a Viceroy butterfly. For survival purposes, the Viceroy butterfly mimics the Monarch, which is well known for its migrations between the United States and Mexico."[35] Butterfly wings are a recurring motif in López's work. Embedded in a lush icon of female fecundity, in López's work they signify "migration, flight, and the hidden intelligence of genetic memory."[36] As she further states: "This work features performance artist Raquel Salinas as a strong *Virgen* dressed in roses, and cultural activist Raquel Gutiérrez as a nude butterfly angel . . . Raquel Salinas, Raquel Gutiérrez and I grew up in Los Angeles with the image of the *Virgen* in our homes and community. The *Virgen* is everywhere. She's on tattoos, stickers, posters, air freshener cans, shirts and corner store murals, as well as church walls."[37]

In spite of the unlimited reproduction of Guadalupe in both secular and sacred contexts, many protesters in the Roman Catholic community of northern New Mexico as well as in the Santa Fe legislature mistakenly perceived López's revision of Guadalupe as blasphemous, indecent, and sacrilegious in intent. Richard Meyer notes that "Shortly after the opening, the Catholic Church publicly reviled López while the curator of the exhibition, Tey Marianna Nunn, received death threats and state lawmakers threatened to pull government funding from the museum unless it removed the offending work. The Archbishop of Santa Fe, Michael J. Sheehan, characterized *Our Lady* as 'repulsive, insulting, even sacrilegious . . . Here is the mother of God depicted like a tart or a call girl. The image of Mary depicted in this way has no place in a publicly supported museum.' "[38]

In turn, López comments that she "was surprised by the violent reaction to *Our Lady* . . . After my initial shock . . . I realized the organizers were primarily men, the Catholic Church, and conservative groups."[39] As she further notes:

> The protest against "Our Lady" is organized and led by community activist José Villegas. New Mexico Archbishop Michael J. Sheehan has

joined him, calling the artwork sacrilegious." Mr. Villegas' first and only attempt to communicate with me was through a threatening e-mail. One week later, on television I saw the rally he organized against the museum.

Mr. Villegas and the Archbishop see the "Our Lady" digital print with exposed legs and belly and a female angel's breasts as "offensive." Yet I know that many churches, in Mexico and Europe and the United States, house images of nude male angels and most prominently, a Crucifixion practically naked except for a skimpy loincloth.[40]

López insists that like her other works *Our Lady* reflects a deeply personal effort to understand a legacy of cultural icons and traditional religious symbols in terms that relate to her multifaceted identity and her own personal life. She says that her aim was "to find a meaningful connection with La Virgen de Guadalupe."[41] Far from any wish to express disrespect, her intention was to explore her personal feelings about Guadalupe. Her depiction was intended as an homage to the Virgin and to the strong women she knows. She states: "As an artist, I feel entitled to express my relationship to her [the Virgin] in a way that is relevant to my own experiences. In doing so, I join many other visual, literary and performance artists, such as Yolanda López, Ester Hernández, Santa Barraza, Delilah Montoya, Yreina Cervantez, Sandra Cisneros and Raquel Salinas, all of whom have shared their personal experiences in their works of the *Virgen de Guadalupe*."[42] Elsewhere she remarks that "Catholic or not, Chicana/Latina/Hispana visual, literary or performance artists grew up with the image of the Virgen de Guadalupe, therefore entitling us to express our relationship to her in any which way that is relevant to our own experiences."[43]

The artist's intention in the case of *Our Lady* was to represent the Virgin as strong and nurturing, quite like the women she knows in the community where she grew up: "When I see "Our Lady" as well as the works portraying the *Virgen* by many Chicana artists, I see an alternative voice expressing the multiplicities of our lived realities. I see myself living a tradition of Chicanas who, because of cultural and gender oppression, have asserted our voice. I see Chicanas creating a deep and meaningful connection to this revolutionary cultural female image. I see Chicanas who understand faith."[44]

The artist's complex relationship to the Virgin of Guadalupe reveals its many nuances when she reinterprets the image from a multifaceted feminist perspective: "Even if I look really hard at my work and the works of many Chicana artists, I don't see what is so offensive. I see beautiful bodies that are gifts from our creator. I see nurturing breasts. I see the strong nurturing mothers of all of us. I am forced to wonder how men like Mr. Villegas and the Archbishop are looking at my work that they feel it is 'blasphemy' and 'the devil.' I wonder how they see bodies of women. I wonder why they think that our bodies are so ugly and perverted that they cannot be seen in an art piece in a museum?"[45] The incident in Santa Fe concluded with a statement by the Museum of New Mexico Committee on Sensitive Materials advising that *Our Lady* should remain on display. But as a compromise the duration of the entire exhibit was curtailed by several months.[46]

The issue at stake in this controversial case is twofold. It can be regarded on the one hand from the viewpoint of the secular realm, and on the other from the realm of the sacred. In the secular realm the center of the debate hinges on the question of censorship—the questionable right of either the state or church to censure a cultural and religious icon that has broken with the normative elements that characterize a tradition sanctioned by a conservative sector within the church. From this point of view the issue concerns an infringement of basic civil rights, namely those relating to freedom of expression. This is the question of the violation of the First Amendment rights of free speech to which every artist in the United States is entitled. In short, in the secular realm *Our Lady* became another battleground over basic civil rights in the United States.

From the viewpoint of the sacred realm, which in this case represents the most conservative element within the Roman Catholic Church, the issue in question is the secularization of a religious icon. The "secularization" that occurred in this case was considered to be a violation of that order which is regarded as sacred, or rather as a destructive act within the sacred order of things. Representatives of both state and church in the Santa Fe community purportedly identified a sacrilegious intention as the motivating factor behind the artist's image. The artist, on the other hand, insisted that *Our Lady* and her other works are a deeply personal attempt to identify, both in thought and meaning, the connections that exist between two seemingly disparate yet deeply related realities: a traditional and religious cultural icon and her own life and identity as an artist. In creating *Our Lady* she did not intend any kind of disrespect whatsoever. On the contrary, she was exploring her own personal feelings about the iconic Guadalupe. Thus, from the point of view of theology, one might say that whether she was aware of it or not, her image reveals that she was deeply involved in both a constructive and a deconstructive process of working through a personally meaningful expression of the divine reality, or what one might call the act of "doing" theology as imaginative construction. The depth of personal investment in such an act attests to the level of motivation behind the artist's ultimate concern.

However one looks at it, the question revolves around the issue of context. The case of context is the following: an image that is inspired by a traditional religious object of devotion is reconstructed from the viewpoint of actual experience. Experience in this case is based on a creative encounter with the artist's own personal reality. She creates a personal image that is a tribute to the Virgin. In a public display at a museum the image is then offered as a personal statement and a work of art, not as an object of veneration. In defense of the freedom of expression, the artist points out the fact that the photo-based digital print in question was on exhibition at a museum and was not intended to be an object of devotion in a church. In a country where state and church operate as separate entities, their respective domains are not to be confused. The image in this case is in the hands of the state and not of the church. Therefore, the church has no right to censure the image's display at a public museum.

In the end the case was settled through a compromise: the image was not removed from the exhibition but the length of the exhibition was shortened. The issue in question, freedom of expression, ultimately won the battle because the image could not be censured in the public domain. An artist's work inspired by an authentic encounter with reality—that is, with the reality of her faith as it was moved to express itself through a particular form that falls within the tradition of a cultural and religious icon—won the battle between the realms of the "sacred" and the "secular." As such it illustrates what John Drury has stated: "The myth has been consumed into the real, the other into the familiar, and has made it wonderful."[47]

The tradition of Guadalupe continues to develop and deliver new and unexpected meanings. The level of depth and power that appears in any particular image—linked to Guadalupe or to any other tradition—is directly related to the quality of the encounter that the artist seeks to express. An artist whose image expresses a personal and authentic encounter with reality will have a greater impact on that image's audience than one whose work does not express such a level of encounter. Consequently, as Rose Marie Berger notes: "Poet Adrienne Rich punctuates the power of art when she says, '[art] wasn't enough as something to be appreciated, finely fingered: it could be a fierce, destabilizing force, a wave pulling you further out than you thought you wanted to be.' A piece of the church's generative power resides with artists' ability to live their vocation fully in the freedom of God. This is the power implicit in prayer; the power of the God of the Tent who won't be confined to temples or museums."[48] No power, therefore, either above or below, can override the freedom of the spirit that the artist participates in through the creative act.

The creative act underlies every authentic encounter with reality. It opens up the depth of reality to its manifold expressions and saves us from the idols of perception, which in the end prove to be oppressive and ultimately self-destructive. In an authentic encounter with reality at its level of depth we begin to perceive the manifold expressions of the creative act (Genesis 1:1–2; John 1:1–3), the reality of which is ever present and fully at work. The iconoclasm that occurs in this act is a natural expression of the process of self-consciously working through theology as imaginative construction. In this process we find that creation and destruction work hand in hand to arrive at the expression of a truth that proves to be liberating and therefore transforming.

The creative act that occurs in an artist's authentic encounter with reality is a liberating event that manifests itself in personal and social transformation. Its hallmark rests on the fact that it radically challenges and even alters a normative viewpoint by opening up reality to the extent that the normative viewpoint is altered. The creative act rescues us from the idolatry of a fixed perception that claims the fullness of truth. Such a perception is sacrosanct only unto itself. For what may be liberating to one perception may be entirely oppressive to another.

The preceding analysis of the mythic vision of the Virgin of Guadalupe, whose origins refer us to symbols of faith, has everything to do with the liberation of a people and with the transformation of their religious symbols in the process of their liberation. This transformation offers a perspective that proves to be liberating. Thus we have found that when distinct cultures encounter one another and coexist under oppressive conditions then religious symbols take the lead that will effect the movement toward liberation. In the case of religious symbols, faith not only receives but also transforms meaning so that what ultimately comes through in the story of faith is a vision that is actualized in the process of imaginative construction. Through that same process the story of Guadalupe came through a vision that developed over the course of time.

Under the impact of prophetic criticism and religious insight Guadalupe's reconstruction is an ongoing process that is sensitive to the struggles of faith. These struggles correspond to the social and historical conditions that are the context of faith. They are embodied in the complex forms that receive their expression in religious symbols. These symbols make themselves known through the power of word and image—that is, through the religious expression they manifest in every form of art.

The fact that theology continues to work with the metaphors, concepts, and images that are rooted in its own mythic origins is evident in the ongoing development of the Guadalupe tradition. After considering the process of imaginative construction through the reconstruction of the Guadalupe image, we are compelled to ask about the theological implications of the iconography that manifests itself in the religious imagination of Latinas.

How can Latina theology benefit by turning its attention to the prevailing iconographic traditions that have their roots in both indigenous and Spanish cultures? It can benefit, first of all, by allowing the image that has been transmitted through the encounter between both cultures to become a vessel for the manifestation of ultimate reality. By opening up to this possibility the theology that is written from the perspective of Latina experience is drawn into the process of imaginative construction. Through religious insight and prophetic criticism the Latina theologian is in a sense already in dialogue with the contemporary artist and with the Guadalupe tradition. In the process of interpreting the image of Guadalupe, the religious symbols of which are rooted in both cultures, the artist can reformulate the tradition from the perspective of contemporary Latina experience. In this process she participates in the imaginative reconstruction of an icon that serves as a vessel for the manifestation of ultimate reality.

To participate in the creative act through the impact of one's ultimate concern is both a liberating and a transforming experience, not only for the artist and for the theologian but also for the person of faith who joins them in dialogue by means of an image that grips them with its power and meaning. Alma López's icon *Our Lady* can thus draw us to participate in the depth content of religious symbols that have the power to transform our perception of ultimate reality.

Can Latina theology benefit by returning to the mythic origins of the Guadalupe tradition and by following its trajectory in the course of history to contemporary representations of *Our Lady*? Without a doubt, both as artists and as theologians, this is what we have been doing all along in the course of our history, through the iconoclastic and reconstructive process of theology as imaginative construction. In so doing we have undergone a process of transformation that to this day we find ourselves participating in by means of a dialogue between the word and the image that reveals our ultimate concern.

Our questions prove their worth when Latinas turn to the proper business of theology, which is the imaginative construction that takes place when we are able to identify the ultimate reality, which though faceless, genderless, and without ethnicity makes itself known to us in an image of someone with whom we can truly identify: a Latina woman. As with the work of some contemporary Latina artists whose vision is liberating in more than one sense, we too can learn how to "do" the visual theologically. We have learned from our Latina artists that while this way of "doing" theology is not out of the ordinary, the process is nonetheless transforming. That is, it can challenge us as theologians, just as it challenges Latina women's reality in general and our society at large.

Notes

1 Kaufman, "Theology as Imaginative Construction," 74. Kaufman rules out some of the traditional ways of understanding what the theological undertaking is all about. The main thesis of his essay lays the foundation by which to identify, by contrast, those practices that are not to be regarded as the chief task of theology. His "thesis A" states: "The proper business of theology (*theoslogos*) is the analysis, criticism and reconstruction of the image/concept of God; therefore theology is (and always has been) essentially an activity of imaginative construction" (74).

2 Elizondo, *La Morenita*, 88.

3 I have used the version of Diego's and Valeriano's *Nican Mopohua* as given by Elizondo in *La Morenita: Evangelizer of the Americas*. Note that all further cites from this work appear as parenthetical page numbers in the text.

4 With its early roots in eastern Christianity, the doctrine of the Immaculate Conception emerged after 1128.

5 Dunnington, *Celebrating Guadalupe*, 57.

6 Ibid.

7 Elizondo, *La Morenita*, 85.

8 Ibid., 84.

9 Ibid.

10 Ibid., 85.

11 Ibid.

12 Ibid., 86.

13 Ibid.

14 Ibid., 91.

15 Dunnington, *Celebrating Guadalupe*, 76.

16 Ibid., 75.

17 A *gachupín* is a demeaning term for a European-born Spaniard living in Mexico (many of whom were hostile to the native-born Mexicans).

18 Dunnington, *Celebrating Guadalupe*, 76.

19 Ibid., 77.

20 Ibid.

21 For a detailed reading of the medieval monastic worldview that this concept represents, see *The Name of the Rose* by Umberto Eco.

22 Cisneros, "Guadalupe the Sex Goddess," 48.

23 Machismo imposes submissiveness on women. It encourages female dependence on men and a passive attitude in the face of male domination.

24 Cisneros, "Guadalupe the Sex Goddess," 48.

25 Kaufman, "Theology as Imaginative Construction," 78.

26 Ibid., 74.

27 Bouchony, *Women*, 165.

28 Lippard, *Mixed Blessings*, 42.

29 Mesa-Bains, *Chicano Art: Resistance and Affirmations*, 137.

30 Yolanda López, quoted in *Yolanda M. López Works: 1975–1978* (San Diego: 1978), 14–15.

31 Gaspar de Alba, *Chicano Art Inside/Outside the Master's House*, 141.

32 "Interview With Alma López," official Web site of Alma López, http://www.almalopez.net (site visited on September 21, 2005).

33 Richard Meyer, "After the Culture Wars," official Web site of Alma López, http://www.almalopez.net (site visited on September 21, 2005).

34 Alma López, "Alma López," University of Nebraska Press, 2002, ProQuest Information and Learning Company, http://www.findarticles.com (site visited on September 21, 2005).

35 Ibid.

36 "Alma López: 2002," California Community Foundation, http://www.calfund.org (site visited on September 21, 2005).

37 Alma López, "The Artist of 'Our Lady,'" LasCulturas.com, http://www.lasculturas.com (site visited on September 21, 2005).

38 Meyer, "After the Culture Wars."

39 Alma López, statement by the artist, official Web site of Alma López, http://www.almalopez.net (site visited on September 21, 2005).

40 López, "The Artist of Our Lady."

41 Alma López, quoted in Hollis Walker, "Depiction of the Virgin of Guadalupe Stirs Objections," *Los Angeles Times*, April 4, 2001; official Web site of Alma López, http://www.almalopez.net (site visited on September 21, 2005).

42 "Interview with Alma López."

43 López, "The Artist of Our Lady."

44 Ibid.

45 Ibid.

46 National Coalition Against Censorship, "Alma López, Our Lady," File Room Publication, http://www.thefileroom.org (site visited on September 21, 2005).

47 Drury, *Painting the Word*, 147.

48 Rose Marie Berger, "Glimpses of God Outside the Temple," *Sojourners*, September-October 1999, 54.

Sheila F. Winborne

RESPONSE TO THE ESSAY BY SUZANNE E. HOEFERKAMP SEGOVIA

In her essay Segovia focuses on both the historical and contemporary significance of icons of the Guadalupe tradition. By rooting her method in the imaginative construction approach of Gordon Kaufman, Segovia shows how a close look at the work of three Latina artists—Yolanda López, Ester Hernández, and Alma López—as imaginative construction can prove useful in developing a theological understanding of the creative act and the image as a means of transformation. With insight Segovia highlights how each of the three artist's critical reinterpretations of icons of the Virgin of Guadalupe may serve as powerful cutting-edge feminist liberation symbols. There are several similarities as well as differences between Segovia's approach to discussing the theological significance of the visual arts and that of my own.

Segovia and I both give attention to the significance of the visual arts in Christian theological development, with a specific focus to how persons of color have been influenced by traditional European iconic approaches. Segovia gives voice to how three artists critically reinterpret traditional iconic subjects in ways that directly speak to the realities of contemporary Latina women. She argues that these new iconic approaches can contribute to the unification of a people. Within a call for greater education and awareness about the significance of the visual arts in historical and contemporary theological development, I focus on some of the ways that "authenticity" has been defined within iconic representations of Jesus Christ. I look at how the "proper" role of visual representations has been defined and debated in the church. I present this focus as background to a discussion on how aesthetics have played a major part in reinforcing as well as countering normative perceptions about individuals of African descent in relation to beliefs about Jesus's race. I discuss how crucifixion imagery and definitions of the black Christ have been interpreted as authentic liberation symbols for African Americans in particular. Segovia too attends to authenticity. She is concerned with authenticity within encounters with reality, and she states that in its depth one can begin to perceive the manifold expressions of the creative act as described in Genesis 1:1–2 and John 1:1–3.

Segovia and I each discuss the influences that European iconic creations have had on minority communities. Segovia is concerned with how representations of the Virgin of Guadalupe shown with European features can be reinterpreted by Latina women. I argue that because most of the images that African Americans see on a daily basis were not created by African Americans, they must be consciously aware of how these images influence self-definitions as well as how they are defined within these images by others. I am not arguing for greater attention to be given to these images than to those created by African Americans. Instead, I am calling for greater education and critical awareness about all art, in particular those works that have the greatest influence on African Americans. I call for greater conscious awareness about how African Americans define themselves as well as how they are defined by others through the visual arts.

Segovia argues that simplistic and dualistic definitions of individuals interferes with seeing their full humanity. She shows how the history of defining women as either ideally submissive and passive virgins or as "sinful" tempests and whores limits women to denigrating roles. Such definitions limit women to being either defined as idealized "holy" virginal figures or devalued as "sinful" tempests. They also rob women of being understood within their full humanity as individuals who are equal to men. My focus includes concern about how simplistic and dualistic definitions of individuals of African descent have been used to reinforce beliefs rooted in colonial ideologies that proclaimed these individuals as inferior to those of European descent.

Segovia argues that the same representational form that may be perceived as liberating in one historical or social context may in another context be perceived as oppressive. For example, she discusses how traditional representations of the Virgin of Guadalupe with her eyes cast down, which icon makers intended to symbolize her humility and compassion, are problematic from a contemporary feminist perspective in that they suggest that women should not project power in overt ways. According to Segovia such representations have contributed to ambiguous and conflicting perceptions of women. This highlights why there is a need for artists such as Yolanda López, Ester Hernández, and Alma López who create and reinterpret traditional iconic representations. There is not only a need for artists who create transformative representations of Latina women but also artists who create transformative representations of all women and all persons of color. This includes a need for representations that embrace womanist and black theologies.

Significant parts of our cultures and faith beliefs are passed on from generation to generation through the visual arts. It is important that communities that historically have been oppressed participate in communicating the truths of personal and communal histories in ways that may inspire and communicate to current and future generations their diversity of experiences. Within this context, like Segovia I recognize that art and artists can provide prophetic criticism and religious insight.

Segovia and I both discuss influences that historical fine art or iconic representations have had on popular media. Segovia gives attention to how representations of the Virgin of Guadalupe as passive and submissive have reinforced the mistreatment of women in the home and workplace. She discusses how the visual arts of the Roman Catholic Church have influenced popular representations of women in Mexican television soap operas. I give attention to how contemporary discussions about representations as "authentic" take place in relation to popular media images such as films that represent biblical events.

A closer look reveals differences in how Segovia and I approach visual theological development. For example, there are differences in our approaches to theological method. Segovia roots her method in the imaginative construction of Gordon Kaufman and applies it to an analysis of the icons of the Guadalupe tradition. I take a more interdisciplinary approach rooted in part in the visual and verbal hermeneutical approach that Margaret Miles uses in works such as *Image as Insight* (1985), and I apply it to an expansive look at "authenticity" in iconic church history. Like Miles I begin from a historical analysis that includes recognizing the approaches to the visual arts taken by historical theologians and art historians. As such, focus may be placed on how issues of race, gender, sexism, and "secularity" may be expressed in texts, and how the visual or written languages of these texts may reflect the issues listed above as they are used in power structures and struggles. This may include discussion about how such issues can be interpreted and implied in artworks, from both the artist and viewers' perceptions. My approach to the visual arts, theology, history, and multicultural issues also includes an expansion upon Rudolf Arnheim's thesis in *Visual Thinking* (1969). This expansion functions as an underlying hypothesis—that is, that visual interpretations have ethical implications that influence both self and communal definitions. Arnheim argues that the task of visual interpretation is a serious cognitive process. Like Arnheim, I acknowledge that sight or the ability to "see" is a primary function and a visual language form to be studied seriously. According to Arnheim, because we cannot understand the things we "see" until they are cast into "manageable models," visual perception, visual artistic creation, and thought are interrelated. Thinking and how it influences art creation and interpretation has self and communal implications.

With a look at the significances of the visual arts in theological development, the possibilities for dialogues between Latino and Latina and African American theologians can be fostered in ways that prove mutually enriching. Areas for discussion may include how individuals of both communities have been influenced and defined through the arts. For example, discussions may focus on how traditional representations of the Virgin Mary, Jesus Christ, and other biblical figures shown with European features have reinforced and influenced individuals of both the Latino and Latina and African American communities in their self-understanding in relation to God. Also, concern may be given to possibilities for reinterpretations of traditional subjects in ways that give attention to some of the diversity of experiences within Latino and Latina and African American communities. This offers an opportunity for dialogue about the importance of persons of color taking critical transformative and liberating approaches to how they have been represented and defined through traditional iconic representations, and about the ways they may create new images that project their self-definitions. These dialogues may be both constructive as well as deconstructive and include a focus on theological concerns from feminist and womanist perspectives. These dialogues also may seek to blend as well as transform ancient and contemporary approaches to representing and interpreting iconic subjects within the Christian church and beyond. As Segovia suggests, contemporary reinterpretations of historical figures may embody a kernel of the original "good news" of the subject represented as well as shed light on the less fruitful aspects that embody and contribute to oppressive views and representational approaches.

Sheila F. Winborne

THE THEOLOGICAL SIGNIFICANCE OF NORMATIVE
PREFERENCES IN VISUAL ART CREATION
AND INTERPRETATION

The scientific, political, or cultural imperative to maintain normative
standards . . . is an outgrowth of society's relentless need to establish
"truth." What determines this "truth" in any society is a system of ordered
procedures for the production, regulation, distribution, and articulation of
the dominant ideologies of the society at large.—Maurice Berger, *How Art
Becomes History*

The visual art forms of various media have functioned as powerful sources
of theological influence throughout Christian history and continue to do
so today. Yet often the significance of the visual arts has been a neglected
topic in theological discussions, as the significance of oral and written expressions of and about "the word" as "truth" has been given priority. It is
through visual as well as oral and written language forms that we encounter representations and interpretations of normative beliefs as accepted
standards and preferred forms of expression. This includes normative
theological beliefs. One of the ways that cultural beliefs and preferences
are passed on to new generations is through the visual arts. In contemporary United States society, which is rooted in the Protestant ethics of
the "founding fathers" and continues to be driven by the Protestant ethics of the majority of our contemporary political leaders, there is a need
for greater understanding and appreciation for the theological roles that
the visual arts play in our lives. This is particularly important at this time

in the United States because increasingly this nation is becoming more of a visually based society than a literarily based one. There is continued growth in the roles that popular visual arts play in influencing the beliefs and daily practices of Americans. As a verification of this trend one need only recognize how most Americans look to popular media for both news and entertainment. Also, there are increases in the number of writings and academic courses across disciplines devoted to United States visual culture.[1] Daily we are exposed to various types of visual art representations through the commercial media of television, cinema, the Internet, books, newspapers, magazines, billboards, and to a lesser extent through fine art displays in museums, galleries, and churches. Although art is still displayed in many churches, many of the pieces originally displayed in churches in past centuries are now in museums and galleries. Because people generally do not go to museums and galleries or churches on a daily basis, increasingly most people are exposed to the visual arts and the normative cultural preferences that are communicated through art by daily exposure to popular or commercial media.

In this essay I address some of the ways that theological "truth" has been discussed within debates about the "authenticity" of specific types of visual representations, both historically within the church and in contemporary society in the United States. I give particular attention to how various representations of Jesus Christ have been defined as "authentic." As a background to my discussion on contemporary imagery I begin by briefly discussing how "authenticity" within iconic representations of Jesus was addressed within several historical debates. Second, I focus on how definitions and representations of Jesus as "authentic" by Europeans and European Americans have become normative, and how African Americans have taken counterapproaches to defining and creating "authentic" representations of Jesus. These discussions are followed by a focus on the structure of debates by church officials and others about one of the most widely viewed recent film representations of Jesus. How these debates reflect the structure of historical iconic debates within the church while also reflecting racial and religious divides in the United States is an issue that I address specifically. In addition, I give attention to the implications of how discussions about "authenticity" may be structured in ways that continue to divide communities or in ways that may encourage dialogue within and between communities. Finally, I address implications for future theological development. I discuss the practical consequences of debates about "authentic" or "proper" approaches to representing Jesus Christ and other sacred subjects. I approach these issues with an awareness that within the "melting pot" ideology of the United States, too often concepts of race and religion are presented as primarily black and white and Christian issues, in spite of the racial and religious diversity that has always been within this nation.[2] I highlight how specific approaches to the creation and interpretation of visual art forms have contributed to as well as critiqued this reality. This essay is not intended to be an all-inclusive discussion about the theological significance of the visual arts or about normative visual preferences but instead is presented as a point of departure for more expansive discussions and dialogues.[3]

The Historical Search for "Authentic" Iconography

To understand how contemporary theologies and related debates are communicated through visual art forms, we need some understanding of the history within which they are rooted. Therefore I take a look at several historic iconic debates in an effort to more fully understand the roots and significance of some of the current approaches to defining "authenticity" and "truth" in visual representations within Christianity. Although often not the most central theological concern, throughout the centuries the "proper" role of visual representations has been a complicated and debated issue in the church. The existence of Christian art in the catacombs in Rome serves as evidence that visual representations were important within Christianity during earlier centuries. In the centuries that followed there was disagreement about how much importance visual representations should be given within Christendom.

A primary focus within iconic debates was the issue of "authenticity." By definition, icons are not just visual representations for appreciation; instead, they recall specific theologies and are used for veneration. Those who supported placing visual representations in the church and those who argued against it disagreed about what should be defined as "holy," "real," "purity of faith," and "authentic." To support their beliefs, individuals on each side of the debates pointed to historical events and artistic styles they accepted as "true" and "authentic" within Christian history. These power struggles influenced structural divisions in the church and what would become normative approaches to defining the "proper" role of the visual arts.

The differences in approaches to the creation and veneration of "authentic" iconography were among the topics of debate that contributed to the eventual permanent divide between the Byzantine Church of the East and the Catholic Church of the West. Not only was the "proper" role of the visual arts a debated issue between the Eastern and Western regions of the church, it was a debated issue within the Byzantine Church and within the Catholic Church, and later as a result of the sixteenth-century reforms within and between various denominations of the Protestant Church. Debates about "authenticity" within the Byzantine Church influenced how later iconic debates between the East and West and within the churches of the West would be structured.

During iconodule periods in the Byzantine Church, icons were usually given the same honor as other "holy" relics and symbols including the cross. At times, icons were defined as equal to the Bible in some respects. The Second Council of Nicaea concluded that both the Bible and icons were means to God's revelation.[4] The council defined icons as having the ability to aid worshippers in gaining access to the holy figure represented—that is, a saint or Jesus Christ. Several types of arguments were cited in support of keeping icons in the church, including the argument that the visual incarnation and virgin birth were evidence of God's approval of visual representations. Often arguments in favor of icons were rooted in the premise that either the first iconic representations of Jesus Christ were created by an "authentic" historical figure who based his or her creation upon an eyewitness account or that Jesus created icons of himself. St. Luke was said to have created the first "authentic" iconic painting of Jesus based upon eyewitness observation. In addition some icon supporters argued that the Veronica and King Abgar of Edessa "holy face" legends were evidence that Jesus himself approved of icons. Each of these legends described how an image of Jesus's face miraculously appeared on a cloth at the moment the cloth came in contact with his face. Within a focus on Jesus's spiritual nature and his relationship with heaven, the cloths were said not to have been made by human hands. Each cloth also was said to have the same miraculous healing powers as Jesus and were accepted as visual proof of his physical existence.[5] Hans Belting defines earlier legends such as these as occurring within periods before the "era of art" or the so-called Dark Ages in Europe, before contemporary conceptions of art as a part of collections and before the fame of artists came into being. He states that "holy face" cloths functioned as secondary forms of "face to face" contact between the viewer and the figure represented. These icons were perceived as objects through which the divine could intervene in the immediate events of human life.

During periods of iconoclasm, various types of arguments were used in support of the destruction of images. Some embraced iconoclasm as a way of defining themselves as followers of Jesus's teachings and in opposition to other faith practices and traditions. In defining themselves in opposition to pagan influences and approaches to imagery, many who opposed icons in the church formatted arguments based upon a specific interpretation of the second commandment—that is, that all created imagery was idolatrous (cf. Exodus 20:4). Others focused on whether the two natures of Jesus Christ could be "properly" represented, namely his natures as both a physical and spiritual being. Still others declared that the Eucharist was the only "true" and acceptable symbolic image of Christ.

The iconic debates reflected important theological differences between the East and West that contributed to what eventually became a permanent divide between the two regions of Christendom. At the meeting of Eastern and Western church officials in Constantinople in 1054, Cardinal Humbert accused the Easterners of worshipping a "dead" Christ because of the distorted representational style of their icons. At the Council of Ferrara-Florence in the fifteen century, the Eastern patriarch Gregory Melissenos voted against a reunion between the two regions by arguing that he could not pray to the more realistically rendered Western images of Christ.[6]

Although there is some evidence that particular artists from each region incorporated stylistic elements used by artists from the other region, in general Eastern artists focused on representing Christ and the saints' relationships with the beings and things of heaven, while Western artists focused more on representing Christ and the saints' relationships with humanity and the things of the earth.[7] For the most part Eastern artists rendered iconic figures of Christ and the saints in distortion and in somewhat static poses as reminders to worshippers of the "other-worldliness" or "heaven-boundness" of the incarnate God and the saints. Eastern icons were meant to reinforce the perception of humanity looking up to God in heaven. The twelfth-century painting *Christ Eleemon* is a well-known example of this Eastern rendering style. The Western stylistic approach was developed partly in opposition to the Eastern approach as the Western church increased its independence from the East. In general, Western artists used more realistic or "expressionistic" styles of rendering intended to symbolically represent the "real presence" of Christ and other biblical figures. The intent of these artists was to give viewers more of a feeling of being in the actual "bodily presence" of the figures represented, and in so doing reinforce the focus on Christ's "earth-boundness" or God's continuing presence in human activities. Michelangelo's work on the ceiling of the Sistine Chapel, created in the sixteenth century, is a well-known example of this Western style. The Eastern and Western stylistic approaches were reflective of the basic theological differences between the churches of the two regions.[8]

The outcomes of the iconic debates were never just symbolic—there were practical consequences as well. Belting states that image theologies have always had practical ends, in that they were used to support specific church theologies—such as the incarnation of God, the virgin birth, and the beliefs that specific images were "holy" and "not made by human hands."[9] Theological disputes within the church carried over into social and political practices. Peter Brown in his discussion about the history of iconoclasm states that "holiness was power; and the symbol of the holy could cover a very real nexus of social influence."[10] Church officials on each side of the debates recognized the power of messages communicated through imagery. Historically, those theologians and rulers who were against iconography in the church as well as those who were for it recognized the tremendous power that images had in influencing the beliefs and worldviews of worshippers as citizens of nations.

A prominent concern within both regions of Christendom was whether church officials could control the theological messages communicated through iconic images. This concern took on new meaning within the Protestant image debates. With the rise of Protestantism the proclamation that the power of images should be secondary to the power of the spoken and written word took on additional prominence. Belting concludes that visual representations lost much of their power for those in the West during the sixteenth-century German Protestant reform. In other words, during this period in the West visual representations were interpreted more as art to be admired than icons to be venerated.

During the sixteenth-century German Protestant reform the use of visual representations in the church was an issue of concern for Martin Luther and his followers who defined much of the Protestant movement's approach to iconography in direct opposition to the Catholic Church's approach of embracing the visual arts. Within the Protestant movement there were two dominant opposing arguments: first, that visual art in the church would lead to idolatry, and second, Luther's argument that visual art did no harm and therefore could be used as reinforcement or illustration of the "word" of God and God as "word" for the illiterate. Both of these arguments placed the visual arts in the background. The first argument reinforced a belief that all visual art was necessarily idolatrous. The second argument confirmed that visual art was useful only as illustrative aids to words. Luther's primary focus was on the written and spoken "word." In an attempt to control how and what representations were used in the early Protestant movement as secondary sources of communication, Luther collaborated with the artist Lucas Cranach the Elder toward creating "authentic" paintings that symbolized and communicated the key beliefs of the movement while also reinforcing his power as interpreter and communicator of the "Word."

The iconodule approaches of Luther and his followers as well as the various iconoclastic approaches continue to influence how the visual arts are understood within much of the church and within many Christian-oriented societies. Although elements of the intended messages of the paintings on which Cranach collaborated with Luther were in opposition to elements in Catholic theology, his painting style was influenced by the realistic styles of representations created for the Catholic Church. The acceptance of representations of Christ by Western artists such as Cranach as "real" and "authentic" contributed to normative beliefs that Jesus looked as he had been represented in most paintings for the Western church—that is, as being part of the white race and having European features. Such representations downplayed or even ignored Jesus's Jewish heritage. Representations of Jesus as white have helped reinforce European and American Christian missionary approaches that have supported colonial ideologies. Colonialism directed greater attention to beliefs about Jesus's physical appearance than to the significance of his actions of love, empathy, and compassion toward the poor and oppressed. Representations of Christ as white by artists of European descent became the norm and were accepted as "authentic" representations, and this type of approach continues to be widely accepted as "authentic."

Normative and "Authentic" Representations of Jesus Christ and of African Americans

Normative ideas, beliefs, and debates about the physical appearance of Jesus as God incarnate, particularly in the West, have often been interrelated with the normative ways that individuals of African descent have been represented. Debates about Jesus's biological makeup and in particular his skin color have helped reinforce ideas about who is more "Godlike" and who is not.

It is not unusual for individuals of all faith traditions to represent their god or gods in their own images. Albert Moore states in *Iconography of Religions* that "if oxen, horses or lions could make works of art they too would depict the gods like themselves in their own animal form."[11] The human tendency to represent one's god or gods in one's own image has had specific implications within colonial practices. Most blacks from Africa who were brought to America as slaves were originally exposed to Christianity by their white slave owners and other supporters of institutionalized slavery. White slave owners and supporters of slavery were the first to expose African American slaves to oral and visual interpretations of Jesus Christ as the Christian God incarnate. When a group with power over others, such white slave owners and their black slaves, represented Jesus in their own images the representations carried oppressive messages. Such representations became visual support of the slave owners' interpretations of scripture. They presented specific interpretations of scripture that supported slavery and that declared whites to be among God's "chosen" as well as more "Godlike" than blacks.

Because historically many political policies and social practices in the United States were developed to reinforce the enslavement and continued servant status of blacks by whites, many of this nation's debates and concerns were originally and continue to be centered on these two groups, often to the exclusion of citizens of other races. Two of the most prominent Christian theological approaches within the United States have been to define and represent Jesus as either white or black. In the sections that follow, I discuss the history of each of these two approaches in relation to the history of defining "authenticity" in Christianity. Globally, Sallman's representation continues to be among the most embraced representations of Jesus.

The Search for an "Authentic" White Christ

Representations of Jesus Christ as white have reflected and supported theologies that reinforce beliefs of white superiority over all other races, particularly the black race. Such representations have a long history within Western art traditions, as do the degrading representations of persons of African descent.[12] These types of representations interrelated with the beliefs of the early European colonists, and the Christian missionary approaches have contributed to ideas of white superiority in America. Warner

Sallman's *Head of Christ* (1940) as one of the most popular modern and contemporary representations of Jesus is rooted in the earlier history of representing Jesus as white and is an example of the continued acceptance of this type of image as among the most "authentic" ways of representing Jesus.

Beliefs about white superiority have often been interrelated with the beliefs that supported ideas of America as the "new Israel" and the United States as a "chosen" nation as well as the missionary approaches toward persons of color. As they began their new lives in America John Winthrop (1588–1649) and the Puritan colonists understood themselves as God's "new chosen" who were entering into a covenant with God.[13] In looking at theologies that have supported ideas of the United States as a chosen nation, the approaches of four Massachusetts-born American historians are relevant. George Bancroft (1800–1891), William H. Prescott (1796–1859), John Lothrop Motley (1814–1877), and Francis Parkman (1823–1893) were among the historians who defined America as "God's chosen nation in which the progressive forces of Protestantism had reached final and perfect culmination."[14] Josiah Strong (1847–1916), a midwestern theologian and minister, also interpreted the United States as the chosen nation. Given that the Puritans and their descendents had in part defined themselves as chosen based upon their interpretations of their agriculturally driven lifestyles as more simple and "pure" than the more urban and industrial lifestyles of Europeans, Strong feared that if the increases in industrialization continued in the United States then the nation's citizens would eventually suffocate under material growth.[15] Strong was among those who argued that a good alternative outlet for the energy that was going into this material expansion was for Anglo-Saxon Protestant Americans to go out as missionaries and convert persons of color to Christianity. Approaches such as Strong's were used to support historical ideas of America as the new or "true Israel"; white Christian Americans as the new chosen; and persons of color as inferior to whites.[16]

Beliefs that America was the new chosen land and white Americans of European descent were God's new chosen people were among the factors used to help unify those living in the territories that became the United States. Renderings of Jesus with European features, which distanced him from his Jewish ancestry, helped reinforce these beliefs. Some of the "founding fathers" and later political leaders believed that if the United States was to successfully function as a united nation there would have to be unity in the citizens' beliefs and tastes as well as unity in their physical look. For example, Ronald Takaki states that the Naturalization Laws of

1790 legally linked race to the republican ideal. These laws were reflective of the belief by many that black skin in particular was counter to the republican ideal, as this ideal pointed to beliefs about "the American dream."[17] For most, the American dream included having at least a middle-class economic status and the "melting" of all Americans into a "civilized" look and lifestyle based upon what was interpreted as the best within European tastes. To create this ideal republic, white Americans chose to inhabit Native Americans' land and to use blacks as well as Latino/as and Asians as laborers.[18] Yet, the presence of blacks as well as other persons of color in America was counter to the ideas of many white Americans about how the people of America as a homogeneous society and a united chosen nation should look.

European Americans were not the first Christians to define themselves as the new or "true Israel." This definition by European Americans can be seen in relation to an earlier declaration by citizens of the Byzantine empire. In the seventh century under the rule of Emperor Heraclius there was an increase in the influence of Hebrew Bible theology. This resulted in the Byzantine people defining themselves as the "true Israel" or God's "chosen people."[19] Just as it was not unusual for groups within particular faith traditions to represent their god or gods in their own images, it was not unusual for various groups within traditions to define themselves as the "true," "chosen," or "authentic" followers of their faith's beliefs and practices. In reaction to the white theologians who had defined themselves and the United States as God's new chosen, black theologians and artists presented counterarguments.

The Search for an "Authentic" Black Christ

The documented history of Jesus Christ as black interrelated with approaches to the black civil rights struggles in the United States dates back to at least the nineteenth century. In opposition to the definitions by whites of themselves as God's new chosen, black Americans understood themselves as chosen. But there were significant differences in the ways that blacks defined themselves and defined whites based upon biblical interpretations. For the most part black Americans neither saw white Americans as the new chosen nor America as the "new Israel" or promised land. Instead, most blacks identified with the Hebrews' plight before the Exodus and understood America as a "new Egypt" or land of oppression.[20] There is a history of visual representations by African American artists that reflects this belief.

Interpretations and representations of America as a land of oppression reflected African Americans' identification with both the suffering of the Hebrews before the Exodus and with the unjust suffering of Jesus during his crucifixion. For example, photographs that document the lynching of African Americans and fine art paintings that represent this chapter in American history have been interpreted as a type of crucifixion imagery. The publication of lynching photographs was prevalent during the late nineteenth century and the early decades of the twentieth century. They were published as journalistic images in newspapers and magazines as well as on postcards as a form of entertainment that reinforced white superiority. The act of lynching a black person was often itself an event of spectacle and entertainment for white accusers and bystanders, as many would travel great distances to witness these events. Also, artists working in various fine art media have created representations of Christ as black that communicate messages about blacks as among God's chosen and function as visual critiques of lynchings and other types of abuse and oppression against blacks. For example, Prentiss Taylor in his lithography *Christ in Alabama* (1932) presents a visual interpretation of Langston Hughes's poem of the same name. Based upon Hughes's poem in which he describes Christ as a "Nigger, Beaten and Black," Taylor presents an image of Christ as a black man with his arms stretched out in front of the cross, while to one side of him is his mother in despair and to the other side is a cotton field.[21] In more recent times artists such as Joe Harris have continued to create representations of Christ as black. In his fine art photographic representation of Christ entitled *Crucifixion #2* (1994), Harris represented Christ on the cross within an urban environment. These types of visual interpretations of the African American experience are a part of and reflective of black theological declarations that Jesus Christ is black, and interpretations of black suffering as akin to that of both the Hebrews in Egypt and Jesus on the cross.

Historically and continuing to this day blacks have identified with the oppression of the Hebrews before the Exodus and have looked to biblical accounts of Jesus's support of the oppressed. Jesus's crucifixion is seen as a liberation symbol in relation to "authentic" definitions of Jesus as black. Within his black liberation theology, James Cone has declared that a theology that identifies with the oppressed is an "authentic" Christian theology, while a white racist theology that supports oppression is a theology of the "Antichrist."[22] Although Cone is credited with bringing black theology and the black Christ to fruition in relation to the civil rights struggles of the 1960s and 1970s, he was not the first to associate images of the black Christ with the civil rights struggles of African Americans. Robert Alexander Young in his *Ethiopian Manifesto* (1829) stated that a black messiah would liberate blacks from slavery. In a speech delivered in 1898 Henry McNeal Turner stated the importance of blacks imagining God and Jesus in their own images. Countee Cullen described Christ as black in works such as his poem "The Black Christ" (1928).[23] As Marcus Garvey (1887–1940), the nationalist and founder of the Universal Negro Improvement Association, stated: "Whilst our God has not color, yet it is human to see everything through one's own spectacles . . . We Negros believe in the God of Ethiopia. . . . we shall worship Him through the spectacles of Ethiopia."[24] Cone's theology can be interpreted as an extension of or as standing on earlier declarations such as these.

Like others before him, Cone and the other contemporary theologians who have based their work upon his have argued that Jesus as God incarnate was black. Cone's theology is a response to the legacies of the enslavement and lynchings of blacks. It is also a response to arguments by white theologians who proclaimed that God as the "father" and as the incarnate "son" was on their side, for they were among the chosen because of their race. Cone points to Jesus as a champion and liberator of the poor and of those who have suffered unjustly. Jesus's crucifixion is a symbol of unjust and sacrificial suffering. Jesus declared that the last shall be first and the first shall be last (cf. Matthew 19:30). Like those before him such as Cullen, Cone argues that because blacks historically have suffered greatly and have been among the least, black people—in particular blacks of African American ethnicity—are among God's chosen. Here Cone implies the suffering of blacks that was due to institutional slavery in the Americas as well as the discrimination and lynching that continued in the United States after slavery was abolished. He argues that African American slaves and their descents reflect God's spiritual and physical image in the suffering of Jesus Christ.[25] In describing Jesus as black and blacks as God's chosen people Cone counters earlier normative images of blacks as necessarily inferior and capable only of positions of servitude to whites.

Although I agree with Cone's statement that no one theology can be for all times, and I recognize the strengths of his theological approach in addressing issues of white racism during the civil rights movement of the 1960s and the periods that followed, I also recognize some limitations in such an approach.[26] I share this view with Kelly Brown Douglas and Victor Anderson, each of whom in their discussions of Cone's theology address

the limitations of his ontological approach to describing Jesus. In developing his theology Cone borrowed from Paul Tillich's ontological theological
approach.[27] In Douglas's critique of Cone, one of the issues she focuses
on is Cone's language. She highlights the fact that part of the problem
with interpreting Cone's ontological approach in works such as *A Black
Theology of Liberation* is the often vague nature of his theological language
in affirming the two dimensions of Jesus's blackness—that is, Jesus's existence as a literal biological being and as a symbol who identifies with the
oppressed and poor.[28]

Anderson also addresses the limitations of Cone's approach. He interprets Cone's theology as bound to white racial ideologies and as embodying some of the same limitations as the white theologies: "In aesthetics,
African American expressive actions are bound denotatively by the dream
of an Africa American form. In politics, African American leadership is
bound by white and black racial ideology, and the politics of exclusion and
inclusion they breed. In religion and theology, church and public theologies are determined by white theology and black theology, the righteous
oppressed and the damnable oppressors. In these cultural spaces ontological blackness binds all."[29] Anderson concludes that Cone's black theology,
like white theologies that justify racism, limits discussions about Jesus to
his physical and symbolic appearance within issues of blackness versus
whiteness. In other words, in justifying his theology in opposition to white
theologies Cone requires white theologies for legitimacy, and he mirrors
their categorical racism in his approach. Cone's theological approach in
works such as *A Black Theology of Liberation* as well as the theological approaches of his white opponents reinforce the dynamics of insiders versus
outsiders. These approaches tend to focus on black and white racial identities to the exclusion of conversations about other races, gender, sexual
origination, and social and economic status. They thus allow whiteness to
be identifiable with what is described within Tillich's theology as "ultimate
concern" or "being" versus "non-being" in relation to God.[30] Anderson is
critical of aesthetic theories and African American practices that continue
to be primarily bound by the structure and questions presented in white
racial ideologies. He also highlights how in most contemporary black theologies there is an absence of discussions about the role that the visual
arts have and continue to play in defining blackness.[31] This is the case in
Cone's theology. Although Cone rooted part of his approach on Tillich's
theology, he does not address the significance of Tillich's in-depth theology of the arts.

Historically, some prominent black leaders and scholars have recognized that aesthetics have played a major part in reinforcing as well as countering normative perceptions about persons of African descent. For example, Frederick Douglass (1818–1895) understood the importance of recognizing the role that the visual arts had played in the oppression of blacks: "Negros can never have impartial portraits at the hands of white artists . . . without most grossly exaggerating their distinctive features. And the reason is obvious. Artists, like all other white persons, have developed a theory dissecting the distinctive features of Negro physiognomy."[32] The specific types of representations to which Douglass referred were those by persons of European descent that presented persons of African descent as "savages," as objects for "scientific" discovery and research, as objects of entertainment, and as "exotic" objects of desire.

Historically there have been specific interpretative definitions of Africa in which normative representations of persons of African descent by persons of European descent were rooted. Jan Nederveen Pieterse states that the Western iconography of Africans and African Americans as "savages" was based upon ideas of Africa as a wild and overwhelming landscape with an abundance of flora. As a result, from the nineteenth-century European point of view in particular, the African "savage" was defined by absences and abundances—that is, "absences of clothing, possessions, and attributes of civilization," and abundances of wildness, overwhelming landscapes, and flora.[33] Within his discussion Nederveen Pieterse also states that the act of defining persons of color as "other" and "exotic" has reinforced stereotypes that ultimately suggest the notion of "foreign" as different and inferior. He states that as an "exotic" object "the Other is not merely to be exploited, but also to be enjoyed, enjoyment being a finer form of exploitation."[34] For example, the entertainment qualities of lynchings as events of spectacle can be interpreted from this perspective. The histories of defining black persons of African descent as "savages" and as "exotic" reflect the luxury that those in positions of power have in directing and reinforcing normative perceptions that attempt to negate perceptions of blacks as multidimensional individuals who are a part of a particular race. Problems develop when a normative or stereotypical definition is so prominent and accepted that it becomes all one can see or perceive.

Like Douglass, W. E. B. Du Bois (1868–1963) recognized how the arts have been used to both reinforce the oppression of blacks and to bring about further acceptance of blacks as equal to whites. Du Bois particularly saw the value of the arts in communicating and expressing black cultural experiences. In his seminal essay from 1903 on the "Talented Tenth" and in the essay that followed, Du Bois discussed a number of contributions by blacks to what he referred to as "American civilization." Among the ten, he included three individuals who were involved in the arts; one was the visual artist Henry Ossawa Tanner (1859–1937).[35] Later, Du Bois was supportive of the Harlem Renaissance art movement of the 1920s in which blacks in every area of the arts communicated experiences that countered stereo-typical, one-dimensional perceptions of African Americans. Like Douglass and Du Bois, Anderson recognizes the power of the arts to influence the quality of life for African Americans. He recognizes that one of the ways that which is most prominently accepted as "true" and "authentic" has been communicated and critiqued is through the visual arts. Not only have representations by African American artists such has Prentiss Taylor, Henry Ossawa Tanner, and numerous others reflected and influenced Af-rican Americans' perceptions and definitions of themselves, but also the ways that European Americans have interpreted and represented African Americans, and how these representations have become normative have had a large impact on African Americans' perceptions and experiences. For historically and continuing to this day the majority of representations of African Americans, particularly those that have become normative, have been created by persons of European descent. For this reason, African Americans need to focus on informed understandings of both how they interpret themselves visually as well as how they have been and are still interpreted visually by others. Historically, the most prominent ways that both European Americans and African Americans have defined and rep-resented Christ have been interrelated with their definitions of each other and themselves as Christians.

The Contemporary Search for an "Authentic" Christ

When comparing historical theological debates about "authenticity" of im-agery to those of today, many of the underlying concerns are often the same. As it was during previous periods, today concerns about visual "au-thenticity" often have to do with power, regardless of which medium is being discussed. Image debates about representations of Jesus Christ, for example, still often reflect concerns about who should have power and privilege, and who should not. Much of the discussion within these de-bates is often centered on conclusions about who bears responsibility for Jesus' death and injustices against his followers. Just as had been the case in historical debates, these types of concerns bring to the forefront tensions and disagreements about which groups and individuals within Christianity are the most faithful followers of Jesus' teachings, most "God-like," and God's "true chosen." Contemporary debates often continue to be interrelated with issues about who groups and individuals within the church "see" as enemies of the church and as enemies to their preferred ways of life.

Within these debates, how are issues of theological "truth" and "authenticity" as they relate to visual representations of Christ most often discussed and represented? Which representations of Jesus Christ most often capture the popular American imagination today? Because the limits of this essay do not allow me to present an in-depth discussion of the contemporary history of how race and "authenticity" of Christ imagery have been interpreted and critiqued in various visual media, I have chosen to focus this discussion on one of the most debated and influential contemporary representations, and discuss how the debates around this contemporary representation reflect many of the ways "authenticity" and theological "truth" were defined historically. I recognize that to a lesser extent than in previous centuries, within some churches today there is still veneration of icons. Pilgrimages to see icons and relics believed to have miraculous healing powers still take place. Also, there are occasionally debates about the appropriateness of some fine art representations of Jesus or the saints.[36] But, the representations that usually receive the most attention across faith traditions and across Christian denominations are those represented in film. In other words, often with as much intensity and vigor as historical iconic debates about paintings and statues in the church, today's debates about "proper" approaches to representing Christ are centered around film representations, with Mel Gibson's *The Passion of the Christ* (2005) being one of the most debated recent representations.

In recent years, various representations of Jesus' life presented through film have been seen by numerous viewers around the world, and have generated a great deal of debate and controversy. Although there has been some variety in the ways God has been represented in popular comedy films, including as a white woman in *Dogma* (1999) and as a black man in *Bruce Almighty* (2003), for the most part the most popular representations continue to reinforce images of God Incarnate as a white man with little focus on his Jewishness. For the most part, this has also been the case in popular representations of Jesus Christ. Although Gibson has stated that his intentions in *The Passion of the Christ* were in part to highlight Jesus's

Jewishness and the "truth" of his crucifixion based upon the Gospels, Gibson's critics have accused him of presenting the opposite. This has been one of the most debated representations of Jesus Christ in recent years, with many supporting Gibson's film as progressive and many others criticizing the film as stereotypical.

Gibson's representation of Jesus has been accepted by many as an "authentic" representation, and interpreted by others as anti-Semitic and counter to biblical descriptions. Gibson presents an intense portrayal of the last twelve hours of Jesus's life, with focus on the violence of his crucifixion and his suffering. The reach of Gibson's representation expanded beyond film audiences, in that the debates about *The Passion of the Christ* have carried over into other media. The film captured the attention of a sizable percentage of the United States population. Numerous Internet sites—entertainment, faith-based, and scholarly—have been devoted to discussions about this film. Upon the release of this film, the points of debate about the film were presented in newspapers, magazines, on some local television news reports, and on so-called "soft news" television entertainment shows such as *Entertainment Tonight*. On some programs, Gibson explained and defended his intent. Other programs presented scholars and persons of various faith communities debating the "authenticity" and significance of the film. Also, several popular as well as scholarly volumes and articles have been devoted to discussions on the significance of the film.[37] Some accused the filmmaker of perpetuating normative stereotypical imagery of Jews as well as presenting imagery of extreme violence that was not in keeping with the Gospels. Others praised him for creating a progressive representation of the "truth" of the Gospels. Numerous ministers of various Christian denominations recommended the film to their congregations as an "authentic" and "true" representation, with some actually taking their congregations to view the film. In contrast, others of the Christian faith as well as some of the Jewish faith declared the film offensive and anti-Semitic. Much of the discussion about Gibson's film was centered on questions about the filmmaker's agenda and intent.

Just as style of representation was a dividing issue historically between the Eastern and Western regions of the church, style of representation was a dividing issue within some of the debates about Gibson's *Passion of the Christ*. For example, many argued that the realism of the violence against Jesus in the crucifixion scenes in the film was beyond what was acceptable based upon contemporary movements against excessive violence in films. Others argued that Gibson's representation could not be considered "authentic" based upon descriptions in the Gospels. Still others were moved by the violence in these scenes, in that they felt as if they were in the "real presence" of Jesus at the moment of crucifixion. Jesus's pain and suffering became real for them. Based upon each of these conclusions by viewers of the film, Gibson's representational approach can be said to be in keeping with earlier Western approaches to representing Christ's "earth-boundness," i.e., with focus on his humanity and relation to the persons and things of the earth vs. greater attention to his relation to the spiritual things of heaven as was the style of early Eastern icon makers. The realism of the Western style was intended to symbolically give the viewer the feeling of being in the actual bodily presence of Jesus. Gibson highlighted the physical pain Jesus felt.

In looking at the debates about the film, it is interesting to note what was not among the main issues of concern as well. For example, in his essay about the debates that have surrounded *The Passion of the Christ*, Robert A. Faggen states that few have focused on whether the film itself succeeds as a devotional work of art, or what the popularity of the film might suggest about the future of religious art. Instead, most of Gibson's critiques have focused on whether the film supports the politics of anti-Semitism and the often lack of focus within Christianity of Jesus as a Jew. Some voiced concern as to whether Gibson has perpetuated anti-Semitism during a time when many Americans already have heightened fears about non-Christians and enemies of the United States due to the terrorist attacks by a group of fundamentalist Muslims on September 11, 2001. Also, most of the public debate about the film has been centered on questions about who was to blame for Jesus's Crucifixion, and other questions that reinforce divides between and within faith communities. These types of questions reinforce ideas of inclusion or exclusion over and against pluralistic approaches. Faggen presents examples of theological questions that may prove more fruitful in creating dialogues within and between groups:

> How is it that God is active in history and determines its outcome but at the same time allows his creatures freedom of will and holds them morally accountable for their actions? How can it be that Jesus can be fully divine and yet a vulnerable human being who suffers when he is tortured? How can one uphold God's power and foreknowledge but not hold him culpable for humanity's transgressions and degradation? How do we uphold justice against brutality and evil and at the same time enact the kind of mercy that the Passion story might want us to embrace?[38]

In addition to Faggen's questions, questions such as the following may lead to expanded and fruitful conversations: Based upon what types of historical visual representations, written and oral descriptions does Gibson as a filmmaker root the "authenticity" of his representation of Christ? How does this influence the messages communicated through the film? How were those historical visual representations and scriptural descriptions upon which the filmmaker rooted his approach understood and used by communities in the past, in relation to how they are used, viewed, and discussed today? How are issues of the "holy," "real," "purity of faith" presented in relation to "authenticity" of look and message? What aspects of Jesus' life are presented and which are not presented, and why? What theological messages are most powerfully suggested or stated within the film? What is presented as the most significant points of Jesus' teachings, and which of his teachings are not presented? Questions such as these are not new within Christianity. But, including focus on these types of questions in discussions about representations of Christ may help viewers as well as creators of visual representations focus on issues of individual accountability in the world and the nature of God, and not just divisional debates that primarily highlight simplistic answers about which groups or individuals were to blame for Jesus' death. This is not to say that the reality of the divisions and why they exist should be ignored. They are important, and works such as Gibson's film help bring some of the underlying tensions between groups and individuals to the surface. The roles visual representations, such as this film, play in bringing to the forefront viewers' concerns and the realities of religious and racial divides is important. For, the difficult realities of our situations and beliefs first must be recognized if constructive changes are to take place. But, in addition to presenting counter arguments against oppressive systems and theologies, we may also want to ask what types of conversations can bring us to further consciousness about group dynamics and individual relationships between persons of different races, faith traditions, and denominations within traditions.

Implications for Further Theological Development

Visual representations have tremendous influence on our beliefs and perceptions about ourselves in relation to God, humanity, and "truth." Among the normative assumptions about visual art has been the belief that visual art has little intellectual or spiritual value and is therefore only worthy of being hobby work. In reality, the significance of the visual arts in influencing theological development within the church and in influencing our larger worldviews is more complicated than this assumption suggests. One of the ways our ethics, cultures, normative social preferences and beliefs are transmitted is through the visual arts. The visual arts have direct influences on our worldviews, and our worldviews are in part learned and reinforced through representations rooted in cultural norms. Our worldviews determine our understandings of God and humanity, how we approach our roles within existing social and economic systems, and our ideas of hierarchy and justice. Also, our worldviews include ideas about physical and spiritual worth, social prestige, and power dynamics. Our ideas and beliefs about these issues drive our values and principles of conduct, and therein whether we define an individual or group as among our friends or enemies.

Whether one is conscious or unconscious of their significance, visual representations influence our worldviews. Whether one is consciously aware of how iconic, fine, and popular media images influence our views about self in relation to God and others or not, these images do often influence, reflect, or bring to the surface our underlying assumptions about these relationships. For example, recent debates about Mel Gibson's film, like some historical iconic debates, were centered on issues about differences within and between groups regarding which type of representations should or should not be accepted as "authentic," "holy," "real," and supportive of a "purity of faith."

Historically and still the proper role of visual art has been much debated, with "authenticity" in representing Jesus Christ one of the most debated issues. Debates about what is a "proper" and "authentic" representation of Jesus are often rooted in specific theologies about the Incarnation of God or about who are among God's "chosen," for example. Black theologies that declare Christ is black and the chosen status of blacks exist in opposition to white theologies that have declared that Christ is white and white Americans in particular to be God's new "chosen." Within these opposing views are disagreements about "authenticity" in defining and representing Christ. The outcomes of these debates are not just symbolic. There are practical consequences, for often the outcomes have been influential in determining who will have the greatest power in declaring what will become acceptable and normative within and outside of the church. Debates about visual representations have contributed to divides within the Christian faith as well as divides between members of the Christian faith with persons of other faiths.

Within contemporary United States society, most are exposed on a regular basis to a variety of visual representations from numerous sources. Yet, often there is little discussion about the theological significance of these representations within or outside the church. Many churches, for example, have stain glass imagery and altar paintings. But, there is usually little to no discussion within congregations about why these art works are there, what they symbolize, or the theologies on which they are based. Particularly within many Protestant denominations there is the belief that stained glass imagery and altar painting are mere distractions from the spoken and written "word" and therefore should not be placed in the church, or when they are, they function as illustrations and should be given a minimal amount of attention. This belief has its roots in the sixteenth-century iconic debates. The reality of having representations that are not discussed proves particularly problematic when images of a white Christ without reference to his Jewish heritage are present in black churches and other churches attended by persons of color, and little to no explanation is given to congregations as to the history and symbolism of such representations. Often such representations reinforce for many viewers consciously or unconsciously beliefs that Jesus as God Incarnate is white, and that therefore white persons are more "God-like" than persons of other races. Today, it often takes a controversial popular film representation of Christ, such as Gibson's *The Passion of the Christ* for the underlying assumptions about the value and influence of visual representations on theological, racial, and social beliefs in relation to practices to become a part of the public discourse.

There is a need for greater awareness and appreciation for both the reflective and critical roles various types of visual art representations have and do play in theological development. My approach is based upon the conclusion that to truly understand the role of contemporary popular visual art forms and debates, we need to have some understanding of the history within which these debates are rooted. In other words, I call for greater focus in theological discussions in particular about visual art forms and the importance of artists' roles in theological and other cultural developments. This may include education and discussions about how we consciously and unconsciously learn about our world, our God or gods, and ourselves in relation to other persons and things through various forms of visual media. These issues are particularly important in the development of theologies by persons of color, in that often our own and others' definitions of us in relation to faith beliefs and practices is interrelated with how we are defined and represented visually in relation to "sacred" figures such as Jesus Christ. Scholars such as Victor Anderson have recognized the power of the arts to influence the quality of our lives.

Oral and written theologies are influenced by and reflected in visual representations within and outside of the church. In shaping our beliefs, visual representations often function as more than just secondary illustrative works. David Freedberg describes the power of images in the history of human development as follows: "People are sexually aroused by pictures and sculptures; they break pictures and sculptures; they mutilate them, kiss them, cry before them, and go on journeys to them; they are calmed by them, stirred by them, and incited to revolt. They give thanks by means of them, expect to be elevated by them, and are moved to the highest levels of empathy and fear. They have always responded in these ways; and they still do."[39] Within his work, Freedberg focuses on some of humanity's responses to images of all kinds that reflect deeply rooted beliefs and perceptions that often are not directly acknowledged within the church or "secular" societies. Deeply rooted beliefs and counter critiques within Christianity about Jesus, race, gender, and other faith traditions are but a few of the issues that historically have been and still are reflected within our ways of creating and ways of responding to popular imagery. As Robert Faggen has argued, how the questions and topics are formatted within a debate can help determine if those on opposing sides will focus more on their differences and issues of blame than on their similarities and issues of empathy and compassion.

As historical iconic debates as well as the recent debates around Gibson's film have shown, often tensions between and within faith traditions come to the surface through exposure to particular types of visual interpretations. These debates have often contributed to widening the divides between those with opposing viewpoints. Different beliefs about "authenticity" in representing Jesus and other biblical figures have contributed to and helped reinforce divides between Catholics and Protestants, whites and blacks, and Jews and Christians, for example.

Attention to the roles visual artists and their works play in theological development is particularly important in the United States as this nation continually becomes more of a visually based society. Historically, the most vigorous theological debates about "authenticity" in visual representation were about iconic representations for the church. Today, such debates are usually about popular film representations. Much is at stake within debates about how Jesus should be represented, for example. Just as historical iconic debates were ultimately about issues of power as to who had the right to define how imagery would or would not be used in support of particular theologies, contemporary debates such as that surrounding Gibson's film are about power struggles within and outside of the church and what will be accepted as normative.

It is a part of our reality that today many messages and ideas about God and community are often reflective and influenced by approaches to popular media imagery. Also, most of the representations of persons of color we encounter on a daily basis that are significant in shaping our worldviews, are not created by persons of color. In studying the significance of images of African Americans, Latino/as, and other persons of color, it is important not only that we give attention to the diversity within how we have represented and defined ourselves and God, but that we give attention to how representations and definitions of ourselves have been influenced by normative approaches embraced by those outside of our immediate communities. We must give attention to how various theological debates divide as well as unite us with each other and with persons outside of our primary communities of experience. If our theologies are to be significant in improving dialogues and in addressing quality of life issues based upon how we actually receive and interpret information in the twenty-first century, we must expand our approaches to address not just how normative approaches within and outside of the church have been created and sustained through written and oral language forms, but through visual language forms as well. Greater awareness of how many contemporary debates about visual representation reflect and are rooted in our histories may be a starting point from which we can begin to move toward more fruitful action.

Notes

1 For more information, see Morgan, *Protestants and Pictures*; and Berger and Holloway, *American Visual Cultures*.
2 The United States "melting pot" ideology is rooted in the belief that all people should conform to the dominant ways of life within United States society, which have been based primarily upon European philosophies and cultural tastes interrelated with Protestant beliefs and practices. The United States "melting pot" ideology is rooted in the Protestant beliefs of the country's "founding fathers" and the various Protestant beliefs of the majority of those currently in power.
3 I recognize that part of my argument may also be applicable in discussions about other art forms, such as music, dance, and drama. In addition, I recog-

nize the differences between the purposes and uses of the fine and popular or commercial arts, and differences in how artists in each form define themselves and their roles within societies. I also recognize that some commercial or popular media forms (e.g., television and film) that I reference are not just visual media, but may be more specifically defined as multimedia in that they also include sound and movement. Nevertheless, for the purposes of this study my focus is on some of the ways that fine and popular art forms each function as carriers of culture and societal norms and on the visual aspects of popular multimedia forms.

4 Moore, *Iconography of Religions*, 247.

5 Koerner, *The Moment of Self-Portraiture in German Renaissance Art*, 80–126.

6 See Belting, *Likeness and Presence*, 1.

7 In spite of the basic differences between their approaches, artists of the East and West at times looked to each other's work for inspiration. For example, the Western artist Jan Van Eyck (ca. 1390–1441) embodied elements of earlier Eastern aesthetics within his Western-style representation of Christ to give credibility to his approach as "authentic." El Greco (1541–1614) also incorporated elements of the Eastern style in his artwork. In the West, during the periods of these two artists and later, classical Greek art was held as an ideal standard. Both Van Eyck and El Greco interpreted Byzantine art as having a direct and "authentic" link to earlier Greek culture and art. Historically, claims of "authenticity" in art representations have often been based upon the standards of previous periods as more "true" and "authentic." For more on this subject, see Koerner, *The Moment of Self-Portraiture in German Renaissance Art*.

8 I recognize that many historians do not accept all Western church art as "true" icons in the sense that Eastern icons are understood. I argue that Western church art may be understood as icons of a different sort, and that some Western art has been venerated like Eastern art and used in devotional practices to various extents.

9 See Belting, *Likeness and Presence*, 3, 139.

10 Brown, "A Dark-Age Crisis," 5–6.

11 Moore, *Iconography of Religions*, 94.

12 For more information, see Porter, Hayes, and Tombs, *Images of Christ*. Although my focus here is on the more degrading ways that persons of African descent have been represented in Western art, I also recognize that in some Greco-Roman and early European art Africans were presented as kings and warriors of the highest honor. As the enslavement of persons of African descent by persons of European descent increased so did the Western preference for degrading representations of persons of African descent. For more information on the variety of ways that persons of African descent were represented historically, see Bugner, ed., *The Image of the Black in Western Art*, vos. 1, 2, and 4; Snowden, *Blacks in Antiquity*; and Nederveen Pieterse, *White on Black*.

13 See Mitchell, ed., *Winthrop Papers, 1623–1630*, vol. 2, 232; and Bercovitch, *The Puritan Origins of the American Self.*

14 Noble, *The Progressive Mind*, 16.

15 For more information on the Puritans' association of agricultural lifestyles with ideas of "purity" and beliefs about their chosen status, see Lockridge, "A Utopian Commune, 1636–1686," in *A New England Town*, section 1.

16 For more on this topic, see Noble, *The Progressive Mind*; and Gutjahr, *An American Bible.*

17 Takaki, *Iron Cages*, 15, 113.

18 See ibid.

19 Brown, "A Dark-Age Crisis," 24.

20 See Raboteau, "African-Americans, Exodus, and the American Israel." See also Cone's references to the oppression of black Americans in relation to the oppression of the Hebrews in *A Black Theology of Liberation*, 18–22.

21 Apel, *Imagery of Lynching*, 113–15. See also James, *Without Sanctuary.*

22 Cone, *A Black Theology of Liberation*, 25.

23 See Douglas, *The Black Christ*, 31–33.

24 Garvey, *Philosophy and Opinions of Marcus Garvey*, 44.

25 See Cone, *A Black Theology of Liberation.*

26 Ibid., xi.

27 See Tillich, *Systematic Theology.*

28 Douglas, *The Black Christ*, 58–59.

29 Anderson, *Beyond Ontological Blackness*, 119.

30 Ibid., 85.

31 Ibid., 84, 85, 86, 91–92. See also Tillich, "Art and Society," in *On Art and Architecture*, for discussions about "ultimate concerns" and theological development in relation to art.

32 Frederick Douglass, "A Tribute for the Negro," *North Star*, April 7, 1849, 2. See also Willis, *Reflections in Black*, xvii.

33 Nederveen Pieterse, *White on Black*, 35.

34 Ibid., 95.

35 See W. E. B. Du Bois, "Possibilities of the Negro, The Advance Guard of the Race"; and Lewis, "Harlem Renaissance."

36 For more information, see Belting, *Likeness and Presence*; Morgan, *Visual Piety*; and Freedberg, *The Power of Images.*

37 For example, for more information on the film *The Passion of the Christ*, see Corley and Webb, *Jesus and Mel Gibson's The Passion of the Christ*; and Landres and Berenbaum, *After the Passion Is Gone*. For more information on representations of Jesus in film, see Baugh, *Imaging the Divine.*

38 Faggen, "'But Is It Art?'" 122.

39 Freedberg, *The Power of Images*, 1.

Suzanne E. Hoeferkamp Segovia

RESPONSE TO THE ESSAY BY SHEILA F. WINBORNE

The central question in Sheila Winborne's esssay is the question of truth or authenticity insofar as it concerns the visual portrayal of Jesus Christ. In the context of the racist reality that has historically characterized the social situation in the United States, this question highlights the brutal ideological consequences that blacks have suffered at the hand of a historically biased representation of Jesus as white. With this chief concern in mind, Winborne directs the reader to the problem of the social consequences that result from resorting to false criteria for determining truth and authenticity in the portrayal of Jesus. The central concern behind Winborne's argument is the reality of racial oppression suffered by blacks at the hand of whites. This type of oppression is justified and perpetuated through a limited and false rendering of the central message of the Gospels. In what does this fallacy consist? Winborne searches the historical roots of the problem in her interpretation of the fallacy. In the end she points to the consequences of the European and colonial rendering of Jesus as white with European features. Incidentally, she states, "it is not unusual for individuals of all faith traditions to represent their god or gods in their own images. Albert Moore states in *Iconography of Religions* that 'if oxen, horses or lions could make works of art they too would depict the gods like themselves in their own animal form.'" With this truth in mind Winborne frames the central focus of her argument.

Winborne argues further that this particular social situation continues to affect the contemporary devotional setting of the church in ways that are sometimes unconscious. Aware of the cultural violence that this situation incurs, Winborne supports her central argument by pointing to the issue of race as the defining criterion of truth in the visual representation of Jesus. She develops the theological content of her own argument along the lines of race. Is an approach or method that is defined and represented along the lines of race necessarily theological?

Following the chronological order of the author's argument I begin my discussion by identifying some key words that deserve further attention. Adjectives such as "proper" and "authentic" are misnomers when it comes to identifying the criteria that distinguish the central issue in the iconoclastic debates, namely the fundamental question of representation. The issue of what is "proper" refers only to the conventional artistic style that represents a given theology. This is a question of mastering a method. Thus the proper mastery of an artistic style will best communicate the underlying theological position that the style represents. Behind any "proper" style of representation lies a distinctive theology. A properly rendered representational (that is, realistic) style would support the theological perspectives of the Western church, namely to focus on giving "realistic" human form to the image of Jesus and making his presence real for the viewer. A properly rendered iconographic style based on the artistic standards of the Eastern church would, on the other hand, focus on representing the divinity of Jesus Christ. This style breaks away from a realistic or representational rendering and emphasizes the divinity of Christ in elongated symbolic form. The theological differences that each style represents are essentially Christological in content.

Throughout the history of the iconoclastic controversy the question of what is authentic has had to do with that which is venerated—the icon itself or the prototype. After the first iconoclastic period, which lasted until 780, the bishops at the Seventh Ecumenical Council affirmed that, in the words of Jim Forest, "it is not the icon itself that is venerated but the prototype whose image is represented in the icon. A careful distinction is made between the image and the person to whom it refers, without denying the powerful connection between the two—a distinction not always appreciated by those outside the Orthodox tradition who too easily suspect idolatry."[1] With this statement in mind, I turn to a well-known figure whose nineteeth-century work has documented a historical quest, the underlying question of which is somewhat similar, although it is not limited to the issue of race. Albert Schweitzer suggested in his famous book *The Quest of the Historical Jesus* that the nineteeth-century liberal critics who attempted to use the Gospels as sources for a "historical" life of Jesus necessarily fell back on their own presuppositions and their own imagination, since the

Gospels do not supply the information that is necessary for a genuinely historical portrayal. These critics, according to Schweitzer, were like a person who looks down a well. They merely saw in the water at the bottom of the well the reflection of their own face. In the words of Schweitzer we can also see the reflection of our own contemporary situation. Just as we are, Jesus was a culturally conditioned historical being whose physical appearance we know nothing of other than that he was of the Semitic race.

Winborne has discussed what she considers to be the historical and contemporary problem of the visual representation of Jesus Christ. The chief focus of her discussion is the question of what is true and what is authentic when it comes to depicting images of Jesus. This question becomes problematic from the point of view of the racist ideology that characterizes the historical and contemporary social situation in the United States. What does the Christian message have to say to this reality?

When it comes to representing the biblical portrait of Jesus, the question of authenticity is relevant only insofar as it refers to what can be identified as an authentic encounter with the truth of the Gospel message. Thus one can say that an artist's encounter with the reality of Jesus is "authentic" in that he or she experiences him as the Christ or the liberating reality. The authenticity of this encounter is what the artist expresses in his or her rendering of Jesus—that is, in a portrait of the new being that he or she has experienced as the Christ in himself or herself. The image is "authentic" only insofar as it is true to the Gospel message of that new being that the artist has known firsthand or "in the flesh." In what does this authenticity or truthfulness consist? It consists in an encounter with a reality that truly liberates and transforms.

In Paul's second letter to the Corinthians we find the message of a "New Creation": "If anyone is in union with Christ he is a new being; the old state of things has passed away; there is a new state of things" (5:17). An authentic encounter with the new reality in our being moves us to turn away from that in us which is plagued by sin, irrational biases, and racism. It calls us to let go of the old state of things and to welcome the new reality that has appeared with Jesus, who for this reason is called the Christ.

From the perspective of the new reality or the new being we have in Christ, what is authentic and proper in the visual portrayal of Jesus is the ability to transcend irrational biases and issues of race that hold a claim on the true identity of Jesus on the basis of his whiteness or blackness, or on the basis of his Semitic race and Hebrew culture rather than on the basis of his embrace of all people and all creation.

Jesus surrendered himself as Jesus, or as a culturally conditioned historical individual (2 Corinthians). His historical situation—that is, the particularities of his race and cultural condition—are not the factors that identify him as the Christ or the new reality. His identity as the Christ is revealed in the surrender of all that he was as Jesus. The sacrifice of his historical particularity, the end of Jesusology, prepares the way for the arrival of the new reality that embraces the uniqueness of all creation. The identity of Jesus as the Christ, or as the new reality that embraces all, appears with the surrender of a particular Jesus of Nazareth. An authentic and proper visual representation of Jesus is neither Jesus as white, black or brown but rather as the Christ or the divine reality we see in our black, white, brown, red, and yellow sisters and brothers.

The historical criteria for the visual portrayal of Jesus that Winborne identifies and interprets under the categories of "proper" and "authentic" were originally intended to represent Christological positions, the differences of which were identifiable in the religious images of the Eastern and Western churches. The historical criteria for identifying the proper artistic styles that are required for representing the authentic Christological positions of the Eastern and the Western churches have nothing to do with issues of race. The historical iconoclastic controversies were based on fundamental Christological differences in church doctrine.

It is misleading to refer to these debates as the relevant historical background for identifying the contemporary ideological criteria for what is a "proper" and "authentic" rendering of the biblical image of Jesus. The majority of the contemporary debates surrounding the representation of Jesus in film are not fundamentally Christological in character. They lack the essence of Christianity, which is the message of a "New Creation." This means that a new reality has appeared in which we *are* reconciled, and this reconciliation makes our reunion possible. The new state of things overcomes our separation. This new reality is the essence of Christianity. A "proper" artistic rendering of this reality, usually not in keeping with common notions of "propriety," elicits an authentic response. The only "proper" response to the new reality that is expressed in artistic form is a response that is authentic. To recognize the Christ in a truly moving image of Jesus is to experience the new reality of the Christian message. An artistic creation that results from an authentic encounter with the new reality does not presume to fall within the categories of what is considered to be normative. The new reality breaks through the prison of normative forms that have become enslaving and thus idolatrous.

As Winborne states in the context of her discussion on implications for future theological development: "Among the normative assumptions about visual art has been the belief that visual art has little intellectual or spiritual value and is therefore only worthy of being hobby work." This may well be the case in the highly materialistic culture of the United States. But it is not the case in most countries of the world, where artistic expression is both an intellectual and a highly spiritual activity. At its deepest levels of reflection, the creative act is essentially an activity of communion. Art is the highest consequence of love, the reunion of the separated. It is therefore in the power of the arts to "do" the visual theologically—that is, it is possible to bring word and image together to create a new and meaningful understanding. In my dialogue with Winborne I am in solidarity with her on calling for greater focus on the vital function of artists' roles in furthering theological developments within the Christian tradition.

Note

1 Forest, "Through Icons," 89–90.

PART SEVEN   FOOD AND RELIGION

Lynne Westfield

◉

SHE PUT HER FOOT IN THE POT: TABLE FELLOWSHIP

AS A PRACTICE OF POLITICAL ACTIVISM

Black folk have a saying—"She put her foot in the pot." This means that the dish prepared by a cook is delicious beyond compare. The cook is said to have in effect put her self—her sole or her soul—into the dish. The flavors thus are exquisite—the envy of angels. Putting a foot in the pot means that the cook can take ordinary or even undesirable food and make it extraordinary. Hog guts become chitterlings; overripe peaches become cobblers; yams become cakes, pies, soufflés, candied, and casseroled. This kind of cooking, this practice of hospitality for survival and resilience, is often the centerpiece of church and family gatherings. An appreciation of and dependence upon the women (and in many cases men) who put their feet in the pot is for the African American community an acknowledgment of the complexity of survival for black folk in the United States.

My work focuses on the practices that African American women have developed and honed to sustain, nurture, and remain resilient. In my first book, *Dear Sisters: A Womanist Practice of Hospitality* (2001), I contend that African American women use "concealed gathering" as a way to provide hospitality to themselves and to each other for resilience. With this work in mind I turn my attention now to the intersection of hospitality and activism—that is, hospitality as a tool for activism.

My hunch is that the meals prepared by a woman who is known to be able to put her foot in the pot and that are shared by the family and church oftentimes provide the venue for reconnection, conflict resolution, affirmation, and deep conversation about vitally important things in the community and shared life. As Jualynne Dodson and Cheryl Townsend Gilkes, authors of "There's Nothing Like Church Food," state: "African American church members in the United States feed one another's bodies as they feed their spirits or, more biblically, one another's 'temples of the Holy Spirit.' In the process, an ethic of love and an emphasis on hospitality emerge, especially in the sharing of food, which spill over into the larger community. Ritual moments of most African Americans occur at home and in their churches, and they are connected to food, meals, and their remembrance."[1] In light of these words by Dodson and Gilkes, what happens when in the sharing of food the ethic of love and hospitality spill over into the larger community, particularly when the "larger community" includes white people in a racist society? In this essay I am concerned with what happens at a table filled with delicious soul food when the guests are white people in power while the host and cook is a black woman with a specific political agenda for community organizing. To address this concern I explore the ritual moments of African Americans that occur at home when food and dining are the impetus for an ethic of love through profound gestures of hospitality for white folk in an attempt to transform a racist school system. More specifically, as a womanist pedagogue I make use of lived experience as a critical framework for analysis. In this essay I draw on my recollections and conversations with my mother who fused her role and responsibility as a volunteer community activist with her culinary skills to transform the Philadelphia public school system. As such my work here is a celebration of the manner in which the art of dining was used by my mother as a practice for creating conversation between unlikely partners around a table.

In *Dear Sisters: A Womanist Practice of Hospitality* I include a kind of disclaimer that I also include here. My chosen style of reasoning and writing is one of reflective, analytical narrative. While some scholars would say that the term analytical narrative is an oxymoron, womanists are concerned with the need to write in reflective modes as a gesture of integrity, scholarship, and affirmation to the unique voice and perspective of the black woman. Alice Walker, the progenitor of the term womanist, as well as many black women scholars of religion and theology (particularly those I quote throughout this essay), have embraced the necessity for a womanist epistemology that affirms the use of personal experience and personal narrative to better relate and convey black woman's history, religious experiences, and approaches. All of this is to say that I am with great intent similar to my womanist counterparts in attempting to craft a scholarly approach and writing style that listens for and to African American women; that thinks with African American women and then with intellect and imagination creates an essay that considers the aesthetic mode and aesthetic conceptualizations as critical aspects of scholarship. With this in mind, I focus my reflection and analysis with the following questions: Given the identity politics of African American women, what does it mean for us to use the breaking of bread—that is, dining and fellowship—as a subversive political practice for justice? What if sharing a meal together creates an uncommon space where the oppressed and the oppressor can be in genuine conversation? Is it possible for enemies to become friends and allies? Can coalitions based upon the notion of friendship transform oppressive, racist, classist, and hegemonic systems? In other words, when my mother put her foot in the pot—what happened and why?

My Mother's Reputation

My mother's reputation as a cook who can put her foot in the pot is far reaching and widely known. Nancy Bullock Westfield puts her whole self into her pots. Daily throughout her entire adult life she prepared meals for her family. Knowing that my mother was an excellent cook and that she cooked more than enough for the four of us, dinnertime in our household often included extended family, neighbors, and friends. My mother, now seventy-seven years old and married to my father for more than fifty years, still lives in Philadelphia, and though her body is riddled with arthritis she still insists on preparing dinner for the two of them every afternoon.

Throughout this essay I will tell you more about my mother's use of cooking, dining, culinary arts, and table fellowship in her efforts as a political activist to transform the Philadelphia public school system. My mother believes that as a Christian she is duty bound to use her gifts and graces for the betterment of the black race and all God's children. It just so happens that my mother's gifts and graces include political genius. My mother engaged in a religiously informed praxis that successfully transformed the Philadelphia public school system. With pride and appreciation, I add my mother's name to the list of African American Christian women exemplars who became community activists out of a sense of Christian tradition and obligation. These women, including my mother, met the challenge of this racist society and fought to improve the circumstances for black folk. My mother, like the other activists, is steeped in the Christian tradition; her father was a Baptist minister and school principal and her mother was a teacher and a devout Christian. With the Christian tradition as her foundation, my mother used her culinary arts as grounds for a religiously informed activism.

Other Black Women Exemplars

My hunch is that my mother's practice of cooking as a strategy of political activism is not unique but has gone unexplored and undocumented as an approach to activism. Though they provide focused analysis, texts on food and African American women along with texts on African American women and activism do not address the intersection of food and activism. For example, Doris Witt, the author of *Black Hunger,* provides a thorough analysis on the role of food in African American culture. Using vaudeville, literature, film, visual arts, and cookbooks Witt focuses upon the creation of mythology about black women and food. Witt's contribution clearly documents the place and role of food as one of complexity; however, the use of food and dining for activism is not emphasized. Concerning activism, the work of Rosetta Ross gives insight into stories of seven African American women of the Civil Rights era. Ross's work *Witnessing and Testifying: Black Women, Religion, and Civil Rights* is a superb remembrance and analysis of the work of religious black women during the civil rights era. As a womanist ethicist Ross documents the lives and contributions of Ella Baker, Septima Clark, Fannie Lou Hamer, Victoria DeLee, Clara Muhammad, Diane Nash, and Ruby Doris Smith Robinson. In my recent conversation with Dr. Ross, she told me that for various reasons the women in her research who were married were able to leave behind the routine and responsibility of cooking to go outside of the home to work for justice. The record of women utilizing their homes for activism is scant. That notwithstanding, Ross argues that the activism of these women was due primarily to their religious moral practice. Ross suggests that these women were able to leave the constraints of the kitchen and traditional "women's work" in order to pursue work and activism in the public arena. Ross joins with the voice of the noted womanist sociologist of religion Cheryl Townsend Gilkes to further frame the work of the women as community builders outside of the home. Gilkes believes that the eradication of systemic racism is the goal of their community-sustaining practices. Specifically, the practices of community building cited by Ross and Gilkes include "arguing, obstructing, organizing, teaching, lecturing, demonstrating, suing, writing letters."[2]

In agreeing with and building on the work of Witt, Ross, and Gilkes, my hunch is that breaking bread, eating together, dining, and table fellowship is a significant practice of African American women community activists to challenge and fight racism and empower their communities to survive, revitalize, and grow in a hostile society. I believe that my mother as a community activist in the 1970s in Philadelphia used the breaking of bread as a political practice for the eradication of racism and to improve the Philadelphia public schools for black children in the tradition of the earlier women activists who worked for justice. My Christian, black mother used the resources available to her to fight for justice in the public school system. In her case her resources were spatula, ladle, fried chicken, collard greens, and peach cobbler.

Nancy's Story

Nancy Bullock Westfield was born on October 18, 1929. Wife of Lloyd and mother of Brent and Lynne, she was also an activist around the issues of education and justice for more than twenty years. The pinnacle of her work came with her election as the first African American woman president of the Philadelphia Home and School Association (Philadelphia's version of the PTA). The volunteer parent group, one of the largest in the country, serves as a parent watchdog group over the Philadelphia public school system. My mother, the first and only two-term president (the constitution was changed so that her leadership might be extended) was president from 1974 to 1978.

My mother's political activism for education began in 1965 when she was a volunteer parent in my brother's kindergarten class at George Washington Carver Elementary School North Philadelphia. During this time North Philly was a predominantly low- and lower-middle-class black neighborhood, and like most black neighborhoods it was considered to be the "inner city." North Philly was a well-established neighborhood with a sense of community, but it suffered from lack of city services, little attention from local and city government, and rising incidences of drug-related crime and teenage gang warfare. As a volunteer at Carver my mother did fund-raising and organized the parents into a cohesive group that both supported the school administration and held them accountable for quality education.

By the late 1960s my mother's volunteer efforts and activism had moved beyond our elementary school and into the district schools. Parents and school officials recognized her ability to inspire and network people. She had singularly focused her activism upon issues of education for all children with an emphasis upon African American children and poor families. Through her efforts teachers were receiving needed equipment, weak administrators were being replaced with administrators who had a vision for quality education, new funding sources were being tapped for schools with particularly low test scores, and parents had a significant voice in the decision making of both local and city-wide politics. Nancy Westfield was the voice of the Philadelphia parent.

By the mid-1970s Nancy had the ear of the school board members, city councilors, the mayor, and the media. With an office and secretary in the school board building in 1974 my mother's volunteer position looked like the job of an elected official with meetings, conferences, and more meetings for forty to sixty hours per week. She made regular appearances on radio and TV and was often quoted in the *Inquirer* and *Bulletin*, Philadelphia's major newspapers. When the public school budget was threatened with draconian cutbacks by state legislature in Harrisburg my mother organized the parents to protest the cutbacks. On June 6, 1976, having rented every available bus in the Delaware Valley, my mother, the mayor, his cabinet, and ten thousand parents marched on the state capital. Mom, accompanied by Mayor Rizzo and his cabinet, met with Governor Milton J. Shapp and his cabinet, while most of the state legislators refused to meet with the parents. Though I was not present for this historic moment, my mother's friends reported that her speech and conversation with the governor was one of her finest hours. Needless to say, the funds were reinstated to the Philadelphia public schools.

The political climate in Philadelphia at the time that my mother was an activist was notoriously racist and especially anti-Black. Frank Rizzo, formerly a Philadelphia police officer then police commissioner, held the mayor's office from 1972 to 1980. As a policeman he was one of the first Italian immigrants to successfully break into the Irish-controlled police force, and he soon had the reputation of being one of the toughest cops in the city. Rizzo took his "tough-guy" attitude into the police commissioner's office. It was this attitude, along with his old-world Italian charisma, that won him the mayor's seat. Rizzo was a self-declared racist and an outspoken chauvinist who was loved by few and feared by most. Among Rizzo's duties as mayor was the appointment of Philadelphia's school board members. Members of the school board, having been appointed by Rizzo, often made decisions that kowtowed to Rizzo's partisan, racist politics. A major part of my mother's job was to attend school board meetings to speak on behalf of the parents. Many of my mother's efforts to put her foot in the pot as president of the Home and School Association were spent intervening, negotiating, and thwarting Rizzo's prejudiced politics.

The Most Significant Practice

Today, almost thirty years later since she was last in office, I recall my mother's days as a volunteer politician, activist, advocate for poor families, and champion for better education and I marvel at all she accomplished. My memory says that she was a smart "wheeler and dealer" who was able to be articulate when called upon to speak and cunning enough to know when not to speak. This is what successful politicians do, or so I thought. In a recent conversation with my mother about her activist days she told me that her speeches, letter writing, and marching were not the most significant and influential practice she employed. Instead, she claimed, her most effective practice for community organizing was to invite people to her home to share a meal. When she said this a flood of memories returned to me. I had watched her prepare many of the meals and I was at the table for the majority of the conversations.

Her dining practice for political activism began when she invited my brother's kindergarten teacher for lunch. Soon she was inviting the school counselors and the principal. In a short time parents from surrounding districts convened for meals. A few years later, city council members, lawyers, school board members, pastors, bishops, reporters, and I think on one occasion the mayor dined at our house. My mother organized people by inviting them to eat at her table. It was not until this recent conversation that I realized the significance of this fact.

In retrospect I have vivid memories of my mother's practice. As she planned the menus and cooked she would talk out loud making mental notes about the agenda she would put forth during the meal and the outcome for which she was hoping. It was like she was praying the outcome directly into the recipes, into the pots, and into the rouxs and stuffings. I helped my mother set the table and greet our guests at the door. People would often remark about the delicious aromas wafting around and ask to go straight to the dining table. My mother would smile and I would help put the food on the table and then call the guest into the dining room. When we were all seated, with my mother at the head of her table, she would say grace. Her meal prayer, whether the guests noticed or not, included the agenda she had in store for the conversation during the meal.

After the prayer my mother would serve each guest the entrée, then invite them to help themselves to the three or four side vegetables. The conversation did not end until after dessert. Satisfied in belly, Mom's guests left having been thoroughly convinced by her that whatever need she was negotiating was to be met.

At this point I want to reflect on my mother's practice of using food and dining as a political strategy. First, a good cook using her skills to create a space for difficult and critical conversations is an ancient practice. What is new, I would suggest, is the audacity of the one who cooked the meal to then sit at the head of the table as host and moderate and mediate the conversation—in essence, to control the encounter. A black woman "flipping the script" by ceasing her relegation to the kitchen and then using that relegation as a tool for activism is a powerful way to reconstruct, reimagine, and transform societal norms. I would also liken these efforts with the lunch counter sit-ins of the civil rights movement. Second, while I suggest that in her efforts my mother was crafting a political strategy, she insists that her work came out of the Christian notion of friendship. Though I disagree with her reflection, in what follows I wish to explore the notion of friendship as coalition building and, finally, suggest that my mother's practice of hospitality rooted in justice and compassion is a strategy of nonviolence designed to combat the twenty-first-century insidious version of racism that permeates society in the United States.

Flipping the Script

The identity politics of African American women is about both succumbing to and overcoming marginalization and oppression. The struggles and challenges of African American women are well documented by such scholars as Patricia Hill Collins in *Black Feminist Thought* (1990) and *Politics of Empowerment* (1991); Katie Cannon in "The Emergence of Black Feminist Consciousness" (1985), *Black Womanist Ethics* (1988), and *Katie's Cannon: Womanism and the Soul of the Black Community* (1995); Cheryl Townsend Gilkes in *If It Wasn't for the Women . . . : African American Women, Community Work, and Social Change* (1994); and Rosetta E. Ross in *Witnessing and Testifying: Black Women, Religion, and Civil Rights* (2003), to name only a few. These scholars argue that African American women, though oppressed, have made inconceivable strides for survival of self and the entire race. The "script" or narrative given to oppressed African American women is one of distorted myths that proclaim that black women are inferior to whites, men, and the wealthy. Like all African American women, my mother suffers the ravages of patriarchy, sexism, racism, classism, and imperialism. The truncated American imagination envisions African American women with the possibilities of only being animated stereotypes of Aunt Jemimas, Jezebels, whores, or superwomen. In rejecting these stereotypes my mother as a political activist and community organizer became an agent for change for tens of thousands of children in the Philadelphia school system. In effect, my mother "flipped the script." She brought the privileged and the mighty to her turf on her terms and she did it not with force or aggression but with graciousness, humility, and hospitality. She did it by cooking. She created a space where she had a modicum of power in which her words had to be taken seriously and considered deeply. She made herself vulnerable by inviting influential people into her home—her most intimate space—and though humble in this gesture she used her vulnerability to disarm those with power over her. Had she invited them to a restaurant to share a meal or prepared a meal and taken it to their offices the outcome would have been drastically different. A woman who sits at the head of her table, prays over her table, then serves the food to her guests is unquestionably the woman who is in power at the table, is in control of the table, and has authority when she speaks at the table. My black mother, relegated by society to the "Aunt Jemima" role of cook for all and host of none, flipped that role to become host of her own table in her own home over food prepared by her own hands.

At first glance this social "bottoms-up" might sound absurd or even deceitful, but the work of the biblical scholar John Dominic Crossan provides insight and clarity into the biblical and theological significance of this invitational and hospitable practice for political gain. Crossan writes that a table is a map of social boundaries and barriers. It is, by his description, a "miniature map of society's vertical discriminations and lateral separations."[3] In quoting the anthropologists Peter Farb and George Armelagos, Crossan writes: "To know what, where, how, when and with whom people eat is to know the character of their society."[4] As it was then, and still is today, eating together demonstrates the power dynamics of relationships in a community. The relationships between host and hosted symbolize the strata of status and power in the community. In stark contrast the message of the Gospel as described by Jesus is that the kingdom of God is a place where all are equal and where there are no social or political layers. In the kingdom of God all are welcomed and all are treated with the same amount of respect and deference. In describing the kingdom of God Jesus suggests an egalitarianism that is a radical threat and a fundamental danger to the status quo both then and now. Jesus, in parable form, suggests that the kingdom of God is symbolized by a nondiscriminating table depicting in miniature a nondiscriminating society. This notion is captured in Luke 14:15–24 and in Matthew 22:1–13:

> One of the dinner guests, on hearing this, said to [Jesus], "Blessed is anyone who will eat bread in the kingdom of God!" Then Jesus said to him, "Someone gave a great dinner and invited many. At the time for the dinner he sent his slave to say to those who had been invited, 'Come; for everything is ready now.' But they all alike began to make excuses . . . Then the owner of the house became angry and said to his slave, 'Go out at once into the streets and lanes of the town and bring in the poor, the crippled, the blind, and the lame.' And the slave said, 'Sir, what you ordered has been done, and there is still room.' Then the master said to the slave, 'Go out into the roads and lanes, and compel people to come in, so that my house may be filled. For I tell you, none of those who were invited will taste my dinner.'"

In this parable the host opens his doors and invites all who would come regardless of social location, class, or societal importance. Matthew says that by the host's instructions the servant brought in "all whom they found, both bad and good." The table at this party broke all of the societal norms and conditions. The social strata no longer had authority. At the kingdom table, classes, sexes, and ranks all mix together, all dine together, and all are in conversation together. Crossan emphasizes that this political shift of dining companions is more than a change in table fellowship. He stresses that "it means the rules of tabling and eating as miniature models for the rules of association and socialization. It means table fellowship as a map of economic discrimination, social hierarchy, and political differentiation."[5] Jesus in his parable and in his living advocates for an act of eating together that resists or denounces the miniature map of society's prejudices. The kingdom of God thus has moments or occasions when this radicality is embodied. My hunch is that my mother had the audacity to embody the kingdom of God at her table. In thinking herself equal she flung open the doors of her home and invited in to dine at her elegant table those who were more powerful than she was. Her table became the place where the kingdom of God was made manifest and where the norms of society were demolished and the stereotypes of black women were confounded. For a victim of oppression, for one touted as being an "Aunt Jemima," becoming the host is a radical event. The host is one who has authority and privilege. The host is the one who people seek out and want to be around. My mother hosted dignitaries and politicians who were used to being hosts themselves. Their version of hosting included my mother as the person who cooked and served the food but never sat at the table, and certainly never sat at the head of the table as the one who would dictate the conversation. In their version, my mother's place was relegated to the kitchen. The place for my mother in the kingdom of God is at the head of the table. By taking the meager materials available to her, fried chicken and peach cobbler, she sought resolution for her human problems through divine intervention.

The Lunch Counter Sit-ins in the 1960s

My mother's political strategy is reminiscent of the efforts of the lunch counter sit-ins by college students that began in 1960. On February 1 of that year four African American freshmen enrolled at North Carolina Agriculture and Technical College entered the F. W. Woolworth Company in Greensboro, North Carolina and sat down at the segregated lunch counter.[6] The students were then forced to leave the store without having been served. The next day a larger group of students returned to the lunch counter and asked for service. Again, they were refused service. The wire service picked up the story and the civil rights organizations began to spread the word to other college campuses urging them to engage in sit-ins at their local department store lunch counters. When students in the North heard of the protests by sit-in taking place in the South, they decided to help by picketing local branches of the chain stores that practiced segregation. By August 1961 over seventy thousand people had been part of the lunch counter sit-ins and over three thousand people had been arrested. The lunch counter sit-ins are said to have been a major catalyst for the formation of the Student Nonviolent Coordinating Committee (SNCC), and without their work the Civil Rights Act of 1964 would not have occurred or would have been profoundly delayed.

Eating at table and sharing a meal together is a universal metaphor for humanness, and ultimately for equality. The experience of gathering at the table for a meal and fellowship is readily familiar and produces understanding, insight and empathy for those denied the experience of the table. To be denied that right is to be forced to be less worthy and less human. The symbolism of being denied the right to sit at table for a shared meal captured the imaginations of black and white Americans when they saw the college students turned away from the table. Through TV footage America witnessed the absurdity of college students being refused service at lunch counters in public places as a fundamental denial of human rights that is at the heart of segregation. The symbol of the meal table helped to persuade Americans that segregation and Jim Crow were wrong. In the 1970s my mother used the same powerful metaphor and embodied experience to persuade people of privilege and voice to transform the racist educational system. If individuals can come to the table to share a meal and have a conversation, if they can look each other in the eye as they talk and eat, then they are equals who are able to make new decisions about old problems, able to speak and listen, and able to hear in new ways.

Political Strategy or Faith Practice? A Disagreement

While talking with my mom about her days as an activist and politician I suggested that her meals were a cunning political strategy. She frowned at me the way black Christian mothers do when their grown daughters refuse to understand the deeper wisdom of complex situations. In response to my comment my mother stated that from her perspective my calling her invitations a "political strategy" trivialized her efforts. For her politics was about folly, personal ambition, and self-aggrandizement. She said that she invited those people to her house not because she was a politician looking for political gain but rather because she wanted them to be her friends. She understood that her Christian obligation was to build the community as a coalition of friends.

I have always known my mother to be gentle and modest, but I have been very clear not to mistake her meekness for fear, inferiority, weakness, or naiveté. That not withstanding, her answer surprised me. I pushed back in our conversation by reminding her that I was at many of the meetings and heard many of the conversations. I was privy to her leadership style on display in front of the TV cameras as well as her style behind closed doors. I recounted for her the strategies and counterstrategies that she and her guests had formulated and utilized. I told my mother that there were times when her office reminded me of a military post or a professional football camp. I recounted how she would deploy her so-called friends like soldiers or warrior athletes into battle and they would return with news, bruises, or both. I told her that I thought her notion of "friendship" was seen through rose-colored-glasses and that her emphasis on this notion lacked a resolute understanding of the impact of the political machine upon the lives of black people and poor people. I told her that to befriend politicians is not to have friends. I recounted Psalm 23:5 to suggest that God was preparing a table for her in the presence of her enemies. To this my mother shook her head vehemently and said that she invited the politicians, media, and parents—both black and white, rich and poor, powerful and nonthreatening—to her table to be her friends because they were not her enemies, opponents, or adversaries. She said that it was the conversation among friends that made the lasting difference for the community. She believes that had they been politicians meeting across the table the transformation would not and maybe even could not have happened because communal responsibility and obligation would have taken a backseat to a win-lose mentality and to opportunism and fear. So was this political strategy or faith practice of friendship? My mother and I agreed to disagree.

Though I disagree with my mother, I am challenged to understand her perspective and approach—her faith practice. And though we have differing labels for her approach, we concur that its foundation is justice. With justice and liberation as the impetus of her activism, my mother set about building relationships for justice. She nurtured coalitions whose primary reasons for being were to nurture the wider community and to include black children and poor children. My mother's decidedly Christian activism was not about winning, besting, or being competitive. Her act of cooking and inviting people to her table was a modeling of genuine cooperation and acknowledgment of interdependence and the need for transformation through relationship building. My mother was concerned with relationships that grow into friendships because friendships have staying power and reciprocity. For my mom, Christianity calls us to be more than "friendly." Being friendly is about being nice—politics is too often merely about being nice. Being nice is often demonstrated in trite behaviors of pleasantries that are not heartfelt or meaningful and are often deceitful—this is why transformation often does not happen. The politics that grows out of a bureaucratic system like that of the Philadelphia public school system demands that huge amounts of time and effort be spent simply to maintain oppressive structures. Resource-laden gestures masked in highly choreographed meetings, inflammatory press releases, and bogus budget negotiations only serve to preserve the oppressive status quo. Little room is made in these structures to effect change, to establish true relationships, or to improve education. Friendship, on the other hand, is a deep, heartfelt relationship filled with gestures of love, healing, and care. Time and effort need to be taken to have deep, genuine conversations about significant issues of contention and those obstacles to their resolution.

Societal transformation on a significant scale (such as for the public schools) requires partnership with others and alliances with those who possess power and authority to effect change. Institutional transformation becomes possible when meetings are humanized with the expectation of friendship and when friendships are nurtured with meals that are shared. My mother was about the kind of friendship that nurtured coalition building and was imbued with accountability. Friends who are partners, who are members of the coalition, are asked not to retreat into the bureaucratic malaise but must come to the table with the expectation of conversation and negotiation.

Contemporary American society has reduced the notion of neighbor to the geographic proximity of those who reside closest to you. Neighbors or friends were meant to be relationships of intimacy and closeness. The ideology of radical individualism has proven to erode the interdependence of our society. According to Paul Wadell our society sees us "not primarily as social and relational beings who need others in order to develop and flourish but as essentially private, solitary, and autonomous individuals for whom relationships are more likely an unwanted restriction than the key to our humanization."[7] The foolishness of the success of autonomy is that loneliness and isolation are debilitating to the mind, body, and soul: "Individualism dead-ends in loneliness because human beings are inherently and inescapably social beings who need to live in deep, intimate, enriching relationships with others."[8] My mother's reliance upon friendship recognizes that it is not through a withdrawal from complex, messy, and difficult relationships but rather an immersion into them that transformation is possible.

What would governmental politics be like if my mother's notion was pushed beyond her own volunteer activism? What would our senate look like or act like if they were trying to be friends? Would Condoleezza Rice and Clarence Thomas have made different decisions if their efforts were predicated on the notion of friendship building? What would it mean for this notion of friendship to dramatically influence our black church denominations and instead of ignoring or envying each other we found ways of collaboration and deep conversation? In what ways would theological and religious education be improved if our jobs as faculty were to befriend our students? These are intriguing questions indeed. In all of these arenas we avoid difficult and potentially transformative conversations to avoid the conflict, the hurt, the argument, or the war. My hunch is that difficult conversations are less deadly while sharing a meal prepared and served with care. My mother's table was never a place of ambush or strong arming. The conversations, like the food, were open, honest and meant to heal. My mother does not categorize or compartmentalize her political actions from her efforts to establish friendship relationships. Perhaps it is time to call our democratic governmental officials, our church leaders, and our scholarly leaders away from animosity and partisan politics toward a more just society.

A Strategy of Non-Violence: A Commitment to Justice

My mother grew up in the black church where the favorite stories were of Moses leading the Hebrew children out of bondage and where the answer to the question of what the Lord requires was always answered with the word of justice. From the story of the creation when God proclaimed that all is good, to the call of the stuttering Moses, to the sometimes withering accusations of the prophets, to the lunch counter sit-ins of the 1960s, to my mother's dinner table, we know that God is the God of the poor and oppressed. The God of the oppressed is both sovereign over creation and intimately in relationship with us. God is on the side of the oppressed and, while yearning for justice, enters into the suffering, brokenness, and lovelessness of the world bringing justice, peace, and love. Our knowing of God comes from God's involvement with us. We experience God who continually experiences our suffering. God suffers as we suffer; God participates actively in our pain; God knows and hears the cries of the oppressed. God grasps, with divine understanding, the crushing cruelty of injustice, and God inspires people like my mother to set about changing the world.

My mother's use of hospitality and her employment of shared meals to build friendships and coalitions for justice is buttressed by the notion of compassion. Many believe that societal transformation must happen through some kind of violence or some kind of force. My mother's call for friendship and use of hospitality is a reliance on the oppressed having compassion for the oppressor and treating the oppressor with the kind of dignity that the oppressor has denied or refused the oppressed. When those who are marginalized and deemed inferior look with dignity into the eyes of the mighty and choose to unclench their fists and unfurl their brows, perhaps a deeper power is tapped for transformation. The setting of a table with the expectation of nurturing friendship is a compassionate act when the cook and the one at the head of the table is a black woman in her home with a conversational agenda for freedom. Compassion of the oppressed for the oppressor is not a gesture of an "Uncle Tom" or a sell out. Compassion by the have nots for the haves was a central virtue in the nonviolent philosophy and theology shared by Mahatma Gandhi and Martin Luther King. The nonviolence advocated by Gandhi and King had a critical effect when the police were swinging batons and the dogs were attacking. As a result of their nonviolent strategies, no longer are there signs over public water fountains prohibiting equal access. Yet in the twenty-first century, I would argue, a silent, invisible, lethal form of racism permeates our society with a violence that is not readily documentable but is just as debilitating. My mother's hospitable table is a strategy of nonviolence and compassion in an era when racism is seemingly invisible yet permeates and annihilates. The compassion at my mother's table where conversations on justice are primary is elucidated in the Negro spiritual "Down by the Riverside." This popular spiritual was sung during the North American enslavement of Africans and during the civil rights movement, and it is sung now:

> Goin' to lay down my sword and shield,
> Down by the riverside . . . To study war no more . . .
> Ain't goin't study war no more . . .
> Goin' to lay down my war shoes,
> Down by the riverside . . . To study war no more. . . .
> Ain't goin't study war no more.[9]

Cooking for friends and gathering them at her dining table was my mother's response to the needs of her community. She worked hard at coalition building because from her vantage point relationship building is what we are to do as children of God in an unjust world. She saw that the needs, though huge, were not insurmountable. My mother knew that it would take the crossing of many racial, religious, and cultural barriers to transform the education provided to all children, especially to the poor and black children. My mother used her own dining room table as a place of conversation for this barrier crossing and as a place to welcome her neighbors in love for the transformation of the Philadelphia school system.

Notes

1 Dodson and Gilkes, "There's Nothing Like Church Food," 519–20.
2 Ross, *Witnessing and Testifying*, 10.
3 Crossan, *Jesus*, 69.

4 Ibid., 68.

5 Ibid.

6 Lisa Cozzens, "Sit-Ins," June 22, 1998, http://www.watson.org/~lisa/black history/ (site visited on October 10, 2005).

7 Wadell, *Becoming Friends*, 44.

8 Ibid., 45.

9 Boyer, *Lift Every Voice and Sing II*, 210.

Angel F. Méndez Montoya

回

RESPONSE TO THE ESSAY BY LYNNE WESTFIELD

It was a truly exquisite experience to read Lynne Westfield's essay. In her work Westfield shows her own "culinary-narrative" skills, which bring together critical analysis (social, political, cultural, and so forth) with a concrete story about her mother's cooking and sharing of meals—a practice of hospitality that proves to be particularly effective when it is offered to people in power (in this case to white folks).

One of the points in Westfield's essay that I found most striking is the notion of black women's act to "flip the script," wherein food and hospitality at the table serve as nonviolent tools for reimagining and recrafting the social and political structures of society. My own essay on the Mexican mole similarly points out how the making of this dish by women during the colonial baroque times in Mexico was a culinary practice that often reversed the social roles of a strong patriarchal and colonial system, and instead embodied a world wherein elements (material and spiritual), traditions, and people coabide in a harmonious and peaceful difference.

This flipping of the script is a practice that echoes the Gospel message that imagines God's reign as a banquet reversing the sociopolitical structures of a secular world. Food and table manners are indeed embodied practices, and so the flipping of the script is a form of embodying here and now God's reign. Westfield wonders whether this practice mirrors a notion of Christian friendship or, rather, a political strategy. Are we here talking about faith or politics?

I agree with Westfield that justice could be a common source between faith and politics. For at the table when all classes, races, and powers are gathered together, it could help in nurturing coalition building and hopefully bring about individual and social transformations. Nancy's cooking and hosting meals is a wonderful example of this. But it seems to me that at times Westfield's treatment of faith and politics as separate spheres might create a greater dichotomy between the two. This attitude could, at best, imply a favoring of one over the other; or, at worst, it could antagonize them.

From a biblical perspective, faith and politics are not antagonistic but instead constitute one another. God is not indifferent to the human drama, but out of profound compassion and love (*caritas*) desires to be near humanity. God shows a radical solidarity toward humanity, becomes one of us, and displays a preferential option for the poor and outcast in a way that God's own gesture is an idiom to be imitated by God's children. It is with the performance of divine caritas—a recognition of the dignity of all human beings envisioned as children of God—that justice can fully take place. This is to say that justice, without a practice of divine caritas, leaves us malnourished, if not starving.

Since I speak from a Catholic tradition I would like to add that God's desire to be near creation is even more radicalized in the Eucharist, in which God not only is a host of an all-inclusive banquet but also becomes the food. The Eucharist displays faith and politics as mutually constituting. Herein is a rich source (though it is not the only one) for speaking on behalf of a "theopolitics": the sharing of the Eucharistic crafts a communal polis where humanity (inter-humanity) and divinity (inter-Trinitarian) coabide. This points to the body politics of the ecclesia—a Eucharistic community. This is not to say that without a sacramental and liturgical practice the church fails to imitate divine caritas. Indeed, one could well argue that Westfield's mother's cooking and hosting meals for the oppressors is also "Eucharistic," for it mirrors God's gesture of compassion as alimentation while it is also a call to transform structures of injustice—particularly those expressed by the debilitating and malnourished forms of racism that so dreadfully permeate society in the United States.

I shall briefly explain what I mean by theopolitics and why I insist on an alternative Eucharistic discourse (which is a form of imagining or envisioning) in order to avoid a dichotomy between faith and politics—most particularly when one attempts to make an argument in favor of alimentation as an extension of table fellowship, which I believe is what Westfield tries to do.

If William Cavanaugh is correct in his argument that politics is "a practice of the imagination" (because it constructs space, time, a sense of civil, national, and global territoriality and identity, and so forth), then alimentation in general, and the Eucharist in particular, manifest a political reality as well.[1] Alimentation is a practice of human imagination that reflects complex interactions and exchanges that go from local and micro realities to more global or macro ones. Carole Counihan and Penny Van Esterik similarly argue that alimentation is "a central pawn in political strategies of states and households. Food marks social differences, boundaries, bonds, and contradictions. Eating is an endlessly evolving enactment of gender, family, and community relationships."[2] The political reality of alimentation reflects, among other factors, the willingness and capacity of individuals and societies to express solidarity by sharing food, while "food scarcity damages the human community and the human spirit."[3] From a Eucharistic angle, food is a practice that imagines divine sharing as the locus (spatial and temporal) of "holy communion" with one another and with God—the one who is a loving community. The political dimension of divine Eucharistic sharing allows us to envision alimentation as incorporation into Christ's body (an intercommunal body). This alimentary divine-human body is the "endlessly evolving enactment" of mutual transformation, harmonious difference, reciprocal relations, and ecstatic love. This eating, however, is neither an "erasure" of sin nor an attempt to go back into Eden but rather a recognition or awareness that God loves and generously shares divinity despite of and in the midst of sin (the refusal to God's gift). Yet such a divine generous sharing is transformative: from sin to redemption and deification, from scarcity to superabundance, from individualism to communion. The Eucharist speaks of the body politics of "coabiding": the Father with the Holy Spirit in the Son, Christ in the Eucharistic elements and in the partaker, and the material elements as well as the partakers into Christ and in the Holy Spirit. This complex coabiding relies on the theopolitics of alimentation, which is endlessly enacted through this communal sharing in the body of Christ.

I use the term theopolitical because politics here is not envisioned as an autonomous element apart from God. My political perspective is fundamentally theological simply because my understanding of the Greek term *polis* (a city or "community embodying the fulfillment of human social relations") is intrinsically derived from a vision of divine sharing, a coabiding in the body of Christ, and which constitutes the ecclesial body; a divine-human *body politics*.[4] Just as humanity does not *have* a body, but *is* a body, the church, as James Smith rightly points out, "does not have a politics; but it *is* a politics."[5] The church expresses a corporate existence where divine agency interacts with human affairs, and such an interaction is nurturing—that is, it gives life and shape to the ecclesial body. Again, the theopolitics of Christ's body in the Eucharist is rooted not exclusively upon power but rather, in a more primary sense, its root is divine caritas, which is expressed with a radical gesture of kenosis, reciprocity, and concrete communal practices. This is not to say that power is herein dismissed, or that the Eucharist is a sign of disempowerment. There is a politics of power here. Yet, it is a power that integrates plenitude of desire; the paradoxical force of sacrifice on the cross; the humble power of bread broken into pieces for the purpose of sharing; the washing of feet that means a life of service to one another; and the power of giving life for the other. In other words, this is the theopolitical power of divine caritas, where the extraordinary embraces and transfigures the ordinary: God's "sovereignty disclosed at the breaking of the bread," as Samuel Wells remarks.[6]

I hope that my bringing to the table an alternative discourse on the Eucharist and the theopolitics of alimentation may help to avoid a dichotomous discourse in which faith and politics are treated as separate spheres. I believe that Westfield's telling of the story of her mother can also help bring both together, and more so, create a true communal sharing.

I hope table-sharing practices like that of Westfield's mother will be encouraged among African Americans, Latinos and Latinas, Asians, and all other ethnic communities (and indeed, among all cultures, classes, and religions). In our current time when politics is becoming more and more an empty rhetoric tool for achieving a privatized and elitist power than an effective locus of true action and transformation, perhaps this more modest, yet powerful faith practice may create a space for real communities where difference and peace are the main items of a divine-human menu.

Notes

1 Cavanaugh, *Theopolitical Imagination*, 1.
2 Counihan and Van Esterik, *Food and Culture*, 1. For a relationship between food and politics, see Mintz, *Tasting Food, Tasting Freedom*. See also Nestle, *Food Politics*; and Bell and Valentine, *Consuming Geographies*.
3 Counihan and Esterik, *Food and Culture*, 1.
4 This definition is cited by Matthew Whelan in "The Responsible Body: A Eucharistic Community," 376. In addition, "body politics" is defined as "people organized and united under an authority."
5 Smith, *Introducing Radical Orthodoxy*, 253.
6 Wells, *God's Companions*, 210.

Angel F. Méndez Montoya

⊡

THE MAKING OF MEXICAN MOLE AND

ALIMENTARY THEOLOGY IN THE MAKING

Sor Andrea de la Asunción is in a great hurry. She is a Dominican nun living in the convent of Santa Rosa de Lima (the Dominican convent of Saint
Rose of Lima). It is near the end of the seventeenth century (around 1680)
in Puebla de los Angeles, Mexico (then known as La Nueva España, the
New Spain). Sor Andrea de la Asunción is hurrying and feels anxious because as the assigned cook for the convent she has been given the difficult
task of preparing a lavish banquet for the arrival of "don Tomás Antonio de
la Cerda y Aragón, marques [marques of] de la Laguna y conde [count of]
de Paredes, virrey [viceroy of] de México y esposo [and husband of] de doña
María Luisa Manrique de Lara, novia espiritual [spiritual girlfriend of] de
sor Juana Inés de la Cruz."[1] In her haste and anxiety for having to host
such a distinguished figure, Sor Andrea has a gastronomic vision: she will
mix up all sorts of ingredients and spices, even contrasting elements such
as various chiles and chocolate, to create a lavish and extravagant sauce
that she will then cook with turkey. The result of Sor Andrea's providential
and eccentric culinary creation was baptized as *molli* (mole) because, the
story goes, she spent many hours *muele y muele* (grinding and grinding)
various extravagant spices in order to achieve its final consistency. In so
doing she created a true gastronomic ecstasy for her guests and for all
peoples thereafter.

   Paco Ignacio Taibo I points out that the origins of this story lie in folk-
lore, the creation of popular narrative. And there is yet another popular
story that also takes place in the monastic world of colonial baroque Mex-

ico in Puebla de los Angeles. Like Sor Andrea, Fray Pascual Bailón was the main cook of his monastery.[2] Also like Sor Andrea, Fray Pascual was in a hurry and anxious because a very important archbishop was coming for a visit. The convents and monasteries (of which there were many, particularly in Puebla) were quite famous in colonial Mexico for their sophisticated cuisine and gastronomic inventions. Preparing banquets and eating was, as in most Mexican fiestas, a central event. The success of a feast depended upon how gastronomically impressive was the food served at the gathering. It goes without saying that in preparing this meal Fray Pascual had a massive responsibility upon his shoulders.

The story goes that while Fray Pascual Bailón was preparing the main dish he accidentally dropped a huge piece of soap in the cooking pot and thus ruined the meal. He became furious with himself for making such a catastrophic mistake. In his fury, he started throwing all sorts of ingredients and spices, including chocolate and various chiles, into another pot where a turkey was cooking. But immediately after his attack of fury, a sudden feeling of repentance overcame him. He dropped to his knees and with all his heart he begged for God's forgiveness and help. The story relates that the miracle was granted to him, and the result was the birth of the "mole poblano," an extravagant stew or sauce concocted of a symphony of flavors that would delight not only the monastery's honorable guest but was to become one of the worlds most glorious culinary achievements. Such was his success that Fray Pascual was beatified by the church and is now known as the patron saint of cooks. He is a saint not found in the clouds of highest heavens but in the pots, fire, spices, smells, and flavors of the kitchen. When it is time to cook, many people in Mexico (myself included) still pray to the saint-chef in these words: Pasculito muy querido / mi santo Pascual Bailón / yo te ofresco mi guisito / y tu pones la sazón[3] (Very dear little Pascual / my holy Pascual Bailón / I offer you my dish / and may you offer your distinctive "culinary touch").[4]

These stories illustrate that one of the "origins" of the mole is the popular imagination in the form of allegorical stories that were passed orally from one community to the other. These stories were also the recipes that were part of the culinary tradition of convents and monasteries, families, towns, and regions that were then further transformed by other generations, with each bringing their individual touch to the mole. The number of ingredients in the mole varies according to regional and personal tastes. Some may have as few as five ingredients while others may have more than thirty. There are an infinite number of moles, for mole is an eccentric alimentary hybrid that changes, transforms, and adapts itself according to the particular tradition, taste, and fancy of the cook. Some people like their mole spicy; others prefer to taste the sweetness of chocolate and cinnamon or anise; still others may be inclined to intensify the taste of almonds, walnuts, or pistachios, and so on. Nevertheless, the hybridity of mole is not the mere result of spices and ingredients plus an added personal touch. Mole is also a cultural hybrid—a mixture of multiple culinary worldviews and cosmovisions.

By taking the Mexican mole as a metaphor as well as a cultural, material, and concrete practice, my aim in this essay is to increase the awareness of what it means to theologize in general, and to partake of the Eucharistic banquet in particular, with both being eccentric alimentary hybrids that feed our hunger. I argue that theology's vocation is to become a form of nourishment to people. Thus, I look at food (in this case the Mexican mole) as a paradigm of engaging in the crafting or making of theology; likewise, I speak about theology *as* food. I use the term "alimentary theology" for these interrelated and mutually constituting matters of nourishment and theology. I speak from my experience as a Catholic and as one who is increasingly becoming "tricultural" (from my experience of Mexico, the United States, and the United Kingdom). I hope that my particular angle may provide some food for thought to people from diverse religious and cultural practices who wonder how religious beliefs become transformative and nourishing. Mole and theology are not identical, of course, and so this comparison might sound contrived. My intention is not to collapse the differences and clear distinctions that exist between them. My only desire is to stretch the theological imagination regarding thinking and talking about God as well as practicing the Eucharist, which I firmly believe has to do not only with reason, faith, and doctrine, but also is the result of bringing together complex elements or ingredients such as the body and the senses, materiality and the spirit, culture and meaning construction, and a divine-human blending of desires.

Molli: Divine Alimentation

Many of those working in historical and anthropological research point to the fact that mole was an important part of the pre-Columbian cuisine, particularly within the region of Mesoamerica.[5] Héctor Bourges Rodríguez argues that Mesoamerican cuisine enjoyed a high reputation as a result of "its great development, complexity and wisdom, for it had millenary roots." He also suggests that the Mesoamerican cuisine had an "exceptional aesthetic sensibility and a distinguished nutritional balance suggesting specialized nutritional knowledge."[6] The banquets prepared for the Aztec emperor Moctezuma are a telling example of this highly developed culinary sensibility.[7] Early Spanish historians reported with great awe that about three hundred different dishes were prepared everyday for Moctezuma's banquets.[8]

The Mesoamerican alimentary practices had a profound religious significance as well. Maximiliano Salinas Campos, in *Gracias a Dios que comí: El Cristianismo en Iberoamérica y el Caribe, siglos XV–XIX* (Thanks to God I Ate: Christianity in Iberoamerica and the Caribbean during the XV–XIX centuries), analyzes the centrality of food in pre-Columbian traditions and shows how these traditions were strongly linked with religious symbols and rituals. Life and death, communal relationships, and peoples' relationship with their deities were deeply embedded within food practices and alimentary symbols. Along this same line of thought, Davíd Carrasco argues that Mesoamerican cosmology—particularly within the Aztec world—was deeply rooted on food and eating symbolisms.[9] According to Carrasco, there is an important aspect within the Aztec cosmic worldview whereby eating played an important part of a sacred economy that transformed everything into food, and such a transformation was a means of the cosmos' divinization, including humans.[10] In this particular Aztec cosmovision, both the earth and the human body were conceived as food, as is noted in a line from a mythical song: "We eat the earth and the earth eats us."[11] The earth was depicted as a large mouth and a sacred digestive system for the cosmos. Humanity was first created out of corn by the gods; and at the moment of death humans nurtured the gods. Death was not viewed as final but rather as a transformation into a source of cosmic energy to the extent of becoming nourishment for divine hunger. The human heart and its blood were the most important sources of fuel for the recycling of cosmic energy. In this context, human sacrifice—and its dramatics of the excision of the heart—was not conceived as mere cruelty but rather as a highly honored ritual and liturgical act that contributed to the recycling of energy and the preserving of the cosmic sustenance.[12]

The Mexican mole became an archetype of this cosmic-divine nourishment. The first invention of the mole goes far back, toward the Aztec world and the cuisine of the so called *mexicas* of Tenochtitlán in central Mexico.[13] In fact, the word *mole* comes from the Náhuatl term *molli*, meaning sauce, mixture, or stew.[14] Or at least this was the interpretation made by the early conquistadores from Spain. Yet before that meaning, which is not totally unrelated to the Spanish understanding, molli actually meant *alimento* (alimentation or nourishment).[15] The molli of the mexicas was a thick sauce made of a great variety of chiles and spices, plus chocolate, to which was most commonly added different sorts of meat, particularly *huexolotl*, or what we now know in Spanish as *guajolote* or *pavo* (turkey).[16] Chiles and chocolate (as cacao) were highly valued, for they were, just as the huexolotl, Aztec deities. To eat molli thus was a way of eating the gods who in turn would eat humans at their moment of death.

As one of the most popular dishes in pre-Columbian civilization, molli was mainly served at important festivals and consumed in religious rituals. Molli was also a gastronomic delight at the banquets of the Emperor Moctezuma and the social and religious leaders of Tenochtitlán. The mexicas preferred to serve molli with beans and corn tortillas. As with chiles and chocolate, beans and corn were highly valued because they were different representations of Aztec gods. Because of the main ingredients of chiles and chocolate, plus the elements of corn and beans and the additional cooking with turkey, the Aztec molli was not an ordinary dish but rather a food of the gods and thus a divine alimentation.[17]

Alimentary Hybridization and the Craving for Spice

Because of the deep religious, social, and cultural significance of molli, it is thus not surprising to observe that it survived the systematic extermination of the European *encubrimiento* (covering up) of America, to use the term developed by Enrique Dussel.[18] In fact, one of the socio-religious and cultural practices that the Spanish conquistadores had most difficulty wiping out was the dietary customs of the mistakenly called "Indians." But during colonial times the exchange and transformation of dietary customs were inevitable. And this transformation occurred in both directions—that is, in the New World as much as in the Old World. What is interesting about the colonial baroque period in Mexico is the resulting hybrid or *mestizaje* not only of races but also of the inherited customs and cultural, social, political, and religious practices. The culinary constructions of the original inhabitants of the Americas, as well as of the European continents, were not an exception to this hybridization of (often) clashing worldviews. From the perspective of alimentation, this complex mixture was what José N. Iturriaga calls *hibridación alimentaria*. This "alimentary hybridization" was the way in which all the continents and cultures *mestizaron sus comidas* (mixed up their foods).[19] And we must not forget that in addition to this mestizaje there was also an alimentary *mulataje* that resulted from the African presence in the Americas, as in the Caribbean.

If we examine this closely it is permissible to say, as Iturriaga does, that the alimentary mestizaje of the Mexican colonial period somehow included all of the continents. Prior to the arrival of the Spanish people into the American continent, the medieval Spanish cuisine already enjoyed an impressive international culinary tradition. Spain's cosmopolitan culinary expressions were a product of the medieval Christian Roman and Muslim Arabic influences. As Xavier Domingo explains in "La cocina precolombina en España," (pre-Columbian cuisine in Spain) both Christian and Muslim culinary worldviews aimed for a rich variety of spices and aromas.[20] This excess of spice constituted what Domingo calls "el sabor de la Edad Media" (the medieval flavor).[21] The Islamic occupation from the eighth century to the fifteenth in Spain intensified this syncretistic culinary tradition and its high receptivity to food and gastronomic pleasure.[22] It was indeed syncretistic and hybridized, for the Christian Roman and the Muslim Arabic culinary traditions resulted from prior historical explorations and exchanges with the Asian and African continents that greatly influenced both cuisines. Therefore, complex elaborations of food and a taste for spice were central aspects of Spanish cuisine before its arrival to the American continent. In fact, as the interdisciplinary research shows, one of the main reasons for Christopher Columbus's explorations—which eventually took him into the American continent—was this European craving for "exotic" spices.[23] George Armelagos in his essay "Cultura y contacto: El choque de dos cocinas mundiales" (Culture and contact: The clash of two world cuisines) also shows that "the Europeans had an insatiable desire for spices, and this was a great impulse for the [trans-Atlantic] exploration." This craving, he argues, was "even greater than their greed for gold."[24] And they did find in America a true paradise of gastronomic delights, particularly with products such as chiles, chocolate, corn, tomatoes, potatoes, beans, and so forth. America's exportation of its products to the Old World further influenced the latter's cuisine and dietary customs.[25]

Subversive Mole

The "early" stories of the creation of mole in the kitchen spaces of convents and monasteries are significant. Of course, often these narratives assumed a colonizing form that obliterated the entire history of pre-Columbian cultures and belief systems, including dietary and gastronomic indigenous traditions. From the baroque period to the present, the narrative that most Mexicans know of mole's origin is the one constructed during the colonial period. Yet in a subversive manner the dietary and eating traditions from the original inhabitants have persisted because they were practices of resistance to colonization.[26] So while there is transgression and transformation in the mole, there is also a powerful sense of continuation and determination despite subjugation. And it was in the convents and monasteries where encounter and clash, subjugation and subversion, took its most extravagant form in reinventing the gastronomic hybrid that is the mole. For in the mole not only does the plurality of cultures and culinary traditions, spices, and food elements come together (often conflictingly so) but the gods and goddesses come as well. If in the pre-Columbian times mole was a material expression of divine alimentation, in the colonial and postcolonial periods it intensifies its divinizing presence in a more eccentric fashion. Somehow throughout the centuries the mole managed to continue being a "spiritual alimentation." But more stridently so, and with greater spice.

During the baroque era in Mexico most culinary inventions were mainly created by women—with a few exceptions such as the case of Fray Pascual Bailón described above. In a male-dominated society where women were not allowed to assume roles of leadership in public spaces, women's form of empowerment and self-expression often arose in the kitchens (both in the convents and the homes). In colonial times, space (both geographical and architectural) was delimited and manipulated by a strong sense of hierarchy, class, race, and gender control.[27] In a patriarchal colonial world such as Mexico the kitchen and the refractory were virtually the sole spaces where women were able to express themselves.[28] Such was the case, for instance, of the famous erudite Mexican nun Sor Juana Inéz de la Cruz (1651–1695).[29] From her early childhood (at about three years of age) Sor Juana learned to write and read. Then during her childhood and early adolescence she managed to "trick" the male-dominated system of her time by dressing as a boy and sneaking into school in order to get an education that was exclusively designed by and for men. When she was eighteen years old she entered the convent of San Jerónimo in Mexico and had a prolific writing career, but not without controversy and even public scandal. The ecclesiastical hierarchy eventually forbade her to write and to visit her beloved library and lecture halls, and subsequently she was sent—as a punishment—to the kitchen where women "were supposed to be." But somehow Sor Juana managed to use the kitchen as a space of creativity and liberation, and there is a book of Mexican cuisine recipes attributed to her. Sor Juana even considered the culinary arts as a higher form of knowledge and wisdom than that provided by traditional philosophy and theology.[30]

In her *Libro de Cocina* Sor Juana included her own recipe of a mole named clemole de Oaxaca. Sor Juana's correspondence to food and knowledge suggests that there is a relationship between *sabor* and *saber* (savoring and knowing). Perhaps the kitchen and the library are in fact united by the same splendid desire to savor and know. Sor Juana truly incarnates what Roberto Goizueta describes as the religious worldview of the Mexican baroque era: an experience that is "sensually rich" and of divine nearness that is deeply embodied.[31] In this organic and symbolic world both the intellect and affectivity, the rational and the sensual, and the human and the divine are intimately connected. Moreover, Ada María Isasi-Díaz is right in pointing out that women's empowerment in the midst of disempowerment has been possible because of their "turning the confinement/spaces to which [women] are assigned into creative/liberating spaces."[32] The case of Sor Juana thus attempts to demonstrate how in the mole we find not only harmony as a festive reality but also struggle and subversion. It is hot, spicy, and picante. Thanks to women, the mole has been preserved and re-created, but not without pain, suffering, and struggle.

Alimentary Theology in the Making

The Mexican mole is the result of many ingredients, elements, and realities coming together. Theology is similar to the culinary extravagance of mole, for it is the result of the convergence of many ingredients including revelation, tradition, faith, history, cultural background, popular practice, and so forth. In addition, similar to the case of making mole, theology reflects a situation or locality (a locus), or to be more precise many situations or localities. I shall start here with my own situation. I am a Mexican male and a Dominican friar within the Catholic Church. My own theological voice reflects and is somehow framed by these particular cultural and religious traditions. I have a desire to listen and learn from various religious practices that include diverse Christian as well as non-Christian traditions growing from a genuine interreligious or interfaith dialogue. Another important factor concerning my own way of theology is the fact that I have lived in the United States and the United Kingdom for the past fourteen years (about ten years in the United States and four in the United Kingdom). These situations already shape and frame my theology, for my theology is bicultural or becoming increasingly tricultural. I bring to theology an experience and an angle of mestizaje—that is, an experience that incorporates a mixture of cultural and linguistic worldviews. After living in the United States and the United Kingdom I am sensitive to issues of language, culture, race, gender, and the body. I realize that these issues are not disconnected from political, historical, and economic factors, among others. Just as I am aware of the profound impact that women had and continue to have upon the creation of mole, I am also constantly inspired and challenged by women's theology—most particularly from both feminist Latinas and *mujeristas* theologians. My theology also contains a particular desire to reflect on the body and its impact on theological discourse. My awareness of the body has been the result of my background of ten years as a professional modern and contemporary dancer prior to my becoming a Dominican friar. In addition, my current research is focused on food, eating, nourishment, and the lack thereof. My interest in food reflects, among other possible influences, my own cultural background. As I hope to have shown in the first part of this essay regarding the complexities of mole, in Mexico the role of food, eating, and the kitchen is important in shaping people's lives and understanding of the world and divinity. I must add to this my personal family background as one who grew up with a father who was an excellent cook and who loved cooking and offering hospitality to family and friends and often to strangers as well. I believe that one of my first theological teachings came from the kitchen of my childhood home in preparing and eating food and feasting with family and friends. I believe that our family kitchen was one of the first spaces where I discovered God's grace, self-sharing, and hospitality. As such my interest in the Mexican mole and my wish to make some theological reflections upon it is not accidental but rather echoes my own biographical background that includes multiple situations and localities, influences, and voices—and most mysteriously so, including God's own voice that is intermingled with all these many voices, influences, and situations.

However, while there might be many ingredients in the making of mole and of theology, there are some that are more predominant and indispensable than others. In the making of both mole and theology not just "anything" goes. In the mole, for instance, the chiles and the chocolate are very important or even indispensable. Speaking from a Christian-Catholic viewpoint, theology contains two indispensable elements: first, the element of God's desire to share divinity with humanity (through creation, incarnation, the cross and resurrection, the Eucharist, and so on), and second, the believer's desire to unite with God in and through community relationships.[33] These two desires (divine and human) coming together play an important role in the making of theology—indeed, they are the "chiles and chocolate" of theological practice. Just as the mole is the point of contact between different elements, I believe that theology expresses the in-betweenness, or a hybrid discourse of divine-human encounter. As in the mole, sometimes the elements coming together may reflect a struggle and clash more than a harmonious ensemble or fusion. What is this desire about? Whose voice is it? Whose authority are we talking about? Who is included or excluded in this hybrid discourse? More than offering facile solutions, theology may instead open further questions and critique as a space of unfinished and unresolved conflicting discourses. Theology often exposes us to a space of indeterminacy, fragmentation, and ambiguity. Most often, these unresolved issues create an experience of frustration. For me this experience of unresolvedness in theology usually brings about a sense of perplexity that is similar to tasting the mole whereby one is left with an ambiguity as to what is actually being tasted. What do we "taste" in a theological work? Mole serves as a metaphor of doing theology: like eating mole, this experience of taste in theology is often plural—that is, a complex network of ingredients put together without a final semiotic resting place.

Because of the enormous complexity of mole, it is difficult to delineate it in a neat category. Is it a dish, an intercultural expression, a strident mixture of worldviews, an interreligious cacophony, or a gastronomic manifestation of the struggle of power, race, gender, and class? Even at the level of flavor and taste, it never completely rests at one particular palate's identification corresponding to a specific ingredient. As soon as one ingredient is tasted, suddenly another taste arises to the senses, and then another comes and so on. Without arriving at a final synthesis, there always is still more to taste, still more flavors yet to discover and experience. It is as if the mole acts as a mobile signifier moving beyond the signified. As such it represents a system of continuously displaced signs, for they point to other signs without final semiotic stasis. In the mole there is an experience that is not so much of the "either/or" type but rather a realm of the "both/and." Better yet, in the mole there is a dynamic sense of the in-betweenness at all levels, all layers, and from all angles. The mole, in its continuous re-creation, becomes the paradigmatic example of Iturriaga's term "alimentary hybridization." Such gastronomic eccentricity (of even mythical dimensions) is what makes mole so amazingly playful, perplexing, and pleasurable.

When talking of God it seems inevitable to arrive at this experience of restlessness and perplexity, for God is ultimately excess. God exceeds any discourse (including "official" discourses). Signification falls short of its signified signs, for God is perpetually and dynamically displaced from any sign. Like the nonstatic semiotics of mole, God's significations are likewise excessive or even extravagant. However, this does not mean that God's signification is a perpetual deferral of meaning that ultimately leaves us anorexic. God's signs are nourished by God's plenitude and superabundant gifts. At the same time mole is a product of human creativity; it is a dish whose main purpose is not to be fetishized but to nourish and to be shared in communal meals. Theology is also incarnational and human made, and as such it attempts not to be a fetish that would make of God a static idol but rather is the result of a human dynamic quest for God, or a human response to the initial movement of God's desire to become closer to or intimate with humanity. It is a discourse that expresses and hopefully feeds in one way or another humanity's hunger for God's goodness, truth, justice, and beauty. Theology is also communal, for it is to be shared in the public space and never for exclusive purposes. Both apophatic and cataphatic discourses are thus necessary for a good theological feast that is God's own excess (who even exceeds both apophatic and cataphatic discourses). While God's excessiveness can never be reduced to language, symbols, concepts, and so forth, God is also a profound nearness to be encountered in loving relations as well as in language, liturgy, and everyday practices—despite the limits and partialities that we always inevitably encounter. Both silence and word nourish the theological vocation.[34] Simply talking about mole does not take one to the actual extravagant experience of eating it. Talking about God from a safe distance for the sake of preserving God's "purity" because of God's being "beyond" situatedness in reality only leaves us empty and malnourished, if not starving. God is also personal, loving, and sharing, and walks with humanity the pilgrimage of history (what faith believes and hopes to be God's orientation toward an eschatological future). Theology's extravagance is to become alimentation—thus the notion of alimentary theology. It must feed human hungers (both physical and spiritual). For this reason theology as alimentation (alimentary theology) is also intimately concerned with and involved in the concreteness of everyday life as well as analogical mediation: language, the body, materiality, and so on. And yet this situatedness is not totally "it." Without ever transcending situatedness, and yet because of its participation to the excess of divine's desire, theology is also perpetually opened and unfinished. Like the tasting of mole, in theology there is still more to taste and more flavors yet to discover.

Making an exquisite mole is not an easy task. It takes time, discipline, effort, personal engagement, and a sense of being self-involved. It is more than merely following a recipe. It is a meticulous crafting that could be compared to an art form. Like making art, making mole involves self-sharing, with much of the cook's person and personality put into the mole, which then is further shared in the communal banquet.[35] Alimentary theology is also a crafting, for one learns it in the making of it. Still, alimentary theology is not a recipe or a mixture of various recipes. It takes time and effort, and often great sacrifices.[36] It does require self-involvement, and there is a sense of self-fulfillment. Yet at the same time, there is a joy (at least in my own experience) of sharing the product. This is a "kenotic delight"; that is, a rejoicing of dispossession for the purpose of feeding the concrete (not abstract) other. In a way similar to the making of the Mexican mole, alimentary theology can be said to be a "culinary art": a vocation that is simultaneously gift and reception, preparation and sharing, contemplation and consumption, materiality and transcendence, human and divine. Theology as a culinary art points to the necessity of integrating an ethics that questions our system of global exchanges. Alimentary theology is food for thought, a gift to be shared in spite and in the midst of sacrifices and limitations.

Divine Desire and Embodiment: A Culinary Narrative

I noted above that theology is a hybrid of divine and human desires. While this blending of desires activates the intellect and spirit, it is nevertheless, like cooking and eating, a deeply embodied experience. Divine desire takes its more extreme form of intimate self-sharing in Christ's incarnation, the Logos of God, the word made flesh (John 1:14).[37] This is at the core of John's theology and the foundation of Christian theology. Flesh is the most primary sense of embodiment. It is the realm of the experience of extreme proximity with humanity's pathos that, as Michel Henry describes, is "pure affectivity, pure impressionness, that which is radically immanent auto-affection."[38] God's incarnation takes this human flesh at its extreme materiality in order to divinize it from the flesh itself (from *within* and not from without). In this act the God-human conjoins what appears to be a mutually exclusive ontology of divinity and humanity and maximizes a new hybrid ontology that is nondualistic but participatory and reciprocally related. This is a new ontology revealed as *relationality*. As a living organism the flesh performs in the body a sharing with life itself, which is already divinized but in a way that it does not do violence to or leave behind its own human condition but rather intensifies and celebrates its own human dimension. Flesh *is* difference and flesh *as* difference. This reality of the human flesh delighting in a divine embrace posits difference as not indifference but as sharing and return.

In words and deeds Jesus Christ—the one who enjoys eating and drinking with the excluded ones—teaches about a God who nourishes and who wants to celebrate love and solidarity with us in the midst of a shared table.[39] He teaches us to tenderly call God *Abba*, and as God's children to ask our loving Father for our daily communal bread, *el pan para todos*.[40] Jesus Christ (the God-human) is the "master of desire" who incarnates God's own desire to feed all our physical and spiritual hungers and who promises us that the kingdom of heaven will be a lavish banquet and a big fiesta (indeed, a feast of love or a wedding feast).[41] Yet, our feasting shall not wait until that final promised day. The new Paschal mystery is a continuation and culmination of the first one that celebrated God's liberation of the chosen people from a condition of slavery. The lamb offered at the altar is now Christ's death on the cross, giving his life for the forgiveness of sin. The new Exodus celebrated by Christians is Christ's victory over death, which was gained at his resurrection. Moreover, after Jesus's ascension into heaven God sends the Holy Spirit as *donum*—a divine gift that is the power and guidance to our desire to practice reciprocity within an all-inclusive communal feasting. In and with the Holy Spirit we learn that *imitatio Dei* is in fact *imitatio Trinitatis*. In and with the Holy Spirit community shall already take place here on earth at the locus of a collective table that is our solidarity to all.

But that is not the end of this culinary narrative. Divine self-sharing performs a more radical gesture of kenosis at the Eucharist, where God who nourishes God's people becomes food: the most excessive form of self-presencing as nourishment itself. God becomes the cook, the host, and the food itself in this Eucharistic banquet. Desire in the Eucharist is the active agent in our relationship with God and with one another. Both divine and human desires are eternally united not in the abstract but rather in an incarnate fashion. Here our food is the body of Christ and our drink is his blood, and this through the materiality of bread and wine. Like the Mexican mole, the Eucharist is a banquet for the senses. More intimately, it is a feasting to the sense of touch because eating and drinking are extreme forms of proximity. Above all it is the sense of taste (in lips, mouth, and tongue) that moves us toward the most intimate ecstatic union with God. What could be more intimate than "ingesting" God?[42] In eating this divine food, sensuality—particularly the sense of taste—is paradoxically intensified to the point of becoming a powerful mystic experience, yet in a way that does no violence to the material. In the Eucharist the sense of taste becomes the medium and guidance to the soul and the intellect (rather than the other way around) to our unity with God, to our deification. In this *sacrum convivium* the sense of taste—which is prior to any sensory data, and even prior to the intellect—turns into a foretaste of the beatific vision, as Thomas Aquinas realized.[43] Yet to call it a (beatific) "vision" no longer fully tells us of the tremendousness of such an alimentary beatitude. For in the Eucharist the beatific vision is not primarily a visual experience but rather is a reality that has to do with touching, tasting, drinking, and eating. It has to do with the sensuality of being nourished: a festive partaking as tasting of God's divine banquet or, to be more precise, a "beatific savoring." The Eucharist evokes the ecstatic realm of beatification as itself being a gastronomic event.

The Eucharist, like the mole, is an alimentary hybrid—a complex interplay that *embodies* multiple narratives.[44] The Eucharistic body (the hybrid of humanity and God, materiality and divinity) speaks of the body as a sharing of differences whereby difference is not eliminated but celebrated: people of all races, classes, gender, sexual orientation, and condition all are united by the one and excessive same divine perpetual love that nourished body and soul.[45] Recall when I indicated earlier that one drop of mole contains the entire world for it brings together different nations, cultures, races, and so on. Likewise, the Eucharistic body is a body that nourishes in its act of sharing and celebrating difference. The Catholicity of the body celebrates a corporeal reality bringing together both the local and universal bodies that coincide in the one body of Christ. Under this Eucharistic construction the "alien other" must no longer be rejected but included. Still more challenging, the other is alien no longer. In the Eucharist, self and other are no longer juxtaposed, and neither do they collapse into one another but instead preserve difference in a stage of mutual constitution. That is the challenge that the Eucharist presents—particularly to those who belong to the Catholic Church. The painful fact is that in societies (and Catholic-Christian social groups are not an exception to this reality) some bodies are not desired but are rejected and outcast because their embodiment is depicted by those in power as "imperfect" or "impure": black and brown bodies, female bodies, disabled bodies, and so on.[46]

Daily Bread and Daily Hunger: Sharing God's Nurturing Gift

Like cooking a lavish meal, alimentary theology arises from concrete practices—linguistic, doctrinal, pastoral, liturgical, and so on—and is called to feed and thus shape communities through such alimentary performance. For this reason, alimentary theology must not be indifferent to the question of why it is that there are so many people in the world that are not well fed and even dying of starvation. Frei Betto rightly insists on reminding us that our planet suffers because of the great number of human bodies dying of hunger and malnutrition. And this horrific fact reflects people's indifference and selfishness:

> According to the FAO, 831 million people are now living in a chronic state of malnutrition. Every day, 24,000 die of hunger, including a child under five years of age every minute. Why is it that there are so many campaigns around other causes of premature death, such as cancer, accidents, war and terrorism, without the same being true of hunger, which produces many more victims than these? I can think of only one explanation, and that is a cynical one: that, unlike those other causes, hunger is a respecter of class. It is as though we, the well fed, were saying, "Let the wretched die of hunger; it doesn't affect us."[47]

Hunger has a physical and existential as well as an ethical-political dimension. Humans are hungry beings, for without eating we die of starvation. But hunger is also a reflection of ethics and politics, for it involves power relations and the sharing of God's gifts or lack thereof.

Hunger reflects society's practice of disempowering by removing communal vision, virtue, and caritas.[48] Why is it that hunger is predominantly related to issues of ethnicity, race, gender, sexuality, and social class? Patricia Hill Collins advocates paying greater attention to black feminist thought that does not ignore these correlated factors. She also argues that black feminist thought contributes to the development of what she calls a "politics of empowerment," precisely because it challenges one to think or to develop an epistemology from the perspective of just and unjust power relations.[49] This challenge must also move beyond mere epistemology in

order to integrate a theological vision of nourishment and communal sharing as the locus of divine self-expression. Bread and the lack thereof has
to do with the power of sharing and the refusal to share. It is therefore a
profoundly theological issue, for I think it has to do, ultimately, with God's
gift and the sharing (or refusal to share) this gift among one another. That
is why the "Zero Hunger" project developed by Betto and others was a
commitment act that expressed the voice of dozens of religious denominations (Christian and non-Christian) under the communal conviction that
"hunger results from injustice and represents an offense against the Creator, since life is the greatest gift of God." Project members also expressed
their belief that "to share bread is to share God."[50]

Further, just as the Mexican mole is made up of the personal touch of
individuals, communities, and traditions, so alimentary theology invites
us to bring our own selves into it, to add our spices, and thus make it more
spicy. Theologians should offer their own particular situatedness, gender,
sexual orientation, race, ethnicity, culture, social class, and so on. The
making of this theological mole shall include as well people's own stories of hope, suffering, and struggle. Spiciness is a kind of subversion: its
sharpness is picante—it stirs our tongues and mouths and wakes us up.
That which is spicy makes us alert, attentive, responsive, and responsible.
Thus to bring our own spices into the theological mole also implies the
acquisition of a piquant, prophetic voice. This prophetic "spicy theology"
urges us to speak up about the concrete instances when communities fail
to feed people's hungers and when there is a refusal to welcome otherness
(both human and divine) into the communal feasting.

Making mole and the making of alimentary theology is not an attempt
to collapse all differences and boundaries into a homogenizing category
of nouvelle cuisine.[51] In the mole and in the making of alimentary theology, harmonious difference is welcomed and celebrated. This notion of
harmonious difference is keen to John Milbank's argument in favor of
the construction of a "gothic complex space" that allows the intersecting
and even overlapping of bonds, ways of life, and identities.[52] In addition to
complex space, alimentary theology integrates Talal Asad's notion of heterogeneous time, which includes "embodied practices rooted in multiple
traditions, . . . the differences between horizons of expectation and spaces
of experience—differences that continually dislocate the present from the
past, the world experienced from the world anticipated, and call for their
revision and reconnection. These simultaneous temporalities embrace
both individuals and groups in complexities that imply more than a simple

process of secular time."[53] But these notions of heterogeneous space and time do not imply that alimentary theology is a new sort of religion made up of all religions. Neither is it a theology made of all theologies cooked together in one single pot. It is instead an attempt to think and discern about the complexity of food and the lack thereof. And food is not "just food" but rather an expression of multiple connections (with our bodies, the earth, local and global economies, God, and so on). Food is also a construction of people's identities: national, political, economic, social, cultural, religious, somatic, sexual, and so on. Alimentary theology envisions theology as food and food as theology: for both theology and food exemplify the need or hunger for a communal practice of delight and sharing.[54] Not surprisingly, food has been one of the most paradigmatic symbols in many ancient religious practices (as that of the Aztecs in the case of mole, for instance) as well as current ones.[55] Most importantly, alimentary theology is an invitation to bind (interlace) people's conviction and power to eradicate spiritual and material malnutrition and starvation, which all have to do with bodies—individual, communal, and ecological.

To be sure, this is an issue deeply rooted in the daily practices of sharing and refusing to share. Being attentive and caring means not only reflecting upon relationality and reciprocity among individuals and societies but also becoming aware of humanity's relationship toward animals, plants, and the planet's resources in general. Alimentary theology is critical of any form of power that is exercised as violent subordination of others: not only of a small group over the larger groups but also in an ecological power whereby humanity is on top.[56] After all, humanity is part of the larger ecological body for it is not an "other" to us. I am aware that this coercive power has been often implemented and carried out by Catholic-Christians throughout the past and in the present.[57] Because of this reality, alimentary theology insists on *metanoia*—that is, a continuous process of conversion that must start first from within. I envision alimentary theology as a practice of power that is noncoercive, communal, and rooted in nurturing loving care for one another and imitating God's own radical gesture of love. I hope this form of envisioning will move us beyond a social practice of mere mutual "tolerance" and instead welcome an effort to a simultaneously local and global ecological embodiment of communion expressed as hospitality and mutual nurturance. With God as our table companion we shall be constantly re-created in the performing of nurturing embodied caritas for every body. The making of alimentary theology may hopefully become a true sharing of food for thought, soul, and body—the human delight in God's self-sharing.

Finally, like the Mexican mole the making of alimentary theology requires creativity, imagination, and God's inspiration, just as Sor Andrea and Fray Pascual Bailón were inspired in making the baroque mole. Alimentary theology integrates God's gift that surpasses calculations and is forever opened to transcendence—God's actuality in surplus. It is also interesting to note that both Sor Andrea and Fray Pascual came up with the idea of the mole in the midst of pressure and anxiety, even chaos. Likewise, alimentary theology often results from uncalculated outcomes or a sudden "event" that arises from a divine donor (God's plenitudinous sharing), or even sometimes from chaotic contexts as church historians remind us. With the reception of divine inspiration we do not even know the full implications and even the full meaning of what has been inspired. But this, of course, requires deep discernment in faith as well as charity and hope.

As we make our journey of this culinary adventure that is the making of alimentary theology, may we invoke Fray Pascual Bailón and Sor Andrea de la Asunción so that we truly savor God's abundant gifts and share them with everyone everywhere.[58] *Buen provecho!*

Notes

1 Taibo, *El libro de todos los moles*, 51.
2 Both stories of the baroque mole created by Sor Andrea and by Fray Pascual are oral tales that have been transmitted throughout the centuries. Here I am primarily using the version related by Taibo in *El libro de todos los moles*.
3 Regarding Pascual Bailón, see Taibo, *El libro de todos los moles*, as well as Pérez Martínez, "La comida en el refranero mexicano."
4 The word *sazón* is difficult to translate into English because it means more than just "seasoning." *Tener sazón* means to have a natural gift for cooking delicious foods. It is a special culinary touch that makes the prepared dish something extraordinary.
5 Most of my historical and anthropological research on food both in the pre-Columbian and colonial times in Mexico is mainly taken from the volume *Conquista y comida*, edited by Janet Long. This volume originated at the international and interdisciplinary symposium 1492: El Encuentro de Dos Comidas, which took place in Puebla, Mexico, in July 1992. In addition to *Conquista y comida* I have relied on the works by Esteva and Marielle, *Sin maíz no hay país*; Pilcher, *Vivan los tamales!*; and Salinas Campos, *Gracias a Dios que comí*.

Regarding the term Mesoamerica, David Carrasco explains that it is "given by scholars to designate a geographical and cultural area covering the southern two-thirds of mainland Mexico, Guatemala, Belize, El Salvador, and parts of Honduras, Nicaragua, and Costa Rica." For further analysis on Mesoamerica in pre-Columbian times, see Carrasco, *Religions of Mesoamerica*, 1.

6 Bourges Rodriguez, "Alimentos obsequio de México al mundo," 124, 125 (my translation).

7 For more information on the Aztec culture and Moctezuma's empire, see Carrasco, *Religions of Mesoamerica* and *City of Sacrifice*.

8 This historical testimony is mainly taken from Bernal Díaz del Castillo's *Historia verdadera de la conquista de Nueva España*. This version is taken from Boruges Rodríguez, "Alimentos obsequio de México al mundo," 124.

9 As Carrasco writes in *City of Sacrifice*: "[The Aztecs] developed a sophisticated cosmology of eating in which gods ate gods, humans ate gods, gods ate humans and the sexual sins of humans, children in the underworld suckled from divine trees, gods in the underworld ate the remains of humans, and adults in the underworld ate rotten tamales! It is also important to note that at certain points in their sacred history, the Aztecs conceived of beings in their sky as a devouring mouth and the earth as a gaping jaw" (168).

10 Not all of the Aztec cosmovision was based on food and eating symbols and practices. However, for the purpose of this essay I concentrate on this particular symbolic aspect to provide some explanation (and not all) of why food practices in general, and mole in particular, were important in the Mesoamerican culture. I am grateful to Vanessa Ochs for suggesting this important clarification to me.

11 Carrasco, *City of Sacrifice*, 172.

12 This is the main argument in Carrasco's *City of Sacrifice*, particularly in chapter 6, "Cosmic Jaws: We Eat the Gods and the Gods Eat Us," 164–87. For a similar argument, see Duverger, "The Meaning of Sacrifice." Regarding the Aztec's notions of the human body as part of "a cosmic banquet" or an "eating landscape," see López Austin, *The Human Body and Ideology*. Finally, for an analysis of the Mesoamerican notions of the body, particularly regarding the body as nourishment, see Sergio Raúl Arroyo, "In Praise of the Body."

13 For a further analysis on mexicas and Tenochtitlán, see Carrasco, *Religions of Mesoamerica*.

14 Náhuatl was the official language—or the "truly lingua franca" as Miguel León Portilla puts it—of the Mesoamerican culture. For a further analysis on the Náhuatl language, culture, and cosmovision, see León Portilla, *La filosofía náhuatl*.

15 Taibo, *El libro de todos los moles*, 108.

16 In the mexica mythology the huexolotl was revered as a deity. It was also considered a symbol of great nobility (hence the use of its feathers for the emperor's crown). For more on this topic, see Heyden and Velasco, "Aves van, aves vienen."

17 For a more detailed information on the historical roots and religious symbolism of chilies, see Patricia Van Rhijn, *La cocina del chile*; for chocolate, see Gozáles de la Vara, "Orígen y virtures del chocolate"; for beans, see Kaplan

and Kaplan, "Leguminosas alimenticias del grano"; and for corn, see Esteva et al., *Sin maíz no hay país*, and Pilcher, *Vivan los tamales!*

18 Enrique Dussel argues in *The Invention of the Americas* that what actually took place at the conquistadors' arrival to the American continent was not a "discovery," as it has been commonly understood. Instead, it was a "covering up" (*encubrimiento*) due to the systematic obliteration of the inhabitants' customs, belief systems, and lives.

19 Iturriaga, "Los alimentos cotidianos del mexicano o de tacos, tamales y tortas," 399.

20 Domingo, "La cocina precolombina en España," 17–28.

21 Domingo in "La cocina precolombina en España" states that this medieval flavor was made up of the following products and spices: "La albahaca, la canela, el cardamomo, el culandro, el clavo de olor, el comino, el tomillo, el hinojo, la galanga, el jengibe, el hisopo, el perejil, la hierba luisa, el romero, la menta, la mostaza, la nuez moscada, el oregano, la pimienta negra y la blanca, la ruda, el azafrán y la salvia" (25). (Basil, cinnamon, cardamom, coriandor, clove, cumin, thyme, fennel, galangal, ginger, hyssop, parsley, lemon, verbena, rosemary, peppermint, mustard, nutmeg, oregano, black and white pepper, rue, saffron, and sage.)

22 For a further analysis on the Islamic culinary influence in Spanish cuisine, see Riera-Melis, "El Mediterráneo, crisol de tradiciones alimentarias." Riera-Melis analyzes five main products that were brought to Spain by the Arabs: sugar (from canes), rice, a variety of citrus fruits, eggplant, and spinach. These ingredients were later imported into the Americas where they influenced the dietary customs of the New World, of which the Mexican cuisine was a result. On the influence of Islamic culinary traditions on Spanish cuisine, see Salinas Campos, *Gracias a Dios que comí*, esp. 86–117.

23 As Domingo writes in "La cocina precolombina en España": "Este gusto por las especias exóticas, uno de los motivos del viaje de Colón, se prolongó durante muchos años y caracterizó la cocina española del tiempo de la Casa de los Austria. Eran sabores que costaban mucho dinero y abaratar su precio, importando las especias por rutas más cortas y al mismo tiempo acabar con la dependencia de los comerciantes de las ciudades-republicas italianas, de los turcos y de los portugueses, entró en línea de cuenta, sin duda, a la hora de financiar el viaje de Cristobal Colón" (19). (This taste for exotic spices, which was one of the reasons of Columbus's explorations, was prolonged for many years and became a characteristic of Spanish cuisine in the times of the House of the Austria. These were expensive spices, and lowering their price by importing them through commercial pathway shortcuts, as well as by ending the dependence on traders from Italy, Turkey, and Portugal, doubtlessly became an important factor at the time of deciding to finance Christopher Columbus's expedition [my translation].) Domingo's argument echoes the main line of reasoning in the book *Conquista y comida*.

24 Armelagos, "Cutura y contacto," 108 (my translation).

25 For an analysis and an index of food products exported from the American continent, see Boruges Rodríguez, "Alimentos obsequio de México al mundo." The book *Conquista y comida* also contains a series of essays exploring this aspect of native food products and their influence on world cuisine.

26 For a study on a history of Mexican resistance to colonization through food and dietary customs, see Esteva et al., *Sin maíz no hay país*; Pilcher, *Que vivan los tamales!*; and Salinas Campos, *Gracias a Dios que comí*.

27 On this issue of controlling space by colonial power, see for instance, Mignolo, *The Darker Side of the Renaissance*.

28 In the history of Christianity, this patriarchal controlling of space and the restriction of women to the kitchen has a long precedence. For example, Caroline Walker Bynum in *Holy Feast and Holy Fast* argues that women during the medieval period (particularly religious women) had an intense relationship with food and sometimes displayed extravagant eating behaviors. Many women's mystical experiences were intensely somatic and closely related to food and the Eucharist. Bynum explains that this somatic relationship with food (feasting and fasting) was a form of empowerment in the midst of marginalization.

29 Most of this reflection on Sor Juana Inés de la Cruz and her relationship with cuisine and the kitchen in a patriarchal society is taken from Morino, *El libro de cocina de Sor Juana Inés de la Cruz*.

30 As Sor Juana Inés de la Cruz writes in *Obras Completas*: "Qué podemos saber las mujeres sino filosofías de cocina? Bien dijo Lupercio Leonardo, que bien se puede filosofar y aderezar la cena. Y yo suelo decir viendo estas cosillas: si Aritóteles hubiera guisado, mucho más hubiera escrito" (838–39). (What could we women possibly know if not philosophies of cuisine? Lupercio Leonardo said it so well: it is certainly possible to do both philosophizing and seasoning a supper. And my custom to say when I see this sort of thing is that had Aristotle cooked, he would have written a good deal more [my translation].) For an English version, see Sor Juana Inés de la Cruz, *The Answer/La Respuesta*, 75.

31 Goizueta, "The Symbolic Realism of U.S. Latino/a Popular Catholicism."

32 Ada María Isasi-Díaz, "*Burlando al Opresor*," 346. There is the possibility, of course, of reading too much of liberation and empowerment into these events in Sor Juana's life because it very well might have been the opposite case, as Vanessa Ochs has pointed out to me. There are, however, elements in Sor Juana's life of what Isasi-Díaz calls "mocking/tricking the oppressor": she dresses as a man to get into school, she writes on matters related to food and has high regard for cuisine, and so on. To what extent were Sor Juana's actions instances of empowerment? My guess is that this is a question that can be answered from different angles. I am inclined to make a more positive reading because of how foodways manage to survive despite colonization (here as obliteration of culture and values), as was the case with pre-

Columbian cuisine. Such a reading I propose, following Isasi-Díaz, does not undermine the aspect of suffering and struggle both in Sor Juana's life and in the survival of the mole.

33 Because this view is partial and limited I know that not all Catholic-Christians would agree with my prioritizing of elements in this particular religious tradition. If this is the case for those who belong to the Catholic-Christian tradition, I imagine that the disagreements with my viewpoint might be even greater among people from other religious traditions. Again, this is only my personal experience and viewpoint and not a generalization. This same point applies for what I say about theology in the rest of this essay.

34 See, for instance, Davies and Turner, *Silence and the Word*.

35 I am reminded here of several now classic novels that present cooking as an art form, as self-expression, and as a means of transforming or transfiguring those who partake of such exquisite meals. See Esquivel, *Like Water for Chocolate*; and Dinesen, "Babette's Feast."

36 For instance, many of those who have gone through doctoral studies know very well how painful at times this enterprise is (particularly those doctoral students who are married and have children). As a Dominican friar, becoming a theologian is never seen as a mere individual achievement but rather is a communal task done for the main purpose of serving the church and the world around us. Some theologians have even suffered harsh criticism, imprisonment, torture, and even death because of the political and social implications of their theological statements. In the mostly male-dominated academy of theology, many women theologians can speak of the experience of being ostracized.

37 Divine self-sharing in and through the incarnation does have a precedent: God's trinitarian reciprocity and exchange, God's creation, God's caring and nurturing people. For a biblical anthology of this relationship between nourishment and God's self-sharing, see López Rosas, *Comer, beber, y alegrarse*. Also, for a reflection on God's making of companionship in and through the sharing of food, see Wells, *God's Companions*.

38 Henry, *Encarnación*, 159 (my translation).

39 For a New Testament analysis of table sharing, see Aguirre, *La mesa compartida*. See also Pikaza, *Pan, casa, palabra*.

40 See López Rosas and Landgrave Gándara, *Pan para todos*. See also López Rosas, *Comer, beber, y*.

41 See Leclerc, *El maestro del deseo*.

42 See Webster, *Ingesting Jesus*.

43 This particular reading on Aquinas regarding taste as foretaste to the beatific vision and deification is inspired by Milbank and Pickstock, *Truth in Aquinas*, esp. chapter 3, "Truth and Touch."

44 See, for instance, Smith, *From Symposium to Eucharist*. Smith rightly argues that the Eucharist does not exist in its own "purity" but rather is a hybrid

constructed by many traditions and narratives (such as Jewish, Greco-Roman, medieval, and so forth). And I must add that the Eucharist continues to be re-shaped by history, cultures, and communities; simultaneously, the dynamism of the Eucharist also shapes or makes the Church. See also McPartlan, *The Eucharist Makes the Church.*

45 In the Catholic tradition, the nondualistic relationship of the soul and body is very important and serves as a reintensification and celebration of the body and the material. As such it can become a solid foundation for sacramental theology.

46 For a striking reflection on how in fact this violent politics of exclusion of the "imperfect bodies" echoes a colonial Christian missionary agenda, see Betcher, "Monstrosities, Miracles, and Mission." I am grateful to Mayra Rivera who so generously gave me a copy of this essay.

47 Betto, "Zero Hunger," 12.

48 I agree with Frei Betto that alleviating hunger is not just the outcome of giving food to people or making donations but also requires a more holistic action that targets structural change: "The aim is to mobilize world resources, under the UN supervision, in order to finance entrepreneurial schemes, co-operative movements, and sustainable development in the poorest regions. Hunger cannot be fought just through donations, or even by transfer of funds. These need to be complemented by effective policies of structural change, such as agrarian and fiscal reforms that are capable of lessening the concentration of income from land and financial dealings. And all this has to be guaranteed by a daring policy of loans and credit offered to the beneficiary families, who must become the target of an intense educational programme, so that they can become socio-economic units and active agents in political and historical processes" (Betto, "Zero Hunger," 13).

49 As Patricia Hill Collins states: "First, Black feminist thought fosters a funda-mental paradigmatic shift in how we think about unjust power relations. By embracing a paradigm of intersecting oppressions of race, class, gender, sexu-ality, and nation, as well as Black women's individual and collective agency within them, Black feminist thought reconceptualizes the social relations of domination and resistance. Second, Black feminist thought addresses ongo-ing epistemological debates concerning the power dynamics that underlie what counts as knowledge. Offering U.S. Black women new knowledge about our own experiences can be empowering. But activating epistemologies that criticize prevailing knowledge and that enable us to define our own realities *on our own terms* has far greater implications" (*Black Feminist Thought*, 273–74).

50 Cited by Betto in "Zero Hunger," 11.

51 The warning in this statement regards homogenization more than the notion of nouvelle cuisine as such. Surely, mole was and is continuously being re-created. And so is theology. I am not arguing to return to a lost "origin." As such, the notion of nouvelle cuisine could well apply to both practices. How-

ever, I want to suggest that alimentary theology, like the mole, is not about homogenizing but is instead about allowing difference and contrasts, ambiguity and perplexity.

52 See Milbank, "Against the Resignations of the Age."

53 Asad, *Formations of the Secular*, 179.

54 In very general terms, this is the main thesis throughout Jung's *Food for Life*.

55 See, for instance, Schmidt-Leukel, *Las religiones y la comida*.

56 With this statement I do not mean to say that humanity does not enjoy a special place in all creation (as the biblical narratives and Christian orthodoxy rightly teaches). Humanity occupies a privileged position in creation, including that over the angels. Instead, my statement attempts to denounce the exercise of power as coercion and destruction or violence, and thus as the betrayal of humanity's vocation to be good stewards of creation and to promote harmonious and peaceful relations (including ecological ones).

57 See, for instance, Catherine Keller's arguments in her essay "The Love of Postcolonialism."

58 I am very grateful to Joel Marie Cabrita for her editorial work on this essay.

Lynne Westfield

▣

RESPONSE TO THE ESSAY BY ANGEL F. MÉNDEZ MONTOYA

Alimentary practices have profound religious significance as portals into mystery. Mystery is not that about which you cannot know anything. Rather, it is that about which you cannot know everything. God is mystery. While no practice or belief will provide insight into the "everything" of mystery, Montoya and I both argue that practices involving food, cooking, and dining can be spirit-filled, sacramental experiences that provide glimpses of insight into mystery. Montoya and I, albeit from different cultural, gender, and religious perspectives, try to describe and illumine the experience of mystery as we have personally known it through food, cooking, dining, hospitality, and the Eucharist. Each of our essays grapples with mystery as being profound, illusive, and indisputably craved by humanity. Gastronomical miracles as encounters with mystery are available to all through the breaking of bread, the giving and receiving of hospitality, and the invitation to a stranger to become a guest.

The hunger for intimacy by humanity is a longing for God's love coupled with a deep need to belong. Theological reflection concerning the need for community, the need for a personal relationship with God, and mystical encounters are often limited to description and analysis that is exclusively cognitive. Further, the writing of theology is too often an event that occurs only in the head, thereby excluding other parts of the body. These disembodied descriptions and depictions leave those in the academy as well as in the local church dry, parched, and starving for reflection that conveys the succulence and savor of the experience. As a corrective to malnourished and ill-thought theology, Montoya approaches theology as a nourishment to people. Theology, from this perspective, is food, is nourishment, and is sustenance for body, mind, and spirit. Resonating with his thesis, I contend that theology is the doing of liberation in which it is never politically neutral and where dining tables are the locations of death-dealing and life-sustaining negotiation—food for the hungry and power for the poor. The doing of theology is hard work for body, mind, and spirit. The work of theology is the activities of justice and liberation achieved through culinary delight and satisfied appetite.

Learning and doing theology begins at a young age and continues for a lifetime. I learned the liberative aspects of theology from my mother as she negotiated over her dining room table for better schools for poor African American children. Montoya likewise reflects upon his learning of theology as it happened in the kitchen of his childhood. As he writes, "I believe that one of my first theological teachings came from my home's kitchen, preparing and eating food, feasting with family and friends. I believe our family kitchen was one of the first spaces where I discovered God's grace, self-sharing, and hospitality." As a girl watching my activist mother use her culinary skills to fight for the nourishment for poor children, I learned that fight for liberation and freedom had to be done using the resources at hand. For women sequestered to the kitchen, the theological enterprise of liberation is not stifled. Women still do what women have done since Hagar—that is, to rethink and reshape ladles, spatulas, and pots into formidable tools of freedom.

Montoya's statements concerning the gender and class politics of the kitchen are well informed and vitally important for all minoritized communities, especially for the Latino and Latina and African American communities. While women of color have historically been relegated to the kitchen, the stories of women like my mother and the women in Montoya's essay reveal the kitchen as a place of creativity and liberation because women have had the audacity it make these spaces vital, vibrant, and holy. It is understandable, even expected, that a womanist scholar will critique domination—this is precisely what I did in my essay. It is of critical importance that men with authority criticize patriarchy and sexism and not leave the condemnation of patriarchy to women as "women's work." Montoya's efforts in appreciating and incorporating the stories of women and in bringing to bear analysis that condemns the oppression and alienation of women is using his power of male privilege and authority as a tool to eradicate sexism. We need more male allies, especially men of color, who will be as forthright and unequivocal in their fight for agendas of freedom for women as they are concerning issues of racism. The struggle must be recognized as our struggle if racism and sexism are to be eradicated.

I am struck as much by Montoya's style of writing as I am with what he has written. Montoya gently weaves narrative with scholarly speech. I suspect he works very hard at writing in a way that allows his authentic voice as a man, as a Latino, and as a church leader deeply committed to justice. I, too, have attempted to write in a style that conveys my intellectual rigor in a voice that is unmistakably woman, African American, and Christian. As church leaders and theologians, stretching the theological imagination of our communities in part means writing in ways that are new and innovative to the academy and needed by the wider world. The task is a formidable one that includes nurturing the writing of theology in voices that convey vigorous analysis while at the same time making use of old ideas to interpret new ones; synthesizing seemingly unrelated theories in poetic forms; experimenting with new arguments for solving ancient problems; weaving experience with theory and resisting the false dichotomy that action and reflection can be separated; connecting everyday life with basic theological notions; and integrating an awareness that body, mind, and spirit must stay in dynamic tension for authentic expressions of theology. I argue for conversation concerning scholarly writing that makes our work accessible to our communities in new ways, and I welcome conversation that can teach us ways of making our work available to our peers while at the same time making it available to our mothers, uncles, cousins, and children.

Bibliography

Aaron, Charles. "What a White Boy Means When He Says Yo." In *And It Don't Stop: The Best American Hip-Hop Journalism of the Last Twenty-five Years.* New York: Faber and Faber, 2004.

Abrahams, Roger D. *African Folktales: Traditional Stories of the Black World.* New York: Pantheon Books, 1983.

Acosta-Belén, Edna. *The Puerto Rican Woman: Perspectives on Culture, History and Society.* New York: Praeger, 1986.

Aguirre Monasterio, Rafael. *La mesa compartida: Estudios del NT desde las ciencias sociales.* Santander, Spain: Editorial Sal Terrae, 1994.

Alarcón Segovia, Donato, and Héctor Bourges Rodríguez. *La Alimentación De Los Mexicanos.* Mexico City: El Colegio Nacional, 2002.

Aldama, Frederick Luis. *Brown on Brown: Chicano/a Representations of Gender, Sexuality, and Ethnicity.* Austin: University of Texas Press, 2005.

Allen, James. *Without Sanctuary: Lynching Photography in America.* Santa Fe, N.M.: Twin Palms, 2000.

Allen, Robert Clyde, ed. *To Be Continued . . . : Soap Operas around the World.* London: Routledge, 1995.

Als, Hilton. "No Respect: A Critic at Large." In *And It Don't Stop: The Best American Hip-Hop Journalism of the Last Twenty-five Years.* New York: Faber and Faber, 2004.

Althaus-Reid, Marcela. "El Tocado (Le Toucher): Sexual Irregularities in the Translation of God (the Word) in Jesus." In *Derrida and Religion: Other Testaments,* edited by Yvonne Sherwood and Kevin Hart. New York: Routledge, 2004.

Anderson, Victor. *Beyond Ontological Blackness: An Essay on African American Religious and Cultural Criticism.* New York: Continuum, 1999.

Anzaldúa, Gloria. *Borderlands/La Frontera: The New Mestiza.* 2nd ed. San Francisco: Aunt Lute Books, 1999.

Apel, Dora. *Imagery of Lynching: Black Men, White Women, and the Mob.* New Brunswick, N.J.: Rutgers University Press, 2004.

Appiah, Anthony, Henry Louis Gates Jr., and Microsoft Corporation. *Encarta Africana.* CD-ROM. Bellingham, Wash.: Microsoft Corporation, 1999.

Arias, Santa. *Retórica, historia y polémica: Bartolomé de las Casas y la tradición intelectual renacentista.* Lanham Md.: University Press of America, 2001.

Armelagos, George. "Cutura y contacto: El choque de dos cocinas mundiales." In *Conquista y comida: Consecuencias del encuentro de dos mundos,* edited by Janet Long. 2nd ed. Mexico City: Universidad Nacional Autónoma de México, 1997.

Arroyo, Sergio Raúl. "In Praise of the Body." *Artes de México* 69 (2004): 75–77.

Asad, Talal. *Formations of the Secular: Christianity, Islam, Modernity (Cultural Memory in the Present).* Stanford, Calif.: Stanford University Press, 2003.

Baker-Fletcher, Karen. "The Erotic in Contemporary Black Women's Writing." In *Loving the Body: Black Religious Studies and the Erotic,* edited by Dwight N. Hopkins and Anthony B. Pinn. New York: Palgrave Macmillan, 2004.

Baldwin, Davarian L. "Black Empires, White Desires: The Spatial Politics of Identity in the Age of Hip-Hop." In *That's the Joint! The Hip-Hop Studies Reader,* edited by Murray Foreman and Mark Anthony Neal. New York: Routledge, 2004.

Baldwin, James. *The Fire Next Time.* New York: Modern Library, 1995 [1963].

Bañuelas, Arturo J. *Mestizo Christianity: Theology from the Latino Perspective.* Maryknoll, N.Y.: Orbis Books, 1995.

Baugh, Lloyd. *Imaging the Divine: Jesus and Christ-Figures in Film.* Kansas City, Mo.: Sheed and Ward, 1997.

Beauvoir, Simone de. *The Second Sex.* Translated by H. M. Parshley. New York: Knopf, 1993.

Begbie, Jeremy. *Beholding the Glory: Incarnation through the Arts.* Grand Rapids, Mich.: Baker Academic, 2003.

Bell, David, and Gill Valentine. *Consuming Geographies: We Are Where We Eat.* London: Routledge, 1997.

Bellah, Robert Neelly. *The Broken Covenant: American Civil Religion in Time of Trial.* 2nd ed. Chicago: University of Chicago Press, 1992.

Belting, Hans. *Likeness and Presence: A History of the Image before the Era of Art.* Translated by Edmund Jephcott. Chicago: University of Chicago Press, 1994.

Beltrán, Mary C. "The Hollywood Latina Body as a Site of Social Struggle: Media Constructions of Stardom and Jennifer Lopez's 'Cross-over Butt.'" *Quarterly Review of Film and Video* 19, no. 1 (2002): 71-86.

Benhabib, Seyla. *Situating the Self: Gender, Community and Postmodernism in Contemporary Ethics.* Cambridge: Polity, 1992.

Bercovitch, Sacvan. *The Puritan Origins of the American Self.* New Haven, Conn.: Yale University Press, 1975.

Berger, Martin A., and David Holloway, eds. *American Visual Cultures.* New York: Continuum, 2005.

Berger, Maurice. *How Art Becomes History: Essays on Art, Society, and Culture in Post–New Deal America.* New York: Icon Editions, 1992.

Betcher, Sharon. "Monstrosities, Miracles, and Mission: Religion and the Politics of Disablement." In *Postcolonial Theologies: Divinity and Empire,* edited by

Catherine Keller, Michael Nausner, and Mayra Rivera. St. Louis, Mo.: Chalice, 2004.

Bethell, Leslie. *The Cambridge History of Latin America.* Cambridge: Cambridge University Press, 1984.

Betto, Frei. "Zero Hunger: An Ethical-Political Project." *Concilium* 2 (2005): 11–23.

Bhabha, Homi K. *The Location of Culture.* New York: Routledge, 1994.

Bhabha, Homi K., and César Aira. *El lugar de la cultura.* Buenos Aires: Manantial, 2002.

Bloom, Harold. *Where Shall Wisdom Be Found?* New York: Riverhead Books, 2004.

Bouchony, Claire Tron de. *Women: From Witch-Hunt to Politics.* Paris: UNESCO, 1985.

Bourges Rodriguez, Héctor. "Alimentos obsequio de México al mundo." In *La alimentación de los Mexicanos,* edited by Donato Alarcón Segovia and Héctor Bourges Rodríguez. Mexico City: El Colegio Nacional, 2002.

Bowser, Frederick P. "Colonial Spanish America." In *Neither Slave nor Free: The Freedman of African Descent in the Slave Societies of the New World,* edited by David W. Cohen and Jack P. Greene. Baltimore: Johns Hopkins University Press, 1972.

Boyd, Todd. *The New H.N.I.C. (Head Niggas in Charge): The Death of Civil Rights and the Reign of Hip Hop.* New York: New York University Press, 2002.

Boyer, Horace Clarence. *Lift Every Voice and Sing II: An African American Hymnal.* New York: Church Publishing, 1993.

Brown, Peter. "A Dark-Age Crisis: Aspects of the Iconoclastic Controversy." *English Historical Review* 87 (January 1973): 5–6.

Buber, Martin. *I and Thou.* Edited by Walter Arnold Kaufmann. New York: Scribner, 1970.

Bugner, Ladislas, ed. *The Image of the Black in Western Art.* Vols. 1, 2, and 4. The Menil Foundation; distributed by Harvard University Press, 1976, 1979, 1989.

Butler, Judith. *Gender Trouble: Feminism and the Subversion of Identity.* New York: Routledge, 1999.

Bynum, Caroline Walker. *Holy Feast and Holy Fast: The Religious Significance of Food to Medieval Women.* Berkeley: University of California Press, 1987.

Cannon, Katie G. *Katie's Canon: Womanism and the Soul of the Black Community.* New York: Continuum, 1995.

Carrasco, David. *City of Sacrifice: The Aztec Empire and the Role of Violence in Civilization.* Boston: Beacon Press, 1999.

———. *Religions of Mesoamerica: Cosmovision and Ceremonial Centers.* Prospect Heights, Ill.: Waveland Press, 1998.

Castillo, Ana. *Goddess of the Americas: Writings on the Virgin of Guadalupe.* New York: Riverhead Books, 1996.

Cavanaugh, William T. *Theopolitical Imagination:Discovering the Liturgy as a Political Act in an Age of Global Consumerism.* London: T&T Clark, 2002.

Cepeda, Raquel. *And It Don't Stop: The Best American Hip-Hop Journalism of the Last Twenty-five Years.* New York: Faber and Faber, 2004.

Cisneros, Sandra. "Guadalupe the Sex Goddess." In *Goddess of the Americas: Writings on the Virgin of Guadalupe,* edited by Ana Castillo. New York: Riverhead Books, 1996.

Cohen, David William, and Jack P. Greene. *Neither Slave nor Free: The Freedman of African Descent in the Slave Societies of the New World.* Baltimore: Johns Hopkins University Press, 1972.

Collins, Patricia Hill. *Black Feminist Thought: Knowledge, Consciousness, and the Politics of Empowerment.* Rev. ed. New York: Routledge, 2000.

———. *Black Sexual Politics: African Americans, Gender, and the New Racism.* New York: Routledge, 2004.

Cone, James H. *A Black Theology of Liberation.* 2nd ed. Maryknoll, N.Y.: Orbis Books, 1986 [1970].

———. *God of the Oppressed.* Rev. ed. Maryknoll, N.Y.: Orbis Books, 1997.

Cone, James H., and Gayraud S. Wilmore. *Black Theology: A Documentary History.* 2nd ed. 2 vols. Maryknoll, N.Y.: Orbis Books, 1993.

Corley, Kathleen E., and Robert L. Webb, eds. *Jesus and Mel Gibson's the Passion of the Christ: The Film, the Gospels and the Claims of History.* London: Continuum, 2004.

Costas, Orlando E. "Evangelism from the Periphery: A Galilean Model." *Apuntes* 2, no. 3 (autumn 1982): 51–59.

———. "Evangelism from the Periphery: The Universality of Galilee." *Apuntes* 2, no. 4 (winter 1982): 75–84.

———. "Hispanic Theology in North America." In *Struggles for Solidarity: Liberation Theologies in Tension.* Minneapolis: Fortress Press, 1992.

———. "The Meaning of Christian Mission from the Periphery of History." Lecture presented at the Southeastern Baptist Theological Seminary, October 5, 1982.

Counihan, Carole, and Penny Van Esterik. *Food and Culture: A Reader.* New York: Routledge, 1997.

Crossan, John Dominic. *The Dark Interval: Towards a Theology of Story.* Sonoma, Calif.: Polebridge Press, 1988.

———. *God and Empire: Jesus against Rome, Then and Now.* New York: HarperCollins, 2007.

———. *Jesus: A Revolutionary Biography.* San Francisco: HarperSanFrancisco, 1994.

Cruz, Juana Inés de la. *The Answer/La Respuesta: Including a Selection of Poems.* Edited and translated by Electa Arenal and Amanda Powell. New York: Feminist Press, 1994.

———. *Obras Completas.* 14th ed. Mexico D.F.: Editorial Porrúa, 2004.

Davies, Oliver, and Denys Turner, eds. *Silence and the Word: Negative Theology and Incarnation.* Cambridge: Cambridge University Press, 2002.

Davis, David. *Inhuman Bondage: The Rise and Fall of Slavery in the World*. New York: Oxford University Press, 2008.

———. *The Problem of Slavery in Western Culture*. New York: Oxford University Press, 2008.

Dawson, Michael C. *Black Visions: The Roots of Contemporary African American Political Ideologies*. Chicago: University of Chicago Press, 2001.

Derrida, Jacques, and Gianni Vattimo. *Religion: Cultural Memory in the Present*. Stanford, Calif.: Stanford University Press, 1998.

Detweiler, Robert. "Theological Trends of Postmodern Fiction." *Journal of the American Academy of Religion* 44, no. 2 (1976): 225–37.

Devisse, Jean, and Michel Mollat. *The Image of the Black in Western Art. Part 2: From the Early Christian Era to the "Age of Discovery."* New York: W. Morrow, 1979.

Díaz, Miguel H. *On Being Human: U.S. Hispanic and Rahnerian Perspectives*. Edited by Robert J. Screiter. Maryknoll, N.Y.: Orbis Books, 2001.

Díaz del Castillo, Bernal. *Historia verdadera de la conquista de Nueva España*. Barcelona: Círculo de Lectores, 1989.

Díaz-Stevens, Ana María, ed. *An Enduring Flame: Studies on Latino Popular Religiosity*. New York: The Bildner Center, 1995.

———. *Oxcart Catholicism on Fifth Avenue: The Impact of the Puerto Rican Migration upon the Archdiocese of New York*. Notre Dame, Ind.: University of Notre Dame Press, 1993.

Dinesen, Isak. "Babette's Feast." In *Anecdotes of Destiny and Ehrengard*. New York: Vintage International, 1993.

Dodson, Jualynne E., and Cheryl Townsend Gilkes. "There's Nothing Like Church Food: Food and the U.S. Afro-Christian Tradition: Re-Membering Community and Feeding the Embodied S/spirit(s)." *Journal of the American Academy of Religion* 63 (fall 1995): 519–20.

Domingo, Xavier. "La cocina precolombina en España." In *Conquista y comida: Consecuencias del encuentro de dos mundos*, edited by Janet Long. 2nd ed. Mexico City: Universidad Nacional Autónoma de México, 1997.

Douglas, Kelly Brown. *The Black Christ*. Maryknoll, N.Y.: Orbis, 1994.

Douglas, Mary. *Natural Symbols*. London: Routledge, 2003.

Drury, John. *Painting the Word: Christian Pictures and Their Meanings*. New Haven, Conn.: Yale University Press, 1999.

Duany, Jorge. *The Puerto Rican Nation on the Move: Identities on the Island and in the United States*. Chapel Hill: University of North Carolina Press, 2002.

Du Bois, W. E. B. "Possibilities of the Negro, The Advance Guard of the Race." *Booklovers Magazine* 2, no. 1 (1903): 2–15.

———. *Writings*. Edited by Nathan Irvin Huggins. New York: Library of America, 1996.

Dunnington, Jacqueline Orsini. *Celebrating Guadalupe*. Tucson, Ariz.: Rio Nuevo Publishers, 2004.

Duverger, Christian. "The Meaning of Sacrifice." In *Fragments for a History of the Human Body,* edited by Michel Feher, Ramona Naddaff, and Nadia Tazi. New York: Zone Books, 1990.

Dussel, Enrique D. *The Invention of the Americas: Eclipse of "the Other" and the Myth of Modernity.* Translated by Michael D. Barber. New York: Continuum, 1995.

Dyson, Michael Eric. "The Culture of Hip-Hop." In *That's the Joint! The Hip-Hop Studies Reader,* edited by Murray Foreman and Mark Anthony Neal. New York: Routledge, 2004.

———. *Holler If You Hear Me: Searching for Tupac Shakur.* New York: Basic Civitas Books, 2001.

Earl, Riggins Renal. *Dark Symbols, Obscure Signs: God, Self, and Community in the Slave Mind.* Maryknoll, N.Y.: Orbis Books, 1993.

Eco, Umberto, *The Name of the Rose.* Translated by William Weaver. New York: Everyman's Library, 2006.

Elizondo, Virgilio P. *Christianity and Culture: An Introduction to Pastoral Theology and Ministry for the Bicultural Community.* Huntington, Ind.: Our Sunday Visitor, 1975.

———. *The Future Is Mestizo: Life Where Cultures Meet.* Rev. ed. Boulder: University Press of Colorado, 2000.

———. *Galilean Journey: The Mexican-American Promise.* Rev. ed. Maryknoll, N.Y.: Orbis Books, 2000.

———. *A God of Incredible Surprises: Jesus of Galilee, Celebrating Faith.* Lanham, Md.: Rowman and Littlefield, 2003.

———. *La Morenita: Evangelizer of the Americas.* San Antonio, Tex.: Mexican American Cultural Center, 1980.

Ellacuría, Ignacio. "The Historicity of Christian Salvation." In *Mysterium Liberationis: Fundamental Concepts of Liberation Theology.* Maryknoll, N.Y.: Orbis Books, 1993.

Ellacuría, Ignacio, and Jon Sobrino. *Mysterium Liberationis: Fundamental Concepts of Liberation Theology.* Maryknoll, N.Y.: Orbis Books, 1993.

Espín, Orlando. *The Faith of the People: Theological Reflections on Popular Catholicism.* Maryknoll, N.Y.: Orbis Books, 1997.

Esquivel, Laura. *Like Water for Chocolate: A Novel in Monthly Installments, with Recipes, Romances, and Home Remedies.* Translated by Carol Christensen and Thomas Christensen. New York: Doubleday, 1992.

Estés, Clarissa Pinkola. *Women Who Run with the Wolves: Contacting the Power of the Wild Woman.* London: Rider, 1992.

Esteva, Gustavo, Catherine Marielle, Griselda Galicia García, and Museo Nacional de Culturas Populares (Mexico). *Sin maíz no hay país: Culturas populares de México.* Mexico City: Consejo Nacional para la Cultura y las Artes; Dirección General de Culturas Populares e Indígenas; Museo Nacional de Culturas Populares, 2003.

Esteves, Sandra Maria. "It Is Raining Today." In *Puerto Rican Writers at Home in the USA*, edited by Faythe Turner. Seattle, Wash.: Open Hand Publishing, 1991.

Evans, James H. *Spiritual Empowerment in Afro-American Literature: Frederick Douglass, Rebecca Jackson, Booker T. Washington, Richard Wright, Toni Morrison.* Lewiston N.Y.: E. Mellen Press, 1987.

———. *We Have Been Believers: An African-American Systematic Theology.* Minneapolis: Fortress Press, 1992.

Faggen, Robert A. " 'But Is It Art?' A Prelude to Criticism of Mel Gibson's *The Passion of the Christ.*" In *After the Passion Is Gone: American Religious Consequences*, edited by J. Shawn Landres and Michael Berenbaum. New York: Altamira Press, 2004.

Feher, Michel, Ramona Naddaff, and Nadia Tazi. *Fragments for a History of the Human Body.* Cambridge, Mass.: Zone, 1989.

Ferré, Rosario. *Eccentric Neighborhoods.* New York: Farrar, Straus and Giroux, 1998.

———. *The House on the Lagoon.* London: Abacus, 1996.

———. *The Youngest Doll.* Lincoln: University of Nebraska Press, 1991.

Florensky, P. A. *Iconostasis.* Translated by Donald Sheehan and Olga Andrejev. Crestwood, N.Y.: St. Vladimir's Seminary Press, 2000.

Forest, Jim. "Through Icons: Word and Image Together." In *Beholding the Glory*, edited by Jeremy Begbie. Grand Rapids, Mich.: Baker Academic, 2001.

Fraile-Marcos, Anna Maria. "Hybridizing the 'City Set upon a Hill' in Toni Morrison's *Paradise. MELUS* 28, no. 4 (2003): 3–33.

Fraser, Nancy. *Justice Interruptus: Critical Reflections on the "Postsocialist" Condition.* New York: Routledge, 1997.

Freedberg, David. *The Power of Images: Studies in the History and Theory of Response.* Chicago: University of Chicago Press, 1989.

Friedman, Susan Stanford. *Mappings: Feminism and the Cultural Geographies of Encounter.* Princeton, N.J.: Princeton University Press, 1998.

Fusco, Coco. *English Is Broken Here: Notes on Cultural Fusion in the Americas.* New York: New Press, 1995.

García Canclini, Néstor. *Hybrid Cultures: Strategies for Entering and Leaving Modernity.* Minneapolis: University of Minnesota Press, 1995.

García Coll, Cynthia T., and María de Lourdes Mattei, eds. *The Psychosocial Development of Puerto Rican Women.* New York: Praeger, 1989.

García-Rivera, Alex. *St. Martín de Porres: The "Little Stories" and the Semiotics of Culture.* Maryknoll, N.Y.: Orbis Books, 1995.

Garvey, Marcus. *Philosophy and Opinions of Marcus Garvey.* Edited by Amy Jacques Garvey. New York: Atheneum, 1977.

Gaspar de Alba, Alicia. *Chicano Art Inside/Outside the Master's House: Cultural Politics and the CARA Exhibition.* Austin: University of Texas Press, 1998.

Gee, Alex, and John Teter. *Jesus and the Hip-Hop Prophets: Spiritual Insights from Lauryn Hill and Tupac Shakur.* Downers Grove, Ill.: InterVarsity Press, 2003.

Gibson, Charles. *Spain in America.* New York: Harper and Row, 1966.

Gilroy, Paul. *The Black Atlantic: Modernity and Double Consciousness.* Cambridge, Mass.: Harvard University Press, 1993.

Goizueta, Roberto S. *Caminemos con Jesús: Toward a Hispanic/Latino Theology of Accompaniment.* Maryknoll, N.Y.: Orbis Books, 1995.

———. "The Symbolic Realism of U.S. Latino/a Popular Catholicism." *Theological Studies* 65, no. 2 (June 2004): 225–74.

Gonzáles de la Vara, Martín. "Orígen y virtures del chocolate." In *Conquista y comida: Consecuencias del encuentro de dos mundos,* edited by Janet Long. 2nd ed. Mexico City: Universidad Nacional Autónoma de México, 1997.

González, Justo L. *Santa Biblia: The Bible through Hispanic Eyes.* Nashville, Tenn.: Abingdon Press, 1996.

Gonzalez, Michelle. *Afro-Cuban Theology: Religion, Race, Culture, and Identity.* Gainesville: University Press of Florida, 2007.

Grant, Jacquelyn. *White Women's Christ and Black Women's Jesus: Feminist Christology and Womanist Response.* Atlanta, Ga.: Scholars Press, 1989.

Greene, Meg. *Lauryn Hill.* Philadelphia: Chelsea House, 2000.

Guerrero, Andrés Gonzales. *A Chicano Theology.* Maryknoll, N.Y.: Orbis Books, 1987.

Gutjahr, Paul C. *An American Bible: A History of the Good Book in the United States, 1777–1880.* Stanford, Calif.: Stanford University Press, 1999.

Hall, Calvin S., and Vernon J. Nordby. *A Primer of Jungian Psychology.* New York: Taplinger Pub. Co., 1973.

Hall, Stuart. *Stuart Hall: Critical Dialogues in Cultural Studies.* Edited by David Morley and Kuan-Hsing Chen. London: Routledge, 1996.

Hammon, Jupiter. *America's First Negro Poet: The Complete Works of Jupiter Hammon of Long Island.* Edited by Stanley Austin Ransom. Port Washington, N.Y.: I. J. Kennikat Press, 1970.

Hanke, Lewis. *All Mankind Is One: a Study of the Disputation between Bartolomé De Las Casas and Juan Ginés De Sepúlveda in 1550 on the Intellectual and Religious Capacity of the American Indians.* DeKalb: Northern Illinois University Press, 1974.

Hardt, Michael, and Antonio Negri. *Empire.* Cambridge, Mass.: Harvard University Press, 2000.

———. *Multitude: War and Democracy in the Age of Empire.* New York: Penguin, 2004.

Harris, Melanie. *Uncovering Womanism: Ethical Themes and Values in Alice Walker's Non-Fiction Work.* New York: Palgrave Macmillan, 2010.

Hebdige, Dick. "Rap and Hip-Hop: The New York Connection." In *That's the Joint! The Hip-Hop Studies Reader,* edited by Murray Foreman and Mark Anthony Neal. New York: Routledge, 2004.

Henry, Michel, Javier Teira, Gorka Fernández, and Roberto Ranz. *Encarnación: Una filosofía de la carne.* Salamanca, Spain: Sigueme, 2001.

Heyden, Doris, and Ana María L. Velasco. "Aves van, aves vienen: El guajolote, la gallina y el pato." In *Conquista y comida: Consecuencias del encuentro de dos mundos,* edited by Janet Long. 2nd ed. Mexico City: Universidad Nacional Autónoma de México, 1997.

Hirsch, Edward. *The Demon and the Angel: Searching for the Source of Artistic Inspiration.* New York: Harcourt, 2002.

Hofstadter, Richard. *Anti-Intellectualism in American Life.* New York: Knopf, 1970.

Holloway, David, and John Beck. *American Visual Cultures.* London: Continuum Logo, 2005.

hooks, bell. *Yearning: Race, Gender, and Cultural Politics.* Boston: South End Press, 1990.

Hoover, Stewart M. *Mass Media Religion: The Social Sources of the Electronic Church.* Newbury Park, Calif.: Sage Publications, 1988.

Hopkins, Dwight N. *Being Human: Race, Culture, and Religion.* Minneapolis: Fortress Press, 2005.

———. "Black Theology on God: The Divine in Black Popular Religion." In *The Ties that Bind: African American and Hispanic American/Latino/a Theologies in Dialogue,* edited by Anthony B. Pinn and Benjamín Valentín. New York: Continuum, 2001.

———. *Down, Up, and Over: Slave Religion and Black Theology.* Minneapolis, Minn.: Fortress Press, 2000.

———. *Introducing Black Theology of Liberation.* Maryknoll, N.Y.: Orbis Books, 1999.

———. *Shoes That Fit Our Feet: Sources for a Constructive Black Theology.* Maryknoll, N.Y.: Orbis Books, 1993.

Hopkins, Dwight N., and George C. L. Cummings. *Cut Loose Your Stammering Tongue: Black Theology in the Slave Narratives.* 2nd ed. Louisville, Ky.: Westminster John Knox Press, 2003.

Hopkins, Dwight N., and Anthony B. Pinn, eds. *Loving the Body: Black Religious Studies and the Erotic.* New York: Palgrave Macmillan, 2004.

Horsfield, Peter G. *Religious Television: The American Experience, Communication and Human Values.* New York: Longman, 1984.

Irigaray, Luce. *This Sex Which Is Not One.* Ithaca, N.Y.: Cornell University Press, 1985.

———. *To Be Two.* New York: Routledge, 2001.

Isasi-Díaz, Ada María. "*Burlando al Opresor:* Mocking/Tricking the Oppressor: Dreams and Hope of Hispanas/Latinas and *Mujeristas.*" *Theological Studies* 65, no. 2 (June 2004): 340–63.

———. *En La Lucha/In the Struggle: A Hispanic Women's Liberation Theology.* Minneapolis, Minn.: Fortress Press, 1993.

———. *Mujerista Theology: A Theology for the Twenty-First Century.* Maryknoll, N.Y.: Orbis Books, 1996.

Iturriaga, José N. "Los alimentos cotidianos del mexicano o de tacos, tamales y tortas: Mestizaje y recreación." In *Conquista y comida: Consecuencias del encuentro de dos mundos*, edited by Janet Long. 2nd ed. Mexico City: Universidad Nacional Autónoma de México, 1997.

Jiménez, Alfredo, Nicolás Kanellos, and Claudio Esteva Fabregat. *Handbook of Hispanic Cultures in the United States*. Houston, Tex.: Arte Público Press; Madrid: Instituto de Cooperacion Iberoamericana, 1994.

Johnson, Paul E. *African-American Christianity: Essays in History*. Berkeley: University of California Press, 1994.

Jung, L. Shannon. *Food for Life: The Spirituality and Ethics of Eating*. Minneapolis, Minn.: Fortress Press, 2004.

Kaplan, Lawrence, and Lucille N. Kaplan. "Leguminosas alimenticias del grano: Su origen en el nuevo mundo, su adopción en el viejo." In *Conquista y comida: Consecuencias del encuentro de dos mundos*, edited by Janet Long. 2nd ed. Mexico City: Universidad Nacional Autónoma de México, 1997.

Käsemann, Ernst. *The Testament of Jesus: A Study of the Gospel of John in the Light of Chapter 17*. Philadelphia: Fortress Press, 1968.

Kaufman, Gordon. "Theology as Imaginative Construction." *The Journal of the American Academy of Religion* 50 (March 1982): 73–79.

Keller, Catherine. "The Love of Postcolonialism: Theology and the Interstices of Empire." In *Postcolonial Theologies: Divinity and Empire*, edited by Catherine Keller, Michael Nausner, and Mayra Rivera. St. Louis, Mo.: Chalice Press, 2004.

Keller, Catherine, Michael Nausner, and Mayra Rivera. *Postcolonial Theologies: Divinity and Empire*. St. Louis, Mo.: Chalice Press, 2004.

Kirk-Duggan, Cheryl A. *Misbegotten Anguish: A Theology and Ethics of Violence*. St. Louis, Mo.: Chalice Press, 2001.

Kirkpatrick, Frank G. "The Logic of Mutual Heterocentrism: The Self as Gift." *Philosophy and Theology* 6, no. 4 (summer 1992): 354–68.

Klein, Herbert S. *African Slavery in Latin America and the Caribbean*. New York: Oxford University Press, 1986.

Knadler, Stephen. " 'Blanca from the Block': Whiteness and the Transnational Latina Body." *Genders* 41 (2005): 1–37.

Koerner, Joseph Leo. *The Moment of Self-Portraiture in German Renaissance Art*. Chicago: University of Chicago Press, 1993.

LaCugna, Catherine Mowry. *God for Us: The Trinity and Christian Life*. San Francisco: HarperCollins, 1991.

Landres, J. Shawn, and Michael Berenbaum, eds. *After the Passion Is Gone: American Religious Consequences*. Walnut Creek, Calif.: AltaMira Press, 2004.

Leclerc, Eloi. *El maestro del deseo: Una lectura del evangelio de Juan*. Paris: Descleé de Brouwer; Madrid: PPC Editorial y Distribuidora, 1997.

León Portilla, Miguel. *La filosofía náhuatl*. 9th ed. México City: Universidad Nacional Autónoma de México, 2001.

Levins Morales, Aurora, and Rosario Morales. *Getting Home Alive*. Ithaca, N.Y.: Firebrand Books, 1986.

Lewis, David Levering. "Harlem Renaissance." In Anthony Appiah, Henry Louis Gates Jr., and Microsoft Corporation, *Encarta Africana*. CD-ROM. Bellingham, Wash.: Microsoft Corporation, 1999.

Light, Alan. *Tupac Amaru Shakur, 1971–1996*. Rev. ed. London: Plexus, 1998.

Lincoln, C. Eric, and Lawrence H. Mamiya. *The Black Church in the African-American Experience*. Durham, N.C.: Duke University Press, 1990.

Lippard, Lucy R. *Mixed Blessings: New Art in a Multicultural America*. New York: New Press, 2000.

Locke, Alain LeRoy. *The New Negro: An Interpretation*. Salem, N.H.: Ayer Co., 1986.

Lockridge, Kenneth A. *A New England Town, the First Hundred Years: Dedham, Massachusetts, 1636–1736*. Rev. ed. New York: Norton, 1985.

Long, Charles H. *Significations: Signs, Symbols, and Images in the Interpretation of Religion*. Philadelphia: Fortress Press, 1986.

Long, Janet, ed. *Conquista y comida: Consecuencias del encuentro de dos mundos*. 2nd ed. Mexico City: Universidad Nacional Autónoma de México, 1997.

López, Ana M. "Our Welcome Guests: Telenovelas in Latin America." In *To Be Continued . . . : Soap Operas around the World*, edited by Robert Clyde Allen. London: Routledge, 1995.

López Austin, Alfredo. *The Human Body and Ideology: Concepts of the Ancient Nahuas*. Salt Lake City: University of Utah Press, 1988.

López Rosas, Ricardo. *Comer, beber, y alegrarse*. Mexico City: Estudios Bíblicos Mexicanos, 2004.

López Rosas, Ricardo, and Landgrave Gándara, Daniel, eds. *Pan para todos: Estudios en torno a la eucaristía*. Mexico City: Estudios Bíblicos Mexicanos, 2004.

López, Yolanda. *Yolanda M. López: Works, 1975–1978*. San Diego, 1979. Online database, asu.edu.

MacMurray, John. *Persons in Relation: Being the Gifford Lectures Delivered in the University of Glasgow in 1954. The Form of the Personal*. Vol. 2. London: Faber and Faber, 1961.

Marques, René. *The Docile Puerto Rican: Essays*. Philadelphia: Temple University Press, 1976.

Martín-Barbero, Jesús. "Memory and Form in the Latin American Soap Opera." In *To Be Continued . . . : Soap Operas around the World*, edited by Robert Clyde Allen. London: Routledge, 1995.

Matsuoka, Fumitaka. *The Color of Faith: Building Community in a Multiracial Society*. Cleveland, Ohio: United Church Press, 1998.

Mays, Benjamin E. *The Negro's God as Reflected in His Literature*. New York: Atheneum, 1973.

Mazziotti, Nora. *La industria de la telenovela: La producción de ficción en América Latina*. Buenos Aires: Paidós, 1996.

McHugh, Francis P., and Samuel M. Natale. *Things Old and New: Catholic Social Teaching Revisited.* Lanham, Md.: University Press of America; Oxford: Oxford Philosophy Trust, 1993.

McLean, Robert, and Grace P. Williams. *Old Spain in New America.* New York: Association Press, 1913.

McPartlan, Paul. *The Eucharist Makes the Church.* Edinburgh: T&T Clark, 1993.

Mesa-Bains, Amalia. *Chicano Art: Resistance and Affirmation, 1965–1985.* Edited by R. G. del Castillo. Los Angeles: University of California Press, 1991.

Mignolo, Walter. *The Darker Side of the Renaissance: Literacy, Territoriality, and Colonization.* 2nd ed. Ann Arbor: University of Michigan Press, 2003.

Milbank, John. "Against the Resignations of the Age." In *Things Old and New: Catholic Social Teaching Revisited,* edited by Francis McHugh and Samuel M. Natale. Oxford: Lanham University Press of America, 1993.

Milbank, John, and Catherine Pickstock. *Truth in Aquinas.* London: Routledge, 2001.

Mintz, Sidney Wilfred. *Tasting Food, Tasting Freedom: Excursions into Eating, Culture, and the Past.* Boston: Beacon Press, 1996.

Mitchell, Stewart, ed. *Winthrop Papers.* Vol. 2: *1623–1630.* Boston: Massachusetts Historical Society, 1931.

Mitchem, Stephanie Y. *Introducing Womanist Theology.* Maryknoll, N.Y.: Orbis Books, 2002.

Monmonier, Mark S. *How to Lie with Maps.* Chicago: University of Chicago Press, 1991.

Montanari, Massimo, and Jean-Pierre Devroey. *El mundo en la cocina: Historia, identidad, intercambios.* Buenos Aires: Paidos, 2003.

Moore, Albert C. *Iconography of Religions: An Introduction.* Philadelphia: Fortress Press, 1977.

Moraga, Cherríe. *Loving in the War Years: Lo Que Nunca Pasó Por Sus Labios.* Boston: South End Press, 1983.

Morgan, David. *Protestants and Pictures: Religion, Visual Culture and the Age of American Mass Production.* New York: Oxford University Press, 1999.

———. *Visual Piety: A History and Theory of Popular Religious Images.* Berkeley: University of California Press, 1998.

Morino, Angelo. *El libro de cocina de sor Juana Inés de la Cruz.* Translated by Juan Pablo Roa. Bogota, Colombia: Grupo Editorial Norma, 2001.

Morrison, Toni. *Beloved.* New York: Knopf, 1987.

———. *Paradise.* New York: Knopf, 1997.

Morse, Christopher. *Not Every Spirit: The Dogmatics of Christian Unbelief.* Valley Forge, Pa.: Trinity Press International, 1994.

Neal, Mark Anthony, and Murray Forman. *That's the Joint! The Hip-Hop Studies Reader.* New York: Routledge, 2004.

Nederveen Pieterse, Jan. *White on Black: Images of Africa and Blacks in Western Popular Culture.* New Haven, Conn.: Yale University Press, 1992.

Nestle, Marion. *Food Politics: How the Food Industry Influences Nutrition and Health.* Berkeley: University of California Press, 2002.

Nickson, Chris. *Lauryn Hill: An Unauthorized Biography.* New York: St. Martin's Paperbacks, 1999.

Noble, David W. *The Progressive Mind, 1890–1917.* Rev. ed. Minneapolis, Minn.: Burgess, 1981.

Norton, Anne. *Bloodrites of the Post-Structuralists: Word, Flesh, and Revolution.* New York: Routledge, 2002.

Oliver, Kelly. *Witnessing: Beyond Recognition.* Minneapolis: University of Minnesota Press, 2001.

Paulston, Rolland G., ed. *Social Cartography: Mapping Ways of Seeing Social and Educational Change.* New York: Garland, 1996.

Paz, Octavio. *The Labyrinth of Solitude.* New York: Grove Press, 1961.

———. *The Labyrinth of Solitude and Other Writings.* New York: Grove Press, 1985.

Pérez Martínez, Herón. "La comida en el refranero mexicano: Un estudio contrastivo." In *Conquista y comida: Consecuencias del encuentro de dos mundos,* edited by Janet Long. Mexico City: Universidad Nacional Autónoma de México, 2003.

Perry, Imani. *Prophets of the Hood: Politics and Poetics in Hip Hop.* Durham, N.C.: Duke University Press, 2004.

Pikaza, Xabier. *Pan, casa, palabra: La iglesia en marcos.* Salamanca, Spain: Ediciones Sigueme, 1998.

Pilcher, Jeffrey M. *Vivan los tamales! La comida y la construcción de la identidad mexicana.* Mexico City: Ediciones de la Reina Roja, Consejo Nacional para la Cultura y las Artes (Mexico), and Centro Internacional de Estudios de las Sociedades y Espacios Andinos, 2001.

Pinn, Anthony B. "Black Theology in Historical Perspective: Articulating the Quest for Subjectivity." In *The Ties That Bind: African American and Hispanic American/Latino/a Theology in Dialogue,* edited by Anthony B. Pinn and Benjamín Valentín. New York: Continuum, 2001.

———. "Cartography and the Children of the 'Americas' ": Toward a Reconfiguring of Religious Studies as Dialogical Enterprise." Paper presented at a special session of the Fund for Theological Education, Philadelphia, November 15, 2005.

———. *Noise and Spirit: The Religious and Spiritual Sensibilities of Rap Music.* New York: New York University Press, 2003.

———. *Varieties of African American Religious Experience.* Minneapolis, Minn.: Fortress Press, 1998.

Pinn, Anthony B., and Benjamín Valentín. *The Ties That Bind: African American and Hispanic American/Latino/a Theology in Dialogue.* New York: Continuum, 2001.

Porter, Stanley E., Michael A. Hayes, and David Tombs. *Images of Christ: Ancient and Modern.* Sheffield, U.K.: Sheffield Academic Press, 1997.

Raboteau, Albert J. "African-Americans, Exodus, and the American Israel." In *African American Christianity: Essays in History*, edited by Paul E. Johnson. Berkeley: University of California Press, 1994.

Ramsey, Guthrie P. *Race Music: Black Cultures from Bebop to Hip-Hop*. Berkeley: University of California Press, 2003.

Recinos, Harold J. *Hear the Cry! A Latino Pastor Challenges the Church*. Louisville, Ky.: Westminster/John Knox Press, 1989.

———. *Jesus Weeps: Global Encounters on Our Doorstep*. Nashville, Tenn.: Abingdon Press, 1992.

———. "Mission: A Latino Pastoral Theology." In *Mestizo Christianity: Theology from the Latino Perspective*, edited by Arturo J. Bañuelas. New York: Orbis, 1995.

———. "Popular Religion, Political Identity, and Life-Story Testimony in an Hispanic Community." In *The Ties that Bind: African American and Hispanic American/Latino(a) Theologies in Dialogue*, ed. Anthony B. Pinn and Benjamín Valentín. New York: Continuum, 2001.

Rhijn, Patricia van, and Ignacio Urquiza. *La cocina del Chile*. Mexico D.F.: Editorial Planeta Mexicana, 2003.

Riera-Melis, Antonio. "El mediterráneo, crisol de tradiciones alimentarias: El legado islámico en la cocina medieval Catalana." In *El mundo en la cocina: Historia, identidad, intercambios*, edited by Massimo Montanari. Barcelona: Paidós, 2003.

Rodriguez, Jeanette. *Our Lady of Guadalupe: Faith and Empowerment among Mexican-American Women*. Austin: University of Texas Press, 1994.

Rodriguez, Richard. *Brown: The Last Discovery of America*. New York: Viking, 2002.

———. *Days of Obligation: An Argument with My Mexican Father*. New York, N.Y.: Viking, 1992.

Roiheiser, Ronald. *The Holy Longing: The Search for a Christian Spirituality*. New York: Doubleday, 1999.

Rosaldo, Renato. *Culture and Truth: The Remaking of Social Analysis*. Boston: Beacon Press, 1993.

Ross, Rosetta E. *Witnessing and Testifying: Black Women, Religion, and Civil Rights*. Minneapolis, Minn.: Fortress Press, 2003.

Roux, Rodolfo Eduardo de, and Matthew L. Lamb. *Pan para todos: Aportes a una teología por el pobre*. Bogotá, Colombia: Facultad de Teología Pontificia Universidad Javeriana, 2000.

Royce, Josiah, and Frank M. Oppenheim. *The Problem of Christianity*. Washington, D.C.: Catholic University of America Press, 2001.

Ruether, Rosemary Radford. *Sexism and God-Talk: Toward a Feminist Theology*. Boston: Beacon Press, 1983.

Said, Edward W. *Representations of the Intellectual: The 1993 Reith Lectures*. New York: Vintage Books, 1996.

Salinas Campos, Maximiliano A. *Gracias a dios que comí: Los orígenes del christianismo en Iberoamérica y el Caribe, siglos XV-XX.* Mexico City: Ediciones Dabar, 2000.

Santiago, Esmeralda. *América's Dream.* New York: HarperCollins Publishers, 1996.

———. *When I Was Puerto Rican.* New York: Vintage Books, 1994.

Santiago, Roberto. *Boricuas: Influential Puerto Rican Writings: An Anthology.* New York: One World, 1995.

Schmidt-Leukel, Perry, ed. *Las religiones y la comida.* Barcelona: Ariel, 2002.

Schultze, Quentin J. *Televangelism and American Culture: The Business of Popular Religion.* Grand Rapids, Mich.: Baker Book House, 1991.

Schweitzer, Albert. *The Quest of the Historical Jesus.* Minneapolis: Fortress Press, 2001.

Segovia, Fernando. "Two Places and No Place on Which to Stand: Mixture and Otherness in Hispanic American Theology." In *Mestizo Christianiy: Theology from the Latino Perspective,* edited by Arturo J. Bañuelas. New York: Orbis, 1995.

Sherwood, Yvonne, and Kevin Hart. *Derrida and Religion: Other Testaments.* London: Routledge, 2004.

Smith, Dennis Edwin. *From Symposium to Eucharist: The Banquet in the Early Christian World.* Minneapolis, Minn.: Fortress Press, 2003.

Smith, James K. A. *Introducing Radical Orthodoxy: Mapping a Post-Secular Theology.* Grand Rapids, Mich.: Baker Academic, 2004.

Smith, Jonathan Z. *Map Is Not Territory: Studies in the History of Religions.* Chicago: University of Chicago Press, 1993.

Snowden, Frank M. *Blacks in Antiquity; Ethiopians in the Greco-Roman Experience.* Cambridge, Mass.: Belknap Press of Harvard University Press, 1970.

Soto, Pedro Juan. *Hot Land, Cold Season.* Translated by Helen R. Lane. New York: Dell, 1973.

———. *Spiks.* Translated by Victoria Ortíz New York: Monthly Review Press, 1973.

Spelman, Elizabeth V. "Woman as Body: Ancient and Contemporary Views." *Feminist Studies* 8, no. 1 (1982).

Spencer, Jon Michael. *Blues and Evil.* Knoxville: University of Tennessee Press, 1993.

———. *Self-Made and Blues Rich.* Trenton, N.J.: Africa World Press, 1997.

Spillers, Hortense J. *Black, White, and in Color: Essays on American Literature and Culture.* Chicago: University of Chicago Press, 2003.

Stewart, Dianne M. *Three Eyes for the Journey: African Dimensions of the Jamaican Religious Experience.* New York: Oxford University Press, 2005.

Stout, Jeffrey. *Democracy and Tradition.* Princeton, N.J.: Princeton University Press, 2004.

Taibo, Paco Ignacio. *El libro de todos los moles.* Mexico, D.F.: Ediciones B, 2003.

Takaki, Ronald T. *Iron Cages: Race and Culture in Nineteeth-Century America.* Rev. ed. New York: Oxford University Press, 2000.

Tandeciarz, Silvia. "Some Notes on Racial Trauma in Peter Weir's *Fearless.*" *Literature/Film Quarterly* 28, no. 1 (2000): 60–65.

Tate, Greg. "Diatribe." In *And It Don't Stop: The Best American Hip-Hop Journalism of the Last Twenty-five Years.* New York: Faber and Faber.

Taylor, Paul V. *The Texts of Paulo Freire.* Buckingham, U.K.: Open University Press, 1993.

Tillich, Paul. *On Art and Architecture.* Edited by John Dillenberger and Jane Dillenberger. New York: Crossroad, 1987.

———. *Systematic Theology.* Chicago: University of Chicago Press, 1967.

Turchi, Peter. *Maps of the Imagination: The Writer as Cartographer.* San Antonio, Tex.: Trinity University Press, 2004.

Turner, Faythe E. *Puerto Rican Writers at Home in the USA: An Anthology.* Seattle, Wash.: Open Hand Publishing, 1991.

Unamuno, Miguel de. *Tragic Sense of Life.* New York: Dover Publications, 1954.

Valdivia, Angharad N. "Stereotype or Transgression? Rosie Perez in Hollywood Film." *Sociological Quarterly* 39, no. 3 (1998): 393–408.

Valentín, Benjamín. *Mapping Public Theology: Beyond Culture, Identity, and Difference.* Harrisburg, Pa.: Trinity Press International, 2002.

———. *New Horizons in Hispanic/Latino(a) Theology.* Cleveland, Ohio: Pilgrim Press, 2003.

———. "Strangers No More: An Introduction to, and an Interpretation of, U.S. Hispanic/Latino(a) Theology." In *The Ties That Bind: African American and Hispanic American/Latino/a Theology in Dialogue,* edited by Anthony B. Pinn and Benjamín Valentín. New York: Continuum, 2001.

Vasconcelos, José. "La raza cosmica." In *The Cosmic Race/La raza cosmica.* Baltimore: Johns Hopkins University Press, 1997.

Vélez, Diana L. "Cultural Constructions of Women by Contemporary Puerto Rican Women Authors." In *The Psychosocial Development of Puerto Rican Women,* edited by Cynthia T. García Coll and María de Lourdes Mattei. New York: Praeger, 1989.

Von Balthasar, Hans Urs. *Theo-Drama.* Vol. 4. Translated by Graham Harrison. San Francisco: Ignatius Press, 1994.

Wadell, Paul J. *Becoming Friends: Worship, Justice, and the Practice of Christian Friendship.* Grand Rapids, Mich.: Brazos Press, 2002.

Walker, Alice. *Anything We Love Can Be Saved: A Writer's Activism.* New York: Random House, 1997.

———. *The Color Purple: A Novel.* New York: Harcourt Brace Jovanovich, 1982.

———. *In Search of Our Mothers' Gardens: Womanist Prose.* San Diego: Harcourt Brace Jovanovich, 1983.

Watkins, S. Craig. *Hip Hop Matters: Politics, Pop Culture, and the Struggle for the Soul of a Movement.* Boston: Beacon Press, 2005.

Weber, Max. *The Theory of Social and Economic Organization.* Edited by Talcott Parsons. Translated by A. M. Henderson and Talcott Parsons. New York: Oxford University Press, 1947.

Webster, Jane S. *Ingesting Jesus: Eating and Drinking in the Gospel of John.* Atlanta, Ga.: Society of Biblical Literature, 2003.

Wells, Samuel. *God's Companions: Reimagining Christian Ethics.* Malden, Mass.: Blackwell, 2006.

West, Cornel. *Race Matters.* Boston: Beacon Press, 1993.

West, Traci C. *Disruptive Christian Ethics: When Racism and Women's Lives Matter.* Louisville, Ky.: Westminster John Knox Press, 2006.

Whelan, Matthew. "The Responsible Body: A Eucharistic Community." *Cross Currents* 51, no. 3 (fall 2001): 359–78.

Williams, Delores S. *Sisters in the Wilderness: The Challenge of Womanist God-Talk.* Maryknoll, N.Y.: Orbis Books, 1993.

Willis, Deborah. *Reflections in Black: A History of Black Photographers, 1840 to the Present.* New York: Norton, 2000.

Yarbro-Bejarano, Yvonne. *The Wounded Heart: Writing on Cherríe Moraga.* Austin: University of Texas Press, 2001.

Young, Robert. *Colonial Desire: Hybridity in Theory, Culture and Race.* London: Routledge, 1994.

Contributors

▣

Teresa Delgado is an assistant professor of religious studies at Iona College. Her Ph.D. dissertation focused on the development of an emancipatory Puerto Rican theology that employs literature as a critical source. She is author of "Prophesy Freedom: Puerto Rican Women's Literature as a Source for Latina Feminist Theology" (2002).

Cheryl A. Kirk-Duggan is a professor of theology and women's studies and director of Women's Studies at Shaw University. Her research focuses on issues of theology, justice, violence, and the way that religious ritual and music aids notions of liberation. She is the author of numerous books, including *Refiner's Fire: A Religious Engagement with Violence* (2001) and *Exorcising Evil: A Womanist Perspective on the Spirituals* (1997).

James H. Evans Jr. is the Robert K. Davies Professor of Systematic Theology at Colgate Rochester Divinity School. He is also a minister within the American Baptist Churches, USA denomination. As a member of the second generation of black theology, Evans has made a major contribution to the systematic presentation of black theology, as well as being a leader in the theological analysis of literature within the context of black religious studies. He is the author of numerous books including *We Have Been Believers: An African American Systematic Theology* (1992) and *Spiritual Empowerment in Afro American Literature* (1987).

Joseph De León completed his Ph.D. in the arts and religion at the Graduate Theological Union. He is currently an independent scholar.

Suzanne E. Hoeferkamp Segovia recently completed her Ph.D. with a dissertation titled "A Theory of Creativity, Divine and Human." Her research and teaching interests lie in theologies of culture, the visual arts, and systematic theology.

Angel F. Méndez Montoya was born in Mexicali, Mexico, and has lived in the United States for the past fourteen years. He is a Dominican friar (the Order of Preachers) and is a member of the U.S. Southern Dominican Province. Before becoming a Dominican friar, he was a professional dancer for ten years and danced in Mexico, the United States, Latin America, and Europe. He is currently a doctoral student in philosophical theology at the University of Virginia.

Alexander Nava is an associate professor in the Department of Religious Studies at the University of Arizona. He is the author of *The Mystical and Prophetic Thought of Simone Weil and Gustavo Gutierrez: Reflections on the Mystery and Hiddenness of God* (2001).

Anthony B. Pinn is the Agnes Cullen Arnold Professor of Humanities and Professor of Religious Studies at Rice University. His research interests include African American religious history, liberation theologies, African American humanist thought, and religion and popular culture. He is the author or editor of seventeen books, including *The African American Religious Experience in America* (2006) and *Terror and Triumph: The Nature of Black Religion* (2003), and *The Black Church in the Post-Civil Rights Era* (2002).

Mayra Rivera is an assistant professor of theology at the Pacific School of Religion. She teaches and writes across a wide range of contemporary theological studies, in which she engages the symbols of the Christian tradition constructively by drawing from a variety of theoretical sources including feminist and gender studies, poststructuralist philosophies, postcolonial theories, and ethnic studies. Her publications include the anthology *Postcolonial Theologies* and *The Touch of Transcendence: A Postcolonial Theology of God* (2007), which explores the relationship between ideas about God's otherness and models of inter-human difference.

Benjamín Valentín is a professor of theology and culture and the director of the Orlando E. Costas Lectureship in Latino/a Theology at Andover Newton Theological School in Newton, Massachusetts. He is the author of *Mapping Public Theology: Beyond Culture, Identity, and Difference* (2002) and the editor of *New Horizons in Hispanic/Latino(a) Theology* (2003), as well as coeditor with Anthony B. Pinn of *The Ties That Bind* (2001). Valentín's teaching and research interests are in contemporary theology and culture, constructive theology, the relation of religion and theology to American public life, and liberation theologies.

Jonathan Walton is an assistant professor of religious studies at the University of California, Riverside. Prior to this posting he was both a lecturer and research specialist in the Program in African American Studies at Princeton University. Trained as a social ethicist, he earned his Ph.D. in religion and society from Princeton Theological Seminary. His research addresses the intersections between religion, politics, and popular culture in America. He is the author of *Watch This! The Ethics and Aesthetics of Black Televangelism* (2008), and he is currently compiling and editing a volume of essays from leading scholars and preachers tentatively titled *Will the Revolution Be Televised? TV Preachers, Profits, and the Prophetic.*

Traci C. West is a professor of ethics and African American studies at Drew University. She is the author of *Wounds of the Spirit: Black Women, Violence, and Resistance Ethics* (1999) as well as many essays on sexism in the church, welfare policy, and racial justice.

Lynne Westfield is an associate professor of religious education at Drew University, with a joint appointment at the Theological School and the Casperson Graduate School. She is also a permanent deacon ordained in Eastern Pennsylvania Conference of the United Methodist Church. Her scholarly interests include issues of womanist pedagogy, theological education, mysticism, and spirituality. She is the author of *Dear Sisters: A Womanist Practice of Hospitality* (2001) and an essay in *African Americans and the Bible* (2000). Her current research focuses on issues of African American influence in theological education and the prayer of African American people.

Sheila F. Winborne worked in the field of visual arts before entering graduate school at Harvard University where she completed her Ph.D. She is currently an adjunct faculty member at the University of Massachusetts, Boston.

ANTHONY B. PINN is the Agnes Cullen Arnold
Professor of Humanities and Professor of Religious
Studies at Rice University.

BENJAMÍN VALENTÍN is professor of theology and
culture and the director of the Orlando E. Costas
Lectureship in Latino/a Theology at Andover Newton
Theological School in Newton, Massachusetts.

Library of Congress Cataloging-in-Publication Data
Creating ourselves: African Americans and Hispanic
Americans on popular culture and religious
expression / Anthony B. Pinn and Benjamín Valentín,
editors.
p. cm.
Includes bibliographical references and index.
ISBN 978-0-8223-4549-7 (cloth : alk. paper)
ISBN 978-0-8223-4566-4 (pbk. : alk. paper)
1. African Americans—Religion. 2. Hispanic
Americans—Religion. 3. United States—Ethnic
relations. 4. Popular culture—United States.
5. Popular culture—Religious aspects. I. Pinn,
Anthony B. II. Valentín, Benjamín.
BR563.N4C74 2009
201'.6305868073—dc22   2009032841